INSIGHT GUIDES
IN THE SAME SERIES

TITLE	APA ISBN	USA ISBN	UK ISBN	AUST ISBN
ASIA				
Bali	9971-982-01-3	031-056200-9	0245-54119-5	0-7018-1852-2
Burma	9971-982-04-8	013-090902-5	0245-54021-0	0-7018-1861-1
Hong Kong	9971-925-69-9	013-394635-5	0245-54019-9	0-7018-1860-3
Indonesia	9971-925-43-5	013-457391-9	0245-54129-2	0-7018-1836-0
Java	9971-982-00-5	013-509976-5	0245-54118-7	0-7018-1853-0
Korea	9971-982-07-2	013-516641-1	0245-54016-4	0-7018-1859-X
Malaysia	9971-925-95-8	013-547992-4	0245-54121-7	0-7018-1855-7
Nepal	9971-982-08-0	013-611038-X	0245-54020-2	0-7018-1863-8
Philippines	9971-982-09-9	013-662197-X	0245-54017-2	0-7018-1857-3
Singapore	9971-982-10-2	013-810713-0	0245-54120-9	0-7018-1854-9
Sri Lanka	9971-982-11-0	013-839944-1	0245-54025-3	0-7018-1866-2
Taiwan	9971-982-12-9	013-882192-5	0245-54128-4	0-7018-1867-0
Thailand	9971-925-96-6	013-912600-7	0245-54117-9	0-7018-1856-5
AMERICAS				
American Southwest	9971-982-13-7	013-029521-3	0245-54176-4	0-7018-1872-7
Florida	9971-982-02-1	013-322412-0	0245-54022-9	0-7018-1862-X
Jamaica	9971-982-03-X	013-509000-8	0245-54024-5	0-7018-1865-4
Mexico	9971-982-14-5	013-579524-9	0245-54023-7	0-7018-1864-6
New England	9971-982-15-3	013-612854-8	0245-54176-6	0-7018-1837-9
Northern California	9971-982-16-1	013-623562-X	0245-54173-X	0-7018-1869-7
Southern California	9971-982-17-X	013-823600-3	0245-54174-8	0-7018-1870-0
PACIFIC				
Hawaii	9971-982-18-8	013-384529-X	0245-54018-0	0-7018-1858-1
New Zealand	9971-925-49-4	013-621111-9	0245-54177-2	0-7018-1871-9
GRAND TOURS				
Australia	9971-925-48-6	013-053828-0	0245-54184-5	0-7018-1868-9
California	9971-982-21-8	013-112608-3	0245-54182-9	0-7018-1835-2
Continental Europe	9971-982-22-6	013-171422-8	0245-54186-1	0-7018-1838-7

hawaii

Directed and Designed by Hans Johannes Hoefer
Produced and Edited by Leonard Lueras
Research Editor, Nedra Chung
Contributing Editor, Ronn Ronck

APA PRODUCTIONS
PRENTICE-HALL • HARRAP • LANSDOWNE

THE INSIGHT GUIDES SERIES RECEIVED SPECIAL AWARDS FOR EXCELLENCE FROM THE PACIFIC AREA TRAVEL ASSOCIATION IN 1980 AND 1982.

HAWAII

Sixth Edition Published by:

U.S. and Canadian Edition: PRENTICE-HALL INC. ISBN 013-384529-X	British Isles edition: HARRAP LTD. ISBN 0245-54018-0	Australia and New Zealand edition: LANSDOWNE PRESS ISBN 0-7018-1858-1

APA PRODUCTIONS

Publisher and Managing Director: Hans Johannes Hoefer
Executive Director Marketing: Yvan Van Outrive
Financial Controller: Henry Lee
Administrative Manager: Alice Ng
Editor: Stuart Ridsdale
Assistant Editor: Vivien Loo
Production Coordinator: Nancy Yap

Contributing Editors
Ravindralal Anthonis, Jon Carroll, Virginia Hopkins, Jay Itzkowitz, Phil Jarratt, Tracy Johnston, Ben Kalb, Wilhelm Klein, Saul Lockhart, Sylvia Mayuga, Gordon McLauchlan, Kal Müller, Eric M. Oey, Daniel P. Reid, Kim Robinson, Ronn Ronck, Rolf Steinberg, Desmond Tate, Lisa Van Gruisen, Made Wijaya

Contributing Writers
A.D. Aird, Ruth Armstrong, T. Terence Barrow, F. Lisa Beebe, Bruce Berger, Dor Bahadur Bista, Clinton V. Black, Star Black, Frena Bloomfield, John Borthwick, Roger Boschman, Tom Brosnahan, Linda Carlock, Jerry Carroll, Tom Chaffin, Nedra Chung, Tom Cole, Orman Day, Kunda Dixit, Richard Erdöes, Guillermo Garcia-Oropeza, Ted Giannoulas, Barbara Gloudon, Harka Gurung, Sharifah Hamzah, Willard A. Hanna, Elizabeth Hawley, Sir Edmund Hillary, Tony Hillerman, Jerry Hopkins, Peter Hutton, Neil Jameson, Michael King, Michele Kort, Thomas Lucey, Leonard Lueras, Michael E. Macmillan, Derek Maitland, Buddy Mays, Craig McGregor, Reinhold Messner, Julie Michaels, Barbara Mintz, M.R. Priya Rangsit, Al Read, Elizabeth V. Reyes, Victor Stafford Reid, Harry Rolnick, E.R. Sarachchandra, Uli Schmetzer, Ilsa Sharp, Norman Sibley, Leslie Marmon Silko, Peter Spiro, Harold Stephens, Keith Stevens, Michael Stone, Colin Taylor, Deanna L. Thompson, Randy Udall, James Wade, Mallika Wanigasundara, William Warren, Cynthia Wee, Tony Wheeler, Linda White, H. Taft Wireback, Alfred A. Yuson, Paul Zach.

Contributing Photographers
Carole Allen, Roland Ammon, Ping Amranand, Walter D. Andreae, Ray Cranbourne, Rennie Ellis, Alain Evrard, Ricardo Ferro, Lee Foster, Manfred Gottschalk, Allen Grazer, Werner Hahn, Dallas and John Heaton, Brent Hesselyn, Dennis Lane, Max Lawrence, Bud Lee, Philip Little, R. Ian Lloyd, Bret Reed Lundberg, Kal Müller, Ronni Pinsler, Günter Pfannmuller, G.P. Reichelt, Dan Rocovits, David Ryan, Frank Salmoiraghi, Thomas Schöllmarten, Blair Seitz, David Stahl, Tom Tidball, Paul Van Riel, Rolf Verres, Joseph F. Viesti, Paul Von Stroheim, Bill Wassman, Jan Whiting, Rendo Yap, Hisham Youssef.

MARKETING, SALES AND ADVERTISING

Insight Guides are available through the international book trade in 30 countries around the world as single copies or as complete collectors sets at discounts. Visit your nearest bookshop. Should any of the Insight Guides listed below be unavailable or out of stock, please refer to the ISBN numbers when ordering through the bookshop or direct through these distributors.

Distributors:
Australia: Lansdowne Press, 176 South Creek Road, Dee Why, N.S.W. 2099, AUSTRALIA **Benelux:** Uitgeverij Cambium, Naarder-

straat 11, 1251 Aw Laren, The Netherlands. **Denmark:** Copenhagen Book Centre Aps, Roskildeveji 338, DK-2630 Tastrup, Denmark. **France:** Librairie Armand Colin,103 Boulevard St. Michel 75005 Paris, France. **Germany:** Nelles Verlag, Schleissheimer Str. 371b, 8000 Munich 45. **Hawaii:** Pacific Trade Group Inc., P.O. Box 1227, Kailua, Oahu, Hawaii 96734, U.S.A. **Hong Kong:** Far East Media Ltd., Vita Tower, 7th Floor, Block B, 29 Wong Chuk Hang Road, Hong Kong **India and Nepal:** India Book Distributors, 107/108 Arcadia Building, 195 Narima Point, Bombay-400-021, India. **Indonesia:** N.V. Indoprom Company (Indonesia) Ltd., Arthaloka Building, 14th floor, 2 Jalan Jendral Sudirman, Jakarta Pusat, Indonesia. **Jamaica:** Kingston Publishers, 1-A Norwood Avenue, Kingston 5, Jamaica. **Japan:** Charles E. Tuttle Co. Inc., 2-6 Suido 1-Chome, Bunkyo-ku, Tokyo, Japan. **Korea:** Korea Britannica Corporation, C.P.O. Box 690, Seoul 100, Korea, 162-1, 2-ga, Jangchung-dong, Jung-gu, Seoul, Korea. **Mexico:** Distribuidora Britannica S.A., Rio Volga 93, Col Cuauhtemoc, 06500 Mexico 5 D.F. Mexico. **New Zealand:** Lansdowne Rigby, Unit 3, 3 Marken Place, Glenfield, Auckland. **Pakistan:** Liberty Book Stall, Inverarity Road, Karachi 03, Pakistan. **Philippines:** Print Diffusion Pacific Inc., 2135-C Pasong Tamo Street, Makati, Manila, Philippines. **Singapore and Malaysia:** MPH Distributors (S) Pte Ltd., 51 Lorong 3, Geylang #05-09, Singapore 1438. **Sri Lanka:** K.V.G. de Silva & Sons (Colombo) Ltd., 415 Galle Road, Colombo 4, Sri Lanka. **Spain:** Altair, Riera Alta 8, Barcelona 1, Spain. **Sweden:** Esselte Kartcentrum, Vasagatan 16, S-111 20 Stockholm, Sweden. **Taiwan:** Caves Books Ltd., 107 Chungshan N. Road, Sec. 2, Taipei, Taiwan. Republic of China. **Thailand:** The Bookseller Co. Ltd., 67/2 Soi Tonson, Nang Linchi Road, Bangkok 10120, Thailand. **United Kingdom:** Harrap Ltd., 19-23 Ludgate Hill, London EC4M 7PD, England, United Kingdom. **Mainland United States and Canada:** Prentice-Hall Inc., Englewood Cliffs, New Jersey 07632, U.S.A.

German editions: Geo Centre, D7000, Stuttgart 80, Honigweisenstrabe 25, W. Germany. **French editions:** Les Editions Errance, 11 rue de l'Arsenal, 75004 Paris, France.

Advertising and Special Sales Representatives
Advertising carried in Insight Guides gives readers direct access to quality merchandise and travel-related services. These advertisements are inserted in the Guide in Brief section of each book. Advertisers are requested to contact their nearest representatives, listed below.
Special sales, for promotional and educational purposes within the international travel industry, are also available. The advertising representatives listed here also handle special sales. Alternatively, interested parties can contact marketing director Yvan Van Outrive directly at Apa Productions, P.O. Box 219, Killiney Road Post Office, Singapore 9123.

Asia and Australia: Martin Clinch & Associates Ltd., 20th floor, Queen's Centre, 58-64 Queen's Road East, Hong Kong. Telephone: 5-273525. Telex: 76041 MCAL HX.

United States: Sfw-Pri International Inc., 1560 Broadway, New York, N.Y. 10036, U.S.A. Telephone: (212) 575-9292. Telex: 422260.

APA PHOTO AGENCY PTE LTD

General Manager: Sylvia Muttom
Together with our associate. Tony Stone Worldwide, the APA Photo Agency represents the work of many leading photographers for publication rights. More than 150,000 original colour transparencies are in our files and are available in SE Asia and throughout the world for advertising, editorial, cultural and educational uses.

Singapore: Apa Photo Agency Pte Ltd 5 Lengkong Satu Singapore 1441. **London:** Tony Stone Worldwide 28 Finchley Road St John's Wood London NW8 6ES. **New York:** Index-Stone International Inc 126 Fifth Avenue New York NY 10011 U S A. **Paris:** Fotogram-Stone Agence Photographique 45 rue de Richelieu 75001 Paris France **Barcelona:** Fototeca Torre dels Pardals 7 Barcelona 08026 Spain **Johannesburg:** Color Library (Pty) Ltd P O Box 1659 Johannesburg South Africa 2000 **Sydney:** The Photographic Library of Australia Pty Ltd 7 Ridge Street North Sydney New South Wales 2060 Australia **Tokyo:** Orion Press 55-1 Kanda Jimbocho Chiyoda-ku Tokyo 101 Japan.

CARTOGRAPHY

To complement **Insight Guides** and bring readers a more complete package of travel information, Apa Productions — in cooperation with cartographer Gunter Nelles of Munich, West Germany — has begun publication of a series of detailed maps on selected travel destinations. Initial maps cover Asian countries and cities:

INDONESIA MALAYSIA NEPAL PHILIPPINES SRI LANKA THAILAND

In your hands is the sixth annual revised edition of *Insight Guide: Hawaii*, a book which has been embraced in the mid Pacific with nearly as much fervor as hula and poi.

Insight Guide: Hawaii first appeared in the spring of 1980, the initial step in Apa Productions' ambitious East to West publishing program. It has since become the cornerstone of expansion success for founder-publisher **Hans Hoefer** and his growing team of writers, editors and photographers. In the past four years, the company has tripled its book output (from eight to 24), including a half-dozen new titles in North America.

Hawaii germinated from a 1975 meeting between Hoefer and **Leonard Lueras**, a Honolulu-based journalist-traveler. Lueras convinced Hoefer, a German Bauhaus-schooled disciple of the "black arts" of printing based in Singapore and Hong Kong, that a book about Hawaii would be viable and worthy of the kinds of creative energy Apa Productions normally expends on a book.

Lueras

For nearly two years, the *Hawaii* idea floated somewhere at the back of Lueras' and Hoefer's minds, but eventually, on a steamy Singapore day in the spring of 1977, in a pleasant surge of economic serendipity, the scheme was nourished. Into Hoefer's inkstained and four-colored life strolled **Walter Andreae**, a Hawaii-based financial backer, an "angel" if you will, who immediately liked the idea of a book on Hawaii. Andreae almost as immediately plopped necessary book initiation funds onto Hoefer's lap and said – to quote his colloquialism of the time – "Go for it!" Later, Andreae turned his Big Island estate into a home base and editorial workshop for Apa's book-creating team.

Upon receiving support from Andreae, Lueras was invited to return to Apa's headquarters from Seoul, Korea, where he was working on a frivolous but financially rewarding writing assignment. Lueras and research editor **Nedra Chung** flew south to Singapore, and, following a series of late-night editorial meetings with Hoefer, they were dispatched to Honolulu to begin creating this book.

To say that this book was more than two years in the making is really an understatement. *Hawaii* – like other Apa *Insight Guides* – is much more than a mere packaging

exercise. Rather, if one totals up the years our team of authors, artists, photographers and other contributors have spent in the Hawaiian Islands, one can say that this book literally reflects some 300 years of recent, first-hand experiences in Hawaii. All contributors except Hoefer are "local folks," each one intimately acquainted with the subject they were asked to write about, photograph or illustrate.

Andreae

Lueras, for example – who edited and wrote more than half of *Hawaii* – has lived and worked in the Islands since 1963, the year

Chung   *Hoefer*

he arrived from Southern California "to surf." Since that first wet summer he has variously worked for nearly 10 years as a reporter for *The Honolulu Advertiser* and as an editor-at-large for *Pacific* magazine; has co-written and edited an anthology of modern Hawaiiana (*Manna-Mana*, 1973) and a limited edition about traditional barkcloth (*Specimens of Hawaiian Kapa*, 1979); and has produced further *Insight Guides* to *Korea, Hong Kong, Florida* and *Mexico* for Apa Productions. Lueras is now editorial director of Emphasis International, a book-publishing company that maintains editorial offices in Tokyo, Hong Kong and Honolulu. Most recently, he has authored *Surfing: The Ultimate Pleasure* and produced *On the Hana Coast*.

Hoefer's fresh eye has brought a European flavor to some of *Hawaii's* images. During frequent visits to the islands while *Hawaii* was in production, Hoefer focused his 8-by-10 Deardorff and a collection of Leica cameras on the islands' fragile and rugged beauty. His sensitive combination of Old World craftsmanship and New World ideas were integral to the shaping of this book.

Nedra Chung, research editor, was born and raised in Manoa Valley, Oahu, and was graduated from the University of Hawaii at Manoa in 1976. Chung prepared and wrote the entire Guide in Brief section, coordinated the preparation of preliminary texts, cartographic materials and the index-glossary, and served as a copy editor and proofreader during all stages of editorial preparation.

Contributing editor **Ronn Ronck**, who is responsible for *Hawaii* revisions and updates and generally serving as Apa's "man on the scene" in the island state, is travel editor of *The Honolulu Advertiser*. Ronck also authored the exploratory essays on Maui, Molokai and Lanai which comprise a healthy portion of this volume. The author of *Hawaiian Yesterdays* (1982), a monument to pioneer cameraman **Ray Jerome Baker**, Ronck also is editor of *Historic Hawaii* (published monthly by the Historic Hawaii Foundation) and a regular contributor to various Pacific-area magazines.

Baker's early 20th Century photographs are an important feature of this book's pages. A longtime Honolulu photographer, filmmaker, naturalist and social critic, Baker lived in Hawaii from 1908 until his death in 1972 at the age of 91. He left, in public and private collections, what is probably the most extensive single

Baker

visual record of the Hawaiian Islands during that period. Numerous reproductions of his black-and-white photographs and hand-coloured lantern slides appear throughout *Hawaii*.

Other principal photographers were **Frank Salmoiraghi, Boone Morrison, Jim Haas** and **Steve Wilkings**. Salmoiraghi photographed the islands of Lanai and Molokai, and contributed valuable advice and superb photographic images to many other sections of the book. In 1983, he travelled extensively in Taiwan on assignment for an *Insight Guide*. He divides his time between a home at Volcano on the Big Island of Hawaii and Honolulu, where he teaches photography.

Also at home in the Volcano area is *kamaaina* photographer Boone Morrison. The director of the Volcano Art Center, Morrison has had his photo works selected for exhibition in galleries in Hawaii, the U.S. Mainland and Australia. His recent book, *Images of the Hula* (Volcano Press, 1984), is one of numerous publications in which his work has appeared.

Haas is a California-based photographer who specializes in editorial assignments for Pacific-area magazines. His work appears in nearly every section of *Hawaii*. A graduate of the University of Guam, Hass taught himself

photography while island-hopping in Micronesia.

Wilkings, whose surfing and windsurfing photographs have earned him an international following, was graduated from Los Angeles' Art Center College of Design in 1970. The next year he moved to Hawaii and founded Pacific Studios. Since then he has shot mostly advertising agency work, but has also served as the Hawaii-based staff photographer for Surfer magazine (when the surf was up).

Jocelyn Fujii, author of lively essays on *leis* and island food, is a local girl born on the island of Kauai. In recent years, she has toiled as a feature writer for *The Honolulu Star-Bulletin*; as a television reporter; and as a free-lance writer, especially for such local

Ronck

Salmoiraghi

Morrison

J. Charlot

magazines as *Honolulu* and *Aloha*.

Jerry Hopkins, who introduces Hawaiian music and dance, used to write scripts for Hollywood television shows. He also produced the first and finest Elvis Presley biography (*Elvis*) and has been a longtime editor of *Rolling Stone* magazine. These days he continues to write books, including a biography of the rock poet Jim Morrison (No One Here Gets Out Alive) and another on Presley's "final years." His classic study of *The Hula* was published as an *Insight Chronicle* by Apa Productions in 1982.

Haas

Wilkings

Carl Lindquist, who leads readers on a ramble down the heavenly Hana Coast of Maui, is president of Trade Publishing Company, Honolulu, and is active in Hawaii's growing advertising and publishing communities. "Link" is also continuously involved in the perpetuation and preservation of Hawaiian culture and in the restoration of special Hawaiian places.

Our man on the Big Island is **Hal Glatzer**,

a media man who regularly changes editorial hats. He has previously worked as a Big Island bureau chief for *The Honolulu Advertiser* and as editor of Sunday magazine, *Orchid Isle*, published by Hilo's *Hawaii Tribune-Herald*. In recent times, Glatzer has been the Hawaii correspondent for *People* magazine and a documentary producer for Hawaii Public Television.

Kauai specialist **Jan W.P. TenBruggencate** is a Dutch-born journalist who has lived in Hawaii since 1956. Toasted in Kauai media circles as "the barefoot reporter," TenBruggencate has lived on the Garden Isle since 1971, the year he was named Kauai bureau chief for *The Honolulu Advertiser*.

Larry Lindsey Kimura, our expert on speaking Hawaiian, is an instructor and former coordinator of the University of Hawaii's Hawaiian language section. Kimura

Fujii

Hopkins

Lindquist

Kimura

Glatzer

TenBruggencate

also is a published poet and songwriter; moderator and producer of "Ka Leo Hawaii - Hawaiian Voice," a Hawaiian language show aired by Honolulu radio station KCCN. Kimura would like to acknowledge the assistance of **Pila Wilson**, an instructor of

M. Charlot

Hawaiian language at the University of Hawaii's Hilo campus, in the preparation of his essay.

The feature on Hawaiian art was penned by **John Charlot**, formerly the visual arts columnist for *Honolulu* magazine. Charlot has worked in Hawaii and Samoa as a teacher, editor and writer.

Readers of previous editions of *Hawaii* who remarked on the animated petroglyph sequences previously incorporated in these pages may be disappointed not to find them this time. These creations of **Martin Charlot**, a noted painter, writer, filmmaker and the young brother of John Charlot, fell victim to the technical aspects of streamlining this latest revision.

This book's extensive photo coverage includes the work of Big Island underwater photography specialist Chris Newbert and numerous other isle photographers, including Ken Sakamoto, Warren Roll, Craig Kojima, Eric Yanagi, Jerry Chong, Yukie Yoshinaga, Corky Trinidad, Ronni Pinsler, Mike and Bettan Dorn, Peter Simon, Marcus Lee, James Sloan, Frank F. Fasi and Walter Andreae.

A very special *mahalo* (thank you) and professional acknowledgement is due author-scientist O.A. "Ozzie" Bushnell, a good friend and critic whose editorial advice was important and much appreciated. Thank you also to Don Severson and Robert Van Dyke, who generously contributed the use of fine graphic materials from their respective historical collections.

Other persons and institutions who have contributed to Hawaii in one or many ways are Idanna Pucci, Jean and Zohmah Charlot, Gavan Daws, Sandy Zalburg, Thurston Twigg-Smith, Paul Cassidy, Chris Hemmeter, Diane Plotts, Bill Fontana, Tom Chapman, Peter Hutton, Gladys R. Van Dyke, Bob "The Maverick" Bone, G. Kent Andersen, John G. Anderson, Linda Carlock, Ted Sturdivant, Blake Nakanishi, Bertil Werjefelt, the late Aunty Edith Kanakaole, Dee Chapin, Beverly Creamer, Lucille Chung, Brian McGarry, Danny Hashimoto, Mike Yano, Roger Worldie, The Makaha Sons of Niihau, Kamaka Hawaii Inc., The Bernice Pauahi Bishop Museum, *The Honolulu Advertiser*, the *Honolulu Star-Bulletin*, *Ha'ilono Mele*, *Honolulu* magazine, *The Waikiki Beach Press*, *Pacific Business News*, The Hawaii Visitors Bureau, The Hawaiian Historical Society, the State of Hawaii Archives, and many others.

Comments, criticism, corrections and praise are always appreciated, and will be taken into consideration in preparing future editions of this book. Readers are advised to contact contributing editor Ronn Ronck, 4825-B4 Kahala Avenue, Honolulu, Hawaii 96816.

Mahalo plenty and *me ke aloha pumehana*.

– Apa Productions

TABLE OF CONTENTS

TABLE OF CONTENTS

Cover:
—by Hans Hoefer

Cartography:
—by Tony Khoo

To the people of Hawaii

HAWAII: HER BIRTH IN FIRE AND SEA

As in the Hebrew Genesis and other origin works, the *Kumulipo* genealogical prayer chant of the Hawaiians documents in poetic detail The Creation and human times immemorial. But also, appropriately and ironically, its basic message — that life as we know it emerged from dark and distant depths — is indeed the birth and growth story of the Central Pacific chain of volcanic islands, reefs and shoals we know as the Hawaiian Archipelago.

Hawaii did in fact emerge from the *deep-profound-darkness* of the sea. It's impossible to determine exactly when she began her ascent to the sky — geologists guess anywhere from 25 to 40 million years ago — but it is known that the 132 scattered points of land which comprise the Hawaiian group are the tips of huge mountains, or shield volcanoes, which rose from the bottom of the Pacific Ocean through standing vents in the earth's thin crust.

This volcanic creation began during a prehistoric period identified in scientific time scales as mid-Tertiary. During that time, huge volumes of magma from the earth's hot mantle began escaping through fractures on the ocean's floor. These eruptions originated at depths of 2,600 to 2,700 fathoms (or 15,600 to 16,200 feet) below sea level, but eventually they discharged enough volcanic matter to build a series of mountains which broke the sea's surface and sometimes kept growing skyward until they towered some 14,000 feet above sea level

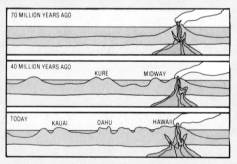

Due to a curious geological phenomenon known as tectonic plate movement, these Hawaiian Islands (or Hawaiian mountain peaks) emerged from the sea one at a time in a sequential W.N.W. to E.S.E. arc across the Tropic of Cancer (between 154° 40′ and 178° 75′ W longitude, and 18° 54′ to 28° 15′ N latitude).

This neat stitching of islands across the ocean floor has occurred because Hawaii sits above a shifting portion of the earth's crust called the Pacific Plate. This plate moves due northwest at a rate of about 5 to 8 centimeters (or 2 to 3 inches) each year. However, while the plate slides along like a conveyor belt, active volcanic vents below remain more or less in place, and continue to punch hot magma through fractures or thin zones in the shifting plate. As a result, each new shield volcano emerges from the sea just due south of a previous one created in this manner.

Following millions of years of sporadic vent activity, and slow but constant Pacific Plate movement, this submerged Hawaiian mountain range now stretches some 1,600 miles across the Pacific Ocean. The archipelago's oldest remains are in the vicinity of tiny Kure Atoll in the far north, and the newest members of the group are on the still fiery Big Island of Hawaii about 200 statute miles southeast of Honolulu.

Many of Hawaii's older islands to the northwest of Honolulu have been eroded into ragged reefbanks and desolate atolls. Others have simply been battered into or have sunk back into the sea. But in the new, southeast end of the Hawaiian chain, where humans now work and play, some of these mountains are still growing, inch-by-infernally-slow-inch.

The most impressive of these volcanic peaks are Kilauea and Mauna Loa on the Big Island. Famed for their memorable "dancing curtains of fire" and flowing "rivers of lava," Kilauea and Mauna Loa have been responsible for most of Hawaii's volcanic activity in recent history. However, geologists caution that these two hot spots could be joined at any time by one or all of three sister volcanoes — Mauna Kea and Hualalai on the Big Island, and Haleakala on the neighboring island of Maui. Those three mountains are officially classified as "dormant," not "extinct," volcanoes.

But whatever their individual activity quotients, all of Hawaii's volcanic mountains must be admired as some of the most massive works ever wrought by nature. Indeed, Mauna Kea, the legendary "White Mountain" which towers above all Hawaii and the Central Pacific, has already reached a height of 13,796 feet above sea level. And nearby Mauna Loa, the sloping "Long Mountain," hovers above clouds at the

13,677 foot elevation. This is not too high and impressive, a world trekker might conclude, but he or she would be surprised to know that scientists often describe Mauna Kea and Mauna Loa as the highest mountain peaks on earth. This is because both of these shield volcanoes rise to a vertical height—from ocean base to summit—of nearly 30,000 feet, or several hundred feet higher than Mt. Everest in the continental-based Himalayas. In terms of sheer mass, broad-based Mauna Loa also is probably the largest individual mountain on earth, having a body weight about 100 times the volume of the celebrated volcanic mountains Shasta and Fuji.

Most of the Hawaiian Islands, or mountain peaks if you will, began emerging from the sea sometime between the Miocene, Pliocene and Pleistocene epochs, or roughly between 2 and 25 million years ago. Therefore, in comparison to the world's major land masses (most of which were well-established about 300 million years ago), Hawaii is a geographical baby and one of the newest places on earth. However, because the Hawaiian Archipelago lies alone more than 2,000 miles away from the nearest continent and about 500 miles away from any other island group, it remained in virtually total isolation for many more millions of years following its late birth. Dinosaurs were lumbering across continents and primitive man was drawing pictures on cave walls as the islands began and completed their final building phases.

An Ice Age froze much of the world during the frigid Pleistocene epoch, and though an Arctic ice cap pushed as far south as New York City, the only chilly effect on Hawaii during that age was the deposition of a 28-square-mile glacier atop Mauna Kea. That tropical glacier's scrape and crunch trails are still clearly visible during non-winter months and the slopes it smoothed out are now being used by snow skiers, who schuss along favorite downhill and cross-country runs during her annual white months.

Meanwhile, in the course of human epochs, Moses commanded, Chinese dynasties patronized poets and philosophers,

Caesars ruled, and Buddha, Christ, and Mohammed preached. But still Hawaii remained untouched, save for the visits of prehistoric whales, dolphins, deepwater fishes and the evolving mosses, landgrasses, Winged Life, Crawlers, Night Diggers, Nibblers and other early creatures identified in *The Kumulipo* creation chant. Eventually, various birds, seeds, insects, barnacles, crabs and an occasional lichen-covered coconut drifted in on sea and wind currents. Coral polyps began clinging to and multiplying on shallow water shoals, and their millions of skeletal remains became fringing, whitewater reefs and lagoon dikes. And so life began appearing.

This growth process was painfully slow, but well worth mentioning, because even today Hawaii is one of the few places on earth where all these prehistoric processes—vulcanism, species introduction and rudimentary reef formation—can be observed and appreciated much as they were by the first dolphin or human eyes who saw them.

During these millenia when primitive creatures began accidentally arriving, the entire island group—both the major Windward or southeastern islands of Hawaii, Maui, Molokai, Lanai, Kahoolawe, Oahu, Kauai and Niihau, and the so-called Leeward, or Northwestern Hawaiian Islands—underwent a series of spectacular natural changes.

For sculptural openers, the unpredictable volcanoes continued to build and destroy land forms as they wished, flinging giant boulders here and there and impetuously upsetting growth processes in well-established neighborhoods. Additionally, the islands were periodically ravaged by violent tropical rainstorms, earthquakes, monster surf, tidal waves, glaciers and every other act of God imaginable. These natural phenomena flattened, steepened, shifted, carved and scooped out the vertical and scalloped valleys, riveted *pali* (cliffs), alluvial plains, tuff cones and knife-edged mountain ridges which make Hawaii a geological and visual delight.

Twain's shippy analogy has been over-quoted by subsequent travel writers, but it's a good one, because for many centuries after they were firmly established, and were teeming with land and sea creatures capable of supporting higher life forms, the Hawaiian Islands waited quietly—like a fleet of newly-launched ships without crews.

Preceding pages, the late Aunty Edith Kanakaole, dancing in a *koa* forest at Volcano, 1977; molten lava flow Kilauea Crater, Hawaii Volcanos National Park.

MIGRATION

kolea. 1. Pacific golden plover (*Pluvialis dominica fulvus*), a migratory bird which comes to Hawaii about the end of August and leaves early in May for Siberia and Alaska.

— *from Samuel Elbert and Mary Kawena Pukui's* Hawaiian Dictionary

The homely speckled plover, also referred to as the American golden plover, doesn't *just* fly to Hawaii. He also wends his way as far south and southwest as the Marquesas, Tahiti and New Zealand. For more than 3,000 miles, save for an occasional pit stop in Hawaii, Christmas Island and other more obscure landing strips in Oceania, the little plover's heart and wings beat rhythmically through Pacific storms, wind-currents and cloud banks until he finds a home in the Central Pacific or South Seas. Once there, the plover spends nine to ten months fattening up on crustaceans, snails and insects, then, mysteriously, flaps away on an annual return journey to Alaska and Siberia at their warmest.

Ancient seafaring Polynesians of the Marquesas and Society groups no doubt observed the comings and goings of this curious golden-backed bird. And they probably wondered just where the touring *kolea* was going every late spring. Certainly not somewhere back of nowhere. Like we humans of the 20th Century, they didn't believe that such a fragile bird could fly too far without food, rest and water. Their wonder fueled speculation, and this bird — and other unexplainable natural phenomena — inspired the launching of northerly expeditions of discovery.

In seaworthy, double-hulled canoes embellished with *aumakua*, carved spirit allies, these water-wary islanders set out in pursuit of the plover and other signs of land to the north. They were led in their quest by birds, but also by leaping dolphin, prevailing winds, ocean currents, shifting cloud masses and, most reliably, stars.

Timid Western man waited until the 15th Century and later before daring to set out on ocean journeys of any significant latitude. However, anthropologists believe that Polynesians were navigating their sturdy sea canoes over distances of 1,000 miles or more prior to 500 A.D. They used absolutely no navigating instruments, relying instead on maritime instincts, their eyes, stars and the aforementioned birds and other natural phenomena.

"Even today," report Bernice Pauahi Bishop Museum astronomers Will Kyselka and George Bunton, "the Marquesans use stars to orient themselves in the 120-mile trip from the north to south islands." The highly competent explorer-navigator Captain James Cook, who first sailed to the South Pacific in 1768 to 1771 to "observe the transit of Venus" for the British Admiralty and Royal Society, watched in a seaman's awe as Tahitians took eyeball bearings on stars and ploughed ahead into uncertain seas.

Based on observational-astronomical data accumulated over the years, it has been established that Polynesians made the 2,000-mile-plus run from their South Seas home to Hawaii by trailing the plover, riding "downhill" tradewinds and fixing on two key stars — Sirius and Arcturus. As Bunton and Kyselka note, "Sirius, the brightest star in the sky, passed almost directly over Tahiti and Raiatea (also called *Hawa'iti*). The present position of Sirius with respect to the equator has changed very little from that of the ancient days of Polynesian voyaging. Arcturus, called by the Hawaiians *Hoku-le'a* and noted for its bright redness off the Big Dipper's handle, presently passes over the northern end of the island of Hawaii. At the time of the great voyaging it passed over the island of Kauai."

A Land of Fire and Gnomes

However they fixed their first courses, the first discoverers and settlers of Hawaii are believed to have been Polynesian natives of the Marquesas Islands, who arrived in Hawaii sometime between 500 and 800 A.D. Early Marquesan landfalls and settlings in Hawaii have been determined by the carbon dating and comparison of fishhooks and adzes found in Hawaiian and Marquesan living sites of approximately the same period.

About 500 or 600 years later, sometime between 1100 and 1300 A.D., similar central Polynesian fleets from the Society, or Tahitian, Islands, began arriving in the land they referred to in Tahiti as *Hawai'ia* — or "Burning Hawaii," which was believed to be a reference to Hawaii's volcanoes. Scholars have speculated that this second wave of Polynesians subjugated the earlier Marquesans and/or drove them north in the Hawaiian chain until they were either assimilated as slaves or completely destroyed. These conquered Marquesans may have been the *manahune*, or *menehune*, mentioned in early Hawaiian and Tahitian chants. The term *manahune* was used haughtily and derisively in the Tahitian homeland to refer to slaves or plebeian castes, but its meaning changed through the centuries to mean, probably sarcastically, a group of mysterious gnomes or dwarfs who lived in the Hawaiian Islands at the time of the great Tahitian migrations.

But gnomes or no gnomes, both Polynesian groups brought to the Hawaiian Archipelago a common basic language, similar foods, related cultural peculiarities and synonymous myths, traditions and gods. They

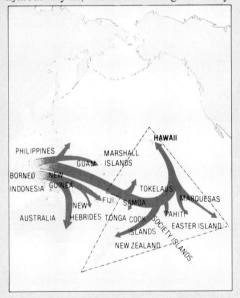

PHILIPPINES
BORNEO
INDONESIA
AUSTRALIA
NEW GUINEA
GUAM
MARSHALL ISLANDS
NEW HEBRIDES
FIJI
TONGA
SAMOA
COOK ISLANDS
TOKELAUS
SOCIETY ISLANDS
TAHITI
MARQUESAS
HAWAII
EASTER ISLAND
NEW ZEALAND

were basically of the same strong Polynesian stock which populated all the island realms throughout the Central and South Seas.

It was the Tahitians, however, who are credited with bequeathing the name *Hawai'i*, which was first given to the major Big Island of Hawaii and later to this island region.

Preceding pages, the "big surf" — January wave-rider at Sunset Beach, Oahu. Above map shows the first Polynesians migrating east from Southeast Asia, and establishing a home base in the Hawaiian Islands.

As the Polynesian bard Kama-hua-lele chanted in centuries past: "Behold *Hawai'i*, an island, a people/The people of *Hawai'i* are the offspring of Tahiti."

Sir Peter Buck, the eminent half-Maori ethnologist who served as director of Hawaii's Bernice Pauahi Bishop Museum from 1936 until his death in 1951, explains the origin of the word *Hawaii* in his 1938 book *Vikings of the Pacific*. He notes that in ancient times "the headquarters of the Polynesian main body was established in the largest island of the leeward group of Tahiti, named *Havai'i* after an ancient homeland."

As Havai'i-based fleets set out to settle the Society Islands, Samoa, Tonga, Fiji, Hawaii and New Zealand—among other scattered places in the Pacific—they established colonies which they often named after their home port-island. Dialectal differences resulted in slight place name variations, or as Sir Buck wrote:

Dialects have developed in various island groups by changes in consonant sounds. *R* and *v* are used in central and eastern Polynesia where *l* and *v* are used in western Polynesia. In some dialects certain consonants are not fully sounded but are represented or should be represented by an inverted comma over its place in the word. In the Society Islands, *k* and *ng* were dropped; so the name for the ancestral homeland, pronounced Havaiki in other dialects of central Polynesia, is here pronounced Havai'i. In New Zealand, where *w* is used instead of *v*, the ancient home is Hawaiki. In the Cook Islands, where *h* is dropped, it is 'Avaiki. In the Hawaiian islands, where *w* is used and *k* is dropped, the largest island of the group is named Hawai'i. In Samoa, where *s* replaces *h*, *v* is preferred to *w*, and *k* is dropped, the largest island is called Savai'i.

An even more conclusive Hawaii-Tahiti relationship is exemplified by the ancient name of a channel located south of the island of Maui between the junior Hawaiian islands of Lanai and Kahoolawe. The channel's Hawaiian name is *Kealaikahiki*. By substituting the *k*'s in the word with *t*'s, we produce the word *Te-ala-i-tahiti*, a term which in translation means "the pathway to Tahiti," or "the pathway to foreign lands."

ILES SANDWICH. UN OFFICIER DU ROI EN GRAND COSTUME.

ANCIENT HAWAII

Hakau-a-Liloa, the high chief who ruled over Hawaii, was one of those laid on the altar as a burnt offering for the god by 'Umi. The story is well known, and thousands of persons were eyewitnesses that the god came down from heaven in a billow of floating clouds, with thunder and lightning and dark clouds, and the tongue of the god quivered above the *lele* (the altar). The god was not seen; his body was in the heavens, but his tongue quivered downward like lightning, and the burnt offering became a billow of smoke and rose up and was gone ...

— *from* Ka Po'e Kahiko, The People of Old, *by the Hawaiian historian Samuel Manaiakalani Kamakau*

When the first Polynesian dug-out canoes were beached on Hawaii's shores — probably first at or near South Point on the Big Island — these islands were as close to being an unspoiled Eden-Shangrila-Bali Hai as had ever been discovered on earth. Biologists say much of the land was somewhat barren, dusty and largely host to scrub plants, but thriving here and there were some 2,200 kinds of higher plants that occur only in the Hawaiian Islands and nowhere else. The islands' undisturbed shoreline reefs and lagoons, fern forests, rich alluvial plains, and well-watered valleys and highlands were verily splashing, crawling and blooming with what had evolved into Hawaii's indigenous flora, fauna, birds and marine life.

"Most visitors and many residents of the State are not aware of Hawaii's unique plants and see very few of them," writes an author in the University of Hawaii's *Atlas of Hawaii.* "The coconuts, orchids, sugarcane, and pineapples of the tourist advertisements are recent immigrants to Hawaii, neither native nor unique. (And) native plants are common today only in such remote places as the headwalls of deep valleys, on steep cliffs, and on mountain ridges and peaks." However, of Hawaii's 2,200 endemic plants, about 30 percent are considered "endangered," or threatened by extinction, most of them the weaker victims of introduced plant species.

Preceding pages, early 20th Century Hawaiians model ancient feather capes, which differ little from the one worn by the helmeted warrior (left) drawn by a French artist who visited Hawaii in 1819.

Nary a Newt, Not Even a Gnat

When the first Marquesans arrived in Hawaii, they found some 67 varieties of endemic Hawaiian birds (about 23 of which are now believed extinct), including large fowl such as the *koloa* (the Hawaiian duck) and *nene* (the Hawaiian goose). But astonishingly, neither amphibia (frogs, newts and the like), nor reptiles, nay, not even pesky mosquitos, lice, fleas, flies or gnats were on hand to bug them. And for nearly a thousand years, until mariners began arriving from the East and West bearing common and social diseases, most of the world's debilitating and lethal germs were also absent. These islands were a pristine place, patiently and naively awaiting the introduction of pestilence and disease.

Among higher animal order representatives, the Polynesians found only two endemic mammals — a small bat, the so-called hoary bat (*Lasiurus cinereus*), which had somehow migrated from either North or South America, and the monk seal (*Monachus Schauinslandi*), a relative of seals previously found in the Caribbean and Mediterranean. The hoary bat, known as the *ope'ape'a* to Hawaiians, still swoops in and out of Big Island nights in the vicinity of Kilauea Crater, but the monk seal, which now survives only in Hawaii, rarely ventures near populated islands for a peek at the colorful jet-set mammals who nearly slaughtered him into extinction for his skin and oil during the 19th Century.

Animal and plant life systems in old Hawaii were very fragile indeed, but how could they be otherwise in what is probably the most perfect climate on earth. Hawaii's environment was then — and still is today — a balmy, mellifluous mix of sunshine, misty rainbows, and regular northeasterly tradewinds which act as one of the planet's finest natural air-conditioning systems.

The first Polynesians from the south, however, immediately upset this finite ecological balance. They fortunately had not yet been exposed to many of the diseases and pests we take for granted these days, but they arrived bearing several forms of domestic foodstuff. In their caches were dogs, pigs and chickens (all three for eating), and, probably unintentionally, the first Hawaiian menace, stowaway Hawaiian rats (*Rattus exulans*). To supplement their diet, the first Hawaiians also introduced the starchy tuber staple known as *taro* (from which the grey, pasty mush called *poi* is made), coconuts, bananas, yams, *kukui* candlenuts, wild ginger, breadfruit and sugarcane. Plus utility plants, such as the *wauke*, the paper mulberry (*Broussonetia papyrifera*), which was beaten and sunbleached into *kapa* (barkcloth), and the *ti* (*Cordyline terminalis*), a lily relative whose roots and leaves are still used as wrapping and matting, and to make *hula* skirts and a liquor called *ti*-root *okolehao*.

But more important than food and fiber stuffs, the Polynesians brought in their minds a remarkable collection of cultural and religious traditions which were directed at the animate and inanimate spirits who ruled their visions of the world and universe.

Most of what we know about "pre-contact" Hawaii is contained in poetic oral traditions, known to the Hawaiians as *mele*. In these *mele*, the Hawaiians' *kupuna* — or ancestors — passed on to their descendants all they knew of their history. Various aspects of physical and spiritual life — from the trivial to the momentous — were reported in this unwritten literature of family genealogies, myths and day-to-day human experiences.

The second best sources on early Hawaii are initial observations made by foreign explorers such as the sea captains James Cook, George Vancouver and Otto von Kotzebue; and the memoirs of early Hawaiian scholars, notably John Papa Ii (1800-1870), Samuel Kamakau (1815-1876), Kepelino Keauokalani (1830-1878) and David Malo (1793-1887). Another good source are the antiquities and folk lores collected by Abraham Fornander (1812-1887), a Circuit Court judge from the island of Maui. Fornander, who spoke and wrote Hawaiian fluently, was married to a Hawaiian woman and took it upon himself to write a history of Hawaii (*An Account of the Polynesian Race: Its Origins and Migrations*) and to collect and translate many ancient Hawaiian chants into English before they were lost.

The above combination of viewpoints differ at times, but they offer enough data to affirm, along with a wealth of surviving artifacts, that the Hawaiians had developed into one of the most complex "Stone Age" cultures ever encountered by outside and "civilized" observers.

The Kapu Way of Life

Hawaiian life was simple but remarkably subtle and regulated under systematic laws known as *kapu*. *Kapu*, a variation of the Tahitian word *tapu* (or taboo), directed daily life and caste relationships. A hereditary group of *alii*, or noblemen, dominated hereditary *makaainana*, or commoners, and there was no way short of revolution that tightly circumscribed *kapu* and bloodlines could be crossed. A common penalty for a *kapu* violation was execution by being stoned, clubbed, strangled, or being buried or burned alive. Sometimes a *kapu*-breaker was singled out merely as a convenient sacrificial victim, say when a chief wanted to appease a certain god, but usually he was sacrificed to graphically exemplify what might happen to other would-be *kapu* transgressors. *Kapu*-breakers, however, were provided with a place of last resort, similar to biblical cities of refuge, where they could seek sanctuary and

A MAN of the SANDWICH ISLANDS, in a MASK.

live unmolested, whatever their crime. These places of refuge, called *pu'uhonua*, had to be reached by a law-breaker before he was caught by a chief's pursuing warriors. A good example of a *pu'uhonua* is located on a lava promontory at Honaunau, Kona, on the Big Island of Hawaii.

This intricate *kapu* system directly or indirectly affected every aspect of Hawaiian life — from birth to death — until it was overthrown in 1819 by the Hawaiian King

The Hawaiian man in gourd mask (above) and similarly masked canoe rowers (right) were sketched in 1779 by John Webber, the artist who accompanied Captain James Cook on his third voyage and discovery of the Hawaiian Islands.

14

Kamehameha II. But until their abolition more than 40 years after the arrival in 1778 of the British Captain James Cook, *kapu* precepts effectively protected the powers of Hawaiian kings and their underlings.

The Hawaiian scholar-historian David Malo recounted that a person could be put to death for merely allowing his shadow to fall upon the house of a *kapu* chief, or for passing through that chief's stockade or doorway, or entering the house before changing his *malo* loincloth, or by appearing there with his head smeared with mud.

More common *kapu* declared that women could not eat pork, coconuts, bananas and shark meat, nor could they eat with men, or vice-versa. Also, certain seasons were established (as conservation measures) for the

from about 1490 to 1521. A chant recorded by Fornander reported that:

> When peace and quiet reigned in the government of Hawaii under Umi-a-Liloa, his name became famous from Hawaii to Kauai. No king was like unto him in the administration of his government; he took care of the old men and the old women and orphans; he had regard for the people also; there were no murders and thievings.

As aforementioned, many heavy-handed — and benevolent — administrative tactics were attributable to the chiefs' ministers, called the *kalaimoku*, the high priests or *kahuna nui*, and various upper, middle or low-ranking *alii*. These royalists were in-

A CANOE of the SANDWICH ISLANDS, the ROWERS MASKED.

gathering or catching of scarce foodstuffs; and sometimes sporting chiefs kapued certain surfing spots for their personal and exclusive pleasure.

Some *kapu* were instigated by Machiavellian chiefs, priests or influential court retainers under the guise of religion, or to arrogantly and tyrannically oppress a person or group of people; but many of the laws were simply of a conservative or rationing nature, designed — much as are modern wildlife regulations — to protect resources from human greed, misuse and pollution.

One Hawaiian *moi*, or king, who was immortalized in song and dance as having been wise and peace-loving was the "mountain monarch" Umi-a-Liloa, who reigned

fluenced, in turn, by staff specialists of the realm — craftsmen, priests, medicine men, artisans, teachers and other wise men — who were collectively known as *kahuna*. These upper castes manipulated the vast working class, known as the *makaainana*, and an "untouchable" minority of outcasts called the *kauwa*. The *kauwa*, a pariah group of people who lived apart from the rest of Hawaiian society, were sometimes marked by tatooing of their foreheads and often were summarily conscripted as sacrificial victims by *kahuna* and executioners (the *mu*) in charge of such "religious" procurements.

Sacrifices — only sometimes of human life — were made to any of hundreds of deities in the Hawaiian-Polynesian pantheon, but the four most powerful gods of Hawaiian Polynesia were always *Ku, Kane, Lono* and *Kanaloa* (known in Tahitian as *Tu, Tane, Rongo* and *Tangaroa*).

Ku, who represented "male generating power," was appealed to for rain and growth, fishing and sorcery, but was best known as a patron god of war. The most well-known Hawaiian images of *Ku,* whose combative title was "the island snatcher," are brilliant wood, wicker and feather sculptures which were carried into battle by Kamehameha the Great and other early warring chiefs. According to oral traditions, these fearsome images—wrought of red *i'iwi* feathers embellished with mother-of-pearl eyes and mouths of jagged dogs' teeth—would utter cries during combat. Good examples of such

retainers on their tribute-tax-collecting tours of the various islands. Benevolent *Lono* was never appealed to with human sacrifices.

Kanaloa, lord of the ocean and ocean winds, oftentimes was embodied in the octopus and squid, but also in other natural things, such as the banana. He was a companion of *Kane,* and according to certain legends the two gods traveled together, "moving about the land and opening spring and water holes for the benefit of men." Kanaloa is also revered as a patron god of healing.

All four deities, and numerous lesser and specialized gods (such as *Pele,* the volcano goddess, and *Laka,* the patron goddess of hula dancers) and personal spirit allies known as *aumakua* (for example, *La'ahana,*

Ku may be seen in the collection of the Bernice Pauahi Bishop Museum in Honolulu.

Kane, the "leading god among the great gods," was the procreator, the ancestor of all chiefs and commoners, the male (*kane*) who dwells in eternity—the god of sunlight, fresh water and forests. Unlike *Ku, Kane* was not fond of human sacrifices.

Lono, meanwhile, was considered a god of thunder (the name means "resounding"), clouds, winds, the sea, agriculture and fertility, but his personage could assume as many as 50 forms. Most notably, he was honored during the annual *makahiki* harvest festivals of November, December and January, when his image was carried by chiefly

the patron *aumakua* of *kapa*-makers) were venerated by Hawaiians of all ranks.

Hawaiians generally worshiped privately and at small shrines they built in their homes or out-of-doors, but the focal points of most major religious observances were large open-air temples known as *heiau.* Ruins of these *heiau* can be seen on all the Hawaiian Islands. In most cases they consist today of rudimentary platforms, terraces and walls made

Above, Pellion engraving shows *kapa*-pounding, the first known study of a surfboard, and Chief Kalanimoku wearing a "mushroom" helmet. Right, temple exterior and carved gods observed by artist-adventurer Arago.

of large lava stones, but previously they housed *kapa*-covered oracle towers, sacrificial platform-altars, carved stone and wooden sculptures, thatch and feather god images, sacred stones, rough-hewn monoliths, groupings of wood and stone sub-temple structures, and often a refuse pit for the disposal of decayed human, animal or plant offerings.

The most complex temples were those built by Hawaiian chiefs to initiate a war. These *heiau waikaua* (war temples) or *luakini* temples were kept spiritually "alive," or current, by the periodic sacrifice of a human or group of humans within their environs. Following a series of such grisly consecrations in honor of Lord *Ku*, the Hawaiians were properly psyched up for periodic acts of intramural hand-to-hand combat, known as *kaua*, or warfare.

Once it had been decided to make war, and proper sacrifices had been made to *Ku*, Malo said, the high chief would call for his *kilolani*, or astrologer, to determine the most auspicious day to do battle. In the event of a surprise attack, he of course had no such supernatural options, but more often than not Hawaiian battles were well-planned and prepared for by both sides.

This system of forearming and forewarning is reminiscent of European days of chivalry when opposing armies would line up and neatly engage one another in proper battle. However, the ritual aspects of Hawaiian wars quickly gave way to brutal, man-to-man affairs not too unlike those waged in later Stone Age periods elsewhere on earth.

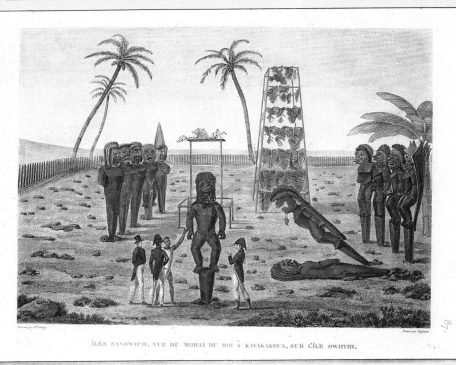

ÎLES SANDWICH. VUE DU MORAI DU ROI À KAYAKAKOUA, SUR L'ÎLE OWHYHI.

Warfare — for Fun, for Real

Given the Hawaiians' disparate, tribal nature, and the generally clannish-feudalistic structure of the society, wars of succession and conquest were somewhat frequent. Consequently, chiefs who wanted to keep their power intact encouraged the study of combat arts such as spear-throwing, spear-thrusting, wrestling, boxing and the like. Periodic, courtly sham-battles were held between the parties of friendly chiefs to keep young warriors prepped and ready for the real thing.

Perhaps there would be some opening decorum (say gladiator-style, where two renowned warriors would fight to the death before two opposing and cheering audience-armies), but more often than not the two forces would meet on an impromptu or chosen battleground, usually during daylight hours and, following an exchange of verbal taunts and insults, would tear into one another with a vicious assortment of war material. Common Hawaiian implements of destruction included spears up to 18 feet in length, shorter javelins, truncheons, bludgeons, assorted exotic daggers (some lined with sharksteeth), rough, smooth and stone-headed clubs. serrated sharktooth clubs and "knuckle-dusters," a variety of sennit and stone tripping weapons, slingshots, strangling cords and any and all crude objects (rocks, boulders, branches and the like) which could be spontaneously introduced into the fray.

Major Hawaiian wars and lesser scrimmages continued through the centuries until 1795 when one chief, Kamehameha of the Big Island of Hawaii, successfully whipped all other *alii* antagonists and consolidated six of the eight Hawaiian Islands into one kingdom.

To be sure, ancient Hawaiian life was not an endless and savage cycle of warmaking, and, more spectacularly, tobogganing (on *holua* sleds which were raced down specially prepared hillside runways) and surfing, known as *he'e nalu.*

'Beauty and Magnificence'

The Hawaiians also created the most exquisite variety of fine artworks and personal adornments found anywhere in Polynesia. Wood and stone sculpture was extremely graphic and vigorous, and ancient featherwork and *kapa* are still considered to be the finest examples of those arts known. Captain Cook, the first "critic" to evaluate the merits of Hawaiian art, said of Hawaiian featherwork he observed that "the surface might be compared to the thickest and richest velvet."

VARIOUS ARTICLES, at the SANDWICH ISLANDS.

oppression and workaday drudgery. The Hawaiians also enjoyed a full share of peace, when games and recreation, fine arts and craftsmanship, song and dance, and lovemaking, superseded war, training for war, *kapu* observances, religious rituals and labor.

In their isolated state, the Hawaiians developed unique forms of "fun" recreation, including such friendly diversions as the flying of large kites (*lupe*) made of barkcloth (*kapa*); the staging of mini-dances and plays using hand puppets; numerous games of skill and chance; archery (used to kill rodents);

His lieutenant, James King, seconded Cook, noting that the "feathered cloak and helmet ... in point of beauty and magnificence, is perhaps nearly equal to that of any nation in the world." The finest of these featherworks, the capes, helmets and cloaks fashioned for high chiefs, are considered priceless today and are among the most cherished objects catalogued in worldwide collections of Pacific art.

Sandwich Islands articles (above) are by Webber; and the hand-colored engraving of a tattooed *hula* dancer in *kapa* skirt (right) is by Arago.

18

It would be impossible today to duplicate one of these cloaks, because most of the birds whose feathers were plucked for their distinctive coloring are extinct. Also, it would probably take a cloak-maker the better part of a lifetime to gather the necessary plumage. In old Hawaii, the king commissioned special groups of royal feather-pluckers — known as *ha'ina-kolo* or *po'e hahai manu* — who stalked and snared preferred prey with nets and long sticky wands. Even with such compulsory labor, a major chief's great cloak might take decades to complete. One such cloak in the Bernice Pauahi Bishop Museum's collection, said to have belonged to Kamehameha I, reportedly required some 450,000 feathers plucked off an estimated 80,000 birds (most of them coming from the *mamo*, or black

head-bands and anklets wrought of flowers, nuts, seeds, shells, ivory, teeth, turtle shell, human hair, and other natural materials, or actual tatooing.

Oftentimes, blistering, burning or tattooing of the skin were done as signs of mourning, as were other forms of bodily defilement, notably the knocking out of front teeth, or the cutting off of one or both ears as a visible sign of grief. The missionary Ellis once saw the Hawaiian Queen Kamamalu, the wife of Liholiho, undergoing a painful ritual tattooing of a line on her tongue. Sometimes the pain was so intense the mourning queen would ask the attending tattooist to rest his needle.

As in other parts of Polynesia (the word *tatoo* is an anglicized version of the Tahitian

Hawaiian honey creeper, which had small tufts of bright yellow feathers growing above and below its tail).

Hawaiian *kapa*, the soft Polynesian barkcloth fashioned from bast of the paper mulberry, also represents a major Hawaiian artistic achievement, one which premier critic Cook greatly praised after seeing it made and worn on the island of Kauai. Unfortunately *kapa*-making is now extinct in Hawaii.

Perhaps the most diverse art practiced by the Hawaiians was adornment of the body, whether in the form of fantastic necklaces,

term *tatau*), Hawaiians — both men and women — tattooed their faces, limbs and torsos with a variety of favorite designs. Some were of a topical tropical nature, but they also were of repetitious motifs resembling barkcloth beater patterns. The design was usually tapped and rubbed into the skin with small sharp needles wrought of fish and bird bones or points of a shell. This form of bodily adornment is still extant in other parts of Polynesia, and has long been popular in nautical circles, but in Hawaii it has largely disappeared as a native Hawaiian vanity.

seven o'clock A. M. a north-easterly breeze springing up, our anchors were ordered to be taken up, with a view of removing the Resolution further out. As soon as the last anchor was up, the wind veering to the east, rendered it necessary to make all the sail we could, for the purpose of clearing the shore; so that before we had good sea-room, we were driven considerably to leeward. We endeavoured to regain the road, but having a strong current against us, and very little wind, we could not accomplish that design. Our Commodore therefore dispatched Messrs. King and Williamson ashore, with three boats, to procure water and refreshments, sending at the same time, an order to Captain Clerk, to put to sea after him, if he should find that the Resolution was unable to recover the road. Having hopes of finding perhaps a harbour, at the west end of the island, we were the less anxious of regaining our former station; but boats having been sent thither, we kept as much as possible to windward, notwithstanding which, at noon, our ship was three leagues to leeward. As we approached the west end, we found that the coast rounded gradually, to the N. E. without forming a cove, or creek, wherein a vessel might be sheltered from the violence of the swell, which rolling in from the northward, broke against the shore in an amazing surf: all hopes, therefore, of meeting with a harbour here soon vanished. Many of the natives, in their canoes, followed us as we stood out to sea, bartering various articles. As we were extremely unwilling, notwithstanding the suspicious circumstances of the preceding day, to believe that these people were cannibals, we now made some further enquiries on this subject. A small instrument of wood, beset with shark's teeth, had been purchased, which, as it resembled the saw or knife made use of by the savages of New Zealand to dissect the bodies of their enemies, was suspected by us to be employed here for the same purpose. One of the islanders being questioned on this point, informed us, that the instrument above mentioned served the purpose of cutting out the fleshy part of the belly, when any person was slain. This explained and confirmed the circumstance before related, of the man's pointing to his belly. The native, however, from whom we now received this intelligence, being asked whether his countrymen eat the part thus cut out, strongly denied it; but when the question was repeated, he shewed some degree of apprehension, and swam off to his canoe. An elderly man, who sat foremost in the canoe, was then asked, whether they eat the flesh, and he answered in the affirmative. The question being put to him a second time, he again affirmed the fact; adding that it was savoury food. In the evening, about seven o'clock, the boats returned with a few hogs, some roots, plantains, and two tons of water. Mr. King reported to our Commodore, that the islanders were very numerous at the watering place, and had brought great numbers of hogs to barter; but our people had not commodities with them sufficient to purchase them all. He also mentioned, that the surf had run so very high, that it was with extreme difficulty our men landed, and afterwards got back into the boats.

On Saturday, the 24th, at day-break, we found that our ship had been carried by the currents to the N. W. and N. so that the western extremity of Atooi, bore E. at the distance of one league. A northerly breeze sprung up soon after, and, expecting that this would bring the Discovery to sea, we steered for Oneeheow, a neighbouring island, which then bore S. W. with a view of anchoring there. We continued to steer for it till past eleven, when we were distant from it about six miles: but not seeing the Discovery, we were apprehensive lest some ill consequence might arise from our separating so far; we therefore relinquished the design of visiting Oneeheow for the present, and stood back to Atooi, intending to cast anchor again in the road, in order to complete our supply of water. At two o'clock, the northerly wind was succeeded by calms and variable light airs, which continued till eleven at night. We stretched to the S. E. till early in the morning of the 25th, when we tacked and stood in for Atooi road; and, not long after, we were joined by the Discovery.

We remained several days beating up, but in vain, to regain our former birth; and by the morning of Thursday, the 29th, the currents had carried us to the westward, within nine miles of Oneeheow. Weary with plying so unsuccessfully, we laid aside all thoughts of returning to Atooi, and resumed our intention of paying a visit to Oneeheow. With this view the master was dispatched in a boat to sound along the coast, and search for a landing place, and afterwards fresh water. In the mean time the ships followed under an easy sail. The master, at his return, reported, that there was tolerable anchorage all along the coast; and that he had landed in one place, but could not find any fresh water: but, being informed by some of the natives, who had come off to the ships, that fresh water might be obtained at a village in sight, we ran down and cast anchor before it, about six furlongs from the shore, the depth of water being 26 fathoms. The Discovery anchored at a greater distance from the shore, in 23 fathoms. The south-eastern point of Oneeheow bore south, 65 deg. E. about one league distant; and another island which we had discovered the preceding night, named Tahoora, bore S. 61 deg. W. distant 7 leagues.

Before we anchored, several canoes had come off to us, bringing potatoes, yams, small pigs, and mats. The people resembled in their persons the inhabitants of Atooi, and, like them, were acquainted with the use of iron, which they asked for by the names of toe and hamaite, readily parting with all their commodities for pieces of that metal. Some more canoes soon reached our ships, after they had come to anchor; but the islanders who were in these had apparently no other object, than to make us a formal visit. Many of them came on board, and crouched down on the deck; nor did they quit their humble posture, till they were requested to rise. Several women, whom they had brought with them, remained along-side the canoes, behaving with much less modesty than the females of Atooi; and, at intervals, they all joined in a song, which, though not very melodious, was performed in the exactest concert, by beating time upon their breasts with their hands. The men who had come on board did not continue long with us; and before their departure, some of them desired permission to lay down locks of hair on the deck. This day we renewed the enquiry whether these islanders were cannibals, and the subject did not arise from any questions put by us, but from a circumstance that seemed to remove all doubt. One of the natives, who wished to get in at the gun-room port, was refused, and he then asked, whether we should kill and eat him, if he should come in? accompanying this question with signs so expressive, that we did not entertain a doubt with respect to his meaning. We had now an opportunity of retorting the question, as to this practice; and a man behind the other, in the canoe, instantly replied, that, if we were killed on shore, they would not scruple to eat us; not that he meant they would destroy us for that purpose, but that their devouring us would be the consequence of our being at enmity with them. In the afternoon, Mr. Gore was sent with three armed boats, in search of the most commodious landing-place; being also directed to look for fresh water when he should get ashore. He returned in the evening, and reported, that he had landed at the village, and had been conducted to a well about half a mile up the country; but that the water it contained was in too small a quantity for our purpose, and the road that led to it was extremely bad.

On Friday, the 30th, Mr. Gore was sent ashore again, with a guard, and a party to trade with the inhabitants for refreshments. The Captain's intention was to have followed soon afterwards; and he went from the ship with that design: but the surf had so greatly increased by this time, that he was apprehensive, if he got ashore, he should not be able to make his way back again. This circumstance really happened to our people who had landed with Mr. Gore; for the communication between them and the ships, by our own boats, was quickly stopped. They made a signal, in the evening, for the boats, which were accordingly sent; and in a short

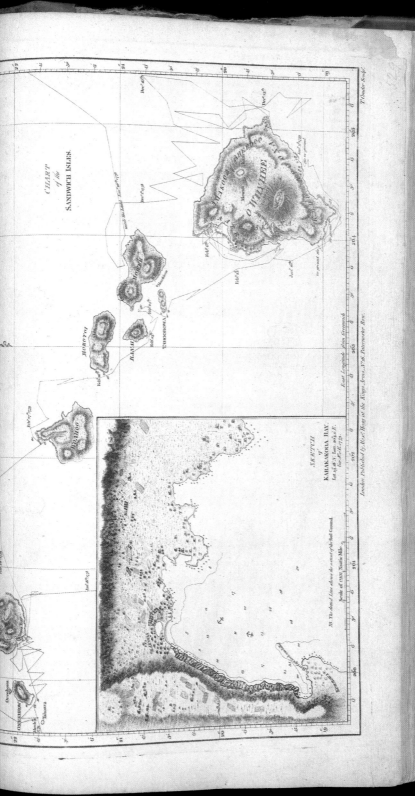

CHART
of the
SANDWICH ISLES.

SKETCH
of
KARAKAKOA BAY.
Lat 19.28.N. Lon. 204.0.E.
Var. 8°E. Dr. 1729.

N.B. The dotted Line shews the extent of the fast Ground.

Scale of 1000 Nautic Miles.

London. Published by Messrs Hogg at the Kings Arms, No. 16 Paternoster Row.

East Longitude from Greenwich

J.Webber del.

CAV

"… On Sunday the 17th, by eleven o'clock A.M. we were safely moored, in company with the *Discovery, in 18 fathoms water. The bay where we lay at anchor, called by the natives Karakakooa, is a convenient harbour; and having suffered much in our masts and rigging, we were happy at last to find so proper a place to refit …*
… After we were moored the ships continued to be much crouded with the natives, and surrounded by a vast multitude of them, besides hundreds that, like fish, were swimming about the two ships. We were struck with the singularity of this scene, and particularly pleased with enriching our voyage, with this important new discovery, owing to the opportunity of thus revisiting Sandwich Islands, and in consequence of not having succeeded in finding a northern passage homeward …

22

KARAKAKOOA, *in* OWYHEE.

... Before we had been long at anchor, the Discovery had so many people hanging on one side, that she was seen to heel considerably; and our people found it impossible to prevent the crowds from pressing into her. Apprehensive that she might receive some injury, Captain Cook communicated his sentiments to Pareea, who instantly cleared the ship of her incumbrances, and dispersed the canoes with which she was surrounded. From this circumstance it appeared to us, that the chiefs of this island exercise a most despotic power over the commonalty ...

Official British Admiralty comments regarding the arrival of
Captain James Cook at Kealakekua Bay, Hawaii, on January 17, 1779.

CAPTAIN JAMES COOK

The ship was first sighted from Waialua and Waianae (on Oahu) sailing for the north. It anchored at night at Waimea, Kauai, that place being nearest at hand. A man named Moapu and his companions who were fishing with heavy lines saw this strange thing move by and saw the lights on board. Abandoning their fishing gear, no doubt through fright, they hurried ashore and hastened to tell Kaeo and the other chiefs of Kauai about this strange apparition.

The next morning the ship lay outside Kaahe at Waimea. Chiefs and commoners saw the wonderful sight and marveled at it. Some were terrified and shrieked with fear. The valley of Waimea rang with the shouts of the excited people as they saw the boat with its masts and sails shaped like a gigantic sting ray. One asked another, "What are those branching things?" and the other answered, "They are trees moving on the sea." Still another thought, "A double canoe of the hairless ones of Mana!" A certain kahuna named Kuohu declared, "That can be nothing else than the heiau of Lono, the tower of Keolewa, and the place of sacrifice at the altar." The excitement became more intense, and louder grew the shouting.
— the Hawaiian version of the arrival of Captain James Cook in Hawaii in 1778, as reported by the Hawaiian author-historian Kamakau.

As Kamakau's prose indicates, the "modern" era in Hawaii's history began with excitement and holy terror when Hawaiian natives on the island of Oahu saw two strange white-winged objects floating by at sea in a northeasterly direction. These "floating islands," as the Hawaiians described them, were British ships — HMS *Resolution* and *Discovery* — commanded by Captain James Cook, the most famous navigator-explorer of his time. While on a search for a Northwest Passage from Asia to Europe, Cook — and the seamen, astronomer and artist assigned to the *Resolution* and *Discovery* by the British Admiralty — had accidentally become the first known non-Polynesians to discover Hawaii.

It was a formidable find, because as it turned out, Hawaii was the last significant land on earth to be discovered by Western man. Even Cook marveled in his journal at

the existence of the Polynesian settlements he had stumbled onto. "How," he asked in his ship's journal, "shall we account for this Nation spreading itself so far over this Vast ocean . . .?"

Seeds of Life—and Death

Cook named these isles the Sandwich Islands in honor of John Montagu, the fourth Earl of Sandwich, First Lord of the Admiralty, and Cook's most enthusiastic patron. In his ship's log Cook later noted that the finding of Hawaii was "in many respects

the most important discovery made by Europeans throughout the extent of the Pacific Ocean."

During his first "discovery" stopover in Hawaii, Cook traded iron and trinkets with natives of Kauai for fresh foodstuffs and water and visited an impressive *heiau* inside Waimea Valley. After five days of replenishing and sightseeing (during which time a Hawaiian man was shot by an over-anxious Cook lieutenant), strong night winds blew his ships away from Kauai and nearer the smaller island of Niihau. On Niihau, Cook's men bargained for salt and yams and, before leaving on February 2 for the Pacific Northwest, left gifts of goats, pigs and seeds of melons, pumpkins and onions. The first specimens of Western flora and fauna were thus introduced at the northernmost populated island in Hawaii on February 1, 1778.

But also introduced, against Cook's explicitly posted orders, were seeds of another kind. During that first two-week stopover in the Sandwich Isles, Cook's men successfully inoculated hospitable females with the venereal diseases syphilis and gonorrhea. These killers, in concert with other lesser Western germs deposited at Kauai and Niihau, began the rapid destruction by disease of the Hawaiian people.

Cook, knowing of this morbid possibility, told his men clearly that no Hawaiian women were to be allowed on board the ships, nor any person "having or suspected of having the venereal disease or any Symptoms thereof, shall lie with any woman," under threat of severe lashing at the masthead. But severe orders or not, these two sexual force fields could not be officially kept apart. The Hawaiian women, they of wanton wiles and

Captain Cook's explorations on the Hawaiian Islands as revealed by travel journal, preceding pages. Cook (left) named Hawaii the Sandwich Islands after John Montagu (above), the colorful fourth Earl of Sandwich.

decidedly promiscuous sexual nature, and the sailors, understandably randy after months at sea, met on Kauai and Niihau sands and spread invisible germs of destruction through ·the heretofore undiseased Hawaiian archipelago.

Thomas Edgar, master of the *Discovery*, said his men employed every devious scheme possible to get women on board the ships, even "dressing them up as Men." But he noted also that the Hawaiian women "used all arts to entice them into their Houses & even went so far as to endeavour to draw them in by force."

Writing 80 years later—after the Hawaiian population had dropped drastically from an estimated 300,000 persons at the time of Cook's visit to about 60,000—the Hawaiian historian Kamakau wrote the following bitter (and exaggerated) commentary on Cook:

> The seeds he planted here have sprouted and grown and become the parents of others that have caused the decrease of the native population of these islands: gonorrhea and other social diseases; prostitution; the illusion of his being a god which led to worship of him; fleas and mosquitoes; epidemics; changes in the air which we breathe; the coming of things that weaken the body; changes in plant life; changes in religion, in the arts of healing, in the laws by which the land is governed ... Because he killed the people, he was killed by them without mercy and his entrails were used to rope off the arena and the palms of his hands used for fly swatters at a cockfight."

Kamakau also alleged that Cook himself received and slept with a Kauai princess named Lelemahoalani, but official British reports of the voyage deny that the conscientious Captain engaged in such a liaison.

Ah, but if Cook was impressed by the way Kauai Hawaiians prostrated themselves in his presence and regaled him with their finest gifts on his first visit to Hawaii, he must have been doubly impressed by the reception he received the second time his "floating islands" made a landing in the Sandwich Isles, this time at the southernmost and largest island of Hawaii.

During the seven months he was in ·the Northwest looking unsuccessfully for an Arctic route to the Atlantic, news of Cook's first visit had been carried to probably every inhabited corner of Hawaii.

Upon returning to Hawaiian waters in November of 1778, Cook's second coming was by all accounts a monumental happening in Hawaii. His ships were first sighted off the island of Maui and were escorted and visited by fleets of curious natives in outrigger canoes. For nearly two months, the *Discovery* and *Resolution* cruised offshore — first alongside Maui, then off the east and south shores of the Big Island of Hawaii, below the snow-covered peaks of Mauna Kea and Mauna Loa.

Finally, on January 17, 1779 the two ships put into a West Hawaii bay known to the Hawaiians as *Kealakekua*, the pathway of the god.

in one place; besides those in the canoes, all the shore of the bay was covered with people, and hundreds were swimming about the ship like shoals of fish." John Ledyard, an American adventurer who had signed on board the *Resolution* as a marine corporal, reported later that two counting officers estimated there were anywhere from 2,500 to 3,500 canoes afloat in Kealakekua's waters.

Ledyard and others also described unusual white *kapa* banners held aloft on crossbars, an ancient symbol of Lono, which, coincidentally, resembled the British ships' masts and sails; and he said that when Cook went onshore the masses of natives "all bowed and covered their faces with their hands until he was passed."

This reverence was followed by a series of

An OFFERING before CAP.^t COOK, in the SANDWICH ISLANDS.

Coincidentally, Cook chose an extremely sacred place to make his second landing in Hawaii; and even more coincidentally, he chose to put into Kealakekua when Hawaiians on shore were celebrating the *makahiki* festival, an annual joyful tribute to a god, *Lono-i-ka-makahiki*, who was auspiciously identified as Cook. Consequently, Cook was afforded the greatest welcome and pomp and ceremony ever accorded a mortal in this land.

Cook's Lieutenant James King estimated that some 10,000 Hawaiians turned out — in canoes, or swimming in the bay, or arrayed on shore — to greet the return of Lono. Cook said in a log entry: "I have nowhere in this sea seen such a number of people assembled

opulent and sacred ceremonies held in Cook's honor during the next two weeks. Indeed, the host Hawaiians lavished every fine gift they could gather on their divine guest, and they entertained him by staging boxing and wrestling matches in his honor. In return, Cook and his men tried their best to please their Hawaiian hosts — with guided tours of their ships, a flute and violin concert, and a fireworks display that both fascinated and terrified the natives.

Captain Cook receives a special *kapa* offering (above) during a welcoming ceremony at Kealakekua; but later (right) he and a group of his marines were attacked and killed by angry Hawaiian natives. Both illustrations are by Webber.

After two weeks of merrymaking and accepting tribute Cook decided to leave Kealakekua. On February 4th the *Discovery* and *Resolution* set sail. Off the Big Island's north shore, they ran into a fierce winter storm that battered them, damaged the *Resolution*'s foremast, and sent Cook-Lono back to Kealakekua for repairs.

The Death of Lono

Upon his return, Cook found that the *makahiki* festival was *pau*, finished, and due to a *kapu* put on Kealakekua Bay by the Hawaiian chief, Kalaniopuu, the area was nearly deserted. The natives who remained resumed their previously friendly relations

Kalaniopuu hostage until the missing cutter was returned. For various untimely reasons this maneuver failed, and, in a violent scuffle which broke out on shore, a large party of Hawaiian warriors attacked Cook and his landing party with stones, clubs and daggers. Five of the marines with Cook escaped with their lives, but four others and the Captain died in the bloody shallows of Kealakekua Bay.

To the horror of Cook's crewmen still on board ships, two delegations of concerned Hawaiians later returned Cook's body in mutilated parts. Some of Cook's anatomy was missing, wrote King, because they had been "cut to pieces & all burnt," and others "had been sent to Kaoo (to perform with it as we suppose some religious ceremony)." One

The DEATH of CAPTAIN COOK.

with Cook and his men, but they were not as generous in their tribute and indeed were surprised that a god's property could be so badly damaged in his domain.

The Hawaiians also were more audacious in their petty thievery, not hesitating to skip off with Western objects which pleased their fancy. They were particularly fond of pieces of the coveted metals. Irritating thievery incidents continued, and increased in frequency and in value of goods being taken, until the night of February 13 when the *Discovery's* cutter was cut loose and stolen.

This infuriated Cook. Upon learning of the cutter's disappearance, he ordered Kealakekua Bay blockaded and went onshore with nine marines to take Chief

bundle of Cook's bones, wrapped in fine *kapa* barkcloth and a cloak made of black and white feathers, included "the Cptns. hands (which were well known from a remarkable Cut) the Scalp the Skull, wanting the lower jaw, thigh bones & Arm bone; the hands only had flesh on them, & were cut in holes, & salt crammed in; the leg bones, lower jaw & feet, which were all that remain'd & had escaped the fire, he said were dispers'd among other Chiefs."

Before leaving Kealakekua Bay (on the evening of February 22, 1779), several of the surviving British seamen attempted to revenge Cook's death by bombarding villages, setting fire to temples, and killing scores of fleeing natives. They even decapitated two

Hawaiian bodies and displayed their heads on the bows of a row boat. The same men who only a few weeks earlier had been reveling in Hawaiian womanhood, song and dance, were now hating and killing.

Hawaii was thus initiated into the modern world of disease and gunfire. And at age 50, the returned god Lono — the greatest navigator the world has ever known — was dead.

Before proceeding with a post-Cook history of Hawaii, mention should be made of the possibility that Spanish explorers may have secretly discovered Hawaii long before the much-credited Cook.

Scholarly speculation that Spaniards were

in Hawaii first has sparked much lively debate in Hawaiian research circles.

One group of historians asserts that several unexplained artifacts prove this theory. Their best evidence is a map taken by the British Commodore George Anson in 1742 from a captured Spanish Galleon, the *Nuestra Senora de Cabadongo*, off Cape Espiritu Santo — on the island of Samos in the

This helmeted Hawaiian warrior by Sarah Stone, circa 1800 (based on an earlier engraving by Webber), does look somewhat like a Spanish grandee; and historians claim that the Spanish map (right) captured by Commodore Anson in 1742 proves that the Spanish knew about Hawaii's (or La Mesa and Los Mojas') existence.

Philippines.

The Spanish map, which was described as "a chart of the northern Pacific which marked the track of the round trip between the Philippines and Acapulco," located a group of islands identified as La Mesa (The Table) and Los Mojas (The Monks) in approximately the same latitude as the Hawaiian archipelago. The charted longitude is shown to be about 10 degrees off but the latitude is correct. However, such longitudinal inaccuracy, scholars contend, was common in early sailing days because longitude usually was roughly calculated by estimating how many leagues a ship had traveled during a given day. Latitude, on the other hand, could be accurately determined.

Additionally, pro-Spanish proponents note that, among other coincidental historical factors:

• The Spanish had made annual commercial voyages from Acapulco, Mexico, to Guam and on to Manila in the Philippines (and vice-versa) for 223 years before Cook ventured into the Central and North Pacific. The chance that one of their ships would happen onto Hawaii at least once between the years 1556 and 1778 was quite good, even though Spain's galleons usually set out on charted sea routes which ran either south or north of Hawaii.

• Unexplained Hawaiian oral traditions speak of the coming of light-skinned people who were given wives and became chiefs; and during the 18th and early 19th centuries Western visitors reported that such reputed descendants of light-skinned visitors had distinctly Caucasian features.

• Anthropologists have always been mystified by the appearance in Hawaii of grand cloaks, helmets and daggers, European-like items which were not in vogue in other parts of Polynesia. They also have wondered why the Hawaiians often fabricated several of their finest featherworks of red and yellow feathers, which coincidentally were and still are the royal colors of Spain.

• Unaccountable also are statuary, anchors and metal daggers found in Stone Age Hawaiian sites. Pacific scholar Robert Langdon of the Australian National University also wonders about, "The discovery at the Bishop Museum in the 1950s of two alien items in the burial casket of a deified Hawaiian chief called *Lono-i-ka-makahiki*, who is estimated to have flourished at the end of the 17th Century. The items are a piece of iron embedded in a wooden handle like a chisel and a length of cloth eight feet long by one wide, having the characteristics of sailcloth."

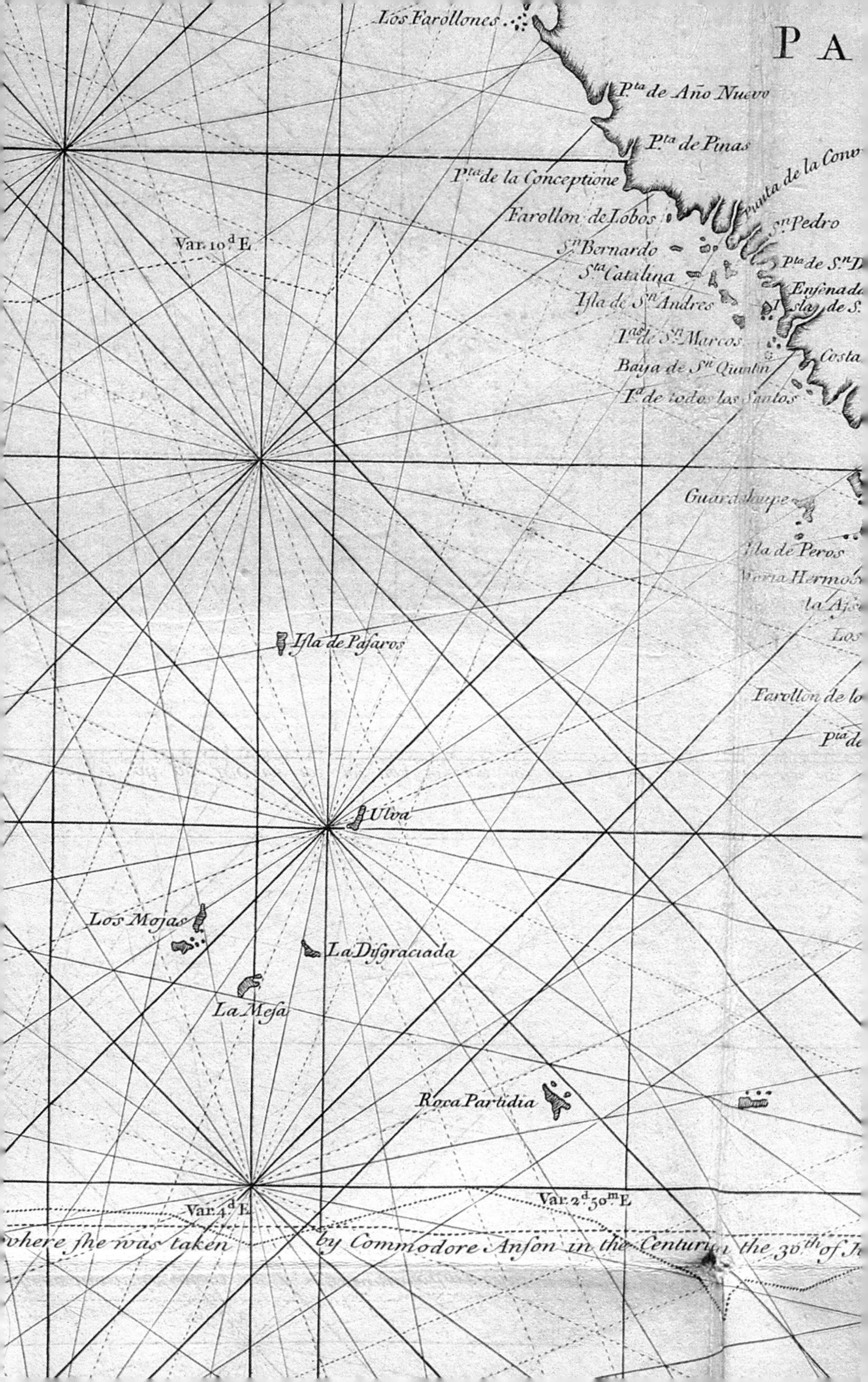

P A

Los Farollones

P.ta de Año Nuevo

P.ta de Pinas

P.ta de la Conceptione

Punta de la Conv

Farollon de Lobos

S.n Pedro

S.n Bernardo

P.ta de S.n D

S.ta Catalina

Enſenada

Iſla de S.n Andres

Iſla de S.

I.as de S.n Marcos

Coſta

Baya de S.n Quintin

Var. 10.d E.

I.ᵃ de todos los Santos

Guardalupe

Iſla de Peros

Noria Hermos

la Aſa

Los

Iſla de Paſaros

Farollon de lo

P.ta de

Ulva

Los Moxas

La Diſgraciada

La Meſa

Roca Partidia

Var. 4.d E.

Var. 2.d 50.m E.

where ſhe was taken   by Commodore Anſon in the Centurion the 30.th of J

Lauvergne del

SCÈNE DE DANSE

THE KAMEHAMEHA DYNASTY

For more than five years after Cook's death at Kealakekua, not an adventurer visited Hawaii's shores, but in 1786 four ships—two from Britain commanded by the sea captains Nathaniel Portlock and George Dixon, and two from France led by Jean-François Galaup de La Pérouse—made calls at different island ports. Thereafter, ships flying the flags of many nations—in particular those of France, England, Russia, Spain and the fledgling United States of America—began stopping at "Owhyee" and courting the natives' favors.

Their usual, practical purpose was to stock up on food and water, but these mariners were also vying for political influence. Cook's men had shown that Hawaii was an extremely convenient stopover point between East and West. Following their esteemed commander's death, the men of the *Resolution* and *Discovery* demonstrated that a trade route from the Pacific Northwest to China via Hawaii was both feasible and valuable. Consequently, from the cold Northwest coast of America, assorted frigates, sloops and smaller schooners stuffed with furs, began putting in at the Sandwich Isles. Most of the ships were bound for the Chinese ports of Macao, Shanghai and Whampoa (on the Pearl River near Canton), where prized American pelts were easily traded for silks, teas and cash. These goods from the Celestial Kingdom in turn produced handsome profits in the eager "Barbarian" markets of Europe and America.

Recuperation and Refreshment

Hawaii—being at the halfway point between these commercial destinations—also provided a most convenient place for recuperation and refreshment. It was a logical place to sojourn before or after facing the ice floes in the North, or grim-faced bargainers in Chinese counting houses.

But these islands of Hawaii were friendly only if the restless natives were at peace. Often they were engaged in one of many bloody civil wars—wars which they were by then waging with muskets and cannon provided by foreigners courting food and favor.

At the center of these controversies, and the key Hawaiian personage mentioned in the logs and diaries of visiting captains and merchants, was a gregarious Hawaiian chieftain named Kamehameha.

Kamehameha, The Lonely One, was born into a hierarchy of great chiefs and his charisma did not go unnoticed even by Cook and his men. Cook's Lieutenant King referred to *Maiha-maiha*, as he called him phonetically, as one of King Kalaniopuu's chief subordinates. King said *Maiha-maiha* was with Kalaniopuu when that aging chief first called on Captain Cook at Kealakekua. *Maiha-maiha's* hair, wrote King, "was now plaisted over with a brown dirty sort of paste or powder, & which added to as savage a looking face as I ever saw, it however by no

means seemed an emblem of his disposition, which was good natur'd & humorous, although his manner shewd somewhat of an overbearing spirit, & he seemed to be the principal director in this interview."

Kamehameha was also very observant, curious and full of questions about the wonderful gadgets these *haole*—or white foreigners—were carrying aboard their floating islands. He quickly developed an appreciation for the advantage one man with a small brass cannon had over several large warriors bearing clubs and spears. And he openly acknowledged the tactical superiority

Preceding pages; French officers and seamen from *La Bonite* enjoy an Oahu hula extravaganza. Above, Kamehameha the Great; and right, a Big Island chief, said to be Liholiho Kamehameha II, lounges in his longhouse while retainers fan him with feather *kahili*.

of Western sailing craft over the functional and streamlined, but tippy and vulnerable Polynesian canoe. To his credit, Kamehameha did not just stare in awe at these wonders; rather, he ordered his followers to acquire as many of the thundering objects as possible, by whatever means. Kamehameha's goal in life was to conquer and rule Hawaii's inhabited islands, and he knew that modern weapons were the means by which he would achieve this end.

His dream quickly and devastatingly became reality. By 1789, the creative and acqui-

1795), then on his home island of Hawaii (1791), and finally on Oahu (1795) — until he had brutally but efficiently conquered six of the eight populated islands in the Hawaiian chain and established what would be known for the next century as the Kingdom of Hawaii.

In 1796 — and again in 1809 — Kamehameha assembled invasion fleets destined for the as yet unconquered northern islands of Kauai and Niihau, but treacherous waters in the channel between Oahu and Kauai (and outbreaks of disease) twice foiled his plans.

sitive Kamehameha was cruising in offshore waters behind a swivel gun mounted securely on a platform bound across the hulls of a large double canoe. And shortly thereafter, he was island-hopping in a fully-armed double canoe bastard-rigged as a schooner, Western-style, with a jib, mainsail and foresail. On the ship's foredeck, riding between two cannon, was the feather-covered image of his war god, the fearsome, shrieking *Kukailimoku* — the Snatcher of Lands.

All this progressive while, Kamehameha also was aggressively enlisting the aid of westerners with military expertise (rewarding their aid and insight with wives, land and other attractive wealth); and he shrewdly and forcefully gained the political support of his people. When the timing seemed propitious, astrologically and militarily, he waged war on the several major chiefs and tribes of Hawaii — first on Maui (in 1790 and again in

Finally, in 1810, following numerous threats and diplomatic overtures, Kaumualii, the esteemed king of Kauai and Niihau, agreed to yield to Kamehameha and serve him as a tributary king.

His dream quickly and devastatingly became reality. By 1789, the creative and acqui-

Many Hawaiians felt Kamehameha was successful in his many wars of conquest because the ancient gods were on his side. They liked to tell of one incident in particular when Kamehameha's major rival on the Big Island, chief Keoua of Puna, was dramatically dealt a military setback by the volcano goddess Pele.

About 1790 (some historians pinpoint the date as November, 1790), when Kamehameha and Keoua were fighting for control of the Big Island of Hawaii, an expeditionary force under Keoua's command was hiking from Hilo to Ka'u via the Kilauea-

Volcano area when its members witnessed huge volcanic explosions on the southeast rim of the Kilauea caldera. The explosions, which reportedly killed some soldiers when flying chunks of lava hit them, threw Keoua's troops into disarray.

Offerings were made to appease the angry gods, but the explosions continued and apparently became more and more dangerous. To escape this untimely interruption of plans, Keoua ordered his men and their accompanying women and children to regroup in three separate divisions and proceed down and away from the volcano at staggered time intervals. The first group passed by the erupting zone safely, but the second party was annihilated. Their remains were found by Keoua's trailing third division.

According to one account of that disaster, the estimated 400 men, women and children in the second division were incinerated in a shower of volcanic mud, sand and cinders. A conflicting version indicates that the 400 or so were found unburned or otherwise visibly injured. Historians will never know for certain what happened, but geologists have theorized that those unfortunate members of Keoua's army may have been killed by suffocating gases released through a rift zone vent during the eruption.

Chief Keoua and his followers were badly demoralized by this omen. Obviously this wartime disaster meant the volcano goddess Pele was siding with Kamehameha of Kona against Keoua of Puna. Whatever Her divine politics, the incident reportedly led to even more deaths as other victims were ordered sacrificed to assuage the angry gods.

Hawaii's State statistician Robert C. Schmitt reported in a recent article on "Castastrophic Mortality in Hawaii" that the 1790 volcanic devastation of Keoua's second division "was the greatest natural disaster in Island history, and ranked second only to the Pearl Harbor attack (in 1941, when about 2,400 Americans and about 100 Japanese died) among all Hawaiian catastrophies." Schmitt also recalled that, "The only other Kilauea explosion recorded in the past two centuries took place on May 17, 1924. This time only one person was killed."

The Olowalu Massacre

During this period of political upheaval and territorial conquests by Kamehameha, foreign sailing craft continued to sail in and out of Hawaii, usually managing to avoid the various Hawaiian hostilities, but in some cases joining in to fight for or against a king,

depending on their politics. Sometimes, however, an arrogant captain would engage in unnecessary violence simply to teach the "savages" a lesson or two.

One of the most tragic such incidents occured in early 1790 off Olowalu, a village south of Lahaina, Maui. To avenge the death of a crewmember and the theft of a small boat at another nearby Maui village, Captain Simon Metcalfe, master of the American trading vessel *Eleanora*, ordered the massacre of natives aboard a fleet of Hawaiian canoes. Under pretense of friendly trade, he directed scores of canoes filled with Hawaiians to gather on the starboard side of his ship. When the natives had clustered about the ship in sufficient numbers, Metcalfe ordered gunwales uncovered and he and his men proceeded to rain fire on the surprised Hawaiians with swivels, brass guns and cannon. "Within minutes," reported one historian, "the sea was red with blood." The *Eleanora* blithely sailed away, "leaving the natives to drag for their dead with fishhooks." More than a hundred Hawaiians died, many more were seriously injured, and the incident became known as the "Olowalu Massacre."

About five or six weeks later the Olowalu Hawaiians were avenged when a second American trading vessel, a schooner named the *Fair American*, anchored off Kona. The captain of the *Fair American* was Simon Metcalfe's son, Thomas Metcalfe. In this case a local chief, Kameeiamoku, who had been struck with a rope and insulted by the senior Metcalfe during a recent visit, took revenge by boarding the *Fair American* and killing the younger Metcalfe and four of his five crew members.

Historians say the two separate Metcalfe incidents—the one on Maui and the other on the Big Island—could not have been related, or of a vengeful nature, because they took place on separate islands ruled by different and uncommunicating Hawaiian chiefs.

Such reprisals became less common once Kamehameha had a firm rein on the islands. He managed the group tightly under the same feudal *kapu* system that had been established by his ancestors. In time he became known as a just, wise and mellow king, but in his younger years he dealt with unfaithful subjects and enemies in a quick and fierce manner. Kamehameha thus was able to keep the islands peaceful and secure until his death in 1819, but with each arrival of foreigners a new series of culture shock waves rolled through his country and battered him and his people's naive sensibilities. Social diseases continued to spread, and so did more common Western ailments such as measles, typhoid fever, whooping cough and influenza. These ailments caused the deaths of thousands, sometimes in epidemics which sent hundreds of Hawaiian people running into the sea in an attempt to cool the fever wracking their bodies. These medical problems were compounded by the introduction of guns, alcohol, tobacco and much coveted western luxuries such as silk, mirrors and other shiny trinkets.

Also, Kamehameha quickly recognized the value of negotiable gold and silver, and to finance his various royal enterprises he monopolized obvious sources of monetary gain. One good example was his control of

When Kamehameha died, on May 8, 1819, at about 63 years of age, he was living at 'Ahu'ena in the Kailua area of the Big Island. His last days were spent in illness near one of his favorite temples, the *heiau* known as *Kamaka Honu*—the Eye of the Turtle. It was one of several *heiau* Kamehameha established in honor of his family ally, the war god Kukailimoku.

As relatives and close friends gathered at his death mat, one of them asked for a final message they might remember and cherish. Kamehameha replied: "*E oni wale no'oukou i ku'u pono'a'ole e pau*—Endless is the good that I leave for you to enjoy."

The Lonely One died in peace, pleased by his accomplishments and surrounded by loving, weeping subjects, but with him died

the lucrative trade in sandalwood, that scented timber which Chinese and other Asian peoples cherish. When Kamehameha discovered that many sandalwood trees grew in his mountains, he forced commoners by the thousands into the cold heights to retrieve it. Many Hawaiians died in this process of sandalwood gathering, but Kamehameha and his son Liholiho, Kamehameha II, continued to harvest that fragrant timber until Hawaii's stands of sandalwood were completely destroyed. In China, because of this early business with Hawaii, the Hawaiian Islands were known for many years as *Tan Heung Shan*, or The Sandalwood Islands. Today, however, only a few stands of sandalwood are visible anywhere in Hawaii.

Above is the first known picture of Honolulu village, circa 1816, drawn by Louis Choris.

the old Hawaii ruled by *Ku, Kane, Lono, Kanaloa* and their last earthly agent.

Ancient Hawaii Dies

Kamehameha the Great's death, and the peculiar political circumstances it created, virtually catapulted Hawaii out of the late Stone Age into a Modern Era of mariners, merchants, missionaries, monarchs, migrants and, much later, *malihini* (as tourists and other newcomers are called). Upon his death, Kamehameha's successor, Liholiho, the heir-designate known as Kamehameha II, was forced to share power with a woman, Kaahumanu, who declared herself Hawaii's first *kuhina nui*, or queen regent. Kaahumanu was the most nagging and shrewish—but also the favorite and most powerful—of Kamehameha the Great's many wives. She was also one of history's most successful women's liberationists.

Shortly after Kamehameha's bones were hidden away where nobody could find and defile them, Liholiho — after much urging by Kaahumanu, other chiefs and priests — overthrew the ancient *kapu* system. To demonstrate his sincerity, Liholiho, in November, 1819, sat down at a feast in Kailua, Kona, and openly, in violation of ancient traditions, ate with women. The symbolic feast was organized by Kaahumanu and his mother, the chiefess Keopuolani.

Concurrent with such *ai noa*, or free eating, Kaahumanu and Liholiho ordered that *heiau* walls were to be desecrated and the many carved wooden idols burned.

This symbolic but shattering renunciation — of ancient Hawaiian gods and of laws which had been observed under their auspices for so long — created a spiritual void. It was a religious vacuum, however, which would soon be filled by a group of Calvinist missionaries, who at the very moment the *kapu* were being overthrown, were en route to Hawaii from their headquarters in Boston on board the American brig *Thaddeus*.

This first party of 14 missionaries, under the sponsorship of the American Board of Commissioners for Foreign Missions (the ABCFM), arrived off Kawaiahae on the Kona Coast of the Big Island on April 4, 1820. The Rev. Hiram Bingham, unofficial leader of the group, was pleased to be in Hawaii, but saddened by what he saw: "The appearance of destitution, degradation, and barbarism, among the chattering, and almost naked savages, whose heads and feet, and much of their sunburnt skins were bare, was appalling. Some of our number, with gushing tears, turned away from the spectacle. Others, with firmer nerve, continued their gaze, but were ready to exclaim, 'Can these be human beings?! ... Can such things be civilized?'"

A new God had come to Hawaii, and though Liholiho had royal reservations, he agreed to let the American missionaries preach Christianity to his people — at Kailua-Kona and Honolulu — on a one year trial basis. Apparently the missionaries spent that first year in a harmless, unthreatening manner, because Liholiho, who was pre-occupied with comfort, alcohol and playing king, let them stay on indefinitely.

In 1822 the restless Liholiho received as a gift from George IV, King of England, a small schooner named the *Prince Regent*. Pleased by this gift, and yielding to a whim, Liholiho left Hawaii to visit King George and negotiate a mutual defense treaty with Britain. He and his party left for England in November, 1823, on board the British whaling ship *L'Aigle*.

Upon arriving at London, Kamehameha II and his entourage were royally feted, but before he could meet with King George, he, Queen Kamamalu, and other susceptible Hawaiians in his suite, caught the measles. Tragically, Liholiho and Kamamalu died On May 6, 1825, HMS *Blonde*, under command of Lord George Byron, cousin of the famous poet, put into Honolulu Harbor with the bodies of the late Hawaiian king and queen.

Before sailing from Honolulu, however, Liholiho had dictated a will which designated that in the event of death his successor was to be his younger brother Kauikeaouli, Kamehameha's sole surviving son. Kaui-

keaouli was to rule under the protection of the queen regent Kaahumanu and the Kingdom's prime minister, Kalanimoku.

'Iehovah is my God, I Fear Not Pele'

Kauikeaouli, Kamehameha III, was only 10 years old when Kamehameha II died, so the early years of his long reign (from 1824 to 1854, the longest for any Hawaiian monarch) were actually the reign of Kaahumanu, who exerted a strong influence on both the handsome boy king and her disoriented people. Probably the most significant occurrence at

During the reign of Kamehameha II (above, lithograph by John Hayter, about 1824) Christianity began to flourish in Hawaii; at right Chief Kalanimoku is baptized by a Roman Catholic priest in 1819, aboard *L'Uranie* (painting by Arago).

the beginning of this third Kamehameha period was the conversion of Kaahumanu and many other powerful Hawaiian leaders to Christianity.

Kaahumanu initially simply tolerated the alien proselytizers from New England, but eventually she learned to read their Bible, was baptized into the faith and, fortunately for the Calvinists, became one of their most enthusiastic converts. One of Kaahumanu's peers, the Big Island high chiefess Kapiolani, became so avid a Christian witness that one day in 1824 she deliberately, defiantly, in the name of Jehovah, denounced the fire goddess Pele on her home grounds.

To discredit and chastize a group of Hawaiian priestesses who insisted upon the continued worship of Pele, Kapiolani staged

Long as tne lava light
   Glares from the lava-lake,
   Dazing the starlight;
Long as the silvery vapor in daylight
   Over the mountain
Floats, will the glory of Kapiolani be
   mingled with either on Hawa-i-ee.

With the Hawaiian hierarchy thus neatly preoccupied with their bibles, the Protestant missionaries forged ahead, building churches and schools on the major islands, and creating an alphabet and a written — and printable — language for the illiterate Hawaiians. To their credit, the *palapala*, reading and writing, were an invaluable contribution to Hawaii's natives. It is true that the missionaries' intention was to use literacy

a Christian religious service at the edge of the Halemaumau firepit in the Kilauea caldera. Declaring "Iehovah is my God. He kindled these fires. I fear not Pele," Kapiolani dared Pele to harm her, hurled stones into the firepit, and ate *ohelo* berries which in ancient times were sacred to the fire goddess and *kapu* to women. Pele did not so much as belch in protest, and ever since that defiant time the story of Kapiolani's courage has been remembered affectionately and reverently by island Christians.

Kapiolani's shrieks at the volcano on behalf of Christianity did not go unnoticed outside of Hawaii. Indeed, more than 50 years after she called Pele's bluff, Britain's poet laureate Alfred, Lord Tennyson (1809–1892), wrote a gushy paean to the brave Christian chiefess Kapiolani. Tennyson proclaimed;

to gain access to the Hawaiians' minds (nearly everything they printed in Hawaiian was religious matter), but at least the Hawaiians could now communicate and document their lives and histories as they wished. As Kaahumanu told the visiting Russian captain Otto von Kotzebue, "Formerly ... she could only converse with persons who were present; now, let them be ever so distant, she could whisper her thoughts softly to them alone."

However, the frock-coated Calvinists were not without fanatical politics. They used their influence in court circles as "messengers of Jehovah" to achieve everything they deemed was best and blest for the Hawaiians. Nudity of any sort was condemned and female converts to the faith were draped in absurd, Mother Hubbard dresses. And the ancient *hula*, even until recently, was denounced in proper Christian circles as being a "lewd" and "lascivious" abomination unto God.

Their Christian biases became most obvious in 1827 and later when French Roman Catholic missionaries began preaching on their Protestant-Hawaiian territory. At that time, the self-righteous Calvinists turned their cheeks away as Kaahumanu nastily persecuted Hawaiians in her flock who dared to follow the teachings of Christians based in Rome instead of Boston. Eventually, in 1839, following the death of Kaahumanu's successor, Kinau, the banished Roman Catholics returned to Hawaii to stay. Today they represent the largest denominational group in the Islands.

Under Kaahumanu's leadership the Hawaiian government began to develop a semblance of laws and administrative form, but when she died in 1832, Kamehameha III embarked on an infamous reign known for its fun-loving rounds of decadence at court. As missionaries gasped and prayed for his salvation, Kamehameha III raced horses, gambled, drank, and danced the hula lewdly or as he otherwise wished. Luckily for the missionaries, Kamehameha III's half-sister, Elisabeta Kinau (Kaahumanu II, 1805–1839), the *kuhina nui* and successor to Kaahumanu, was able to control her brother's debauchery and tend to matters of state during his frequent bouts with the bottle. Through Kinau, the missionaries maintained political power and proceeded to gain Hawaiian converts by the thousands.

By the time of Kinau's death in 1839, Kamehameha III and Hawaii were, in fact, if not officially, being quietly run "behind-the-scenes" by missionaries and merchant friends who had by then been appointed to several important advisory and cabinet posts in the Hawaiian administrative structure.

On Surviving Righteously

Kamehameha III's government was further assaulted by a series of complicated court intrigues, shifts in power, visits by dictatorial captains of foreign ships of war, and nearly comical personality clashes. The following events were among the most important to occur during his chaotic and autocratic 30-year reign:

1839: The Hawaiian Government negotiated, under threat of war, a treaty with France which guaranteed the safety of French Catholic missionaries in Hawaii, judicious treatment of French nationals in Hawaii, and the admitting of French wines and brandy into the kingdom at a fair duty. The government also issued Hawaii's first Code of Civil Laws and an admirable Declaration of Rights.

1840: Kamehameha III announced and granted to the people of Hawaii the kingdom's first constitution, which among other things established an upper ruling house made up of royalty and a lower house of representatives to be elected by the common people. Besides giving the people their first legal access to the country's power structure, the Constitution of 1840 also created Hawaii's first supreme court. During this year government also took over management of elementary schools in the kingdom.

1843: On February 25 a visiting British mariner, Captain Lord George Paulet, commander of the frigate HMS *Carysfort*, after listening to a countryman's imprudent

advice, brashly occupied the fort at Honolulu, raised the British flag, and had his ship's band play "God Save the Queen" to celebrate the ceding of Hawaii to Great Britain at gunpoint. As it turned out, Paulet had acted hastily and contrary to British foreign policy, and six months later his superior officer, Rear-Admiral Richard Thomas, restored Hawaii to a tearful and thankful Kamehameha III. During a moving Restoration Day thanksgiving ceremony on July 31 at Honolulu's Kawaiahao Church, Kamehameha III uttered words of thanks which later became the Hawaiian Kingdom's— and now State of Hawaii's— motto. "*Ua mau ke ea o ka aina i ka pono*," he said—"the life of

King Kamehameha III and Queen Kalama (above) posed for an artist with the Danish corvette *Galathea* in 1846; and Queen Kaahumanu (right) suns herself at the seaside in 1816 Choris sketch.

the land is preserved in righteousness." Also during this year, France, the United States and England signed declarations which recognized Hawaii as a sovereign nation.

1845: The king and his fledgling legislature moved the nation's capital from the whaling town of Lahaina, Maui, to the booming port town of Honolulu.

1848: The king, at the urging and engineering of foreign advisors, divided all Hawaiian lands into three parts—one third for himself and his heirs, one third for the government, and a final third to be distributed among the common people. This land division and its laws—known as The Great Mahele—allowed ordinary native Hawaiians to own property for the first time. Two years later this land reform was fol-

anything in retaliation, so everybody simply waited patiently until De Tromelin had sailed away with his imperious French pride.

Kamehameha III's reign endured more than its fair share of absurd moments, but through them all his people loved him. Following his death on December 15, 1854, his successor-nephew, Alexander Liholiho, proclaimed:

The age of Kamehameha III was that of progress and of liberty—of schools and of civilization. He gave us a Constitution and fixed laws; he secured the people in the title to their lands, and removed the last chain of oppression. He gave them a voice in his councils and in the making of laws by which they are governed. He was

lowed by what would become an even more significant one when foreigners were given the privilege of buying real estate outright and owning it "as freehold property forever."

1849: On August 25, Rear Admiral Legoarant de Tromelin, in a French version of the 1843 British invasion of Hawaii, attempted to negotiate French demands with Hawaii's king, but when Kamehameha III and his advisers failed to comply, De Tromelin landed troops who sacked Honolulu's fort and governor's home, seized a number of artifacts belonging to the late queen regent Kinau, and made off with the king's yacht, the *Kamehameha*. Again, the Hawaiian Kingdom was powerless to do

a great national benefactor, and has left the impress of his mild and amiable dispostion on the age for which he was born.

Today we begin a new era. Let it be one of increased civilization, one of decided progress, industry, temperance, morality, and all of those virtues which mark a nation's advance.

— *comments by Kamehameha IV at his inauguration on January 11, 1855 at Kawaiahao Church*

"New era" was a royal understatement. When Alexander Liholiho took office as the fourth Kamehameha king, his islands were in the midst of a significant economic transition.

Wine, Women and Whales

Since the mid-1820s—following the near total destruction of Hawaii's sandalwood forests and the short-term royal profits they created—the whaling industry had become by far the biggest producer of revenue in the Hawaiian Kingdom. This unsavory business in the blubber, oil and bones of the world's largest mammal, had made Honolulu and Lahaina the two biggest boom ports in the Pacific. As many as 500 whaling ships a year were putting into those and other Hawaiian ports (notably Hilo and Koloa) during whaling's annual spring and fall hunting seasons.

One character who sailed into Lahaina before the mast of a whaler during this period was a young, would-be writer named Herman Melville. Like most budding authors full of notes and little else, Melville arrived in Hawaii broke, and after making his way from Lahaina to Honolulu in 1843, managed to survive during part of a stay on Oahu by working as a pin boy at a downtown bowling alley. This was at a time when he was sorting out plots, soliloquies, and nautical miscellany which would one day become parts of *Typee*, *Moby Dick* and *Billy Budd*.

But besides giving a few unappreciative Mauians and Honoluluans an early look at the youth who would become the greatest American writer of their time, whaling was pouring hundreds of thousands of dollars into island cash boxes. Crowded Lahaina Roads and Honolulu's harbor were floating mines to be worked for all the ships' supplies, shipping-related services, liquor and love their sailors and masters could buy. Frock-coated missionaries complained bitterly about the rampant prostitution, drunkenness and other merry vices which flocked around the coming of every whaler, but their sermons merely ricocheted off royal and commercial ears. Henry T. Cheever, a traveling parson who visited Hawaii in the early 1840s, complained that Lahaina had become "one of the breathing holes of hell" and "a sight to make a missionary weep."

Times were tawdry, but whether old gold and silver were dropping onto the languid laps of Hawaiian ladies on shore or being earned by local lads at sea, whaling—or *o kohola* as the natives called it—kept Hawaii's fragile economy above water for more than 30 years in the middle part of the 19th Century.

However, by the mid and late 1850s, or about the beginning of Kamehameha IV's nine-year reign, a number of crucial marketplace factors killed this lucrative industry. These included a drastic shortage of whales, the new use of cheaper petroleum and coal for heating and lighting, and the outbreak of war between the northern and southern United States. By 1860, the year before the Civil War officially began, the Western whaling industry, like the whales it had harpooned, diced up and boiled into oil, was entering upon a long decline.

A Sweet Alternative

Hawaii's business and government communities knew that something would have to

be done soon to keep Honolulu and Lahaina from becoming once again idyllic clusters of grass shacks by the sea. That something, oddly enough, had been encouraged by the great California Gold Rush of 1849. During that glittering West Coast era, Hawaiian sugar planters—who were a relatively new and small-time lot by world sugar-growing standards—had enjoyed a brief profits boom when the over-populated ports and hills of gold-hungry *Kaleponi* (California) turned to Hawaii as a convenient supply point. Island sugar then was of a substandard quality, but the thousands of miners and migrants amassed in California didn't seem to mind. Usual services and goods of all kinds were so expensive in California in those boom days that miners, it was reported, would send their clothes to Hawaii by ship to have them laundered, pressed and then sent back to California by return ship. Many islanders with gleams in their eyes joined the big rush for gold, but conservative local folks with fiscal foresight stayed at home, minding their stores, sugar crops and the prime Hawaiian lands.

Historian Lawrence H. Fuchs comments on such speculators' land-consolidating ways in his insightful book *Hawaii Pono: A Social History*:

> After the Mahele, foreigners eagerly purchased government lands at moderate prices. Even some of the missionaries found land speculation compatible with spreading the Gospel. One bought and sold forty-seven parcels in his lifetime, and another engaged in thirty land transactions. The ten who did the most

heads in prayer, and when we looked up again the land was gone."

Some *haole* investors bought these cheap Hawaiian lands simply out of greed for vast landholdings, but others bought them speculatively, hoping to plant their hundreds of acres in sweet, money-making sugarcane. It sounded like a good gamble, but once they had the land they were faced with two major problems. First, they didn't trust the king and his administrators; they considered the Hawaiian Government irresponsible and worried that newly-granted property rights would not be honored and protected in the event of a political crisis. Second, and of more immediate concern, they needed laborers to work the plantations they wanted to establish in Hawaii.

land business averaged twenty-two parcels. By 1852, sixteen of the forty-six members of the Congregational mission possessed land titles, averaging 493 acres per man, some of which had come as gifts from chiefs or the King.

Fuchs reports further that the "second generation of missionary families was even more active in land speculation," so much so that by 1886 about two-thirds of all government lands sold had been bought by resident *haole*. As the famous Waikiki entertainer Don Ho says in his nightly cabaret routine, "The missionaries taught us how to bow our

Kamehameha IV (left) steered Hawaii through whaling days; the above engraving, "Boats Attacking Whales," appeared in an 1839 edition of *The Natural History of the Sperm Whale*, published in London for Thomas Beale, Surgeon.

This planters' paranoia resulted in the eventual overthrow of the Hawaiian Kingdom in 1893 by *haole* merchants and plantation barons; and the need for workers created the multi-ethnic society which now populates the Hawaiian Islands.

Only Mad Dogs and Haole

Prospective and already working plantation managers knew that the native Hawaiian population would be almost entirely unsuited to their needs. Diseases and several forms of culture shock had destroyed any potential native-born labor force; also, Hawaiians were not inclined to do back-breaking stoop labor for low wages—not because they weren't good workers, but because they lived in a land that gave them plenty of fish, *poi*, coconuts and other traditional Polynesian foods. They didn't need a menial job to survive. In Hawaii of the 19th Century, only mad dogs, *haole* and imported coolie laborers worked under the midday sun.

This labor shortage resulted in a series of official acts designed to encourage the immigration of competent laborers to Hawaii. A first group of 293 Chinese was brought to Hawaii in 1852, and they were followed over the years by groups of more Chinese, Japanese, Portuguese, Filipino, Norwegian, German, Korean, Puerto Rican, Spanish, Russian, and other laborers. The colorful histories of these ethnic groups is reported in greater detail in the second section of this book.

Kamehameha IV understood his kingdom's population-labor problems, but he stepped into these years of important transition with a well-bred dislike for aggressive Americans and their red, white and blue causes. His anti-Americanism however, was not unfounded. He was educated by Americans at the royal Chiefs' Children's School and, during the years of 1849 and 1850, he and his elder brother, Lot Kamehameha, went on an extensive royal tour of Europe and America. His teenage impressions of that journey reflected his intelligence and precocious sophistication; but they also described travel experience which gave rise to his attitudes towards America and Americans.

One incident which helped him establish a preference for civilized England over frontier America occurred while Kamehameha IV and his brother Lot were in Washington, D.C. A train conductor there mistook the Hawaiian prince for a negro and rudely ordered him out of a railway car. That was an extreme case of bigotry, but only one of many slurs he would experience and hear voiced by "democratic" Americans. Predictably, the king didn't find colonialists and traitorous Americans living in Hawaii much different from their mainland countrymen.

Among accomplishments during Liholiho's administration were the building of Hawaii's first hospital, the Queen's Hospital, named after his Queen Emma; the establishment of a British-style Episcopal Church in Hawaii; and the negotiation of important diplomatic agreements with Britain, France, and the United States.

A Royal Streak of Bad Luck

However, Kamehameha IV's reign of fun and pomp was also a decade marred by a series of unfortunate incidents, including:

• The alarming spread, mostly among Hawaiians, of an ancient and horrible disease called leprosy. Known to the Hawaiians as *ma'i Pake*, or Chinese disease, at that point in medical history there was still no known cure for the ailment. Confirmed cases of leprosy began occurring in all parts of Hawaii during the mid 1800s, but nothing "official" was done about it until 1865, during the reign of Kamehameha V. In 1866 the kingdom's Board of Health established a segregated settlement for the housing and treatment of lepers on the desolate Makanalua Peninsula on the small island of Molokai.

• The shooting of Henry Neilson. In September of 1859, in a burst of unfounded jealousy, the impetuous Kamehameha IV got very drunk and proceeded to gun down, at

very close range, an American named Henry Neilson who was his secretary and, until then, one of his best friends. Neilson took more than two years to die, slowly and painfully, of internal wounds, and throughout Neilson's ordeal and thereafter Kamehameha IV was filled with guilt and remorse for his crime of passion.

• The death of the Royal Prince Albert. On August 27, 1862, the king's beloved four-year-old son, Albert, died of an undiagnosed fever. It was reported that the crown prince became ill not long after his father had drenched him with cold water to punish him

When the Swedish frigate *Eugenies* called at Honolulu in June, 1852, the ship's artists sketched several charming images of old Honolulu. Included here are pictures of a typical island home (above) and a woman and man (right) seen on the streets of Honolulu. From *Fregatten Eugenies, Resa Omkring Jorden, Aren 1851–1853*.

for throwing a childish tantrum. Whatever the cause of death, it greatly depressed his father, and little more than a year later, on November 30, 1863, Kamehameha IV died, at age 29, of an asthmatic attack. Some Hawaiians said he "drank himself to death;" others said he died of a broken heart.

Following the untimely, unexpected death of young Kamehameha IV, there was no question who his successor would be: on the very day Alexander Liholiho died, court heralds rode through the streets of Honolulu and announced at prominent public points that the late king's elder brother, Lot Kamehameha, had succeeded him as Kamehameha V.

Lot, 33, didn't fool around with the royal rhetoric and assumed humility of the pre-

more than a month with much dickering and little achievement, Kamehameha V tired of the proceedings and simply abrogated the Constitution of 1852. Nobles and representatives of the lower house listened stunned as the strong and impatient king told them, "I will give you a Constitution."

A week later Kamehameha V did indeed "give" his subjects a new constitution. The Constitution of 1864 abolished the old, matriarchal office of *kuhina nui*, weakened powers of the royal Privy Council, established a one-chamber legislature for nobles and elected representatives, and required that persons born after 1840 pass literacy tests and meet certain property qualifications before being allowed to vote or serve in the legislature. His act was in effect a bloodless

vious three Kamehamehas. From the start, he took over the Hawaiian Kingdom and ran it as he wished.

Lot refused to take an oath to uphold the liberal Constitution of 1852. He felt that the 1852 Constitution weakened the powers of the Hawaiian monarchy and rendered it dangerously vulnerable to overthrow by non-royalists. Having served under his brother as Minister of the Interior, he knew too well the political ambitions of non-native subjects and expatriates. As different historians have noted, he was a confirmed "nativist," who did all he could "in the olden style" to revive native traditions, including *hula* and *kahuna* practices despised by court Christians.

To set his reign upon a proper course, Kamehameha V, in May, 1864, declared that a special constitutional convention would be held to revise the Constitution of 1852. In August, after the convention had met for

and effective *coup d'etat*.

As "despotic" as some critics said his reign would be, Kamehameha V enjoyed his decade as king with few significant problems.

A Strong Kamehameha Finish

Among Lot's major actions was the establishment of a Bureau of Immigration to help assist the "wants of our agriculture, the dictates of humanity and the preservation of our race." The Bureau immediately began promoting and encouraging the immigration of laborers from abroad to support the booming sugar industry. From sales of 1.5 million pounds of sugar in 1860, business had leaped to sales of 5.3 million pounds in 1864 and more than tripled to 17 million pounds sold by 1872, the last year of Kamehameha V's reign.

King Cane was the obvious financial hope

for Hawaii, so Kamehameha V made two noble efforts — once in 1865 and a second time in 1867 — to obtain an agreeable reciprocal trade treaty with the United States. The bloody Civil War interfered with the first bid for reciprocity, or mutual give-and-take, and the second attempt to gain a treaty was defeated in 1870 by the U.S. Senate.

Kamehameha V's reign was productive in a variety of ways: more important public buildings — including a Central Post Office, government office building (*Aliiolani Hale*), barracks for the Royal Household Troops (Iolani Barracks) and a new Hawaiian Hotel (at the corner of Hotel and Richards streets) were built downtown; tourists such as the writer Samuel Clemens (Mark Twain) and the Duke of Edinburgh gamboled in Waikiki's surf; a new Hawaiian Steam Navigation Company began carrying passengers and cargo to inter-island destinations; and the kingdom negotiated a first friendship treaty with the Imperial Court of Japan.

But the amiable bachelor king never married, or otherwise designated a successor, so when he died on his 42nd birthday on December 11, 1872, the illustrious 77-year-old Kamehameha Dynasty came to an end.

'I Like the Man'

Prince William is a man of fine, large build . . . affable, gentlemanly, open, frank, manly; is as independent as a lord and has the spirit and will of the old Conqueror himself. He is intelligent, shrewd, sensible; is a man of first-rate abilities in fact. I like the man.

— Mark Twain on Prince William Kanaina, who became known as Lunalilo when he succeeded Kamehameha V as Hawaii's monarch.

Lots of people in Hawaii liked King William Charles Lunalilo, known more commonly and personally as "Prince Bill" or the "People's King."

Because Kamehameha V died without designating a successor, the laws of the land, under the Constitution of 1864, authorized the legislative assembly of the Kingdom to elect a native *alii*, a recognized Hawaiian chief or chiefess, to be Hawaii's new ruler. This elected king or queen would then become "a new Stirps for a Royal Family," or in effect the progenitor of a new dynasty.

Four persons — including Lunalilo, Colonel David Kalakaua (a well-known Hawaiian politician and newspaper editor), and the chiefesses Bernice Pauahi Bishop and

Ruth Keelikolani — were promoted by nobles and commoners alike as the kingdom's best candidates. But eventually the choice narrowed down to a campaign between the princes Lunalilo and Kalakaua. Kalakaua ran aggressively against the very popular "Prince Bill," but when a general plebiscite was held on January 1, 1873 to determine the will of the people, Lunalilo soundly defeated Kalakaua. A week later the legislative assembly officially elected Lunalilo and announced to a pleased populace that "Prince Bill" was their new king.

But as popular as Lunalilo was, he, like his three royal predecessors, was partial to unhealthy quantities of alcoholic drink; only 13 months after becoming Hawaii's sixth king he died of pulmonary tuberculosis compli-

cated by alcoholism.

It was a year-long reign, however, full of intrigue — particularly regarding the kingdom's relationship with the United States.

Lunalilo once again made a bid for a reciprocity trade treaty with the United States, but this time his advisers suggested he use Hawaii's largest harbor, the Pearl River, or Pearl River Lagoon, as a bargaining chip to gain trade concessions from the United States. The Pearl River — later to be known as Pearl Bay or Pearl Harbor — was being eyed by the United States as a potential coaling port for American commercial and military vessels, Lunalilo was told. Using the Pearl River Lagoon to gain trade concessions

Kamehameha V (above) was a take-charge king, who ran his kingdom as he saw fit; to right is a rendering of Hawaii's first royal coat-of-arms; and at far right is a portrait of King Lunalilo.

was an interesting political idea, but public opposition to such a leasing of Hawaiian soil killed the idea before the kingdom could begin negotiating with Washington.

During that same year, however, two American generals—Major General John M. Schofield, commander of the United States Army's Military Division of the Pacific, and Brevet Brigadier General Burton S Alexander—paid an attentive visit to Hawaii. They were reportedly in the islands on a vacation trip, but it was revealed many years later that they had been ordered by Secretary of War W.W. Belknap to tour the Hawaiian Islands confidentially "for the purpose of ascertaining the defensive capabilities of the different ports and their commercial

Except for a brief, nearly comical mutiny of the Royal Household Troops against their martinet Hungarian drill-master, Captain Joseph Jajczay, the remainder of Lunalilo's abbreviated reign drifted by uneventfully. As for the mutiny, Lunalilo, in a fatherly sort of way, convinced his royal guards to give up the mini-rebellion and return to their barracks in peace. After mediating that last "crisis" of his life from a sick bed in Waikiki, the beloved "Prince Bill," age 39, died on the night of February 3, 1874.

Like Kamehameha V before him, Lunalilo died a bachelor; but even when asked at his deathbed who should succeed him, the "People's King" refused to name a new monarch. Accordingly, the kingdom's representatives once again had to go about the

PRECURSOR OF HAWAII'S COAT OF ARMS
Prepared in London in 1843-44 at the order of Timothy Haalilio and the Reverend William Richards

facilities, and to examine into any other subjects that may occur to you as desirable, in order to collect all information that would be of service to the country in the event of war with a powerful maritime nation ... It is believed the objects of this visit to the Sandwich Islands will be best accomplished, if your visit is regarded as a pleasure excursion, which may be joined by your citizen friends."

During their two-month spying visit, Schofield and Alexander carefully studied the Pearl River Lagoon, the largest natural harbor in the kingdom and, of more strategic importance, in the entire North Pacific Ocean. The generals' conspicuous interest in Hawaii's geography did not go unnoticed by both Americans and Hawaiians in the kingdom, but by then the *keiki aina*, or children of the land were used to seeing wide-eyed, land-hungry foreigners.

sticky political business of electing a new sovereign.

Before he died, Lunalilo composed a will which asked that his estate be used to build a home for "poor, destitute and infirm people of Hawaiian blood or extraction, giving preference to old people." The original Lunalilo Home was opened in 1883 in the Makiki area of Honolulu (on the present site of Roosevelt High School), but it is located now in Hawaii Kai, on a lower slope of south Oahu's Koko Crater.

The major monument to the time of Lunalilo, however, is a 14,400-acre military reservation in central Oahu near Wahiawa known as Schofield Barracks. This sprawling installation, "the largest permanent Army post in America," was named, of course, after the aforementioned spy-General who came to Hawaii on "holiday" during the short and mostly happy reign of Lunalilo.

HAWAII'S LAST ROYAL DYNASTY

A Royal Free-For-All

Hawai'i pono'i,	Hawaii's own,
Nana i kou mo'i	Look to your king,
Ka lani ali'i,	The royal chief,
Ke ali'i.	The chief.

— *the opening four lines of Hawaii's national anthem, "Hawai'i Pono'i," written by King David Kalakaua*

As it did when Kamehameha V died, the legislative assembly again met to choose a new king or queen among available and interested candidates. This time only the previously defeated Kalakaua and the Dowager Queen Emma, widow of Kamehameha IV, vied for the Hawaiian throne. After a round of colorful campaigning, the assembly (on February 12, 1874) handily elected Kalakaua King of Hawaii by a strong 39 to 6 vote. Kalakaua won by more than a 6 to 1 margin, but the zealous and disappointed backers of Queen Emma rioted in protest. Within minutes after Kalakaua's ascendancy to the throne was announced, several persons were injured, one fatally, in a free-for-all fight inside and outside the courthouse where the election was held. Local authorities had to enlist the help of 150 American and 80 British marines stationed on visiting warships in order to quell this disturbance.

With that inauspicious start behind him, Kalakaua proceeded to rule with a flourish and style which in time would earn him a nickname and reputation as Hawaii's "Merry Monarch."

Royal pretensions were awkward and somewhat primitive during the reigns of the Kamehamehas and Lunalilo, but under "Kalakaua, Rex," as he signed his name to official documents, the Hawaiian Kingdom enjoyed a Europeanesque era that was the toast of courtly romantics, but the absolute misery of the kingdom's sugar planters, merchants and other Americanists who were growing bolder by the month in their calls for the United States to annex Hawaii.

Kalakaua ignored such rabble and ruck and determinedly fashioned his kingship in the grand courtly tradition of Western monarchs. Like numerous royal exemplars he admired, he spent *his* taxpayers' dollars as *he* royally pleased — by building himself a grand $350,000 palace; by embarking on a royal trip around the world (which distinguished Kalakaua as the first monarch to circumnavigate the globe); by presenting gala horse races, grand balls and old-style Hawaiian feasts; by entertaining his many friends and visitors at lavish *hula* spectacles; by keeping a soothsayer-adviser on the Royal Household payroll; and by staging Hawaii's first coronation (of himself and his Queen Kapiolani) before an audience of 8,000 persons gathered at the new Iolani Palace.

But despite these kingly excesses, His Highness David Kalakaua also lived an earthy life noted for its pleasant mix of easy-going

charm and cultivated sensibility. He charmed Queen Victoria with his decidedly British accent, and a literary friend, the usually skeptical Robert Louis Stevenson, called Kalakaua "a very fine, intelligent man." Country folk remembered feeling most comfortable in the presence of their beloved king, who took enormous pride in being Hawaiian. During his reign, Kalakaua openly clashed with educators and church men in fights to restore many of his people's nearly extinct cultural traditions.

Kalakaua, however, was not a king given to blind frivolity; his reign was also dis-

Kalakaua, Hawaii's last king (above), became known as Hawaii's "Merry Monarch" and the ruler of a "Champagne Dynasty." At right he is seen entertaining the Scottish author Robert Louis Stevenson in the poker parlour of his Honolulu Harbor boathouse. Photo taken about 1889.

tinguished by several splendid diplomatic and executive successes.

America's First Royal Guest

Indeed, no sooner had he gotten used to being addressed as "His Majesty" than he traveled to Washington, D.C., in October of 1874 to promote and negotiate the long sought reciprocity treaty with the United States. As befits a visiting monarch, Kalakaua and his entourage were warmly and grandly received by President Ulysses S.

triumph for the new king, but he had to make one Hawaiian concession that crucially altered Hawaii's status as a sovereign nation: Kalakaua agreed to a clause which stated that as long as the treaty remained valid, he would not "lease or otherwise dispose of or create any lien upon any port, harbor, or other territory in his dominion, or grant any special privilege or rights of use therein, to any other power, state or government, nor make any treaty by which any other nation shall obtain the same privileges, relative to the admission of any articles free of duty,

Grant and a joint session of the U.S. Congress as "the first reigning monarch to ever visit the United States." Newspaper reporters described the state banquets and other entertainments arranged for Kalakaua as the most lavish they had ever seen in the nation's capital. Kalakaua's presence on American soil undoubtedly had a positive effect on the controversial bid for reciprocity because he subsequently received strong personal support for his efforts from President Grant and other politicians; by March, 1875, the treaty was approved by the U.S. Senate. The treaty in effect gave Hawaii "favored nation" duty concessions and by eliminating a former tariff of two cents a pound on sugar, it made Hawaiian sugar cheaper and therefore more readily bought. When it was officially implemented in 1876, Hawaii burst into rounds of grand celebrations.

The Reciprocity Treaty was a diplomatic

hereby secured to the United States." The United States was in effect covering its interest in Pearl Harbor, and at the same time was not allowing Kalakaua to use that strategic waterway to gain political or economic concessions from other interested parties, notably Britain and France.

However, the treaty secured Hawaii's immediate economic future. Sugar growers could plan ahead with confidence, even though, ironically, this arrangement also meant that successful sugar-growing interests and their downtown merchant affiliates would be able to exert more and more economic leverage on the Hawaiian monarch and kingdom in general. By helping his chief taxpayers and critics gain economic concessions, Kalakaua at the same time weakened his own and his people's power base.

In an attempt to neutralize the antagonistic, largely missionary-descended power being wielded in his kingdom by a rich *haole* minority, Kalakaua enlisted the political backing and money respectively of two other *haole*. One was his leading adviser, an adventurer-royalist named Walter Murray Gibson, and the other was the enormously wealthy California and Hawaii "sugar king" Claus Spreckels. Kalakaua placed too much faith in the flamboyant Gibson, and both he and Gibson borrowed too much money from Spreckels, and eventually this triple alliance proved to be of great embarrassment to the king and his hopes for a strong Hawaiian Kingdom.

Meanwhile, in January 1881, Kalakaua embarked on a much-celebrated tour of the world, ostensibly to look into the matter of labor immigration (which he did attend to in

Japan and Portugal). He and his suite had a grand time, beginning in Japan where his ship, the *Oceanic*, was greeted at Yokohama Bay by the 21-gun salutes of 13 assorted warships. The Emperor Matsuhito wined and dined Kalakaua to an extreme, and at his Tokyo palace presented him with "The Grand Cross of the Order of the Rising Sun." Kalakaua, in turn, presented Matsuhito with Hawaii's "Grand Cross of the Order of Kamehameha." The Hawaiian king was so impressed by his host that he also proposed a matrimonial alliance between Japan and Hawaii, offering the hand of his 6-year-old niece, Princess Kaiulani, to Japan's Prince

Princess Kaiulani (above, about 1895) was educated at Harrowden Hall near London. She was proclaimed (by Queen Liliuokalani) heir-designate to the Hawaiian throne, but she died young at age 24, six years after the monarchy died.

Hatsu. This offer was politely declined by the tradition-bound Japanese Emperor.

From Japan, Kalakaua proceeded to, among other adventures, lavish banquets with a viceroy of China, the Governor of Hong Kong, the King of Siam, and with official representatives of Singapore, Malaysia, Burma, India and Egypt (where he visited the Sphinx and Pyramids).

A Glittering Social Lion

In Europe Kalakaua was received by Pope Leo XIII, Queen Victoria, the Prince of Wales, and numerous other princes, princesses and heads of state. The King's chamberlain, William N. Armstrong, wrote of Kalakaua's appearance in London:

> The Prince of Wales, as the social chief of the English people, representing the Queen, gave the "tip," or more decorously speaking, fixed the measure of his reception, and the King at once bounded into the glittering arena as a social lion. This was accepted with excellent humour by the aristocracy, who are always charmed with some new sensation ... Instead of staying only three days in London, the King remained sixteen days, during which time he was most royally entertained, and, if a lion fattens on attentions, he finally waddled out of England "as fat as a poodle dog."

Armstrong, whose memoirs of Kalakaua's trip are bitchily recounted in his book *Around the World with a King* (1903), played the role of protective diplomat wherever the King traveled, but sometimes the carefree Kalakaua would steal away for private fun. Or as Armstrong reported from Vienna:

> The King unfortunately, with the Austrian gentlemen attending him, visited one of the noted music and beer gardens, the Prater, and was placed in a conspicuous place; he drank wine and beer, and while walking about the place, was approached by a pretty Viennese girl who bowed to him and asked him to dance with her. He instantly assented, and was soon waltzing, and surrounded by a large crowd, who watched him with much interest.

While on this grand journey, Kalakaua, no doubt royally inspired, commissioned English jewelers to fashion two bejeweled crowns, one for himself and one for Queen Kapiolani. Though the two crowns were modest by European standards (costing only about $10,000 each), the purchase of such imperial ostentations later infuriated Hawaii's resident Americans.

While passing through America, Kalakaua visited with the new American President Chester Arthur (who had succeeded the recently assassinated James Garfield), purchased horses in Kentucky, and shopped and banqueted in San Francisco. Then, shortly after returning home to Honolulu, he announced his most royal pretension yet: he invited thousands of subjects to a magnificent coronation ceremony to be held on February 12, 1883.

'Cry Out O Isles—With Joy'

On Coronation Day, Kalakaua's investiture included a grand combination of feather standard.

The coronation's grandest moment, however, came when the Prince of Hawaii, David Kawananakoa, stepped forward with Kalakaua's crowns, and, while a choir sang "Almighty Father! We Do Bring Gold and Gems for the King," Kalakaua took his crown from the chancellor, placed it upon his head, and then placed a smaller, similar crown on Queen Kapiolani's head. "Cry Out O Isles with Joy!" the choir sang. Immediately cannons on land and at sea barked in salute, and upon conclusion of that ecstatic number, the Royal Hawaiian Band played a spirited "Coronation March."

Kalakaua's will had been done, and to the delight of his native subjects, and the chagrin of planters, coronation celebrations con-

Hawaiian and European regalia which can only be described, like his Iolani Palace, as "Polynesian Baroque." In a pavilion especially built for the occasion, the Chief Justice of the Kingdom, A.F. Judd, placed a Royal Mantle, the large feather cloak of Kamehameha I, on Kalakaua's shoulders and handed him a royal sceptre. Meanwhile, the King's sister-in-law, the Princess Poomaikelani, presented him with a *pulo'ulo'u kapu* stick, a *lei palaoa* (a whaletooth pendant suspended from a necklace of woven human hair) and a *kahili*, or royal

tinued for two more weeks, adding further festive fuel to His Hawaiian Highness' well-earned reputation as a "Merry Monarch."

It was just as well that Kalakaua lived it up as he wished, when he could, because his grandiloquent reign was soon weakened by a series of political scandals, many of them

The Hawaii Tramways Company was a welcome and modern addition to the Honolulu scene. In this 1890 photo tramcar patrons pause for a pose in front of Aliiolani Hale on King Street.

inadvertently created by Gibson and Spreckels. Gibson, as the Kingdom's Prime Minister, stirred up anti-American sentiments and the wrath of the *haole* populace by using race as a dominant political issue. Spreckels, meanwhile, with the blatant help of a puppet cabinet created by Gibson and Kalakaua, gained enormous land concessions on Maui at absurdly low prices. Other political disasters during this period included a mutinous, drunken voyage (to Hawaii's sister Polynesian state of Samoa) by the King's "Navy," a poorly outfitted ship called the *Kaimiloa*; and Kalakaua's alleged acceptance of large cash bribes from two competing Chinese businessmen interested in obtaining a single available license to sell opium in the Kingdom.

predominantly white) minority, because the new Constitution of 1887 included strict provisions which required that voters own at least $3,000 worth of property or have an income of at least $600 a year. That accounted for only about a third of the kingdom's males, and most of them were not Hawaiian.

During 1887, the new Reform Party also renegotiated the Reciprocity Treaty, which coincidentally was up for renewal that year. This time the United States was openly granted the exclusive right to use Pearl Harbor as a port. If Hawaii previously was not directly caught up in America's "sphere of influence," she certainly was now.

Two years later, on July 30, 1889, a fiery part-Hawaiian revolutionary named Robert Wilcox and about 150 armed followers loyal

The 'Bayonet Constitution'

This haughtiness infuriated the *haole* community until it openly revolted on June 30, 1887 against the king and his Gibson-led cabinet. An armed insurrection—led by a *haole* political group called the Hawaiian League, which commanded the services of a few hundred white soldiers called the Honolulu Rifles—forced Kalakaua to replace Gibson and accept a new "Bayonet Constitution" that seriously curtailed his powers and, in effect, made him a figurehead.

This revolutionary Reform Party's bloodless coup created what was basically a constitutional monarchy. Power, however, now belonged to the Kingdom's landowning (and

to the kingdom staged a counter coup against the *haole* businessmen. Wilcox, who had been educated at a military school at Turin, Italy, wore his gold braid and epauleted uniform for the event and, with fellow royalists following, swashbuckled his way past the King's Guards and occupied Iolani Palace's grounds and office structures in the area. Wilcox had noble intentions, but his attempted *coup d'etat* failed miserably. Within hours after the insurrection began, he and the other revolutionaries were flushed out of hiding with rifle fire and crude anti-personnel bombs made of dynamite tied to twenty-penny metal spikes. When Wilcox finally surrendered, seven of his men were dead and another 12 wounded.

Wilcox claimed later that he was promised the personal support of both King Kalakaua and Princess Liliuokalani, but both members of the royal family denied they had offered him such aid and comfort. Whether Kalakaua simply got cold feet at the last minute is not known, but nonetheless he spent the day of the Wilcox Revolution relaxing at his boathouse, not deigning to associate himself with the matter. Wilcox eventually was acquitted of his "treasonous" crime (because no jury of natives would convict him), and in the end the insurrection accomplished little except to make the gutsy Wilcox something of a folk hero and create further racial strife in the Hawaiian Kingdom.

For the remainder of his reign, Kalakaua

Liliuokalani, regent during his absence. Upon receiving her brother's body and news of his death, Liliuokalani became Hawaii's first reigning Queen—and its last monarch.

Aloha Hawaiian Rule

Aloha 'oe, aloha 'oe,
E Ke onaona no ho i ka lipo,
One fond embrace, a ho'i a'e au
A hui hou aku.

Farewell to you, farewell to you,
O fragrance in the blue depths,
One fond embrace and I leave
Until we meet again.
— *Hawaii's famous song of farewell,*
"Aloha 'Oe," written by Queen
Liliuokalani

was for all practical purposes simply a power-less figurehead. For the next two years his life took a somewhat aimless turn, and in 1890 his health began to deteriorate. On January 20, 1891, while visiting in California for his health, the last king to reign in Hawaii died in a suite at San Francisco's Palace Hotel.

Honolulu had been decked out with bunting in anticipation of Kalakaua's return to Hawaii, but when word of his death reached Honolulu with his body, joyous colors and shouts of *aloha* were replaced by black crepe and cries of *auwe*, the doleful wail of a people in mourning.

Before leaving Hawaii in November of 1890, Kalakaua had appointed the heir-apparent, his sister the Princess Lydia

Lydia Paki Liliuokalani, whose mottos were *"Onipa'a!*—Stand Firm!" and "Hawaii for the Hawaiians," was more fervently against annexation than her brother Kalakaua. From the very start of her two-year reign, she made it known that she planned to restore monarchial power and the "rights" of native Hawaiian people.

She and many other Hawaiian liberals were weary of the plodding "Cabinet Government" created by the Bayonet

Queen Liliuokalani (left) in 1893, the year blue-jacketed marines (above) from the U.S.S. *Boston* came ashore and helped a group of Honolulu businessmen overthrow her Hawaiian kingdom. The deposed queen died 20 years later, in 1917.

Constitution of 1887. Liliuokalani and her backers opposed the existing cabinet and its laws, and by January, 1893, she informed court circles that she would soon be issuing a new constitution similar to the Constitution of 1864. Once again, she noted, power would be in the hands of the monarchy and the Hawaiian people instead of in the grasp of a privileged white minority.

In response to this royal intent, pro-annexation leader Lorrin A. Thurston called a secret meeting at his home with members of a group called the Annexation Club. This "club" hastily organized a Committee of Safety which in turn planned the outright overthrow of the monarchy and the initiation of annexation negotiations with the United States.

abdicate her throne to the revolutionaries. She was shocked and indignant, but helpless, the victim of a successful, American-backed *coup d'etat*. As a historian wrote later, "Thirty businessmen, not the 30,000 surviving Hawaiians, determined Hawaii's fate" that day.

'A Great Wrong Was Done'

When newly-elected Democratic President Grover Cleveland received word of the coup involving American troops, he, like the Hawaiian Queen, also reacted with indignation and incredulity. Almost immediately he dispatched a special investigator, James H. Blount, a former Georgia congressman and Confederate Army officer, to Honolulu

On January 16, 1893, the committee launched their revolt after first enlisting the aid of John L. Stevens, the United States Minister in Hawaii. Stevens, an ardent supporter of the pro-annexation movement, ordered, without any authorization from Washington, the landing of U.S. Marines from the visiting gunship USS *Boston*, ostensibly to help "protect American lives and property."

Between 4 and 5 p.m. that day, some 160 armed bluejackets came ashore in a quiet invasion. They positioned artillery pieces and Gatling guns at strategic points, set up guard posts at key locations throughout Honolulu, and by the next day, "without the drawing of a sword or the firing of a shot," a self-proclaimed Provisional Government of Hawaii led by Sanford B. Dole was in power. Liliuokalani, who was summarily overwhelmed by a superior military force, had to

to conduct a study and prepare a formal report on the Hawaiian situation. Blount steamed off to Hawaii and upon his arrival found bitter, resentful Hawaiians and a Provisional Government made up of mostly American businessmen (who had adopted the Civil War song "Marching Through Georgia" as their theme song). American flags were flying above Hawaii's public buildings and the Iolani Palace had been renamed The Executive Building.

Blount was not pleased. He ordered red-white-and-blue ensigns and other patriotic paraphernalia hauled down, U.S. Marines withdrawn from the streets of Honolulu, and

Hawaii's flag comes down (above) on August 12, 1898; and later depressed royalists (right), including Princess Kaiulani (black dress), gather around the deposed Queen Liliuokalani at her Washington Place home on Beretania Street.

the American occupation of Hawaii ended. Then, after 5½ months in the islands, he returned to Washington disgusted and reported to President Cleveland and the U.S. Senate that "a great wrong has been done to the Hawaiians" who were "overwhelmingly opposed to annexation." He suggested that "their legitimate government should be restored" as soon as possible. Blount's suggestion was supported by Cleveland, who asked Congress to "devise a solution [to the Hawaiian problem] consistent with American honour, integrity and morality." Blount and Cleveland were ignored.

On July 4, 1894, the Provisional Government of Hawaii, having grown desperate, simply declared that the Kingdom of Hawaii, succeeded by the Provisional

they planned a counter-coup—once again led by the indefatigable Robert Wilcox. This time the Hawaii for Hawaiians revolution was organized with the support of some 200 staunch royalists and the approval and encouragement of the deposed Queen Liliuokalani. The insurrection, however, was defused at an early stage; before Wilcox and his armed followers were able to launch their attempt, the Provisional Government got wind of their plans and chased Wilcox and other royalist guerrillas around Diamond Head and into the upper reaches of Palolo, Manoa, Pauoa and Nuuanu valleys in back of Honolulu. After 10 days in hiding, and after suffering a few casualties, 191 rebels, were caught and brought to trial for treason before a military commission. Former queen

Government of Hawaii, was thenceforth to be known as the Republic of Hawaii. Sanford Dole was named the Republic's first President, and five men—W.B. Cooper, Samuel Damon, J.A. King, B.L. Marx and W.O. Smith—were designated as ministers of the new state. The Republic's constitution was similar to that of the United States.

During this brief period of the Republic of Hawaii, the Cleveland administration sent a minister to Hawaii to seek the reinstatement of Queen Liliuokalani as Hawaii's constitutional authority, but President Dole and his cabinet refused to surrender their government's power.

Bold Wilcox Tries Again

Liliuokalani and her supporters were furious about this state of their once and happy Hawaiian Kingdom, and in January of 1895

Liliuokalani was arrested in her home.

Liliuokalani denied any guilt in the matter, but the government's attorney pointed out that amidst the fruit trees and flowers in the garden at her home, Washington Place, national guardsmen had found some 21 bombs, 30 rifles, 38 cartridge belts, assorted pistols and swords, and about a thousand rounds of ammunition. Despite persuasive and articulate argument by the deposed queen, the commission found her guilty of high treason and sentenced her to five years at hard labor and a fine of $5,000. The penalties, however, were never enforced.

After enduring humiliating periods of house arrest (in Iolani Palace) and parole for her misdeeds, Liliuokalani was set free late in 1896. For three years after the overthrow, the Republican Congress and Democratic President Cleveland had merely blustered around the Hawaiian issue. Liliuokalani went to Washington in an attempt to rally support for her cause, but by then the U.S. Government was pursuing an expansionist, imperialistic policy which 20th Century historians would refer to as "Manifest Destiny." Also, the Spanish American War was looming, and conservatives knew that Hawaii would become an important mid-Pacific base of operations once U.S. forces were sent to do battle in the Philippines. The timing for a "Hawaii for Hawaiians" argument was bad. Congressional imperialists and hawks could not care less about such native slogans.

Hawaii Is Ours, But ...

The end, politically, came in November, 1897, when President Cleveland lost that

year's presidential election to Republican Candidate William McKinley. Once the Republican Congress and the New Republican President got together on the annexation issue, Hawaii's future became manifest. Less than seven months after he took office, McKinley signed a Joint Resolution of Annexation (on July 7, 1898) which authorized American acceptance of these islands from the Republic of Hawaii. Many Hawaiian tears fell when that news was delivered, but it was too late to cry for the past. Hawaii was no longer a curious little Polynesian kingdom somewhere in the middle of the Pacific Ocean; it was now a

U.S. Minister Sewall (above) accepts Hawaii from President Dole; and in an 1897 cartoon in a German edition of *Puck* (right) an artist satirizes Hawaii's marriage to Uncle Sam.

"possession" of the powerful United States. The "luscious pear," as one pro-annexation editor in California had once described Hawaii, was plucked.

Former President Cleveland later wrote the following personal comment regarding America's annexation of Hawaii:

> Hawaii is ours. As I look back upon the first steps in this miserable business and as I contemplate the means used to complete the outrage I am ashamed of the whole affair.

And ex-Queen Liliuokalani, writing in her memoirs, *Hawaii's Story by Hawaii's Queen*, eloquently and bitterly compared the plight of herself and her subjects to that of America's original Indian inhabitants:

> The conspirators, having actually gained possession of the machinery of government and the recognition of foreign ministers, refused to surrender their conquest. So it happens that, overawed by the power of the United States to the extent that they can neither throw off the usurpers, nor obtain assistance from other friendly states, the people of the Islands have no voice in determining their future, but are virtually relegated to the condition of the aboriginals of the American continent.

On August 12, 1898, Minister Harold M. Sewall, representing the United States, attended a grand "transfer of sovereignty" ceremony in front of the Executive Building. During this ceremony President Sanford B. Dole of the Republic gave Hawaii to the United States. Sewall graciously accepted the gift. A large American flag was raised over Iolani Palace, and Hawaii was now formally and officially a part and parcel of the United States of America.

No sooner had "Old Glory" skipped up the Iolani Palace flagpole and begun fluttering in Hawaii's tradewinds than the U.S. Military Establishment marched ashore. On August 16, four days after patriotic Hawaiians had their last Annexation Day cry, members of the Army's 1st New York Volunteer Infantry Regiment and the 3rd Battalion, 2nd Volunteer Engineers, set to work pitching tents and digging latrines in a large plot marked off at Kapiolani Park. The encampment, across a dirt road from Waikiki Beach and in the morning shadows of Diamond Head, was named, appropriately, Camp McKinley, after the U.S. Commander-in-Chief who signed the final annexation order.

THIS IS IT!—These are the faces of men who've heard the war
is over. This moving moment of history was recorded by a Navy

...hotographer in downtown Honolulu late yesterday. (U. S. Navy photo.)

Honolulu Star Bulletin, Aug. 15, 1945

20TH CENTURY HAWAII

Twentieth Century Hawaii, American Hawaii if you will, was both battered and massaged by people and time. Much related information is reported in other sections of this book, but the following chronological occurrences were among the most significant to take place in Hawaii during the current century:

1900: On January 20, the Honolulu Fire Department purposely started a fire near the corner of Beretania Street and Nuuanu Avenue, near the heart of town, in order to burn out an area where cases of bubonic

plague had been detected in Honolulu's Chinatown. Firemen were on hand to contain the blaze, but strong winds whipped it out of control and before it could be stopped 38 acres of Chinatown were destroyed, leaving about 7,000 Chinese, Japanese and Hawaiians homeless.

1900: President William McKinley signed an Organic Act on April 30 which officially made Hawaii a United States territory. This gave Hawaii's residents certain rights and privileges of American citizens, but left control of local government in Washington's hands. The president appointed the Territory of Hawaii's governor, secretary (as the lieutenant governor was called in those days) and judges; and the governor, in turn, appointed

the administrators of the territory's departments. However, the territory had no vote in Congress, and Congress could veto or change any law passed by the territorial legislature.

1901: James D. Dole organized the Hawaiian Pineapple Company, Ltd., and began to market pineapples successfully on the U.S. Mainland. Within 20 years, pineapples became Hawaii's second most lucrative industry, and Hawaiian pineapples made up most of the world's known market in that sweet fruit.

1902: A communications link was established with the American mainland when the Commercial Pacific Cable Company of California laid a transpacific telegraphic cable between San Francisco and Honolulu. A crew from the ship *Silvertown* landed the cable at Waikiki Beach on December 28, 1902. A second cable section, connecting Hawaii with Midway, Guam and the Philippines, was completed on July 4, 1903.

1905: The Territorial Legislature passed a law which divided Hawaii into five counties — Oahu, Kauai, Maui, Hawaii and Kalawao. Kalawao, the Hansen's Disease (or leprosy) Settlement of Kalaupapa on the Island of Molokai, has since been incorporated into the County of Maui.

1906: Three yachts entered the first Transpacific Yacht Race, which ran between San Pedro, California, and Honolulu. The famous Trans-Pac race is the world's oldest established long distance sailing competition.

World War II came to a cheerful end on "V.J. Day" (previous two pages); above is the famous Chinatown fire of 1900, moments before Kaumakapili Church was consumed by flames; and at right gold medal swimmer Duke Kahanamoku receives a classic laurel wreath from King Gustaf of Sweden at the 1912 Olympics at Stockholm.

1907: The County of Oahu was abolished by the Territorial Legislature, which established in its place the City and County of Honolulu, which is made up of the entire island of Oahu and the numerous islets and atolls which stretch some 1,350 nautical miles northwest of Honolulu to Kure Atoll beyond Midway Island.

1909: Joseph J. Fern, a Democrat, was elected as Honolulu's first Mayor.

1912: Duke Kahanamoku, a young 18-year-old Hawaiian, became the toast of the sports world when he thrashed his way to a

Mausoleum in Nuuanu.

1920: The U.S. Congress passed a Hawaiian Homes Commission Act sponsored by Prince Jonah Kuhio Kalanianaole, Liliuokalani's nephew and then the territorial delegate to Congress. The act set aside about 200,000 acres of land, which was to be allocated to needy Hawaiian people in an attempt to rehabilitate them by returning them to the land. Hawaiians of half or more native blood were given the privilege of applying to a government-administered Hawaiian Homes Department for a 99-year

world's record in the 100 meters swimming event at Olympic Games held this year at Stockholm, Sweden. Until he died in 1967, "The Duke" was probably the most well-known international personality associated with Hawaii. Worldwide surfing enthusiasts still refer to waterman Kahanamoku as the unofficial "father" of that glamorous Hawaiian sport, and his name is recalled with reverence wherever young and older waveriders congregate.

1915: When the submarine F-4, *Skate*, sank in 50 fathoms of water off Honolulu Harbor, all 21 men on board dying with her, the accident was referred to as "the first submarine disaster in U.S. Navy history."

1917: Liliuokalani, Hawaii's last ruling monarch, died on November 11. Her body lay in state at Kawaiahao Church, and on November 18 she was interred in the Royal

lease (at minimal cost) of a small agricultural or pastoral plot. As of 1978, the program was generally considered to be a failure, primarily due to bureaucratic problems.

1922: Prince Kuhio, the last member of the Hawaiian royal family to wield political power, died on January 7 at Waikiki. The popular prince's birthday, Kuhio Day (March 26), is still celebrated in Hawaii as an official state holiday.

1922: On July 16th, an engineer, conductor and fireman were killed when their fast-moving pineapple train derailed about three miles west of Waipahu Mill at the Waikakalaua Gulch on the Oahu Railway and Land Co.'s Wahiawa-Schofield line. Two other persons were injured in what publisher-historian Thomas G. Thrum called "the worst train wreck in the history of the Oahu R. & L. Co." It was the worst railway catastrophe known since 1884, when a passenger freight train on Maui (of the Kahului Railroad) uncoupled, ran away on a sharp grade and collided with another train, killing three passengers and seriously injured three others.

1922: Hawaii's first commercial radio stations began broadcasting.

1924: On September 9th, Governor Wallace R. Farrington had to dispatch Hawaii National Guard troops (6 officers, 85 riflemen and 2 machine-gun squads) to Kauai to restore order, following a labor riot above the town of Hanapepe which caused the death of 16 Filipino strikers and 4 policemen. In the labor dispute's legal aftermath, 101 of 133 strikers were arrested, 76 were brought to trial and 60 received four-year jail

wife of Navy Lieutenant Thomas Hedges Massie — captured the attention of the national press for nearly a year. Allegedly, Mrs. Massie had been raped by a group of "local boys" during the evening of September 12 while she was wandering along through an undeveloped area near Waikiki. The story became more bizarre when on January 8, 1932, Mrs. Massie's mother, Lieutenant Massie, and two accomplices kidnaped one of the five charged suspects, Joe Kahahawai, and killed him. In a spectacular court case which followed these incidents, the Massie family was represented by the famous mainland attorney Clarence Darrow. Darrow, by then 75 years old, eloquently argued his last courtroom case in the Massie family's behalf. On April 29, 1932, Darrow's clients

sentences. The strike, sponsored by the new Filipino Higher Wages Movement, involved three thousand sugar workers and was the biggest such stand by organized Hawaii laborers until the late 1930s.

1927: U.S. Army amphibious planes completed the first successful non-stop flights from California to Hawaii.

1929: The Inter-Island Steam Navigation Company created a transportation subsidiary, Inter-Island Airways (now known as Hawaiian Airlines), which on November 11 began providing Hawaii's first inter-island air transportation with a pair of Sikorsky S-38 amphibious aircraft. Five years later, the new airline began ferrying mail between principal islands of the Hawaiian group.

1931: Radio telephone service to and from the U.S. mainland was initiated.

1931: A lurid and openly racist rape case involving Thalia Massie — the 20-year-old

were convicted of manslaughter and later sentenced to 10 years of hard labor; but territorial Governor Lawrence M. Judd commuted their sentences from 10 years to one hour — which the prisoners served in his office. The controversial Massie Case seriously divided Hawaii's citizens along racial-political lines for many years. Its judicial outcome still inspires bitter arguments among oldtimers who felt that "white man's law" had discriminated against darker and poorer local people.

1935: At 8 a.m. Honolulu time on Wednesday, April 17, a 19-ton Pan American World Airways Clipper Ship landed at the

Tourists of the "Roaring Twenties" era are seen "Toasting postals" in this postcard view of lava flow at Kilauea Volcano; right, stunned servicemen look across a shattered airfield as a fuel tank explodes on Pearl Harbor Day, December 7, 1941.

fleet airbase in Pearl Harbor, completing a 19-hour and 48-minute flight from Alameda Airport near San Francisco. This "exploratory" flight marked the first time a civilian-commercial aircraft had ever crossed the Pacific Ocean to Hawaii. Seven months later, a second Pan Am aircraft, *The Silver China Clipper*, touched down with a cargo of mail, then continued to Midway and Wake island, Guam and Manila, thereby creating the first Pacific air link between the United States, the Philippines and China. And less than a year after that, on October 22, 1936, a third *Hawaii Clipper* skidded across Pearl Harbor's waters with a cargo of paying passengers. The international commercial air age had finally reached out to Hawaii, the Pacific crossroads between East and West, and hot

1938: A workers strike directed at the powerful Inter-Island Steamship Company ended in violence on August 1 when 40 armed policemen attacked a large group of strikers gathered on docks at Hilo, Hawaii, with fire hoses, tear gas bombs and shotguns. None of the strikers was killed, but 50 of the male and female picketers were wounded, several seriously. This early strike — by members of the International Longshoremen's and Warehousemen's Union (ILWU), the Inland Boatmen's Union and the Metal Trades Council — was later referred to by unionists as the "Hilo Massacre."

1941: Shortly before 8 a.m. on Sunday, December 7, two waves of Japanese aircraft, 360 planes in all, dropped below cloud cover above Oahu and attacked every major mili-

on these airtrails came untold millions and ultimately billions of dollars in cargo and tourist dollars.

1935: A National Labor Relations Act passed by Congress this year (and afterwards, in 1937, declared constitutional by the United States Supreme Court) made it entirely legal for workers to organize into unions and press claims against management through collective bargaining. This official support made possible a local workers' revolution, which during the next two decades completely shifted the political power structure of Hawaii — from the hands of conservative "big money" Republicans to the open arms of liberal "working man" Democrats.

tary installation on the island. The surprise attack by Japanese-built Val dive-bombers (Aichi D3AI Model II), Kates (Nakajima B5N2) and Zekes (or Zeros, the Mitsubishi A6M2 Zerosen) devastated the United States' Pacific air and naval forces and initiated World War II in its Pacific theater. A military board of inquiry reported at the end of the war that the "astoundingly disproportionate extent of losses" suffered by the United States on Oahu marked "the greatest military and naval disaster in our Nation's history." As the board noted in its report, "Military and naval forces of the United States suffered 3,435 casualties; Japan, less than 100. We lost outright 188 planes; Japan,

29. We suffered severe damage to or loss of 8 battle-ships, 3 light cruisers, 3 destroyers, and 4 miscellaneous vessels; Japan lost 5 midget submarines."

That same day, following the attack, U.S. President Franklin Delano Roosevelt declared war on Japan, and at 11:30 a.m. Army Lieutenant General Walter C. Short informed the people of Hawaii that they would be living under martial law until further notice.

Some 68 Oahu residents were killed or injured during the attack on Pearl Harbor and other parts of Honolulu, and another group of civilians died at sea on board a steam schooner named the *Cynthia Olsen*. About 13 minutes after the Japanese began bombing Pearl Harbor, the *Cynthia Olsen* radioed frantically from about 1,000 miles

northeast of Honolulu that she was being attacked by a submarine. That was the last ever heard from her; she and 35 persons on board simply disappeared at sea.

During the next seven weeks, two other ships moving through Hawaiian waters were torpedoed by prowling Japanese submarines. On December 18, nine people on board the freighter *Prusa* died when she was hit about 100 miles southeast of Oahu; and on January 28, 1942, another 29 persons perished when the small transport ship *Gen. Royal T. Frank* was attacked while crossing the Alenuihaha Channel between Maui and Hawaii.

1944: In May and June, three separate military-related accidents on Oahu took a total of 187 lives and injured 396. The first

disaster occurred on May 21 at Pearl Harbor's West Loch while a group of LST's were loading mortar ammunition for the Saipan invasion near the Naval Ammunition Depot. One LST-353 caught on fire, blew up spectacularly and set off a chain reaction of loud explosions on five other LST's. That accident killed 163 men and wounded 396 others. Another similar explosion on June 11 killed 10 men who, again, were transferring ammunition at the Naval Ammunition Depot. Meanwhile, on June 8, two Army medium bombers collided in mid-air above Honolulu and crashed into a busy residential area, Kalihi, burning a dozen buildings, and killing 10 women and children and the planes' four crew members. That disaster caused "the greatest number of fatalities from a single fire" in Hawaii's history.

1944: On October 24, by Presidential proclamation, martial law was ended, thereby returning normal legal rights to Hawaii's citizens. During the martial law period, nearly all constitutional rights in Hawaii were suspended. For almost three years the U.S. Army controlled the operation of civil and criminal courts, public health and hospitals, the regulation of labor, licensing (and censoring) of the press, all the normal bureaucratic functions of Hawaii's county and the territorial governments, even the collection of garbage, establishment of traffic control systems and licensing of bowling alleys. The only thing the Office of the Military Governor did not do for Hawaii's civilians was to collect their taxes.

1945: At 1:42 p.m. on Tuesday, August 14, air raid sirens, church bells, honking horns, firecrackers and shouting civilians and military personnel celebrated the news that Japan had unconditionally surrendered to the United States following the dropping of

Newspaper headlines say all that needs to be said: above, on that "day of infamy" in 1941; and (right) in 1959, when the U.S. Congress approved statehood for the then Territory of Hawaii.

atomic bombs on the cities of Hiroshima and Nagasaki. The day became known as V-J Day, for "Victory over Japan Day," and was marked by impromptu parades, singing and weeping in Honolulu's confetti-littered streets.

1946: On April 1 the northern and eastern shores of Hawaii's islands were hit by a huge, devastating *tsunami* (or seismic or tidal wave), the largest ever in recorded local history. About 159 to 173 persons were killed (estimates vary) by a massive wall of water which smashed shoreline areas with a force which destroyed standing structures and pushed cars and trucks around like toys. At Hilo on the Big Island, 96 persons died when the town was inundated. The wave—generated by a submarine earthquake off the north-

economy, which is almost completely dependent on shipping to survive.

1952: Hawaii's first television stations began broadcasting.

1955: A military air transport aircraft (MATS R6-D) crashed into the Waianae Mountains near the Lualualei Naval Ammunition Depot at 2:16 a.m. on March 22 and killed 66 passengers. That was the greatest number of deaths ever recorded in an air accident in Hawaii. Everybody on board the MATS plane—64 armed forces personnel and 2 military dependents—died in the crash.

1959: The Congress on March 12 sent to President Dwight D. Eisenhower a bill (approved by the House of Representatives 323–89 and the Senate 76–15) recommending statehood for Hawaii. Pending approval by Hawaii's citizens it would make Hawaii the 50th State in the United States of America. Eisenhower signed the bill and Hawaii's citizens began to celebrate their new status. In a general plebiscite held in the islands on June 27, Hawaii's eligible voters ratified 17 to 1 the congressional move for statehood. The only precinct of 240 electoral precincts to reject statehood was the island of Niihau, the only place in Hawaii which is populated almost exclusively by Hawaiians. On Au-

ern Aleutian Islands—caused an estimated $10,500,000 in property damage. The last previously known *tsunami* of this power hit Hawaii on April 2, 1868, killing about 46 people on the same Hilo-windward side of the Big Island.

1946: The ILWU staged a very successful 77-day strike against the sugar industry and established itself as one of Hawaii's major new political and economic powers.

1946: Also this year, the Hawaii Visitors Bureau began to aggressively promote Hawaii on the mainland and abroad.

1949: Again the ILWU called a major strike, this time against shipping companies, and a 177-day freeze of Hawaii's dockworkers nearly devastated Hawaii's fragile

gust 21 President Eisenhower issued the final presidential proclamation necessary to admit Hawaii into the Union.

1959: During this year the first regular jet air service was inaugurated between Hawaii and the mainland, cutting travel time from California in half—from 9 propellor hours to $4\frac{1}{2}$ jet hours.

1969: Thousands of cheering Hawaii residents were on hand at Oahu's Hickam Air Force Base on Saturday morning, July 26, to welcome home the first three men to return to earth from the moon. Neil Armstrong, Edwin E. "Buzz" Aldrin, Jr., and Mike Collins, the three astronauts who manned the United States' Apollo 11 lunar landing mission, smiled through the window of a stainless steel quarantine chamber as they were plopped back onto solid ground after their historic journey into nearby outer space. To honor Armstrong's famous "one small step for a man" and "giant leap for mankind" a troupe of Navy wives danced a *hula* for the returning voyagers. In response, spaceman Armstrong picked up an *ukulele* he had taken to the moon and strummed it, eliciting applause from his fellow earthlings. White plumeria leis were draped on the transport chamber's door handle moments before the three astronauts and 47.4 pounds of lunar soil were lifted into a cargo aircraft and flown to the National Aeronautics and Space Administration (NASA) Space Center at Houston, Texas.

1974: George R. Ariyoshi, 48, was inau-

officers and men who were actively involved in that long debacle in Vietnam, Cambodia, Thailand and Laos. Throughout this unpopular war in Southeast Asia, Hawaii served, as she had during the Spanish-American War, World War II and the Korean War, as a major supply and command post, second in importance only to the Pentagon in Washington, D.C.

1976: On January 4, under cover of early-morning darkness, eight young Hawaiians "occupied" Kahoolawe Island, a dusty isle about eight miles southwest of Maui, to protest the U.S. Navy's regular use of it as a bombing and shelling target. The Hawaiians and numerous other citizens and public officials want the bombing stopped and had been lobbying to have Kahoolawe returned

gurated on December 2 as Hawaii's third Governor since statehood and earned the additional distinction of being the first American of Japanese descent ever elected governor of one of the United States. Some 8,000 people attended Ariyoshi's noontime swearing-in ceremony on the grounds of Iolani Palace. "For many in Hawaii, his inauguration symbolized the culmination of a political and social struggle of more than two decades," wrote the politics writer for *The Honolulu Advertiser.*

1975: On April 23 President Gerald R. Ford declared that America's undeclared war in Indochina was over. Thus, Hawaii ceased to serve as a major command headquarters and rest and recuperation center for

to the State of Hawaii and restored to its original condition. The Navy, however, which has been shelling, bombing and detonating ordnance on the island since 1941, claims that the island, the eighth largest in the Hawaiian chain, plays an important role in national defense. The Navy also has argued over the years that so many unexploded bombs, shells and other war material have been embedded in the 45-square-mile

Back on earth, summer of 1969, are happy U.S. astronauts (from left to right) Buzz Aldrin, Neil Armstrong and Mike Collins; and to right, celebrating his 1978 re-election as Governor of Hawaii is George Ariyoshi, former Lt. Gov. Jean King (white hair) and Mrs Jean Ariyoshi.

isle that it could not be safely returned to civilian use.

Kahoolawe had previously been used as a penal colony and for cattle grazing. In ancient Hawaiian times it also was the site of several sacred shrines and was occupied at various times by fishermen and their families.

1978: On August 14, Federal agents and police officers from all of Hawaii's counties (Honolulu, Maui, Hawaii and Kauai) grouped on the Big Island of Hawaii to launch the first of a series of secret dope raids aimed at "eradicating marijuana" and "interdicting drug smuggling" in the islands. The secretive scheme was called "Operation Green Harvest," and before its completion raiding vice officers and feds had sought out, seized and burned millions of dollars worth of cane and pineapple plantations.

Late 20th Century Postscript

Since 1959 and Statehood, Hawaii's Democratic Party has tenaciously held on to its political power, and the only political interest has been generated by colorful intra-party squabbling. In the economic meantime Hawaii's major industries — of sugar, pineapple, Federal spending and tourism — continued to boom as nobody ever dreamed they would. During the 1950s, for example, the construction industry grew slowly, from about $100 million in expenditures to about $200 million. But from the beginning of 1960 to the end of 1970 more than $4.35 billion worth of construction went up in the islands,

marijuana on the various islands.

Local law enforcement officers were concerned about the marijuana, because Hawaiian *pakalolo* (crazy tobacco), or "island buds," had been gaining a notorious reputation in dope-smoking circles on the U.S. mainland and abroad. Certain specially cultivated strains of Hawaiian hemp — such as Kona Gold, Puna Butter, Maui Wowie and Kauai Electric — were selling in mainland smoking salons for as much as $300-plus an ounce, or for more than the marijuana's weighed value in gold. Some State economists guessed that the illegal, tax-free revenues being earned by island marijuana growers and sellers were exceeding local taxable money being earned by legitimate sugar

followed by ever-increasing years of growth until it reached a high of $1.04 billion for a single year in 1974. Sugar and pineapple are in a decline now, and Federal spending has stabilized, but tourism, as they say in the trade, "has taken off" to dizzying dollar heights. In 1972 tourism edged ahead of defense spending to become Hawaii's number-one money earner. In 1977 nearly four times as many people visited Hawaii than live in Hawaii, and, as has been mentioned, that figure is expected to double sometime during the later 1980s. Indeed, the most significant Hawaii story of the 1960s and 1970s, and probably of the 1980s, has been the astounding success of Hawaiian tourism and the related worldwide selling of Hawaii.

IT IS THE MEETING PLACE OF EAST AND WEST,

the very new rubs shoulders with the immeasurably old. And if you have not found the romance you expected, you have come upon something singularly intriguing. All these strange people live close to each other, with different languages and different thoughts; they believe in different gods and they have different values; two passions alone they share, love and hunger. And somehow as you watch them, you have an impression of extraordinary vitality.

— *William Somerset Maugham, commenting on Honolulu in* The Trembling of a Leaf, *1921*

"The meeting place of East and West ..." If the writer were not Maugham, he'd be attacked for resorting to cliche. But wordly Maugham wasn't the first or last scribe to say such simplistic, catch-all things about the people of Hawaii as a group. Recent favorite sobriquets refer to "the golden people," "a social rainbow" and "a preview of ultimate world man." Even James Michener, who authored the weighty epic *Hawaii*, titled his last chapter "The Golden Men" and alluded to "a man at home in either the business councils of New York or the philosophical retreats of Kyoto." All are awful but understandable "melting pot" and "color blind" generalities. But what else can a newcomer say about the only state in the United States, or for that matter in the world, where every racial group is a minority, and where most of these minorities originated in Asia and Polynesia, rather than in Europe or Africa?

Nonetheless, it is best we mention this "galaxy of cultures" concept now, then forget nicknames forever, because the real truth — or truths — about Hawaiian society are much more complex, subtle, and, from anthropological-psychological points-of-view, invisible to the untrained eye, ear and soul.

Localism, or Coexisting Nervously

Perhaps a more enlightened general comment was one in a recent *Hawaii Observer* magazine article which noted skeptically, but knowledgeably, that the Hawaiian Islands are made up of many disparate cultures "that somewhat nervously coexist." It is true that for political and economic "survival" purposes Hawaii's multi-racial citizens and immigrant aliens have congealed. But this viscosity is more jelly than pudding. Inside the transparent mass which is the host Hawaiian Islands, one can clearly observe various ethnic parts, each floating along in a distinct "working" state of suspended animation. In toto they belong to a group consciousness called "localism," an identity which somehow gives "local boys" and "local girls" a kinship rare in other crazy-quilt communities. And with each new generation, with each sexual shuffle of the *local* gene

pool, this island society is creating hundreds of splendid mutations. As Honolulu humorist Tom Horton once asked in a gossip column published by *The Honolulu Advertiser*: "Where else but in Hawaii would nice Japanese girl, Jeanette Sylva, married to nice Portuguese boy, make her nightclub debut as Natasha the belly dancer at the Asakusa on Kapiolani, and be introduced as the 'Queen of Egypt' by a Chinese bandleader, and come out dancing to 'Hava Nagila'?" *Ah so* and *oh wei*. And in what other city of only 700,000-plus residents can you blink at — in the same quarter mile of road — ethnocentric shingles, signs and neons advertising, among other enterprises, H. Yasumoto Tailor, the Portugal Pacific Sausage Company, Knights of England Imported Pianos, the Aloha Plumbing Co., Goto Fishing Supply, Mama's Mexican Kitchen, Uptown Saimin and Fountain and McDonald's Hamburgers? Which are all just around a Kalihi corner from the Dutch Girl Pastry Shop, Park's Korean Foods, Hoy Tin Chop Suey, St. Theresa's Rectory, the Konko Mission of Honolulu and the United Puerto Rican Community Association.

But that's nothing. How about the drive-in restaurant in Moiliili with a fluorescent marquee touting "French Fries and Kim Chee To Go"?

Got a complicated, "international" legal problem? Surely somebody with either Fong, Miho & Robinson, or Damon, Shigekane, Key & Char, or Chun, Kerr & Dodd, or Woo, Kessner & Duca, or Gill, Park & Park should be able to help.

This "chop suey" consciousness even permeates Hawaii's corridors of power. Hawaii's four-man delegation to the U.S. Congress now includes two Japanese (Inouye and Matsunaga), one Hawaiian (Akaka) and a carpetbagger *haole* from Texas (Heftel). And though Hawaii's Governor was Japanese (Ariyoshi), the Mayor of the City & County of Honolulu was an Anglo-Saxon from California (Anderson), and the chief executives of Maui, Kauai and Hawaii Counties were, respectively, a Portuguese (Cravalho), Filipino (Malapit) and Japanese (Matayoshi).

Overall, according to recent census figures,

Hawaii's population of about 900,000 includes about 261,000, or 29% assorted Caucasians; 248,000, or 27½% Japanese; 162,000, or 18% Hawaiians and Part-Hawaiians; 90,000, or 10% Filipinos; 41,000, or 4½% Chinese; 9,000, or 1% Koreans; 9,000, or 1% Samoans; 9,000, or 1% Negroes; and some 71,000, or 8% persons who are identified as "Mixed and Miscellaneous."

On Making the 'Connection'

The most important Hawaii population item, however, has to do with love and marriage. George Tokuyama, the State's expert on that productive subject, reported recently that of Honolulu's approximately 10,000 marriages a year, "about 50 per cent

are now interracial, that is involving brides and grooms who were of a different race." On a world-wide basis, that may well be the highest incidence of interracial marriages being consummated in any known society.

Preceding pages, wide-eyed Hawaiian beauty is a typical island blend of Hawaiian, Chinese, French and German racial ancestry. Hawaii's broad ethnic mix is very clear in slide photo (above) of newsboys, selling *The Pacific Commercial Advertiser* in 1916.

Plus, State health officials feel that Hawaii's annual marital rate — of about 10,000 marriages per year in a total population of less than 1 million — may be the highest in the United States on a per capita basis.

The above facts and figures all add up to virile phenomena which didn't escape storyist Maugham when he passed through Honolulu in 1916. "Though the air is so soft and the sky so blue," observed Maugham, "you have, I know not why, a feeling of something hotly passionate that beats like a throbbing pulse through the crowd. Though the native policeman at the corner, standing on a platform, with a white club to direct the traffic, gives the scene an air of respectability, you cannot but feel that it is a respectability only of the surface; a little below there is a darkness and mystery."

Pierre Bowman, one of Hawaii's few native Hawaiian writers who comments regularly on island life, suggested recently that this Maugham-Hawaii mystery readily reveals itself if a visitor "takes time out of his touristic itinerary to talk to local people."

"So many visitors," Bowman sighs, "walk off their jet, bus to Waikiki and lock themselves into the 'Sheraton Circuit.' They sit in air-conditioned hotel rooms, ride around the island in mirrored, air-conditioned tour buses, eat standard menu foods, then drink and dance themselves to sleep in formulaic, air-conditioned nightclubs. Then they jet home and rave about how nice the weather was. Few of these people ever enjoy the real Hawaii — the people. And it's a pity, because if they would take time to walk downtown, sit on a bench and spend a few minutes talking to a local person, they would learn so much more about Hawaii, and about themselves. It's all so obvious, and so accessible, but few tourists connect."

This Hawaii "connection" is much easier, however, if you know something about the colorful comings and goings of Hawaii's ethnic casts and the dramas they've created on this island stage.

HAWAIIANS

The last prophet was Kapihe, who uttered his final prophecy near the end of the reign of Kamehameha I, saying, *E hui ana na moku, e hiolo ana na kapu akua, e iho mai ana ko ka lani, a e pi'i aku ana ko ka honua* — "The islands will be united, the kapus of the gods overthrown, those of the heavens (chiefs) will be brought low, and those of the earth (the common people) will be raised up."

> — *from the chapter on "Kahuna Orders — The Order of Prophets" in Samuel Manaiakalani Kamakau's* Ka Po'e Kahiko, The People of Old.

"What's a Hawaiian?" the *haole* reporter asked.

The young Hawaiian doctor thought about that inquiry for a moment, looked away, returned with a smile, and answered in a quiet voice:

"On the island of Molokai," he said, "local people say a Hawaiian is someone who eats *palu*."

Palu, he explained, is an exotic Hawaiian condiment made of chopped bits of the head and stomach of fish mixed with dashes of *kukui* nut relish, garlic and chili peppers. The doctor smiled when the perplexed reporter shook his head. "My answer wasn't meant to be facetious," he explained. Rather, he just wanted to point out, in a simple way, that his people, Hawaiians, are different from non-Hawaiians. *Palu* may sound off-the-wall or unsavory, he said, but it is one of few Hawaiian things newcomers haven't managed to change, replace or glamorize. "It's a little identity thing," he winked.

Ironically, some would say tragically, native Hawaiians are now among the most inconspicuous people walking the streets of Hawaii. Indeed, they are there, interacting at all levels of society, but as a reporter observed recently, "It's gotten to where you almost can't see the Hawaiians for Hawaii."

The reason for this dearth of Hawaiians in Hawaii is because during their first 100 years of exposure to Western man, most of Hawaii's native residents were destroyed, mostly by diseases introduced to the Islands during the late 18th and the 19th centuries. They were the genetically weak victims of a physical devastation so swift that by 1893 — the year a group of American businessmen overthrew the Hawaiian throne — Hawaii's aboriginal population had shrunk from an estimated 300,000-plus at the time of Captain James Cook's first visit in 1778 to about 40,000, many of whom by then were of only part-Hawaiian blood. This decimation was so awful and culture-shocking that by the mid-19th Century, many thousands of Hawaiians began dying of sheer psychological depression. "*Na kanaka kuu wale aku no i ka uhane* — The people freely gave up their souls and died," recounts a sorrowful Hawaiian saying of the 1840s when many despondent Hawaiians were wishing themselves dead.

Keiki Aina, Children of the Soil

Since those morbid times, Hawaiians who survived have made a dramatic social

comeback — first by outmarrying into other racial groups, then by producing part-Hawaiian babies at a procreation rate unchallenged by the Islands' other races. As a result, pure and part-Hawaiian people now number about 160,000 and are the fastest-growing ethnic group in the Islands. "If this reproductive pace maintains itself," a demographer notes, "by the year 2000 there will be as many part-Hawaiians in Hawaii as there once were pure Hawaiians."

A *malihini*, or newcomer, might point out that these part-Hawaiians are also "part-

Left, helmeted Hawaiian who performs in Waikiki's Kodak Hula Show for tourists; above, spectator at Hawaiian music festival at Hauula.

something else," but it must be emphasized here that part-Hawaiians, whatever their other exotic parts, nearly unanimously think of themselves as "Hawaiian" and not the "something elses." And with every passing year, it's becoming more and more of a local status symbol to be a *keiki aina*, a child of the soil, a Hawaiian.

Consequently, as "pure" genetic Hawaiians disappear from the planet, they are just as rapidly being replaced by non-thoroughbred Hawaiians who are "psychoculturally" Hawaiian, in heart and soul, if not in body. In recent years, this "psychological rebirth" has manifested itself in a Hawaiian *renaissance* which has been proudly and aggressively salvaging Hawaiian traditions which were on the verge of extinction due to

immeasurably to Hawaii's—and the world's —understanding of Hawaii.

However, as this Hawaiianness evolves, the Hawaiian race's ability to adapt to and successfully assimilate into the many cultures which have migrated to its shores has been a remarkable success and survival story.

Contrary to media impressions which for decades have painted stereotypical pictures of "the average Hawaiian" as an easy-going beachboy, tour bus driver, dancer, musician or kowtowing detective's sidekick, many part-Hawaiians are now among the most powerful people in the Islands. As of now, for example, part-Hawaiians included the Chief Justice of Hawaii's Supreme Court (William S. Richardson), the owner of the largest private ranch in America (Richard

neglect or outright *haole* suppression. More young native Hawaiians than ever before in modern history are enrolling in *hula* and Hawaiian language courses in order to preserve and practice the cultural traditions of their elders, the *kupuna*. They are also becoming more politically active than ever before in this century, fighting for "Hawaiian rights" which they say were unjustly taken from their ancestors following the 1893 *coup d'etat* and U.S. annexation of the Islands in 1898. Critics of this activism fear that such Hawaiian verve may evolve into indiscreet forms of racism with negative social consequences, but many Hawaiians see this resurgence of pride as a positive movement which will strengthen their lot and contribute

Smart), a U.S. Congressman (Representative Daniel K. Akaka), the president of First Hawaiian Bank (John Bellinger), Honolulu's Chief of Police (Francis Keala) and Fire Chief (Boniface Aiu), one of the world's wealthiest entertainers (Don Ho), and the executive director (David Trask) of the 19,000-member Hawaii Government Employees Union, the most powerful labor organization in Hawaii.

On the other hand, Hawaiians and part-Hawaiians make up the largest number of inmates in County jails and the State Prison, the greatest percentage of State and Federal welfare recipients, the majority of school dropouts and juvenile delinquents, and are the number one producers of illegitimate

babies. Plus, in the dubious profession called "organized crime," they are the undisputed heavies.

As the above disparities indicate, it's a subtle thing this Hawaiianness, something aboriginal and abstract beyond a fondness for *palu* and *poi*, outrigger canoe racing, and quiet, communal respect for the works, gods and belief systems of "the people of old."

On Being Hawaiian

Frustrated, the *haole* reporter moved on to other Hawaiians and repeated his question: "What is being Hawaiian?" Answers broke here and there, like waves ricocheting off a jagged coral reef.

George Kanahele, a Hawaiian business-

special pride to being Hawaiian. The Hawaiians were not a middle-class society when Western man came. They were an aristocracy and placed value on things not in terms of possessions, but in terms of genealogy. And because of that, of all the primitive people ever confronted by the white man, only the Hawaiians were ever accepted as equals."

Pete Thompson, a Hawaiian grassroots organizer — "Hawaiians don't differ all that much from other people in terms of the everyday problems people face — stuff like housing and getting one's kids a decent education and all the rest. But in terms of what questions are peculiar to Hawaiians, or give rise and interest to them as a racial group, I would say primarily, from my point of view,

man-intellectual — "These days, any resident of this State who considers Hawaii his home and who has an understanding of the values of Hawaiian culture ought to consider himself or herself a Hawaiian."

Steve Morse, a part-Hawaiian social worker — "Being Hawaiian is being here a long time and getting turned on to what's here — the people, the customs and all that. Just the recognition is important, knowing that a person is a son or daughter of Hawaii. It's like when you see a brother walking up the street. It's just a nod of the head, a flick of the eyebrow, a feeling that somehow you're part of something — something Hawaiian."

Samuel Crowningburg-Amalu, part-Hawaiian newspaper columnist — "There's a

that the biggest Hawaiian issue is the land question. What about the land? If you look at every Hawaiian (political) group that was formed in the past five years, every single one of them has been formed around the question of land. Every last one."

Auntie Abby Napeahi, an elderly Hawaiian matriarch and community leader on the Big Island of Hawaii — "Being Hawaiian today is finally feeling at home after nearly a century of trying to live like foreigners told us we should live in our own land."

Edward Keliiahonui Kawananakoa, the man who would be King of Hawaii if the Hawaiian monarchy had survived — "I guess, generally, I'm just trying to be a good American citizen."

THE HAOLE

In vile Honolulu there are too many
cesspools and beastly *haoles.*
  — *Robert Louis Stevenson*

Mr. Stevenson, himself a *haole* and a
moody man given to Jekyll and Hyde-like
personality shifts, was perhaps being a bit too
harsh on fellow white men living in Honolulu. After all, some of the Scotsman's best
friends, even his wife, were *haole.* Nonetheless, Stevenson was simply being honest and
a typical islander. Since the time of Captain
Cook and thereafter it has been fashionable
in Hawaii for both *haole* and non-*haole* to put
down *haole.*

This "thou is *haole*-er
than me" attitude has
taken on a good-natured
racial connotation in recent
years (depending on the
adjectives or nouns which
precede or follow the word
haole), but for many
years — particularly dur-
ing periods of oppression
— the term was more a
slur than a synonym for
Caucasian or foreigner.

As some Hawaiians
explain it, their ancestors
called the first western
visitors *haole* because
they could not believe that
men with such pale skins
and frail bodies could be
alive. Hence, the coining
of the word *haole*, made
up of the prefix *ha*, which
means breath or the
breath of life, and the
suffix *ole*, which connotes
an absence of. Taken
together—as the word
haole—they mean absence
of the breath of life or, more simply,
without life. Kinder native sons say the
term means only that a person does not
understand the Hawaiian language and
lifestyle.

The *haole* is now the number one ethnic
group in terms of population, having slipped
by the Japanese population during the mid-
1970s. And — given in-migration trends
since Statehood in 1959—his/her caucasian
numbers should continue to increase at a
steady pace. Therefore, the *haole*, whether of
malihini (newcomer) or *kamaaina* (oldtimer)

status, is the new population wave hitting
Hawaii's shores. Like immigrants who preceded him, he is attracted by Hawaii's sun,
sea and sand, but also by the economic
stability of Hawaii's two biggest industries,
tourism and the U.S. military.

'Pre-American' Haole

In Hawaii however, there is one *haole* sub-
category which deserves special mention as a
"pre-American" Caucasion group. They are
the Portuguese, or "Portagee" as they are
referred to in local pidgin dialect, who immigrated to Hawaii in great numbers when
Hawaii was still a kingdom ruled by Hawaiian
kings and queens.

The Portuguese, who are also affec-

tionately known by the island nickname
"guavas," began immigrating to Hawaii in
1878 during the fourth year of King
Kalakaua's reign. As early as 1872 there were
as many as 395 Portuguese in Hawaii, most
of them sailors who had left visiting whaling
ships in favor of a landed life. These
Europeans were well received by both
Hawaiians and *haole* merchants and planters, so in 1878 the Hawaiian Government

Left, spectator at outrigger canoe races, Waikiki,
1979; right, woman surfer at Waikiki, 1915.

and the Kingdom's sugar planters conducted an official labor recruitment campaign in Portugal's Azores and Maderia island groups. By 1899, 12,778 Portuguese (5,362 men, 2,486 women and 4,930 children) had made the rough voyage from their Atlantic islands to Hawaii.

Many of these Portuguese became *lunas*, or foremen, on the plantations, and thus gained a mid-level power foothold much faster than Oriental and Filipino immigrants. Consequently, by the 1930s Portuguese members of the Hawaiian community had succeeded in becoming a Chief Justice of the Territory's Supreme Court (Antonio J. Perry), a territorial Secretary and Acting Governor (Frank G. Serrao) and the Catholic Vicar Apostolic of the Hawaiian Islands

(Reverend Stephen Peter Alen-castre).

In lighter style, the first Portuguese also made a contribution to local culture which has since become an internationally recognized symbol of Hawaii. This was the introduction of a small four-stringed guitar-like instrument — known as the *braquinho* or *cavaghindo* in Portugal — which is now

Portuguese women pose for an early plantation portrait by renowned people photographer Ray Jerome Baker. Right, Honolulu's former Mayor Frank Fasi campaigns.

popularly identified by the Hawaiian word *'ukulele*. The term *'ukulele* literally means "leaping flea," and was said to have been derived from the Hawaiian nickname of an English expatriate named Edward Purvis. Purvis, reportedly arrived in Hawaii in 1879, made friends with newly-arrived Portuguese immigrants, and soon learned how to play their compact little *braquinho* with amazing and entertaining finesse. Purvis was small in stature and at the same time so quick with his hands that his Hawaiian friends nicknamed him *'Ukulele*, the "leaping flea."

The *'ukulele* is probably the only remnant of early Portuguese influences in Hawaii which has drifted beyond these turquoise shores. However, local Portuguese, though more than two generations removed from the "old country," still leap with traditional gusto into Portuguese traditions and festivals which can be traced to the Middle Ages.

A classical example of such activity is a spring time, post-Easter series of *festas*, or festivals, known in Portuguese Hawaii as the Seven Domingas, or Holy Ghost festivals. These seven weekly observances, dedicated to the *Santo Christo* (Jesus Christ), the Holy Ghost and Queen Isabel, a 13th Century queen of Portugal, are sponsored by a handful of surviving Portuguese Holy Ghost societies which maintain clubhouse chapels on Oahu, Maui and the Big Island. During the seven weeks of festa entire families participate in one Portuguese way or another in old-style prayer and merrymaking. Ladies prepare heaps of traditional delicacies such as baked *paodoce* (sweet bread), hot fried *malasadas* (a light Portuguese doughnut), spicy Portuguese bean soup, and beef and fish dishes marinated in tangy *vinha d'alhos*. The men, meanwhile, polish up the Holy Ghost meeting chapels and grounds, pause periodically to drink spirited toasts of thick Port wine to the Holy Ghost and each other, and — God and wine willing — keep an eye on the children, the *crianzas*, who are dolled up in new clothes and shown off at

78

numerous social occasions.

Probably the most obvious Portuguese item you'll notice in Hawaii is the listing of tangy "Portuguese sausage" on breakfast menus alongside bacon, ham and eggs. Any coffee shop worthy of being called "local" includes this spicy selection. Some cafes carry the Portuguese influence further by serving Portuguese bean soup as a standard *soup du jour*. But beyond such established genuflections ·to Portuguese cuisine, the third most noticeable item ala Portuguese is the *malasada* doughnut. At school fairs, other such carnival events, and recently in supermarket parking lots, people of all hungry races queue up in front of red-and-white motor vans which sell these greasy lumps of dough as fast as they can be deep-fried and

years. Others have followed or were born here since. Puerto Ricans have traditionally been classified in Hawaii's census polls as Caucasian, or *haole*, but their early immigrant ranks also included people of creole blood (*mulattos*) and persons of more or less pure Spanish, American Indian and black African descent.

Unlike the gregarious Portuguese, the Puerto Ricans have never established a very solid socio-cultural beachhead in the Islands. Now and then they gather at the United Puerto Rican Civic Association social hall at 1249 North School Street in the Kalihi area of Honolulu for an evening of *salsa* dancing and drinking, but in comparison to other ethnics, the Puerto Rican presence is low key.

sugar-coated.

Another *haole* immigrant group with Euro-Latin origins, Puerto Ricans, began arriving here at the turn-of-the-century. And though they now number an estimated 12,000-plus, they are relatively unknown to most Hawaii residents.

On Salsa Dancing in Kalihi

A first group of these Caribbean laborers disembarked here on December 23, 1900, on the ship *Rio de Janeiro*, and were quickly followed by 10 other shiploads or some 5,200 fellow Puerto Ricans during the next 10

Hawaii's·sugar and pineapple barons also imported assorted Spaniards, Russians, Germans, Norwegians, Austrians, Italians, Scots and black and white Americans to work on the plantations, but few of those laborers stayed in Hawaii long, and if they did were invisibly assimilated into Hawaii's Euro-American *haole* population in general.

Perhaps the most famous of these part-time *haole* laborers were a group of Spanish-Mexican cowboys from old California and Mexico who became known as *paniolo*, after the Hawaiian pronunciation of the Spanish word *Espanôl* (for Spaniard). These *paniolo* were first brought from Mexico to Waimea on the Big Island of Hawaii in about 1830 to teach natives cowboy culture.

JAPANESE

In October of 1975, when Hirohito, the Emperor of Japan, arrived in Hawaii on the last leg of a pleasure and diplomacy visit to the United States, his royal aircraft landed at Honolulu International Airport from a southeasterly approach, instead of from the usual northwesterly side of Oahu. The reason: the Emperor's pilots wanted to avoid flying over Pearl Harbor and subjecting His Highness' mind to thoughts of the vicious war which began there one quiet Sunday morning in 1941.

That was most thoughtful of the pilots, but mention here.

Along the highway from the airport to downtown and Waikiki, Hirohito, his Empress Nagako and their entourage rolled past dozens of business establishments with Japanese names, fleets of fishing sampans wriggling with fresh tuna for Hawaii's *sashimi*-crazy households, and opulent Honpa Hongwanji, Jodo, Soto Zen and Shinto shrines and temples similar to ancient structures at Tokyo, Nara and Kyoto. If he wanted, the Emperor could listen to local Japanese language radio (KZOO), watch KIKU-Channel 13, Honolulu's Japanese language television station, and read either the *Hawaii Times* or *Hawaii Hochi*, the State's two regular Japanese language newspapers. And if he saw it, he probably chuckled aloud

it really didn't matter. By then, 34 years after Japanese forces had obliterated American air and naval forces based in these islands, Hawaii was so Japanese that Hirohito may as well have been landing at Nagasaki. As the smallish Emperor toddled down the ramp of his Japan Air Lines aircraft, he was greeted by thousands of Japanese-Americans waving little Rising Sun flags and occasionally shouting "banzai! banzai! banzai!" And on the airport tarmac was an "aloha" delegation which included three U.S. congressmen of Japanese descent, the recently-elected Japanese-American Governor of Hawaii, a Japanese president of the University of Hawaii and other Japanese-American "power people" too numerous to

at that morning's *Honolulu Advertiser* which, in a "forget the past" gesture unprecedented in American journalism had headlined a front page story about the Emperor's arrival with huge stacked *kanji* characters proclaiming in formal script:

天皇皇后兩陛下御歡迎 (We Joyously Welcome Their Imperial Majesties, The Emperor, King of Heaven, and Empress of Japan.)

Even local Japanese—who could "Remember Pearl Harbor" and the strafing Zeroes with ominous red suns on their wingtips, and huge billows of smoke and, for some, several years of internment in wartime concentration camps—could hardly believe the changes in local social and political circles which had occurred in Hawaii since December 7, 1941 and that much-decried "day of infamy."

To say the Japanese have succeeded in Hawaii is an amusing understatement. In truth, it would probably be safe to assume that until the burgeoning *haole* population takes over the "votes" which determine local political power, Hawaii's Americans of Japanese Ancestry (AJAs) should continue to run Hawaii like no other non-Caucasian group has ever run any other state in the United States.

This Japanese rise to prominence, however, like that of the Chinese, involved extremely humble beginnings, lots of lost but ultimately saved face, and much dedicated work.

Honolulu on board the British sailing ship *Scioto* carrying three-year immigrant laborer contracts. In all, there were 141 men, 6 women and a three-year-old boy named Shintaro.

While at sea, most of the men had cut off their traditional topknots — as a gesture of gratitude to gods whom they felt had saved them from a fierce storm at sea — but as they stepped ashore at Honolulu they were dressed in plantation-issue "coolie uniforms" and their wives were wrapped in *kimono*. All were quickly assimilated into local plantation labor forces at an earning rate of $12\frac{1}{2}$ cents a day or, according to one account, "about twice what they could make in Japan." By 1885 that money-making figure quadrupled to about 50 cents a day, but work in the fields was as hot, dusty and back-breaking as ever.

Strict Japanese immigration laws during reigns of the later Kamehamehas and Lunalilo made it difficult for many Japanese to come to the Kingdom they called "Tenjiku — the heavenly place," but in 1885, during the reign of King David Kalakaua, their numbers began increasing rapidly.

Indeed, if any one person should be credited with establishing the Japanese in Hawaii, it is Kalakaua, their most ardent early patron.

In March, 1881 Kalakaua visited Japan on the first leg of a glamorous tour around the world. While there, he directed his chamberlain, W.N. Armstrong, to initiate treaty discussion with Japan and to place particular emphasis on the matter of Japanese immigration to Hawaii. As historian Ralph Kuykendall notes in the third volume of his *The Hawaiian Kingdom*, "The king let it be known that, in accordance with the policy of the government of Hawaii to increase population by inviting immigration from other countries, any Japanese who desired to settle in the Hawaiian kingdom would be permitted to do so." Kalakaua even went to the diplomatic extreme of proposing to the Emperor Mutsuhito that one of the imperial

Life in 'The Heavenly Place'

A few Japanese survivors of nearby shipwrecks inadvertently visited Hawaii as early as 1832, but it wasn't until 1868, during the first year of Japan's Meiji Emperor, that a first "official" group of immigrants from Japan put into Hawaii. These "Gan-nen-mono," or "First Year Men," arrived at

Left, elderly Japanese zen archers practice their ancient sport at Honolulu's Kapiolani Park, 1979; above, *sumo* wrestling at Lahaina, Maui, 1915.

princes become betrothed to Princess Kaiulani, his six-year-old *hapa-haole* niece and heiress to the Hawaiian Throne. And, "To the emperor privately," reported Kuykendall, "Kalakaua suggested the formation of a federation of Asiatic nations, of which the Japanese ruler would be the head and Hawaii would be one of the member nations."

Both the marriage and the Asiatic federation schemes were lost somewhere in diplomatic history, but Kalakaua's Hawaiian government actively pursued the Japanese immigration issue until it was given official legislative sanction and funding. Consequently, on February 8, 1885, a first large group of 943 immigrants — 676 men, 159 women and 108 children — arrived in

Honolulu on board the Pacific Mail steamer the *City of Tokio*. The *Pacific Commercial Advertiser* described the arrival of these Japanese contract laborers as "the most important event that has happened in Hawaii for many years."

Under Kalakaua's personal direction, the Hawaiian Kingdom rolled out a rainbow carpet for these immigrant Japanese. The Royal Hawaiian Band serenaded them, Honolulu policemen served as tour guides, and all necessary food, shelter and medical needs were taken care of expeditiously by the kingdom.

Life was oftentimes miserable in the camps, mills and fields of Hawaii's plantations but Japanese kept coming to "the heavenly

place" in ever-increasing numbers until, by 1890, there were 7,612 Japanese contract laborers on the plantations, and 12,610 total Japanese in the islands. By 1896 the Japanese population doubled again to 24,407, and by the year 1900 it was up to 61,000, or more than twice the number of Hawaiians (29,799), Caucasians (26,819) or Chinese (25,767). (About a tenth of the immigrants during these years were from the Okinawan Islands, but usually were classified as "Japanese.") From then until the mid-1970s the Japanese remained the Islands' number one population group.

'Going For Broke'
Despite Executive Order 9066

Though their numbers were many, the Japanese, like nearly all of Hawaii's non-*haole* laborers, suffered from racial and economic prejudices under the "colonial" yoke of Hawaii's plantation elite. And when their homeland launched World War II at Pearl Harbor, this situation only worsened. Following the Pearl Harbor attack, many local Japanese were rounded up as "potential traitors," and some 1,444 of them were forcibly removed from island homes and placed in wartime concentration camps on the mainland. This was accomplished under Executive Order Number 9066 signed by President Franklin Delano Roosevelt. The order authorized the Secretary of War to intern any persons he so desired to protect American security interests.

In Hawaii, where Japanese made up 40 per cent of the population and labor force, not everybody could be interned, but under martial law Japanese language schools and radio stations were shut down; Buddhist, Shinto and Zen temples were spiritually deactivated; Japanese newspapers were strictly censored; and the Japanese population in general suffered from both blatant and subtle forms of harassment. Historian Larence Fuch's notes in his social history *Hawaii Pono*: "It was not primarily the legal deprivations that demoralized the Japanese population in Hawaii. The fear and hostility of their neighbors hurt much more. *Nisei* (second generation Japanese-Americans), as well as their fathers and mothers, met discrimination in employment throughout the war."

In an attempt to salvage their discriminated-against pride and prove their loyalty to the United States, *nisei* by the hundreds volunteered for Army duty; but

Above left, Japanese orchid fancier, Honolulu; and right, farmer at Waipio Valley, the Big Island.

they were initially turned away. Eventually, though, the man-hungry U.S. War Department agreed to the mustering of an all-*nisei* Army unit, and on June 5, 1942, a 100th Battalion of *nisei* Hawaii National Guardsmen and draftees was created; a year later, when the Army had more *nisei* volunteers than it could handle in the 100th Battalion, a larger group, the 442nd Regimental Combat Team, was formed. Both *nisei* units were sent to the Italian front, where they met on June 11, 1944, at Civitavecchia, about forty miles north of Rome.

Fighting as the 442nd "Go For Broke" Infantry Regiment, *nisei* from Hawaii became world-famous for their military exploits in France and Italy. Men of the 100th

White House lawn at Washington, President Harry Truman reviewed a 100th-442nd delegation, awarded them their seventh presidential citation, and told them: "You fought not only the enemy but you fought prejudice—and you have won."

Power By the Numbers

Once home in Hawaii, these veterans pursued their education under the G.I. Bill, then teamed up with organized laborers and other fellow Japanese to gain political power in Hawaii, as a *nisei* politician once put it, "by the numbers."

These days, Honolulu residents are very much at home with things Japanese—be they the *zori, tatami, futon* or *o-furo*.

and 442nd earned seven presidential unit citations and almost 6,000 individual awards. But the going for broke was tough: 36 officers and 614 enlisted men were killed and another 4,500 were wounded—a unit casualty rate more than three times higher than the average Army-wide. Back home, however, paranoid and racist opponents were silenced. Not a case of Japanese-American disloyalty or sabotage occurred during the war, and the men of the 100th and 442nd more than distinguished themselves as the "most highly-decorated" American military unit to see action during World War II. When the war ended in Italy, the 100th-442nd *nisei* led a march of Allied Forces into Rome. And later, on July 15, 1946, on the

On New Year's, everybody from the Governor on down to city streetsweepers joins Japanese friends to eat *soba* buckwheat noodles and *mochi* rice soup for good luck. And if a politician wants to make inroads with the powerful "Japanese vote," he'd better be sure to don a *yukata* or *hapi* coat and hit the *O-bon* dance circuit in July and August when members of Japanese temples and missions host joyous drumdancing festivals to honor ancestral souls. A picture in a local daily of a would-be mayor or county councilman in complete *O-bon* regalia and slurping up a juicy cone *sushi* can work miracles come election time. So can a properly produced television spot broadcast at prime time on local Japanese television.

CHINESE

The ball at the Court House on Thursday night last, given to their majesties the King and Queen by the Chinese merchants of Honolulu and Lahaina, was the most splendid affair of its kind ever held in Honolulu ... We have heard but one opinion expressed by those present (which includes all Honolulu and his wife), and that was that the Celestials have outshone the 'outside barbarians' in fete-making for the throne.
— The Polynesian, *November 15, 1856*

... the taste displayed in getting up this feast is a little ahead of anything we have witnessed here or elsewhere.
— The Pacific Commercial Advertiser, *November 20, 1856*

When the top two reviews were composed, Hawaii's Chinese community numbered only an estimated 600 persons. That's a small ethnic constituency in any country, but the party its business leaders hosted on November 13, 1856 — to honor the recent marriage of King Kamehameha IV (Alexander Liholiho) and his bride, Queen Emma (the former Emma Rooke) — was raved about for decades by local socialites, journalists and historians.

"That first Chinese ball of 1856 was unmatched for its gaiety and brilliance," Chinese writer Tin-Yuke Char reported more than a century later in his history book *The Sandalwood Mountains.* The grand ball, however, meant much more to Hawaii's Chinese than mere café society acceptance. More important, it marked the entry of local Chinese into the highest of the Hawaiian Kingdom's economic and political circles.

Verily, the Crown was so pleased that less than a year after the ball, one of its Chinese sponsors, the "merchant prince" Chun Afong, married the foster sister of the future Hawaiian King David Kalakaua. Afong built his part-Hawaiian bride a luxurious Victorian mansion, she in turn bore him 16 children, and in 1879 in the fifth year of Kalakaua's reign, he became the first and only full-blooded Chinese person ever to be appointed a noble of the Hawaiian Royal Court.

At the time of the Grand Ball of 1856, resident representatives of the Celestial Realm — most of them contract workers who began arriving in Hawaii in 1852 — were determined to prove their loyalty to Hawaiian monarchs who had accepted them as desirable immigrants. And so to evidence this fealty, a committee of Honolulu and Lahaina Chinese merchants — identified as Asing, Yung Sheong, C.P. Samsing, Utai, Ahee, Achu and Afong — secured the use of the Old Court House on Queen Street near Honolulu's waterfront, raised $3,700 in entertainment expense money, and treated the town to "the party of the season."

That was a grand evening, but Hawaii's Celestials didn't always have it so good; in the 1890s, for example, jealous *haole* businessmen, in an attempt to restrict the inroads enterprising Chinese were making into local commerce, succeeded in passing legislation which greatly restricted the freedoms of Chinese who immigrated to Hawaii as la-

borers. The Chinese, however, patiently endured such discrimination, ingratiated themselves to more tolerant islanders, and have become one of Hawaii's most prominent, influential, generous and financially successful ethnic groups.

Indeed, ask any island person who the richest men in Hawaii are, and the list will surely include Chinese names. Run your finger down a financial review of major directorships in the islands, and the top twenty will almost always include a Ho, Ching,

Fong, Chang or other such surname. And who was the first person of Oriental descent to ever occupy a seat in the United States Senate? Hiram Fong of Hawaii, of course.

Country of the Fragrant Wood

Opinions differ as to who the first Chinese in Hawaii were, and exactly when they arrived, but as early as 1789 several Chinese crewmen jumped a ship captained by an infamous American trader, Simon Metcalfe. And about two years later, in 1791, the British Captain George Vancouver reported seeing a Chinese man in Hawaii who was one of three "banditti of renegadoes who had quitted different trading vessels." These alleged bandits and other expatriates taught

Kamehameha the Great many useful things about Occidental and Oriental warfare and seamanship and later (as well-rewarded mercenaries) helped him conquer the island of Oahu in his final territorial battles of 1795.

Because of a big sandalwood trade with Hawaii in the early 1800s, Chinese were well acquainted with the Sandalwood Islands, known to them as *Tan Heung Shan*, or the Country of the Fragrant Tree; but the first significant group of Chinese didn't arrive in the Islands until 1852. On January 3 of that

year, 195 coolies from Kwangtung and Fukien provinces in southeastern China put into Honolulu on board the bark *Thetis*. Before they left the Chinese port of Amoy, these Hakka and Punti people signed five year contracts which promised them $36 a year, sea passage, food, clothing and housing, plus "an advance of six dollars each" to be later deducted from their wages. *The Polynesian* reported on January 10, 1852 that their sea passage from Amoy to Honolulu "was accomplished with the loss of but four or five men in 55 days. In addition to the laborers brought under contract there was room in the ship for about 20 more, which was occupied by that number of boys, who have been readily engaged by residents here for five years as house and other servants." The *Thetis* returned to Amoy for more coolies, and on August 2, 1852 arrived back at Honolulu with a second cargo of 98 indentured laborers.

Many of those first Chinese were a transient lot, interested only in putting in their five years, smoking "foreign mud" — as they called their favored drug opium — to anesthetize labor pains, and returning to their clans in China with money. Others, though, aware of vast and mildly competitive commercial opportunities available in the Sandalwood Islands, quietly and efficiently honored their 5-year contracts, saved wages, married Hawaiian women and set up shops in Honoloulu and Lahaina, port towns which during the 1850s were still making much money off a booming and raucous whaling trade. The Chinese were not generally allowed to infiltrate the sugar industry, but their local descendants like to point out with pride that it was a Chinese man, not a *haole*, who grew and milled Hawaii's first sugar. Wong Tse Chun built a sugar mill on Lanai in 1802 and produced what is believed to be the first sugar manufactured in the Islands.

Today, many immigrations and political changes later, the *pake*, as Hawaiians call the Chinese (the word is thought to be a derivative of the Cantonese term *pai kei*, meaning "father"), have indelibly chopped Hawaii's eclectic consciousness with their Celestial character, customs and cuisine. During the annual Chinese New Year, the greeting *kung hee fat choy* is nearly as common as *aloha*. And through any island childhood, chances are that a kid eats more *manapua* (steamed bread stuffed with pork or black beans) and *li hing mui* (preserved fruit) than candy bars. Local Chinese observe Confucian, Taoist and Buddhist holidays in a traditional manner, but these days they are also enjoyed in a celestially kitschy way that's

uniquely Hawaiian-Chinese.

Most Chinese who used to live in Honolulu's so-called "Chinatown" left downtown long ago; they took their newfound affluence to other, ritzier sectors of the community. No more Chinese-style live-upstairs-work-downstairs for them. Following World War II, many Honolulu Chinese bought homes in the Makiki Heights and Bingham Tract neighborhoods, inspiring local people to nickname those communities "Mandarin Heights" and "Chinese Hollywood." A few persistent old-timers stayed behind in Chinatown — where they still mind Hong Kong-style herb shops, acupuncture clinics, open market food stalls, cookie emporiums, noodle factories and restaurants — but they are exceptions who linger in deference to their suburban cousins' cravings for *hahm hah* (shrimp paste), pressed duck, black hundred-year-old eggs, steamed *char siu bao* and *dim sum*, and the occasional potion of dried sea horse, snake oil, powdered deer antler and anise one needs as a decongestant, restorative or aphrodisiac.

The 'Cradle' of China's Revolution

But while modern Chinese youth — like all Hawaii youth — tend to favor more social herbs, and oscilloscopic, multiplexed rock and roll, Chinese grandparents like to steal away from their moon doors, Mercedes-Benzes and Betamaxes in the heights to musty and noisy mahjong parlors on Smith and Maunakea streets downtown. After all, they'll tell you, it was down here where Honolulu schoolmates Ho Fon and Sun Yat-Sen met with mother and father to organize a Kuo Min Tang Society and plan a Chinese Revolution. That secret Honolulu society, first known by the Chinese-Hawaiian name Hsing Chung Hui (Revive China Group) was crucial to the future success of China's revolutionary movement. Dr. Sun, "The Father of Modern China," founded his original revolutionary group at Honolulu in November, 1895, and because Chinese patrons in the islands contributed generous military and financial support to Sun's cause, Hawaii became known in Chinese history books — both Taiwanese and Communist — as "The Cradle of the Chinese Republic."

Downtown Honolulu was also the scene, during the 1910s and 1920s, of another famous Chinese character — this one a Hawaiian-Chinese detective, Chang Apana, whose Honolulu exploits inspired the American mystery writer Earl Derr Biggers

to write a series of stories and screenplays which became internationally known and loved as "The Adventures of Charlie Chan."

In 1925, with the publication of Biggers' novel "House Without a Key," the whimsical Inspector Chan assumed a place in history as one of the world's most well-known fictitious characters. "Ah so," Biggers' Chan would say in non-Chinese Japanese, but later, in the 1920s, 1930s and 1940s, when Hollywood began filming Biggers' "Adventures" series and an additional 46 Charlie Chan specials (such as "Charlie Chan in Egypt," "Charlie Chan at the Race Track," "Charlie Chan in Shanghai," and "Charlie Chan at the Opera"), this Honolulu detective, his Number One, Number Two and Number Three sons and their Honolulu-inspired ad-

ventures became immutably established in cinematic history. Biggers' screenplays, of course, were highly dramatized, and projected dubious oriental ethnic stereotypes to millions of viewers, but nonetheless were born in *pake* Hawaii and enjoyed enormous success.

The "real" Charlie Chan — detective Chang Apana, known to the Chinese of Hawaii as "Kana Pung," died in December, 1933. Apana had retired the previous year after 34 years of distinguished service as a police officer and detective, and at his impressive funeral many fellow police officers, detectives and the Royal Hawaiian Band marched in his cortege.

Left, owner of confectionery shop, Chinatown, Honolulu; above, statue of Sun Yat Sen at entrance to the Cultural Plaza, downtown Honolulu.

KOREANS

"In Hawaii you rarely ever see a group of Koreans, but you see a Korean in every group."

That recent comment by a Honolulu-born Korean businessman isn't entirely true (because Hawaii's Koreans do maintain special Korean clubs and quasi-political-social community associations), but it is a good contemporary comment on the Islands' highly mobile and adaptable Korean community. Unlike more clannish Japanese and Chinese, Hawaii's 9,000-plus Koreans have fanned out and into the society-at-large at a remarkable pace. Their "out-marriage" rate, for example, has been known to run as high as 80 per cent for both brides and grooms, an interracial matrimony factor second only to the convivial part-Hawaiians.

Though they compose little less than one per cent of the local population, their "spice" and "fire" has certainly kindled a distinct flavor in the islands' culture and history.

"It's the *kimchi*," jokes a man who recently married a Korean woman. "Once you start eating your regular food with *kimchi*, you're hooked. You've got to have more and more." Ah-ha, but chilied and garlicked vegetables notwithstanding, some folks are probably also "hooked" by the Korean character. Koreans, whether in the land of Morning Calm or at a Waimanalo Beach barbeque, are, always have been, and probably always will be a fiery, independent, persevering, and down-to-earth lot. They are not known to put lids on their passions. As writers have observed since the late 1880s when Korea was opened to the West, Koreans are the "shouters," the "door-slammers" or — to repeat a popular cliche — "the Irish of the Orient." But in the Hawaiian Islands, probably the most popular name for them is *yobo*. Literally, *yobo* means "my dear" and is a way of addressing one's husband or wife. It is also the informal equivalent of "hello" or "hey there" when used to catch one's attention. "*Yobo-seyo*" — or simply "*yobo* (not quite as polite)" — early Korean immigrants would address one another, and this term stuck with them as an island nickname.

Both long-established and recently-immigrated Koreans have capitalized on their verve, ambitions and versatility to achieve great business and social successes in Hawaii. Their overall education and income levels, for example, are the highest per capita of any one ethnic group in Hawaii. And from their scattered families have emerged a Honolulu City Prosecutor, a State of Hawaii Comptroller, a Federal Circuit Court Judge and a disproportionate (in comparison to other races) number of professional people such as doctors, dentists, engineers and attorneys. As the man observed, "... a Korean in every group." And with a recent flood of Korean immigration to Hawaii (in the United States, Honolulu is second only to Los Angeles in the number of native-born Korean residents living within its city limits), that "in every group" line could be expanded to say "... a Korean cafe in every neighborhood" and "a Korean bar in every arcade, shopping center and commercial strip."

Anymore, despite Hawaii's relatively small Korean population, few suburbs don't

have a cafe sign advertising — in both English and Korean *hangul* scripts — Korean delicacies such as *bi bim bab*, *bul gogi* and *mandu*.

Picture Brides for Picture Grooms

This Korean infiltration began on January 13, 1903, when the Pacific steamer *SS Gaelic* arrived at Honolulu with 2 interpretors, 54 men, 21 women, 13 children and 12 infants who had been recruited as laborers for the Hawaiian Sugar Planters Association.

Left, third generation (*samsei*) descendant of the Korean picture bride and groom, above, who migrated to Hawaii—he in 1904, she in 1914.

From 1903 to 1905, more than 7,000 Koreans, most of them young men (ten for every one Korean woman), signed up for work in Hawaii. However, in April, 1905, Korea's Emperor Yi cut off all labor emigration from Korea after hearing that a group of Korean laborers had been mistreated while working on Mexican hemp plantations. Consequently, until the years 1910 through 1924, when Japanese administrators of their then "Territory of Korea" allowed 951 Korean "picture brides" to join their "picture grooms" in Hawaii, Korean immigration to the Islands was curtailed.

However, following the loss of Korea's independence to imperialistic Japan in 1910, Hawaii became a prime American-Korean source of pro-Korea revolutionary support.

Japan in World War II, Dr. Rhee of Honolulu returned to Korea triumphantly, and on August 15, 1948, at age 70, was inaugurated as the Republic of Korea's first President. Five years later when Hawaii's Korean community was celebrating its 50th Anniversary in Hawaii, President Rhee acknowledged that Koreans in Hawaii had contributed immeasurably to the freedom of their homeland. "In fact," he said, "their strivings for the restoration of Korea's national sovereignty were truly the greatest of all the Korean communities overseas."

Apparently President Rhee felt very much at home in Hawaii, because in 1960, after a Korean military government deposed him as he was beginning to serve his fourth presidential term, he fled to Hawaii, where he

Most of the Korean societies still operating in Hawaii (such as Kuk Min Hoi, the Korean Community Association) originated as "anti-Japan" and "restore the homeland" societies, some of them highly secretive. As Dr. Sun Yat-Sen had done with fellow Chinese living in Hawaii, Dr. Syngman Rhee, an American-educated diplomat, turned to Hawaii's Korean community for revolutionary assistance. In 1920, Dr. Rhee, then a Honolulu school principal, organized a local society known as Dong Ji Hoi (the Association of Comrades) which was dedicated to restoring Korea's sovereignty and promoting education and Korean culture among Korean immigrants.

Eventually, following America's defeat of

died in exile on July 19, 1965. Friends recall that even as former President Rhee was dying, he often would straighten up in a chair and sing favorite Korean marching songs.

Plenty Kimchi and Hwa-Too

Koreans have adapted well to their new environment and, with each sprouting generation, many of their traditions have become more and more muted by the Western world they've joined. *Halmoni* (grandmothers) who first came to Hawaii as picture brides still try

Above, the first official Korean diplomatic delegation to visit the United States; right, senior Korean immigrants pose at Aala Park, Honolulu.

to arrange marital matches in the traditional Korean way, but second and third generation children no longer honor their elders' wishes. However, the generations still thrive together, somehow communicating despite language barriers and lost Confucian ideals. The *haraboji* (grandfathers) still gather at the Korean Community Association's old clubhouse on Rooke Avenue in Nuuanu and spend long hours deep into clacking rounds of an ancient Korean board game, *changgi*, which they call "Korean chess." And on weekends large family groups enjoy beach park barbeques which are quickly and easily distinguished by the pungence of crushed garlic, sesame, soy sauce and notoriously aromatic *kimchi*. Visually, the Korean picnic is also identified by card players who

influences are somewhat scarce. Notable are a springtime Miss Koreana contest which features demonstrations of song and dance by local beauties of Korean descent; and the University of Hawaii's new Center for Korean Studies, which is housed in a neo-traditional Korean structure on the Manoa campus' East-West Road. The Center hosts periodic Korean fine art exhibitions and concerts performed by visiting Korean musicians and students in the University's Department of Ethnomusicology.

Don't Blame Koreans

Mention should also be made of a recent night-life phenomenon commonly referred to

loudly slam down tiny flower picture cards called *hwa too*. The *halmoni* floats about the gathering like a large puffy flower in her long pastel *jo-gori-jima* (traditional Korean dress) and white rubber shoes with upturned toes, encouraging her grandchildren, in broken English, to "Eat rice-oo, *bul gogi*, *kimchi*—plenty, have-oo."

Meanwhile, in neighborly Kalihi is the Joe Kim Factory, home of the first *kimchi* to be exported to the U.S. mainland and Canada in large commercial quantities. And at a health food restaurant in Makiki, a young part-Korean proprietor is driving "natural foods" palates crazy with his peanut butter-and-*kimchi*-on-wholewheat sandwiches.

In the realm of fine arts, local Korean

in Hawaii as the "Korean bar." The term "Korean bar" is actually a local, catch-all euphemism for dozens of Asia-style "hostess bars" which have opened up on all parts of Oahu and in Neighbor Island resort communities. The name probably originated because a couple of early and favorite hostess bars along Honolulu's Kapiolani Boulevard and downtown were serviced by immigrant Korean waitresses and were indeed owned by Korean-American businessmen. But these days the bars are owned by multi-racial entrepreneurs and hostesses recently immigrated from all parts of the Orient. They aggressively ply male clients with *pupus* (appetizers), highballs, very expensive cheap champagne and other flirtatious favors.

FILIPINOS

Appropriately, and with a *fiesta* flair, the first Filipinos to make Hawaii their home were a band of acrobats and musicians who swept into Honolulu in December, 1888, following an entertainment tour of Shanghai, Tokyo, Kyoto and Yokohama.

These Manila-based minstrels arrived during the reign of King Kalakaua on board the clipper ship *City of Peking*, and in true Filipino spirit, immediately set to work entertaining Oahu residents during the two weeks they had to wait for their ship to depart for San Francisco.

"The Filipino troupers pleased their Hawaiian audiences, and the spell of Hawaii upon the performers was even more potent; so much so that when sailing time came and their manager refused to pay their salaries until arrival in San Francisco, they returned to their lodgings and took up their abode in Hawaii. Four of the 12 young men found immediate employment in the Royal Hawaiian band of King Kalakaua. These musicians were Jose Lebornio, Francisco de los Santos, Geronimo Innocencia and Mr. (Lazaro) Salamanca."

This "first Filipinos in Hawaii" intelligence was reported in 1935 by a Filipino scholar-author, Roman Cariaga, who based his information on interviews with Lazaro Salamanca, one of the original 12 Filipino musicians and a 33-year member of the Royal Hawaiian Band. "He (Salamanca) served through the reigns of Kalakaua and Queen Liliuokalani, and after the revolution and establishment of the republic, and then annexation, he remained the only Filipino of the original troupe. Labornio went to Peru where he became a music teacher. The where-abouts of the rest of the group is not known," Cariaga wrote.

Cariaga's words with Salamanca (who was then 72) were published in the May 15, 1935 issue of *The Honolulu Star-Bulletin*, and they successfully debunked a long-held belief that the first Filipinos to settle in Hawaii were 15 contract laborers who arrived in the Islands on December 20, 1906, to work at the Olaa Sugar Plantation on the Big Island. Not that it really makes that much difference who the first Filipinos were, but the report does make for a much happier and more musical story than would another "coolie labor" history. It will also please Hawaii's 90,000-plus Filipinos to know that Hawaii's first Filipinos came bearing good times and were

promptly hired as court musicians by His Popular Majesty Kalakaua.

However, it was the Hawaii Sugar Planters Association (HSPA) more than any other institution or individual which must be credited with having created in Hawaii "the largest Filipino colony in the world outside the Philippines."

Serious Filipino immigration to Hawaii did indeed begin with the arrival of that "second group" of 15 Filipino laborers. Those immigrants, who were recruited in the Ilocos Islands, were described by a reporter as being "small in statures but wiry and healthy looking." It was also observed that one of the men in this group disembarked at Hilo "with a fighting cock under his arm." This was a "grim foreboding," a Filipino

writer recounted later, which caused some local officials to worry "that this new immigration would introduce a new element of lawlessness into the 'low life' of Hawaii."

Lovely but Lonely Hawaii

This "new element" poured into Hawaii at a pace bettered only by the Japanese. Between 1906 and 1946 more than 125,000 Filipinos were recruited by the labor-hungry HSPA. They were predominantly from

Left, Rosalina del Rosario, a daughter of Filipino immigrants; above, lantern slide taken in the early 1910s of a Filipino immigrant woman in traditional embroidered gown with butterfly sleeves.

Ilocos Norte and Ilocos Sur in the Philippines' distant north, but their plantation camps also included Visayans from the south and Tagalogs from the central Philippines. But, alas, of the more than 125,000, only 9,398 were women and 7,006 children. If not lawlessness, this largely segregated group of Filipino bachelors did introduce a great deal of loneliness, and many of them — about half who came to Hawaii — eventually returned home to find wives and begin lives anew with money they had earned picking pineapples and cutting and milling sugar cane.

The majority of those who remained behind either married women from other ethnic groups or continued to lead raucous, happy-go-lucky extended bachelorhoods which in the early part of this century were the scandal

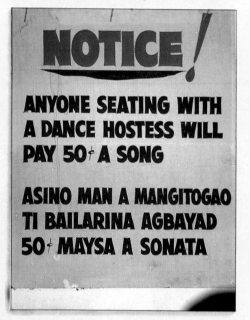

of proper plantation Hawaii. Many were the stereotypical slurs directed at these fun-loving strangers from "P.I." who preferred to travel in groups and "raise hell" on weekends. Harry A. Franck, an author (*Roaming in Hawaii*) who adventured about Hawaii during the middle-1930s wrote the following "typical" *haole* commentary about Hawaii's Filipinos:

> "They are confirmed knife-toters and much given to fighting over women, who are scarce among them. It is a common saying in Hawaii that the Filipino is only one

Above, sign in taxi dance hall, Honolulu. This dance emporium has been operating since 1938, and is patronized mainly by Filipinos.

pair of pants removed from the jungle. And that pair is likely to be purple or strawberry-red or wine-colored or something of the sort, topped by shirts — on gala days whole suits — that make a rainbow seem colorless."

Franck went on to describe the Filipino's fondness for gamecocks imported from Cuba ("the owner grooms his fighting cock more carefully than he does himself") and other "flashy" ways. "Sometimes a whole camp of Filipinos," he said, "will club together and buy a fine new automobile ... A brand-new car wrecked beyond recognition the day after it is bought, or even that same evening, is by no means an unusual holiday stunt in a Filipino camp."

Even today, in the remnants of Filipino cane camps, say around the Waipahu Sugar Mill on Oahu, or at Hanapepe on Kauai, you'll often stumble across a new, super-customized automobile glowing like a gigantic surrealist gem on red dirt roads fronting a row of tiny weather-beaten sugar shacks. And on Maui, young Filipino rogues, nicknamed "bunnies," are noted for sartorial splendor which ranges from basic black slacks, black shoes, black belts and crisp white dress shirts to the aforementioned riot of colors observed by Franck in the Thirties.

But, indeed, how else was a Filipino bachelor going to jazz up life in faraway Hawaii on an isolated and lonely plantation *barrio*.

Machismo and Collective Dignity

One way in which the Filipinos successfully channeled pent-up energies was to organize into some of Hawaii's first labor unions and then strike out collectively and with courage at powerful *haole* employers. The Filipino Federation of Labor, for example, was well organized and actively agitating for employee benefits as early as 1919. And though some of their early labor-management confrontations of the 1920s ended in violence and defeat, their tenacity and eventual successes served as an early indication of the Filipino community's Latin *machismo* and sense of collective dignity. For several decades, the Filipinos, like other ethnic laborers in Hawaii, were oppressed by Hawaii's *kamaaina haole* elite. But *bum-by* (by-and-by), to use a favorite Filipino term, their voices were heard and they emerged powerful.

Today, Filipino names (Bicoy, Cayetano, Aduja and De La Cruz, to name a recent few) stand and are recognized as legislators during regular sessions of the Hawaii State

Legislature. And as of 1981, one of their local kinsmen, Eduardo Malapit, was serving as Mayor of the Garden Island of Kauai. Filipinos also are pursuing remarkably successful careers as journalists, attorneys and judges, union officials, realtors, law enforcement officers, businessmen and musicians.

Filipino food hasn't captivated island tongues as decisively as have the cuisines of Korea, China and Japan; but if you're game for tastes ala Manila or Zamboanga, stroll into the Mabuhay, Filipiniana, Dalisay or Fil-American cafes downtown and wish the smiling mama behind the counter a sincere *mabuhay* (hello). She will then ply you with a complete range of Filipino food fantasies, including *lechon kawali* (baked piglet), *adobo* (a stew prepared with beef, pork or chicken and green papaya chunks) and *pancit bijon* (a gourmet shrimp-pork-vegies creation with Malay, Chinese and Spanish influences). Add all the pungent *bagoong* (fermented fish paste) you can stand, and if that's not enough, fling in a dash or three of horseradish, jute leaves and Malabar nightshade. Still not enough ambience? Then take in a Filipino movie at the nearby Hawaii Theater and follow that "triple Filipino action-tearjerker" with a few rounds of smoky pool at the Mindanao and Cebu billiard parlors on River Street.

Other distinctly Filipino events occur annually during Roman Catholic religious observances. One such occasion is the exotic candlelight festival held every Spring on the Feast Day of Santa Cruz. The biggest annual event, however, is a June Fiesta Filipina, which takes place at different publicized locations on Oahu and the Neighbor Islands. This annual fiesta includes appearances by Miss Filipiniana beauty contestants who wear sequined gowns with stiff bouffant sleeves, and exhibitions of ancient Filipino song and dance, cookery and other home country culture.

A more regular dose of Filipino hospitality and old-time "culture," can be enjoyed nearly every weekend at one of the islands' many "clandestine" cockfighting arenas (but don't tell the police we suggested you attend). Though Hawaii's Finest make periodic arrests of bird handlers and pit bosses, "chicken fights" continue to flourish in rural Hawaii. Hundreds of "cockers," as such afficionados are called, gather at country arenas (Waianae Valley and Waimanalo on Oahu are two of the biggest scenes) to watch specially groomed gamecocks have at it with razor-sharp blades attached to their ankles. In special holding areas, handsome birds in lovingly crafted wooden cages strut, preen and cluck at their owners in haughty anticipation of win or die rounds in the central fighting pit. Meanwhile, a raucous betting crowd, most of them Filipinos, mill about in a carnival atmosphere, pausing now and then to scrutinize a popular bird's finer fighting points, or to patronize cheroot-smoking Filipinas who do a brisk business in hot *adobo* and coconut-milk-rice-banana sweets.

Ask a Filipino

In years past, raiding police officers regularly arrested persons present at these illegal gambling pits, but nowadays, following a court ruling that mass arrests are unconstitutional, only the actual bird hand-

lers and bookkeepers are nabbed. As of press time, tourists, residents and Filipinos who attended these bloody affairs out of "intellectual curiosity" were safe. But how, you ask, does one find these places and gain entrance to them? Ask a Filipino.

And for further Filipino developments read the *Hawaii Filipino News*, tune in to the morning "Saniata Variety Show" on Radio KCCN (AM-1420), or contact Hawaii representatives of the Oahu Filipino World Federation Inc. and the Filipino Federation of America Inc.

Above, cartoon by Corky Trinidad, Filipino artist and syndicated staff cartoonist whose satire appears in *The Honolulu Star-Bulletin* newspaper.

SAMOANS

"I wanna see some mo'a of Samoa," go the pidgin English lyrics to an old *hapa-haole-hula* song which used to be quite popular in Hawaii. For many years, school children and nightclub entertainers would sing that song's whacky lyrics and do a matching comic *hula* which was good-naturedly dedicated to their Polynesian cousins to the southwest.

That was when Samoa was a South Seas vision somewhere way over there. Today, though, Samoans, the newest of Hawaii's non-*haole* immigrants, number more than 13,000 and are flocking to Hawaii at a rapid — though distinctly Polynesian — pace.

Most of them are coming from the six languorous, paradisiacal isles which make up the Territory of American Samoa, a 76-square-mile group located about 2,600 miles due southwest of Honolulu. This oceanic territory, the most southerly of all lands under U.S. ownership, has been a part of the United States since 1899 under the terms of a treaty negotiated with the United Kingdom and Germany. In 1900 and 1904 American Samoa's various ruling chieftains officially ceded their islands to the United States, and for the first half of this century American Samoa was managed by the U.S. Navy. In 1951 the six islands were put under the jurisdiction of the U.S. Department of the Interior, which appoints its governor and lieutenant governor and oversees the election of a bicameral legislature and a Samoan delegate to represent American Samoan islanders' interests in Washington. (American Samoa, however, should not be confused with Western Samoa, a larger island group which is an independent nation.)

After 1951, the Samoans' improved "American" status made immigration to other parts of the United States their constitutional right. Therefore, as early as July of 1952, a first large group of 921 Samoan men, women and children boarded a U.S. Navy transport ship, the *President Jackson*, and set off for new economic opportunities in distant Hawaii.

According to news accounts of their departure, these first immigrants, about half of them American-Samoan Navymen and their dependents being transferred from the Fiti Fiti Guard at Pago Pago to Pearl Harbor, were seen off by some 7,000 persons — "the largest gathering," a reporter wrote, "in Samoan history." Some 500 other Samoans had trickled into Hawaii since about 1919

(most of them to join a Mormon community at Laie on Oahu's North Shore), but never in Samoa's recorded history had such a large group left those idyllic isles at one time. After crossing to the north side of the Equator and docking at Honolulu on July 28, this ship-load of Samoans made up what a reporter for *The Honolulu Star-Bulletin* enthusiastically called "the greatest migration in the history of the Samoan Islands." Less than a thousand people doesn't sound like much of an exodus by world movement standards, but in 1952 that number represented six per cent of American Samoa's population.

These Polynesian newcomers and the many who followed them quickly adapted to Hawaii's similar climate and foods, and they charmed the Islands with their powerful song

and dance, Hawaiian-like hospitality and personalities. But many found it extremely difficult to adapt to the faster lifestyles which were and still are the rule in modern Hawaii.

On Samoan islands these people were used to sharing and sharing alike, whether they owned something or not; but in Hawaii, Hawaiians had long ago abandoned communal ways common to most of Polynesia. Indeed, local folks got downright upset and angry if a neighborly Samoan bade them "*talofa* (their version of *aloha*)" and then unabashedly helped himself to the bread-fruit, mangoes and bananas growing on their

Above, Ato, a Samoan woman who works as a waitress in Tahitian-style Waikiki restaurant.

private property. Even today, newly-arrived Samoans shake their heads and wonder aloud why everybody here is so, as they put it, "greedy."

High Talking Chiefs
Have the Last Say

Such cultural-lifestyle differences and a serious communication gap (by 1952 the Polynesian language was no longer generally understood in Polynesian Hawaii) have caused Hawaii's Samoans assimilation problems; but many of them have patiently stuck out this new life and adapted to American Hawaii while maintaining Samoan customs. When a matter of "Samoan community" urgency, for example, requires proper

Samoan-style attention, duly-elected Paramount High Chiefs, High Chiefs and High Talking Chiefs (who represent the various expatriate Samoan clans in Hawaii) call a special *fono*. At these councils the chiefs establish policy, mediate in the case of intra-Samoan grievances, and, if they feel a Samoan problem requires County, State or Federal government attention, draft mutually agreed upon statements of Samoan solidarity which are presented to the proper individual or agency.

Most Samoan gatherings, however, are of a less heady and more celebratory nature. On

Above, Jesse Sapolu, Samoan, a defensive guard with the University of Hawaii's football team.

such occasions — say for a wedding, or for festivities associated with the selection of a Miss Hawaii-Samoa, or for the investiture of a new chief, or on Flag Day (an annual American Samoan holiday which celebrates the raising of the American flag over Eastern Samoa on April 17, 1900) — Hawaii's Samoans bring out *kava* cups and bowls, oil their bodies, don their most colorful and dressy *lava-lava* sarongs and *puletasi* dresses, spread out finely woven *lauhala* mats, hang boldly block-printed *tapa* cloths, toot on conch shells, bang metal cans with lengths of wood, and dance and chant the day and night away in fine *fia-fia* (feasting) fashion. Hawaii's Samoans often are joined at these nationalistic affairs by fellow Oceanic and like-spirited expatriates from the Tokelaus, Tonga, Fiji, Tahiti and the Marquesas. Nearly all Pacific-area natives appreciate strong dance movements and the numbing intoxication of *kava* juice, and many such a Samoan night becomes day before the last bowls of *kava* and breadfruit have been drunk and consumed.

The Samoan community is fanning out into all sectors of the Hawaii community in a slow and proper island style.

As aforementioned, a large number of Hawaii's Samoans have congregated with Mormon-Samoan brothers and sisters in Oahu's Laie area, but significant communities and councils have also been established along Oahu's west coast and in Honolulu proper's Kalihi-Palama area.

One area of endeavor in which Samoans have fast gained an awesome reputation is in the athletic arena. In recent years American Samoans from Hawaii have become nationally famous as football players. The burly Samoans have always been very good at cricket, soccer and rugby, but following the introduction of American-style football in Samoa in 1968, they leaped into that punch-out full-contact athletic activity like penguins taking to ice. Several of Hawaii's Samoans have dazzled national football crowds with their fiercely competitive football performances. Anymore, few of Hawaii's championship high school football teams don't have one or six Samoan names on their starting rosters, and every year more mainland college and university football scouts are making an expensive detour to Hawaii to check out the latest in American-Samoan gridiron talent.

More detailed information about Hawaii's Samoans can be obtained by contacting representatives of The Samoan Action Movement of America or the local Samoan Council of Chiefs and Orators.

PLACES

But enough of history. Your jet has just shuddered to a reverse-engined stop at the end of the Reef Runway, and no sooner does the pilot turn and head for one of the airport's multi-spoked terminals than the aircraft's speakers begin injecting a mellifluous medley of familiar Hawaiian Muzak into your mainland mind.

"Honolulu Lady, where'd you get those eyes ... I Wanna Go Back to My Little Grass Shack in Kealakekua ... and Beyond the Reef" do indeed exist, as you knew they always did, but you still need a first lungful of balmy tropical air and intoxicating whiffs of *plumeria* (frangipani) and *pikake* (jasmine) to mellow your pre-Hawaiian skepticism:

"ALOHA!" the red-white-and-blue sign leading into Customs proclaims to foreigners: "WELCOME TO HONOLULU, HAWAII, U.S.A."

Ah, yes AHH-LLOW-HUH! Even out there in the computer perfect terminal, as you drift down to other levels of textured concrete and fluorescent efficiency on a stainless steel escalator, those haunting, twangy steel guitar riffs continue to massage your brain and cause palm trees, *hula* girls and flowers to sway through your Everyman's Vision of Paradise. Then — in living quadrophonic, multiplex stereo and laser vivid color — a local lady, a *wahine*, with long reddish hair, cinder eyes and chocolate thighs, approaches you from Somewhere Back of Beyond, drapes a garland of orchids 'round your neck, and with a kiss of sincere affection decisively ejects any jet-set cool you had saved up on the flight over. "Aloha," she says, repeating that pleasant Hawaiian cliche, and you melt into a heap of perfume and smiles.

That fantasy doesn't happen to everybody who first visits Hawaii, but by-and-by every person who has invested sincere time and energy into getting to know local people will admit that it begins to happen, quite regularly in fact, during subsequent returns to the islands. "Aloha," the ancients said as they met one another, left one another, or as they simply, fondly, expressed thanks, love and appreciation to one another for being.

Alo — to face; *ha* — the breath of life. A term which implies reverence for that which has life, and for the *mana*, the power, the spirit, which life implies. With that spirit in mind, we will begin to explore *Hawaii nei*.

STATE OF HAWAII

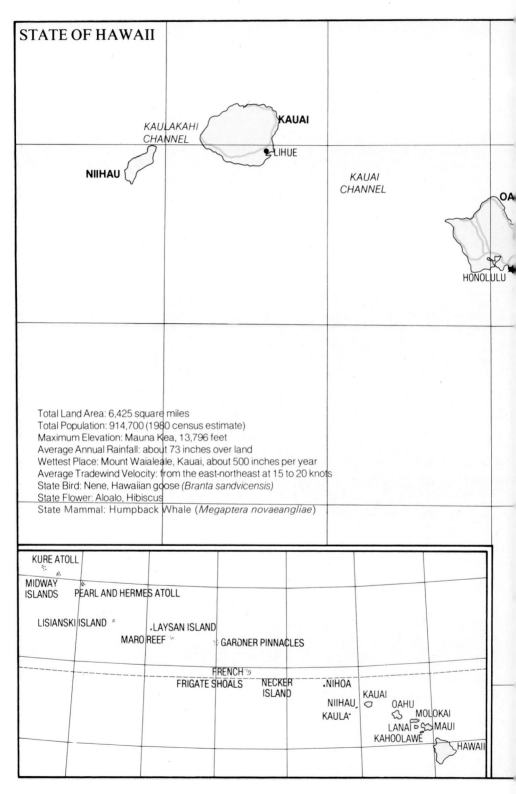

KAUAI

KAULAKAHI CHANNEL

NIIHAU

●LIHUE

KAUAI CHANNEL

OA

HONOLULU

Total Land Area: 6,425 square miles
Total Population: 914,700 (1980 census estimate)
Maximum Elevation: Mauna Kea, 13,796 feet
Average Annual Rainfall: about 73 inches over land
Wettest Place: Mount Waialeale, Kauai, about 500 inches per year
Average Tradewind Velocity: from the east-northeast at 15 to 20 knots
State Bird: Nene, Hawaiian goose *(Branta sandvicensis)*
State Flower: Aloalo, Hibiscus
State Mammal: Humpback Whale *(Megaptera novaeangliae)*

KURE ATOLL

MIDWAY ISLANDS   PEARL AND HERMES ATOLL

LISIANSKI ISLAND   .LAYSAN ISLAND
           MARO REEF   GARDNER PINNACLES

                    FRENCH
                FRIGATE SHOALS   NECKER   .NIHOA
                                  ISLAND
                                      NIIHAU   KAUAI
                                      KAULA·   OAHU
                                           LANAI   MOLOKAI
                                           KAHOOLAWE   MAUI
                                                   HAWAII

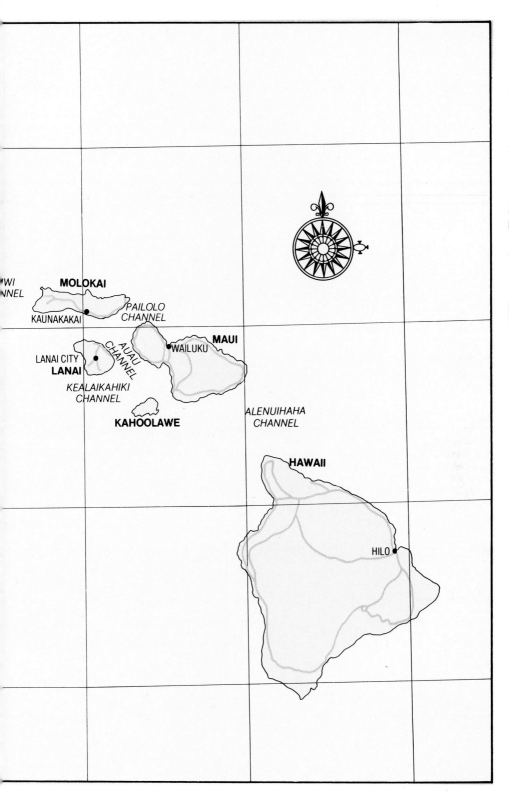

'WI
NNEL

MOLOKAI

PAILOLO
CHANNEL

KAUNAKAKAI

MAUI

•WAILUKU

LANAI CITY •

LANAI

AUAU
CHANNEL

KEALAIKAHIKI
CHANNEL

KAHOOLAWE

ALENUIHAHA
CHANNEL

HAWAII

HILO •

101

OAHU

Kauai
Channel

Kuilima Point
Kawela Bay

Makahoa Point
MOKUAUIA ISLAND
Laie Bay
Laie Point

Waimea Bay

Puaena Point

Waialua Bay

Kaiaka Bay

Kamehameha Highway

Koolau Mountain Range

Kahana Bay
Kaaawa Point

Kaena Point

DILLINGHAM
AIR FORCE BASE

Kaukonahua Road

Wiilkina Drive

CHINAMAN'S HAT

Kawaihoa Point

Yokohama
Bay

Waianae Mountain Range

Kaala (peak)
4,020

SCHOFIELD
BARRACKS

He'eia Kea
Boat Harbor

Kaneohe
Yacht Club

KANEOHE MARINE
CORPS AIR STATION

Kolekole Pass
1,724

WHEELER AIR
FORCE BASE

Kaneohe
Bay

COCONUT ISLAND

Mokapu Point
Mokapu Boulevard

Pokai Bay

Kunia Road

Kaneohe Bay Drive

Kahekili
Highway

Kawai Nui Swamp

Maili Point

Moanalua Road

Kailua Bay

BELLOWS AIR
FORCE STATION

Wailea Point

Kahe Point

Farrington Highway

Fort Weaver Road

FORD ISLAND

Nimitz Highway

Salt Lake

Likelike Highway

Pali

Pali Highway

Kailua

Kalaheo Avenue Road

Nuuanu Pali
1,186

Waimanalo

Kalanianaole

MANANA RABBIT
ISLAND

BARBERS POINT
NAVAL
AIR STATION

Mount Tantalus
2,013

Koko Crater

Barbers Point

Keahi Point

Honolulu Harbor

Mamala Bay

Ala Wai
Yacht Harbor

SAND ISLAND

Lunalilo Freeway

Kalanianaole Highway

Makapuu Point

Palea Point

PEARL HARBOR
US NAVAL BASE

Diamond
Head Crater

Maunalua
Bay

Kupikipikio
(Black) Point

Kaiwi
Channel

Land area:
592.7 square miles
44 miles long,
30 miles wide
Population:
City and County of
Honolulu:
722,400 (1978 census estimate)
Honolulu: 352,516 (1978)
Kailua: 36,553 (1978)
Waipahu: 30,886 (1978)
Pearl City: 28,760 (1978)
Kaneohe: 28,678 (1978)
Wahiawa: 17,489 (1978)
Aiea: 13,025 (1978)
Highest elevation:
Mount Kaala: 4,020 feet
Airport:
Honolulu International
Main seaports:
Ala Wai Harbor
Honolulu Harbor
Kewalo Basin

Points of Interest

29 Brigham Young College
24 Byodo In Temple
28 Crouching Lion (Kauhi)
40 Del Monte Pineapple Pavilion
10 Diamond Head Order
1 Downtown
32 Fishing Shrine (Kalani Point)
25 Fishponds (Along Kaneohe Bay) Golf Courses
20 Hawaii Kai Executive Golf Course
35 Kuilima Golf Course
46 Makaha Valley Golf Courses
22 Olomana Golf Course

13 Waialae Country Club
17 Halona Blowhole
34 Hawaii Nudist Park
49 Hawaii Raceway Park
41 Healing Stones (Wahiawa)
3 Honpa Hongwanji Mission (Nuuanu Valley)
33 Kahuku Sugar Mill
48 Kamaile Heiau
45 Kaneaki Heiau
44 Kaneana Cave
18 Koko Head Crater Botanical Park
19 Koko Head Stables
47 Kolekole Pass
36 Kuilima Hotel
38 Kupupolo Heiau
16 Lanai Island Vantage

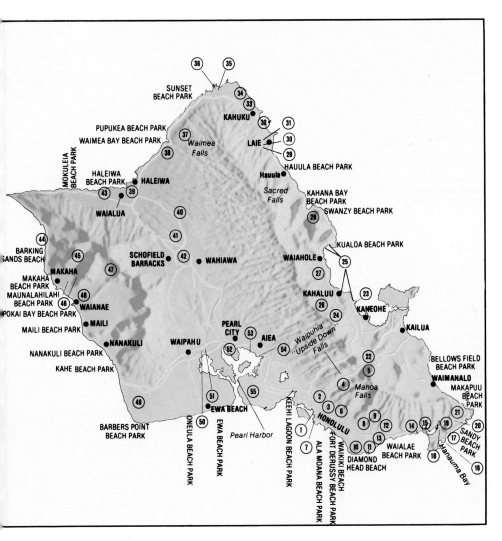

2	Liliuokalani Gardens	39	Queen Liliuokalani Church
43	Mokuleia Polo Farm	42	Sacred Birth Stones (Kukaniloko) (Wahiawa)
31	Mormon Temple (Laie)	21	Sea Life Park
6	National Cemetery of the Pacific	23	Ulu Mau Village
5	Nuuanu Pali Lookout	8	University of Hawaii, Manoa Campus
55	Pacific Submarine Museum	26	Valley of the Temples
52	Pearl City Tavern (Monkey Bar and Japanese *bonsai* miniature tree collection)	9	Waahila State Park
		27	Waiahole Poi Factory
30	Polynesian Cultural Center (Laie)	51	Waipahu Botanic Garden
37	Pu'u o Mahuka (*heiau*)	50	Waipahu Sugar Mill
4	Queen Emma Summer Palace (Nuuanu Valley)	42	Wahiawa Botanic Garden
		53	Kam Drive-In Theatre
		12	Waialae Drive-In Theatre

● Shopping Centers

7 Ala Moana Shopping Center
15 Hawaii Kai Koko Marina Shopping Center
11 Kahala Mall Shopping Center
14 Niu Valley Shopping Center
54 Pearl Ridge Shopping Center Swap Meets

● Surf Spots

1 Ala Moana Beach
4 Banzai Pipeline
10 Barbers Point
7 Chun's Reef
2 Diamond Head Beach
9 Makaha
5 Pupukea
3 Sunset Beach Tracks (Kahe Point)
6 Waimea Bay
8 Yokohama

HONOLULU, 'SHELTERED BAY'

From way up there, where sea blue becomes bullet grey, and where cameras peeking out of satellites and spaceships take infrared photographs of the whirling planet Earth, the small island of Oahu looks like an Indian arrowhead with rough chipped edges, or perhaps, if you get high enough, like a tiny spinning top or jagged coral bead—one of 132 which make up the loosely strung Hawaiian Islands chain.

Oahu—pronounced oh-ah-hoo. The word floats like a smoke ring or soft yodel from the back of your mouth. In the ancient Hawaiian language it probably meant something very special, perhaps the name of a god or brave chief, but its original meaning has remained buried with early Hawaiians. Like hazy Polynesian fables about lost lands of *Mu* and *Hawaiki*, the word Oahu faded into pre-history and now remains in use simply as a name for a particular Hawaiian place, an island. Scores of Hawaii-related guide books, history books and magazine articles continue to publish an erroneous theory that *Oahu* means "the gathering place," but that translation is a mistake.

However, because the **City and County of Honolulu** and the island of Oahu are one and the same place, let us turn to that second place name—*Honolulu*—for practical intelligence and exploratory inspiration.

Honolulu—Ho-no-loo-loo. Again the word rolls out like a soft Swiss yodel. But this time the meaning is clear: *Hono*, a bay; *lulu*, sheltered. Sheltered bay.

No mystery about that word's origin, and it explains the importance of Honolulu—and why Oahu-Honolulu has been the business, political and cultural center of the Hawaiian Islands since the early 1800s. Until Pearl Harbor was made navigable early in this century, Honolulu's harbor was the only protected body of water of its size within 2,000 miles of Hawaii.

Unless you are one of the rare few who first land at Hilo on the Big Island, your first Hawaiian experiences will take place on, in and about Honolulu, where 80 per cent of Hawaii's 900,000 people live, work and play. Meanwhile, fasten

Preceding pages, Waikiki at twilight from the seaside brow of famous Diamond Head Crater.

your seat belts.

As your aircraft drops low into Hawaiian skies after five or more monotonous hours of high altitude clouds, sky and shiny sea, deep Hawaiian waters below begin to make a subtle but striking transition from dark inky blue to aquamarine. As a writer of an 1875 guide to Hawaii observed from his sailing vessel, you will pass "through all shades of the maritime spectrum" until Blue Hawaii visions end abruptly just off land's edge with flashes of bone white surf spilling like drawn cream against offshore coral reefs, lava, sand beaches and the narrow buoy-marked entrance to Honolulu Harbor.

On final approach to the island's new **Reef Runway**, you'll see straight ahead, in a southerly direction, Honolulu Harbor, downtown Honolulu and, at the far southside, Waikiki Beach and the familiar Honolulu landmark, Diamond Head. To the port side is a much larger and famous waterway, **Pearl Harbor**, but as the stewardess-turned-tour guide probably will explain over the aircraft's sound system, this former oyster-growing spot was a land locked and shallow lagoon until 1911.

More important historically, and geographically, is much smaller **Honolulu Harbor**, formerly known to Hawaiians as Kou. It was this "sheltered bay" of Kou which made Honolulu the most important and only city in the Central Pacific; and it was the city, in turn, which made Hawaii more than just another island group out in the middle of blue nowhere.

Violence at "Fair Haven"

Though Honolulu's harbor was always conveniently there, waiting for weary ships to sail into her comfortable waters, explorers didn't find her for more than 16 years after the coming of Captain James Cook in 1778. This was probably because the navigable channel leading into the harbor was only about 550 feet wide and easily overlooked, but also because in those early post-contact days the Big Island of Hawaii and the island of Maui were greater centers of Hawaiian power than Oahu.

However, one day in late 1792 or early 1793 (nobody's sure of the exact date), Captain William Brown, master of the

English ship *Jackall*, accidentally discovered this inlet, which he described in his logbook as "a small but commodious bason with regular soundings from 7 to 3 fathoms clear and good bottom, where a few vessels may ride with the greatest safety." Brown, whose ships were involved in the fur trade between the Pacific Northwest and China, but at that time also in a new and lively Hawaiian gun trade, explored the anchorage and named it "Fair Haven," a term almost synonymous with the Hawaiian name *Honolulu*.

Ironically, Brown's life ended violently at Fair Haven, when on January 1, 1795, he and another British skipper (identified only as Captain Gordon of the *Prince Lee Boo*) were killed during a massacre led by Oahu's ambitious King Kalanikupule. Kalanikupule wanted to use the two British ships, their guns and captured crewmen to attack Hawaii's well-armed and advancing King Kamehameha. But the Oahu king's naval strategy was a bit late; about four months later, Kamehameha invaded Oahu and dealt Kalanikupule and his Oahu soldiers a series of devastating defeats which ended in a final and ultimately unsuccessful last stand at the Battle of Nuuanu Valley. As for Kalanikupule, he was captured 13 months later and ended his life on Oahu as a human sacrifice to Kamehameha's war god Kukailimoku.

Meanwhile, in Kamehameha's hands, Honolulu became the most important stopover point in the mid-Pacific ocean. Within a few years, dozens, then scores, and eventually hundreds of ships a year were lying yardarm-to-yardarm in Honolulu's harbor. It didn't matter to them that Honolulu — or the surrounding plains of Kona — was a minor habitation site of fishermen's shacks and dusty slopes; what mattered more was that ships anchored offshore didn't have to worry about being swept onto jagged coral reefs and rock shores by sudden shifts in surf, wind and sea.

Hawaiians on Oahu had always preferred, as do tourists today, the soft sands, surf, breezes and coconut groves of Waikiki and other cooler seaside resorts, but with the coming of sailing vessels, trinkets, gunpowder, alcohol and a *haole* concept called money, the more *akamai*, or smart, Hawaiians, including Kamehameha the Great, began moving to Honolulu's harborfront.

Kamehameha himself was only able to tolerate this commercial chaos for about eight years (from about 1803-1804 to about 1812), but though he eventually moved away and spent his life at quieter Kailua-Kona, his Big Island "capital," he closely monitored money-making matters at Honolulu until his death in 1819. And so did his sons, Kamehameha II and Kamehameha III. With the coming of whaling-related revenues, the Kamehamehas moved Hawaii's capital to the booming whaling town of Lahaina; but eventually the Hawaiian elite conceded that the real action was taking place at Honolulu and in 1845 Kamehameha III moved — lock, stock and legislature — to that south Oahu port town. On August 30, 1850, Kamehameha III officially declared Honolulu to be the capital of the Hawaiian Kingdom.

Ticky-Tacky Paradise

If only because it's logistically easier, and also because Honolulu and Waikiki Beach are the only places in Hawaii most people have heard about, perhaps 99 out of 100 first-time tourists begin

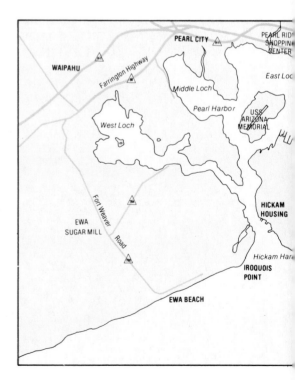

their tours of Hawaii at **Honolulu International Airport** and spend their first night on Oahu in one of the more than 25,000 hotel rooms at **Waikiki**, "the most famous beach resort in the world."

Which is just as well, because Honolulu, Waikiki and other Oahu environs are probably the best place in the islands to make the mind-dusting transition from mainlander (whichever mainland or other populated place you come from) to short-term islander — or as the locals will call you, *malihini* (newcomer).

Also, whether you choose to ride Oahu's gaily striped TheBus for 50 cents, or cruise into town and Waikiki in the air-conditioned splendor of a black or white Cadillac limousine taxi, the five to eight mile ride from Honolulu International Airport to your hotel is the best *first thing* you can ever do in Hawaii. That's because you will be driven past the very worst ticky-tacky, military-industrial, beep-beep, warehouses, wrecking yards, commercial kitsch, oil tanks, used car lots and *yecch* you never expected to see in the much-touted Paradise of the Pacific.

State and City lawmakers have prom-ised for years to do something to disguise this unaesthetic entry to greater Honolulu, but as of today the situation is status quo.

However, it's best to experience the worst first, and last, in order to appreciate all the enormous beauty available between takeoffs and landings. Be patient, because as you near Honolulu's city center on broad Nimitz Highway, quaint reminders of harbor days past begin to improve the industrial ambience. One very pungent all-Hawaiian assault occurs just as you leave the district known as **Kalihi** and cross the Kapalama Canal into **Iwilei** (pronounced ee-vee-lay). To your left — in sectors which years ago were known as **Hell's Half Acre** and **Old Chinatown** — are the famous and constantly fragrant canneries of the **Dole Pineapple Company**, the world's foremost purveyor of that sweet yellow fruit. If you didn't recognize the syrupy scent that wafts through your car like the aroma from a bootlegger's fermenting mash, a visual reminder rises high above the old canneries on Iwilei Road: This is the **Dole Pineapple**, a water tank high on stilts which was painted and enhanced, com-

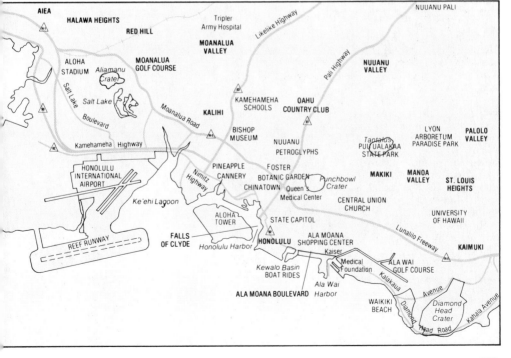

plete with green crown and yellow-brown prickles, to look like the hugest pineapple on earth.

Long before that prickly pine rose over Iwilei, this area was more well known as the location of "Horny Lulu's" notorious and historic harborfront "red light" district. Oh, how the rum did flow in those sinful cribs when the visiting pirate Bully Hayes and his marine moll, Stormbird Emma, staggered with their maties past Old Chinatown's opium dens, grog shops and cat houses. An old Hawaiian folk song, "Sassy," celebrates the "Girl of Iwilei/sassy straying/always eating black crabs/sassy straying." And in his Samoa-based short story "Rain," author Somerset Maugham firmly immortalized Iwilei by introducing literature to Miss Sadie Thompson, a harlot Maugham met on a ship cruise from Honolulu to Pago Pago after she had eluded a big 1916 police raid on Iwilei's resident professionals.

In those days, Maugham wrote, Iwilei was a place of row upon row of neat little green houses, each holding two women, each simply furnished with beer and gin for visitors. "When you go in the blinds are drawn down and if someone knocks, the answer is: Busy. You are at once invited to drink beer and the woman tells you how many glasses she has had that day. She asks you where you come from. The gramophone is turned on. The price is a dollar."

Hapa-Haole Hula-Hula

Upon crossing the **Nuuanu Stream** at Honolulu Harbor's western edge, Nimitz Highway becomes Ala Moana Boulevard, and smack on the waterfront stands a less commercial landmark — the **Aloha Tower**. This pleasing structure is only 10 stories high — or 184 feet from the ground to the top of its clock tower — but when it was erected in 1926 it was the tallest building in Hawaii. Thirty story skyscrapers across the boulevard dwarf the Aloha Tower now, but it lingers proudly as the most well-known building in the harbor area, second in symbolic fame only to Diamond Head Crater.

As recently as the 1940s and 1950s, the Aloha Tower's four clock faces and maritime signals for harbor traffic smiled down upon Hawaii's famous

The Dole Pineapple.

"Boat Days," when luxury Matson liners, the *Malolo* and *Lurline* in particular, would arrive and depart at Piers 10 and 11 in a hail of flowers and *hapahaole hula-hula*. On and off the ships would go huge steamer trunks, pink children, valets, nurses and private physicians of prominent mainland folks in white linen suits and be-ribboned picture hats; at pierside brown-skinned native boys would dive for coins tossed into the water; and while the Royal Hawaiian Band played "Aloha 'Oe"— up-tempo if a ship were arriving, almost funereally if it were leaving — the ships' horns would bellow a long salute to the giddy or sad masses on shore. "Boat Day" is just a memory nowadays, but the Aloha Tower still serves proudly as the state's harbor headquarters and official maritime signals point.

And speaking of ships and sea, two of the most recent and obvious arrivals on the Honolulu waterfront are now permanently docked just around the corner from the venerable old Aloha Tower. These are the big and Celestially kitschy *Oceania*, a Chinese floating restaurant which was towed to Honolulu in 1972 from the Hong Kong suburb of Aberdeen; and, at Pier 7, the splendidly rakish *Falls of Clyde*, the world's only surviving full-rigged, four-masted sailing ship. Both will sail fast past your Waikiki-bound taxi, but keep them in mind for future close-up study.

As you continue along Ala Moana Boulevard past the new **Prince Jonah Kuhio Kalanianaole Federal Building**, harbor and sea will disappear behind walls and buildings, but perhaps a mile further on you'll flash past four other "file away" spots worth visiting later. These include the **Kewalo Marine Basin**, next to the Fisherman's Wharf Restaurant, where the remnants of Honolulu's *sampan* fishing fleet return with their days' catch; and about a block farther, to your right, **Ala Moana Beach Park** and the relatively new **Magic Island Lagoon**, two "local" recreation sites which are probably the most popular sandy spots in the greater Honolulu area.

Directly across Ala Moana Boulevard from this more than 100 acres of parks, beaches and swimming and surfing sites, is the mammoth, triple-tiered **Ala Moana Shopping Center**, a mega-market place of more than 150 shops, depart-

The *Falls of Clyde*.

ment stores and restaurants which used to be called the "world's largest modern shopping center." Whatever its market-place standing these days, this vast complex of consumers and that which they voraciously consume is one of the island's finest people-watching spots, seven days a week.

On the extreme south end of Ala Moana Beach Park, where a bridge rises over the wide **Ala Wai Canal**, you will get a last glimpse of turquoise waters before entering famous Waikiki and its concrete interior. To the left of the **Ala Wai Bridge** in the canal itself is a favorite training area for outrigger canoe paddlers; and to the right, bobbing in place and tacking hither and thither in snappy tradewinds, are dozens of spindly sailing craft. This is the **Ala Wai Harbor** and yacht basin. Many of these sailboats belong to members of the harbor's spiffy and private Waikiki and Hawaii Yacht Clubs, but nearly as many are skippered by transient live-aboards passing through on their way to and from dreams in the South Pacific. This snug little harbor is usually a quiet place, but in June and July of odd-numbered years (e.g. 1979, 1981 and 1983), it is the glamorous focus of the international yachting fraternity. At that time, media eyes are on the deck hands and super yachts competing in the biennial **Transpacific Yacht Race** from Los Angeles to Honolulu. Upon completion of this 2,225 mile race, the world's oldest established long-distance sailing competition (initiated in 1906), the Ala Wai Harbor's "Transpac Row" becomes a rich and raucous who's who of the world's yachting elite. Renowned racing craft with names like *Ragtime*, *Ondine*, *Windward Passage*, *Merlin* and *Drifter* gleam like the oceangoing spaceships they are; and their well-burnt and pampered crews uninhibitedly engage in a post-race drinking competition which lasts about as long as the crossing itself. As of 1980 the Transpac crossing record was held by *Merlin* of Santa Cruz, California, which sailed the 2,225 miles in 8 days, 11 hours, 1 minute, and 46 seconds. And so goes your arrival and the road to Waikiki: a Polynesian panorama of petroleum refineries, the harborside perimeter of Honolulu, small boat basins and adult-size sandboxes by the sea.

The 84-foot ketch *Ondine* winning a recent Transpac regatta; and (right) yachts in the Ala Wai boat harbor.

WAIKIKI

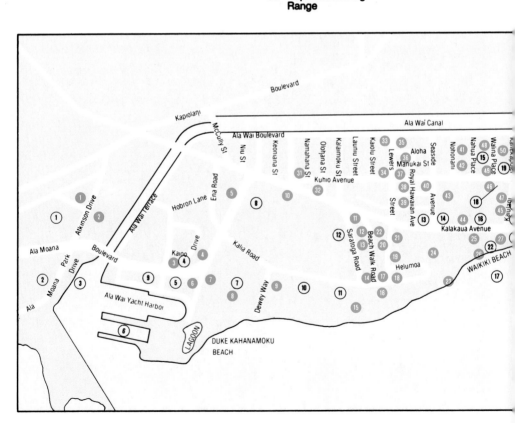

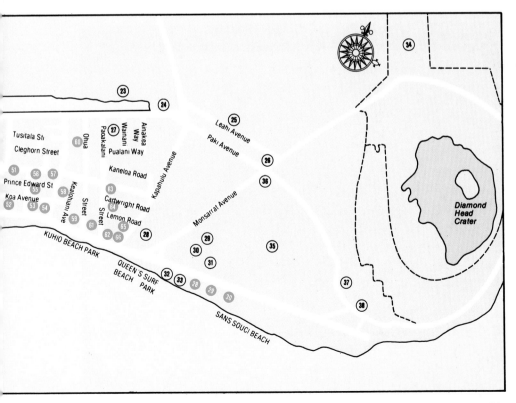

WAIKIKI

"*Ho-ni Ka'ua, Wi-ki-wi-ki*," *
Sweet brown maiden said to me,
As she gave me language lessons
On the beach at Waikiki.

 —*from* "On the Beach at
 Waikiki," *lyrics by G.H. Stover,
 music by Henry Kailimai, 1915*

 * translation: "Kiss me quickly."

Early Hawaiians named this mile-
and-a-half long strip of beachside land
Waikiki, or spouting water, because it
was previously a swampland kept wet
and mushy by mountain-fed streams
and gushy springwaters. As recently as
the 1920s, Waikiki's interior was a bog-
gy place populated by burping buffos,
quacking waterfowl and other damp
creatures which frolicked in its fishponds, taro patches and rice paddies.
Waikiki's inland swamp was a somewhat smelly place, but from ancient
times its seaside beaches, coconut groves
and fish rich reefs made this south shore
fishing village a favorite Hawaiian resort. Ancient chants identify five important surfing breaks at *Waikiki—Aiwohi,
Kalehauwehe, Kapua, Kapuni* and
Maihiwa—and one of these five,
Kalehauwehe, was renowned as a *kapu*
surfing place for chiefs and chiefesses
who rode its exclusive waves on 18-foot
olo surfboards, made of planks hewn out
of the trunks of *koa* and *wili-wili* trees.

During the early 1800s the Kamehameha kings built and maintained a
beach retreat at Waikiki, but it wasn't
until the 1860s that a dirt road was built
to comfortably link Waikiki's cool surf
with hot and dusty Honolulu. In the
1880s a mule-drawn omnibus began
making daily round trips to Waikiki,
and by 1888 regular tramcar service
was initiated. Until the late 1880s and
early 1890s, when a few cottages were
converted into guest bungalows, most
tourists stayed with island friends or in
one of downtown's hostelries, notably
the Hawaiian Hotel on Hotel Street.

In 1884 Allen Herbert opened one of
these "family resort" operations at
Waikiki and named it *Sans Souci*
(French for "without a care") after the
Potsdam Palace of Frederick the Great,
King of Prussia. Five years later, in

Waikiki in
the 1920s.

1889, Herbert hosted one of Waikiki's most famous early tourists, the Scottish author Robert Louis Stevenson, of *Dr. Jekyll and Mr. Hyde* fame.

Stevenson, who apparently enjoyed his Waikiki vacation and the good times spent with the hard-drinking King Kalakaua and his royal cronies, wrote the following endorsement into the Sans Souci's guestbook: "If anyone desires such old-fashioned things as lovely scenery, quiet, pure air, clear sea water, good food, and heavenly sunsets hung out before his eyes over the Pacific and the distant hills of Waianae, I recommend him cordially to the 'Sans Souci'."

Even today those same riotous sunsets take place within easy eyeshot of the surviving Sans Souci near Diamond Head, but one wonders if Stevenson would have approved of Waikiki even 12 years later, in 1901, when a group of Honolulu businessmen opened Waikiki's first real hotel, a whitewashed, five-story Colonial-style structure named the **Moana Hotel**. Chances are good that the moody Stevenson would have been infuriated by the way this shiny structure full of steamer-set tourists would block his view of central Waikiki's coconut groves. Indeed, one doesn't even try to wonder what he would think today, when one can hardly see Waikiki for the hotels.

Paradise Paved

The inevitable development of Waikiki as a major "planned" resort center began in earnest in January of 1922 when a Waikiki Reclamation project, as it was called, capped and drained the area's "spouting water," and, as the once-popular Joni Mitchell folk song about Hawaii noted, proceeded to "pave paradise and put up a parking lot." The end results of this dredging, draining and filling in and paving are now eminently obvious and not yet finally realized. Verily, the Hawaiian word *Waikiki* does not just rhyme with the Florida Indian word *Miami*; rather, both places have been decisively converted from idyllic places by the sea into America's two biggest hotel-to-hotel, parking-lot-to-parking-lot tourist enclaves. Waikiki is praised by some critics as being "one of the most well-planned and executed visitor destinations on earth," and panned by

Modern Waikiki's skyline from Magic Island.

others as a prime example of "future schlock." Some jet-set travelers don't even want to be heard mentioning the word Waikiki, and others return year after year to the same room where they met and danced and danced and danced many a romantic island night away under big *hula* moons, kerosene "tiki torches" and swaying palms with loud-speakers and colored glass balls tucked among their fronds. It's a safe and con-servative appeal easily understood by the silent majority who flock here by the 747-load.

The Wizards of Waikiki

But whether you look at Waikiki through the silver-mirrored windows of an air-conditioned tour bus or while dodging day-glo colored boulevardiers on flashy **Kalakaua Avenue**, Waikiki does have her redeeming qualities. Take for example the little-known **"Wizard Stones of Waikiki"** which vibrate quietly at **Waikiki Beach Center**.

These unimpressive-looking boulders sit under a small *hala* (pandanus) tree on the Diamond Head side of the **Surfrider Hotel**. However, approach the stones with respect, because according to Hawaiian oral traditions they possess the *mana*, or spiritual powers, of four Tahitian *kahuna* priests, wizards if you will, who were renowned throughout Polynesia for their wisdom and abilities to cure and heal. These four wizards— Kapaemahu, Kahaloa, Kapuni and Kinohi—came to Oahu from Tahiti in the 16th Century, long before the reign of Oahu's King Kakuhewa, and (as a metal plaque on the first stone notes) "before vanishing, the wizards trans-ferred their powers to these stones."

Consider the surrealistic setting of these four stones—across the street from the 40-story twin towers of the **Hemmeter-Hyatt Regency Hotel and Shopping Center**. At this sacred Waikiki epicenter you are about three outrigger canoe lengths away from the most trod upon stretch of imported sand in the world. Hours can be spent here people-watching.

In a seaward, or *makai*, direction are crocheted and *pareu* cotton bikinis drenched in coconut oil and cocoa but-ter, mayonnaise-white tourists who are painfully ignoring every anti-sunburn precaution ever preached by the Red Cross, and da beach boys, big brown

blalahs, as they call themselves, who are paddling oversized orange surfboards out to "Queen's," "Populars" or "Canoes," their chins resting pointedly on the excited fannies of a middle-aged matriarch or giggling adolescent blonde from Missouri. "Eh, geev 'um!" yells the chang-a-lang gang on shore as a brud-dah and would-be surfer girl disappear under a foamy Waikiki wave. Many are the local songs which have immortalized this age-old Waikiki pastime. "Coeds here, coeds there/coeds sitting 'round everywhere/in short shorts and muu-muus too/trying to do like the Hawaiians do," is one, and another recalls: "I took my girl for a surfboard ride/*e lei ka lei i lei*/the surfboard *huli* (turned over)/so she grabbed onto my (oops ... bleep!)." It's all part of Waikiki's nasty but nice mystique.

Christians and Krishnaites
Plus 'Poopooly's Papaya'

The *mauka* view across Kalakaua Avenue is not as refreshing, but just as fanciful: neatly organized ranks of Japanese tourists are following a leader behind a little flopping flag that says "Jalpak Hawaii 802"; blonde surfer boys and coast ladies in cutoff denims and braless tanktops are rolling by in "open-air pedicabs," trishaw cycles, which they lease by the mile to moms and pops in matching floral *muumuus* and *aloha* shirts; and a Tropical Trolley

The world's most famous beach (left) and (right) portrait of a portrait.

drawn by mules wearing diapers jingles past like a Gay Nineties apparition. And the hits keep right on coming: On one side of the street a clutch of born-again Christians are competing for alms with a platoon of saffron-robed devotees of the local temple of the International Society for Krishna Consciousness. The lyrics of "It's because of Jesus in my soul" collide with the mantra "Hare Rama, Hare Rama, Hare Krishna, Hare Hare."

But somehow, from somewhere in that cacophony, the blasphemous refrains of a strolling 'ukelele musician emerge and attract a large crowd of people to a plinkety-plink rendition of Harry Owens' song about "Princess Poo-poo-ly, who has plenty of papaya."

With every passing block, wicked Waikiki gives of herself with little effort on your part. At the **King's Village**, a Disneyland-like shopping complex off Kaiulani Avenue, a white-faced mime identified as Chanelle Akamine, slithers in and out of imaginary barrels and other such surrealistic situation. Meanwhile, behind a Kuhio Avenue gift arcade which deals in carved Filipino kitsch, and plastic, wind-up pineapples that walk, would-be Japanese cowboys are paying to pump twelve 22-magnum slugs into a moving target range. The guns are conveniently chained to the aiming counter, says the manager, "to keep people from shooting themselves." Wide-eyed passersby drift by like technicolor ghosts, then disappear into Pancho Goldstein's for a Grand Marnier soufflé. Bikinis in banks, afternoon tea dances, GIs on the prowl — all are mad facets of the *kapakahi* (out of kilter) kaleidescope called Kalakaua Avenue. For many years the **International Market Place**, at 2330 Kalakaua Avenue, has been the unofficial "Tropical Times Square" of Waikiki. This acre or so of supper clubs (Cock's Roost, Tavana's, Trader Vic's and the Tiki Broiler), trendy shops (The Little Glass Shack), and kiosks selling everything from sno-cones to computer printout portraits, used to be a pleasant, tropical sort of place full of twittering birds, a large central greensward and a good share of curious local folk. But in recent years, with Waikiki space becoming more and more dear, the Market Place has been overcrammed with every possible bit of commerce, and tourists, it can hold. From the shop at the entrance which sells Tongan and Samoan tapas and grass skirts — to the psychic reader who leases a soothsaying space inside the tendrils of a large banyan tree — and the Hula Dolls shop where for a fee you can have your picture taken with a real Polynesian beauty in full Tahitian regalia — the place is a veritable volcano of free enterprise.

Upon visiting Hawaii several years ago, the well-known Soviet poet-journalist Yevgeni Yevtushenko wrote a poem, "The Restaurant For Two," about a small treehouse office high in a banyan tree at the entrance to the International Market Place. He sang of "mermaidenly thighs ... glinting trinkets in shopwindows ... heedless brown hands ... pilings of palm ... baked shark's fin steeped in pineapple ... the samba's throb ... and flat champagne." Then, as he recalls, a man stepped up to the banyan tree, threw a switch and turned on "the bird song tape-recorded to lend the illusion of Paradise."

Indeed, that's a far technological cry from Waikiki, 1913, when another poet, the Britisher Rupert Brooke (1887–

1915), composed a sonnet, "Waikiki," which sighed about "warm perfumes" drifting "like a breath from vine and tree" and recalled hearing in the dark, "hidden from eyes," the sounds of an *eukaleli* which "thrills and cries/ And stabs with pain the night's brown savagery." Brooke heard "Dark scents whisper; and dim waves creep to me/Gleam like a woman's hair, stretch out, and rise/And new stars burn into the ancient skies/Over the murmurous soft Hawaiian sea." Oh, Rupert, ol' bean, if you could only be here now ...

Since the mid-1950s, hotels in Waikiki have sprouted like topless mushrooms in a cow paddock; even today, a new one with some vaguely Polynesian or other resortish name routinely announces its opening every five months or so. As fast as pile drivers can sink posts and cement mixers can pour concrete into uninspired forms, these sleeping blocks rise to the sky and add to what surfers call the Great Wall of Waikiki. However, for most of this century only two Waikiki hotels have managed to retain a bit of "old style Waikiki" charm. These are the aforementioned **Moana Hotel** and the **Royal Hawaiian Hotel**. Both

Puka shell necklaces. Tavana's "Polynesian Spectacular."

beachfront places are still regarded with a certain amount of hostelry respect by *kamaaina* folks who "knew them when." Their nostalgic importance was officially acknowledged in 1967 when the Mayor's Historic Buildings Task Force selected them as "Waikiki's foremost landmark buildings." The **Halekulani Hotel** used to be on this list but its famous wooden bungalows have recently been replaced by a concrete high rise. Only the former main building, dating from the 1930s, is left standing to echo the hotel's legendary past.

The **Moana**, which fronts Kalakaua and the ocean about 100 yards the airport side of the Wizard Stones, is the big white *tutu-kane* (granddaddy) of them all. Its colonial white columns and verandahs have remained white and intact, and its century-old banyan still shades her open courtyard.

Until recently the stately Moana has received more contemporary fame as the site of a pulsing and very sexy Polynesian song and dance revue known as "Tavana's Polynesian Spectacular." This extravaganza, now moved across the street to **Tavana's** in the International Market Place, takes its name from its

creator-choreographer Chief Tavana Anderson, a longtime South Seas and Waikiki character-diplomat known for his savage ways and generous heart. The Moana now has a new Polynesian dance troupe which wails away nightly with fast hips and flaming five knives in the same Banyan Court where aristocrats once drank away tropical nights playing poker and backgammon.

Between 1935 and 1972, the Moana's Banyan Courtyard became internationally famous as the favorite home of "Hawaii Calls," a Hawaiian music show which was once known as the oldest and most widely listened-to radio show on earth. Some 1,900 "Hawaii Calls" shows, sometimes carried by as many as 600 radio stations around the world, were broadcast and relayed live from Hawaii. And the show's emcee, Webley Edwards, became famous as the golden-throated "voice of Hawaii" and "Mr Hawaii Calls." Listen closely and over the soothing roll of surf and tradewinds whooshing through the Moana's banyan, and you may still hear Edwards' voice signing off with "all of us wish you were here with us — here in Hawaii — on this beautiful day. Come over and see us sometime! *Aloha — Aloha nui loa.*"

When the Matson Navigation Company and Territorial Hotel Company unveiled their $4 million "Pink Palace" at Waikiki on February 1, 1927, Honolulu's jaded *kamaaina* elite shifted their frivolous focus from the 26-year-old Moana to this pseudo-Moorish-Spanish hostelry constructed on the site of the former summer home of the Kamehameha kings. Properly social Honolulu and San Francisco were atwitter when the Royal's completion date neared. An advance *Honolulu Advertiser* story promised that the Royal's opening "will be one of the greatest social events in the history of Hawaii." "There will be softly thrumming music upon the air. There will be the powerful fragrance of flowers. There will be the pomp and brilliance of social glory," a reporter wrote.

And indeed there was. Some 1,200 formally gay *haole* and Hawaiian guests turned out to witness a "semi-barbaric pageant" produced and directed by Princess David Kawananakoa, the hotel's first official guest and wife of the late Prince David Kawananakoa (her common maiden name was Abigail

Aerial view of Waikiki, 1929, with the pink Royal and red-roofed Moana in clear view.

122

Campbell). Princess Kawananakoa's pageant, which began in offshore Waikiki waters, was a splendidly campy restaging of the 1795 landing at Waikiki of the conquering Hawaiian King Kamehameha the Great. From the Royal's pink balcony, Princess David hand-directed the movement of a fleet of 15 outrigger canoes and dozens of native Hawaiians outfitted in pseudo-Hawaiian warrior regalia.

Ah, it was a grand debut, but just the shiny start. During the next 15 years, the Royal became *the place* in Hawaii where the Hollywood likes of Mary Pickford and Douglas Fairbanks and Al Jolson and Ruby Keeler joined Duponts, Rockefellers, Fords and assorted presidents and *real royalty* in chit-chat over Green Turtle Soup Kamehameha, Medallions of Sweet Breads Wilhelmina, Royal Hawaiian Givree, Gourmandise and Moka in the tapestry-filled Persian Room, now known as the Monarch Room.

With Hawaiian standards flying above its pink bell towers, and white bush-jacketed beachboys and Chinese bellhops chasing after missy's needs, the Royal cruised through the Depression and later Thirties. But in 1941 World War II flew into Pearl Harbor, barbed concertina wire was rolled across the sands of Waikiki, and tourism sought refuge in less vulnerable resort areas. Few of the world's big spenders could dance during blacked-out nights and in the ominous sight of Army beach sentries carrying M-1 rifles, machine guns and hand grenades, so the Royal mothballed her tapestries and was leased to the U.S. Navy. From January 20, 1942, until February 1, 1947 she "Served Proudly" as a rest and recreation center for armed forces personnel, mainly submariners.

That martial experience, however, took the tradewinds out of her social sails; and though she prospered once again under Matson management in the late Forties and into the middle Fifties, she eventually was bought in 1959 by the Sheraton Corporation of America, then later by Japanese investment tycoon Kenji Osano.

Her rouge has caked and run a bit, and she has been dwarfed by young but towering neighbors, but on a good night, with waves lapping offshore, and moonbeams dancing through a palm tree, the

Opening night at the Royal Hawaiian Hotel, February 1, 1927.

old Pink Palace still gleams like the classy and period gem she is.

The Royal is easily spotted from the beach, but if you have a difficult time finding her from the mountain side, just look up in a seaward direction until you spot the 31-story **Sheraton Waikiki**, Hawaii's biggest hotel (with 1,900 rooms). Walk toward the looming, curving Sheraton, and just to its left, on the Diamond Head side, you'll see a pink cupola peeking through floodlit palms. That's part of what visibly remains of Waikiki's "Pink Lady."

Although the Halekulani, on Kalia Road isn't what it used to be, it's worth a visit even if you aren't staying there. Originally founded in 1907 as the Hau Inn, the Halekulani (literally, the house befitting heaven) was the last of the low-rise hotels on Waikiki Beach. The quaint bungalows are now gone and in its place is a 450-room "inn" managed by the Regent International Hotels. The new hotel, however, is a modern wonder and the beautiful guest rooms are contained in a cluster of buildings that are terraced back from the beach in rising levels to a height of 14 stories.

You can still find a few *hau* trees and bold sparrows haunting the grounds where, in the early 1900s, American author Jack London drank hard, chain-smoked and spun surfing stories on his typewriter. It was here, too that writer Earl Derr Biggers was staying when he first heard of Chang Apana, who was to become the model for Briggers' famous fictional crime-solver, Charlie Chan. The Halekulani's bar, "The House Without A Key," takes its name from the title of the first Charlie Chan novel, published in 1925.

Freebies by-the-Sea

But if old hotel lobbies and bold sparrows are not your cup of Kona coffee, then *hele* (walk) on down to one of the following "free" Waikiki attractions:

• The **U.S. Army Museum of Hawaii** at Fort DeRussy on Kalia Road, where implements of destruction collected during the American Revolution, Spanish-American War, the Boxer Rebellion, Philippine Insurrection, World Wars I and II and the Korean and Vietnam Wars are on display inside Battery Randolph, a massive bunker with 22-

The Royal as seen from beyond the reef.

foot-thick concrete walls. Battery Randolph, built in 1911 to house 14-inch shore guns, was so dense and indestructible the Army couldn't afford to tear it down; so instead of waiting for a direct hit to do away with it, the battery is now being used to house assorted martial arts goodies such as Nazi Reichmarshall Herman Goering's ruby and diamond-studded gold-ivory-platinum field baton; a miniature Japanese submarine that was snagged by anti-sub nets strung across the Pacific end of the Panama Canal; assorted uniforms, howitzers and tanks; and even a Japanese lantern salvaged from the "Death Railroad" which used to chug to and from Thailand's infamous bridge on the River Kwai. This macho museum is open from 10 a.m. to 4:30 p.m. daily except Monday.

• **The Queen Kapiolani Rose Garden** at the corner of Paki and Monsarrat avenues just beneath Diamond Head's Waikiki-side brow and across the street from the *mauka* side of the Honolulu Zoo. This garden, designated an All-American Rose Garden in 1972 by the American Rose Society, was named after Queen Kapiolani, the wife of King David Kalakaua. In its fertile plots you'll find the fragrant *lokelani*, a small and somewhat rare Hawaiian rose, but also dozens of off-the-wall rose varieties named after, among others, Lady Bird Johnson, Princess Grace of Monaco and various towns and people in the Americas, Europe and Asia. Though roses usually do not fare well in tropical climates, the garden's longtime curator, Paul Yamanaka, has had astounding success with his thorny plants. One result of this was the naming of the Queen Kapiolani Rose Garden as the world's first tropical, sea-level rose-testing site for the World Conference of Rose Societies. It is open for sniffing and browsing 24-hours-a-day, everyday.

• The corny and campy but free and fun **Kodak Hula Show**. This touristic one-hour performance takes place at 10 a.m. Tuesday, Wednesday and Thursday (and on Fridays during the summer) on a bleachers-bordered greensward adjacent the **Waikiki Shell** amphitheater at **Kapiolani Park.** *Hula* dancers in authentic ti-leaf skirts (not phony "grass" skirts, please) do their vampy thing in front of a thatch hut and to music sung and strummed by

Windsurfers jumping waves off Diamond Head.

tutu wahine (grandmothers) in bright *holoku* dresses and flower-banded *lauhala* hats. A regular feature of this show, which has been staged since 1937, is the climbing of a coconut palm by a "young Hawaiian native." As he performs in perfunctory fashion this Polynesian palm-climbing act, scores of instamatic cameras click, flash and record the event for Uncle Herman and Aunt Mabel back home. Once down from the tree, he hacks open a coconut with a machete and offers the happy *malihinis* a sip of its sweet milk. Eastman Kodak's revue is worthwhile if only to watch tourists watching Hawaiians.

● **Diamond Head** landmark itself. Few tourists ever find out through normal coconut wireless information channels that they can actually walk or drive into this extinct volcano crater and — if they've got the time, energy and an adventurous spirit — hike 760 feet up its inside walls to the rim of its seaside peak. The view of Waikiki and Oahu's south coast from up there is one of the most memorable on the island. And it's also a superb spot, atop one of its abandoned World War II gun emplacements, for an open-air picnic. Permits and hiking directions for this purpose can be obtained from the State Parks Department, 1151 Punchbowl Street, downtown.

"Diamond Head," if a tour guide hasn't already told you, is a nickname given the crater in 1825 by British sailors who found worthless calcite crystals there which they thought were diamonds. Its original Hawaiian name was *Lae'ahi*, which means brow (*lae*) of the *'ahi* fish. Hawaiian legends say fire goddes Hi'iaka, Pele's younger sister, noticed the resemblance between Diamond Head's profile and that of the *ahi* (yellow-fin tuna) and so gave it that name, *Lae'ahi*, which in later years, for some unexplained reason, was shortened by map-makers to *Leahi*.

Long before this volcanic tuff cone became Hawaii's most famous landmark and internationally recognized symbol, *Lae'ahi* was widely known to Hawaiians as the site of the Papaenaena Heiau, one of the major religious sites on Oahu. According to historical accounts, some of the last human sacrifices ordered by Kamehameha the Great took place at this *heiau* following the decisive Battle of Nuuanu Valley in 1795. Early descriptions indicate that the Papae-

naena Heiau was located just beneath Diamond Head's jutting brow and slightly to its Waikiki side.

● **Kapiolani Park**. This vast complex of beaches, grassy picnic areas, amphitheaters, jogging courses, gardens, the **Honolulu Zoo**, **War Memorial Natatorium** and the **Waikiki Aquarium** was dedicated on June 11, 1877, Kamehameha Day, as Hawaii's first public park. King Kalakaua named the park after his beloved wife, Kapiolani, and opening day was celebrated at a slate of high stakes horse races held on a new racetrack oval laid out just below Diamond Head.

The park's big Kamehameha Day races ended after the turn-of-the-century, when temperance and anti-gambling forces outlawed them, but since those days of the Hawaiian Jockey Club and thoroughbred runs, Kapiolani Park has steadily remained one of the most enthusiastically patronized recreational facilities on Oahu. Whether one prefers cricket, soccer, kiteflying, surfing or simply long tranquil walks under monkeypod, royal poinciana, scrambled egg or ironwood trees, this royal park has got you covered. Joggers, who are

Gate at the Waikiki Natatorium and War Memorial, Kapiolani Park.

more visible in Hawaii than mynah birds, say the park's 1.8 mile exercise circuit is one of the most ideal anywhere. It wends past picnickers, soccer matches, a driving range, archery cove and free ethnic music and dance concerts held in the park's bandstand. Across the street at **Queen's Surf Beach Park**, gay beach-boys gather for long sultry days of sun, fun and volleyball, and to listen to impromptu conga drum, guitar and flute music concerts held under a banyan, especially on weekend afternoons.

Meanwhile, at the park's Honolulu Zoo, one can enjoy the typically zooey antics of assorted monkeys, big cats, elephants, giraffes, camels, and alligators. Also, and this is of great importance to island children, the zoo is the only place in Hawaii where you can observe a real live snake. Not until 1971, following four years of spirited debate in the State Legislature, was a serpent allowed into Paradise. The first one, a little red rat snake from Florida, was followed into Hawaii's only snake pit by a Burmese python and an Arizona king snake. All slither behind a bulletproof glass case not far from three Malayan sun bears — Jan, Ken and Po — and a 450-pound gorilla who recently was provided with a tug-of-war rope which allows him to match strength and wits with *Homo sapiens* passersby.

Probably the rarest creature in the Honolulu Zoo is a monk seal caught in nearby Hawaiian waters. This seal and a lowly hoary bat are the only two mammals known to have been native to Hawaii when the first Hawaiian settlers arrived from southern Polynesia in about 500 A.D. Every other mammal now present in Hawaii was introduced by human carriers.

Appropriately, this park has also become one of the running world's most well-known competition meccas, because its **Kapiolani Park Bandstand** is the annual finishing point of the famous **Honolulu Marathon**, an endurance race which attracts several thousands of local and imported long-distance runners. That December marathon race (of 26 miles, 385 yards) and numerous other running programs in Hawaii have made Hawaii what one sports reporter recently called "The Runningest State in the Nation." Perhaps because of the islands' conducive environment. Hawaii is said to have the greatest number of

Sunset from the Kuhio Beach breakwater.

runners per capita in the United States, or about 10 times the national average.

Oh, Waikiki, "my whole life is empty without you, you've got that magic about you," the lyrics to the song "Waikiki" lament. And, they might add, "you make so much money." On this 7/10 of a square mile of recycled sand and concrete, 25,000-plus hotel rooms, and rolling, rentable surf, tourists annually spend more money than the State makes off military spending and the sugar and pineapple industries all together. As a Honolulu journalist said of Waikiki recently, "She is the bane of our existence, but apple of our economic eye."

Many Honoluluans consider Waikiki a kind of foreign country, or foreign trade zone, where stereotypical products and services Made in Paradise are packaged prettily in cellophane, glass bottles, concrete and air-conditioned comfort for the 24-hours-a-day enjoyment of big-eyed visitors. Some local folks venture into this zone to sell goods and services, but others avoid Waikiki entirely. As a well-known Honolulu newspaper columnist explained recently: "Yes, we enjoy the economic benefits of the tourist industry, and the military industry for that matter, but we stay the hell out of both. The point is, you eat the chicken, but you don't necessarily walk into the chicken coop."

Ask a "local" what he'd recommend seeing in Waikiki, other than things already mentioned above, and suggestions range from amateur strip tease night at the Lollipop, to Prince Hanalei's "flaming *okole* (rear end)" act, to Don Ho's nightly "Suck 'Em Up," "Tiny Bubbles" act at the geodesic **Hilton Hawaiian Village Dome**. Ho, a self-described former "Air Force pilot and psychology major" has become one of the world's highest paid nightclub entertainers on the basis of a mumbly nightclub show he hosts. Ho sings very little, horses around a lot, and has made a great commercial thing out of inviting nervous and aging women from the United States and Canada onto his stage for an open-mouthed kiss. These mainland *wahine* (and their curious husbands) obligingly pay upwards of $15 each for two drinks and a chance (for her) to thus buss Ho on stage. Unbelievable, you say, but it has made Ho one of the richest entertainers on earth, and his show a Waikiki institution.

Art in Waikiki? Such an eclectic range of creations you will rarely ever see in the same 7/10 of a square mile anywhere. From an important 9 x 28 foot fresco mural ("Early Contacts of Hawaii with Outer World") at the Waikiki Branch of First Hawaiian Bank (2189 Kalakaua Avenue) by the late and internationally renowned French artist Jean Charlot, to the most awful tropical kitsch, all forms of "art" can be found in Waikiki.

Walk over to the Waikiki Shopping Center and there — in **Center Art Gallery** — you will find to your delight or dismay the heart-piercing works of Margaret Keane, a shy lady painter from Tennessee who made little children with huge doleful eyes her internationally-recognized art mark. A sign card above an enlarged promotional eye titled "Window of the Soul" notes that Mrs. Keane's "works have drawn comparison with Grant Wood, Boticelli and Modigliani, the latter being her own favorite." Hmmm — but if lithe and lonesome-looking waifs in *kimono, muumuu* and polka-dot party dresses don't catch your eye, also on regular display and for sale are clown paintings

Don Ho

128

and prints by Red Skelton, Woody Woodpeckers by Walter Lantz and primitive "folk-art" paintings by actress Elke Sommer.

Those *who know* also recommend a peek at Edward M. Brownlee's 28-foot and obliquely phallic sculpture in the lobby of the Waikiki Branch of Bank of Hawaii (2220 Kalakaua Avenue), and in the same bank lobby a five-panel tapestry by Ruthadell Anderson (made of *hau* fiber, banyan roots, split bamboo, mango seeds, bunya-bunya cones, night blooming cereus roots and other natural materials).

Like your art big? Try the mosaic rainbows which arch across the 30-story high **Hilton Rainbow Tower** (at 2003 Kalia Road). These vertical murals made of 16,000 ceramic tiles and designed to be seen two-and-a-half miles at sea, are billed as "the world's tallest murals." But if it's quantity you're after, take in the Saturday Art Mart from 8 a.m. to 4 p.m. every Saturday at the Honolulu Zoo's Monsarrat Avenue fence. Some 50-plus island artists display and sell their creations there under big and shady monkeypod trees.

But perhaps the most *touching* work of art in Waikiki is a wall mural at the **Hawaii School for the Deaf and Blind** (at 3440 Leahi Avenue) which ceramicist Kay Mura and students at the school created for people who cannot see artworks. Its tactile theme is Hawaiiana, and includes canoes, fishes, birds, flowers and other Hawaii symbols in its sculpted and glazed expanse.

Entrepreneurs say Waikiki is second only to Las Vegas' Nevada in the number of commercial entertainment distractions available to tourists in one place, but as in show biz everywhere, these day and night diversions open and close so often that it would be improper to mention them in this brief introductory review. For further up-to-date information, consult leisure time calendars and advertisements in Honolulu's two daily newspapers (*The Honolulu Advertiser* and *Honolulu Star-Bulletin*), *Honolulu Magazine*, Waikiki's two major tourist give-aways (*The Waikiki Beach Press* and *The Hawaii Tourist News*) and — for Hawaiian music — the Hawaiian Music Foundation's monthly publication *Ha'ilono Mele*.

ate
night action
at The Wave,
Waikiki

DOWNTOWN HONOLULU

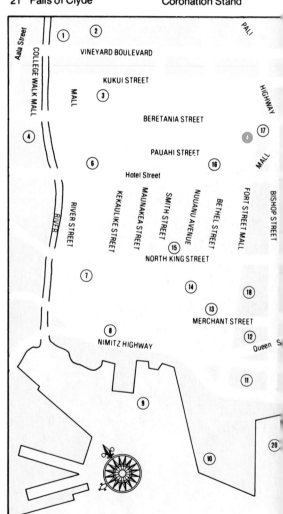

11	Irwin Park	7	Oahu Open Market	47	State Office Building
37	Judiciary Building (Aliiolani Hale)	20	Oceania Floating Restaurant	53	Thomas Square
13	Kamehameha V Post Office	17	Our Lady of Peace Cathedral	26	War Memorial
43	Kawaiahao Church	22	Pacific Trade Center and Mall	56	Ward Warehouse
57	Kewalo Basin	16	Pantheon Bar	25	Washington Place
36	King Kamehameha I Statue	40	Royal Brewery	23	YWCA, Richards Street
1	Kwan Yin Temple	24	St. Andrew's Cathedral		

11 Irwin Park
37 Judiciary Building
    (Aliiolani Hale)
13 Kamehameha V
    Post Office
43 Kawaiahao Church
57 Kewalo Basin
36 King Kamehameha I
    Statue
 1 Kwan Yin Temple
33 Library of Hawaii
42 Lunalilo Tomb
14 Merchant Square
    (shaded area)
50 Mission Houses
    Museum
45 Mission Memorial
    Building
39 New Federal Building
51 News Building and
    Contemporary Arts
    Center of Hawaii

 7 Oahu Open Market
20 Oceania Floating
    Restaurant
17 Our Lady of Peace
    Cathedral
22 Pacific Trade Center
    and Mall
16 Pantheon Bar
40 Royal Brewery
24 St. Andrew's
    Cathedral
46 "Sky Gate"
30 State Archives
    (Kekauluohi
    Building)
32 State Attorney
    General &
    Ombudsman's
    Building and Ancient
    Threshold Rock of
    Liloa
27 State Capitol

47 State Office Building
53 Thomas Square
26 War Memorial
56 Ward Warehouse
25 Washington Place
23 YWCA, Richards
    Street

● **Banks**
 1 Bank of Hawaii
 2 Deak-Perera Hawaii
    Inc.
 3 First Hawaiian Bank

Hotels
 5 Armed Services
    YMCA
 4 Blaisdell Hotel

Hospitals
 6 Queen's Medical
    Center
 7 Straub Clinic &
    Hospital

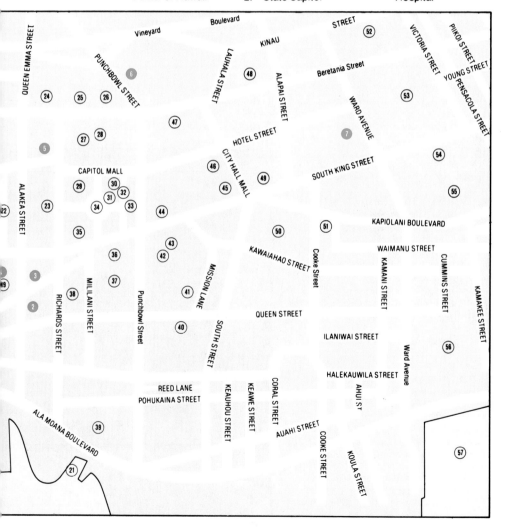

DOWNTOWN HONOLULU

As the popular song goes, if life gets lonely or you've had your touristic fill of the hustle, astro turf and *mai-tais* of Waikiki, "you can always go downtown." Downtown Honolulu — or "Old Honolulu" — or simply "town," as locals prefer to call Honolulu proper — is but 50 cents and a 15-minute air-conditioned TheBus ride away from your Waikiki hotel. But once there, you'll find your sunburned body deposited into a walker's delight, where you can kill entire days, weeks or even months poking around in back lanes, dusty junk shops and odd bars where at least one street character will talk pidgin English into your ear and woo you back for another *aloha* beer.

Even the standard Woolworth's and Kress five and dime stores, where *saimin* noodles and preserved mango and ginger coexist on the same menu with fried chicken and chocolate milk shakes, are a rare traveler's treat. All-America, yes, but as a Honolulu editor once wrote of Honolulu, "about as American as apple *poi*."

As in any slow-rolling place like Honolulu, where tradewinds and bikinis attract more money than stocks and bonds, the key to unlocking her intrigue is to treat her not like a city, but like the small painted lady she is. Putter about her serendipitously, from park bench to palm tree and Anglican churchyard to Filipino pool hall, looking for whomever or whatever your amused, confused eye happens to see. Like da gang at the old Rialto Bar (at 22 S. Hotel Street) suggests: "Try go easy, bruddah."

Pupus, Mahus and Tattoos

But to set you on your *aloha* way, follow the advice of the boys in the Royal Hawaiian Band and begin your downtown pavement pounding by attending one of their free Friday noon concerts held at "the gazebo," or **Coronation Stand**, on the grounds of **Iolani Palace**. Some tourists like to combine this concert with a tour of the *koa* and gold gilt palace itself, but what many of the band members do is *holo-holo* (stroll) over to the nearby Union Street Mall where they order a "plate lunch" stacked high with local-style beef teriyaki, *kalua* pig or stew and rice, and sit on a bench slurping and blinking at an improbable promenade of soap-box evangelists, giggling steno poolers, junior executives, winos, and eclectic multi-ethnic others who either race along the mall like whirlwinds or float by looking like drugged birds of paradise.

Want to see what this place looked like a hundred years ago? Don't touch that dial. Simply dispose of your plate lunch refuse, about face, stroll *mauka* up the mall to the **Bishop Building** at 1136 Union Mall and scan the handy, multi-paneled mural just inside the front door which depicts "Honolulu — 1876" by six well-known local artists (Juliette May Fraser, Shirley Kuuleimokihana Yong, Mataumu Toelupe Alisa, David G. Asherman, Bruce C. Ha'o and Mark S. Lang). This informative artwork is a quite thorough briefing on many historical areas — the waterfront, **Merchant Street**, **Chinatown** and numerous royal remnants — you can visit within a half-mile radius of this building.

That intelligence tucked away, proceed with inspiration and appreciation

Bishop Street, downtown, 1979.

132

through the bluestone, brick, coral, lava and wood frame charm of **Old Honolulu**. Marvel for a moment at mirror-tinted and chromium skyscrapers which reflect sunlight onto Bishop and Merchant streets, but allot just as much or more time for the bustling Chinese open market at King and Kekaulike streets, the Armenian gypsy fortune tellers who grab your arm and pat your pockets as you turn up Nuuanu Avenue, and the tattoo artists at China Sea and Floating World who creatively peck away at people's privates with the very latest in highspeed and electro-ink injection needles.

Still jaded? Then boogie with the Rolling Stones "live" at the 8,500-seat **Blaisdell International Center Arena** or swoon with the Honolulu City Ballet and Symphony, also alive, at the **Honolulu Concert Hall** next door. Then ... slow down by taking in the opulently outrageous "Boys Will Be Girls" transvestite-*mahu* revue at **The Glade** on Hotel Street. Commit all the above to latent memory by quaffing a few potent toddies at any of downtown's three Irish pubs (Jameson's, or O'Toole's), and — if

you are not yet gasping for air or in a tropical trance — stir in a Chinese *wushu-kungfu-shiao-lin* triple feature at the **Golden Harvest Theatre** ("in Mandarin with English subtitles") and add a dash of *da kine* Hawaiian music, *pupu* (Hawaiian *hors d'oeuvres*) and Primo beers in the campy courtyard of the old Blaisdell Hotel on the **Fort Street Mall.**

Some people like to neutralize this eclectic mix with coffee and coconut pie at the all-night Columbia Inn "at the Top of the Boulevard" on Kapiolani, but Uncle Moki suggests a different course: "The morning after," he says, can be remedied by first quaffing a sure-fire and ancient hangover potion prepared by the Bo Sau Ton or Chee Wo Tong herb shops in Chinatown, then — after a long walk around the elderly Filipino checkers-players and adolescent skate-boarders in Aala Park — by drinking a thick Bloody Bullshot at the Cheerio Room. Or, if you're a vegetarian, a papaya-mango-banana-and-*lilikoi* smoothie at one of downtown's many health bars.

But don't get hung up for too long in the clatter, clink, neon and honky-tonk of whiskey bars, prowling servicemen,

Fort and Hotel, Streets, downtown, 1893.

blue police lights, Smith Street soul brothers, porno arcades, chop suey houses and the Don and Flo and Tweetie and Clyde "live sex acts" which crowd commercial quarters on the *Ewa* side of Bishop Street. Save quiet, less blasphemous moments for a good peek at places such as the impressive and historic **Iolani Palace**.

America's Only Palace

The grand old Iolani Palace (on King Street, of course) is where King Kalakaua and his successor-sister Queen Liliuokalani, lived, held royal court and dreamed Royal Hawaiian dreams from 1882 until January 17, 1893, when a group of American businessmen— backed by 160 heavily-armed American Marines—staged a *coup d'etat* and abolished the monarchy.

This impressive structure, the only royal palace on American soil, was built in what its three architects (Thomas J. Baker, C.J. Wall and Isaac Moore) called an "American Composite" or "American Florentine" style. It was completed in December, 1882, during the eighth year of King Kalakaua's reign, after three years of labor and at a cost of just under $360,000. In 1969, after more than 75 years of official neglect and misuse of its superstructure and grounds, the State and a private non-profit group, The Friends of Iolani Palace, began a massive restoration effort designed to restore the Palace to its original splendor. In 1978, after nine years of meticulous labor and some S6 million in restoration funds, Iolani Palace was officially reopened to visitors.

Many original furnishings are still missing or are being replaced with facsimiles of original pieces, but the Palace proper — its Corinthian columns, etched glass door panels, chandeliered, mirrored and gilded Throne Room and spectacular three-story *koa* stairwell with carved balusters—now glow as they did when Kalakaua and Liliuokalani hosted formal banquets and grand balls in the large Dining Room and adjacent Blue Room. Also back in operation are the first flush toilets known to have been installed in any palace anywhere, and Hawaii's first intra-house telephone and electric light systems.

Iolani Palace.

Iolani, Hawaiian for "The Hawk of Heaven," a symbol of highest royalty, soared majestically for a glittering and noble decade before being shot down by the succeeding Provisional Government of Hawaii and being renamed "The Executive Building." But *auwe,* alas, royal humiliation did not end there. In January, 1895, following a futile counter-revolution led by sympathetic royalists, ex-Queen Liliuokalani was charged and convicted of high treason, and returned to Iolani Palace where she spent most of 1895 living in the second floor rooms of her former palace — this time under "house arrest" as a prisoner of the Provisional Government.

Since the 1893 coup, the palace has been used as a capitol for the Provisional Government of Hawaii, Republic of Hawaii, Territory of Hawaii, and State of Hawaii. But in 1969 the State Legislature and Administration moved to the impressive new grounds and Capitol just *mauka* of the palace, so it was finally left vacant, unused and restorable.

In recent years, however, Iolani Palace has not been without its truly royal moments. Now and then, with little public fanfare, collateral descendants of the Kalakaua Dynasty participate in discreet meetings on the Palace's grounds with visiting monarchs from other Polynesian "kingdoms," such as Tahiti, Tonga and Maori tribes of New Zealand. On these unheralded occasions, the man who would be King of Hawaii, Edward Keliiahonui Kawananakoa, his sisters, the Princesses Poomaikelani and Kapiolani Kawananakoa, and a cousin, Kekaulike Kawananakoa, gather on the palace's *mauka* portico to welcome and toast their royal Polynesian peers in a manner befitting such visiting and receiving dignitaries. These private affairs are purely symbolic in nature, receiving no support or recognition from the State of Hawaii, but they are a poignant, living reminder of Royal Hawaiian days past.

Of additional interest on the Palace grounds are:

• The gaily-painted **Coronation Stand** built in 1883 for King Kalakaua and Queen Kapiolani's grand coronation ceremony. The stand originally stood at the foot of the King Street steps of the Palace, but following the coronation was moved to its present location in the

Edward Keliiahonui Kawananakoa, the would-be King of Hawaii.

Ewa-makai corner of the grounds. The stand's foundation was rebuilt of concrete during 1919-1920, but the copper dome is original and now shelters Friday noon public concerts by the Royal Hawaiian Band.

• The **Iolani Barracks**, a stone structure which served as headquarters and home for the Royal Household Guards from 1871 until the overthrow of the monarchy in 1893. The barracks originally stood on Hotel Street on the new State Capitol grounds, but was moved piece-by-piece to its present location alongside Richards Street in 1965. The State is now restoring Iolani Barracks. It may use the barracks as a museum and as a permanent palace administration headquarters.

• The **Royal Burial Ground and Tomb**. This inconspicuous grass-covered mound surrounded by sacred *ti* plants in the *Diamond Head-makai* corner of the grounds was the location of the first Royal Mausoleum, "built in 1825 to house the remains of King Kamehameha II and Queen Kamamalu who died in England in July 1824." Later Hawaiian *alii* were also buried there, but in 1865, after the crypt had become over-crowded with royal remains, all were ceremoniously moved to a new and larger Royal Mausoleum in Nuuanu Valley.

Also on the palace grounds, in the *mauka-Diamond Head* corner, alongside the Library of Hawaii next door, are two contemporary structures — the **State Archives Building** (the Kekauluohi Building) and the **State Attorney General and Ombudsman's Building** (the Kanaina Building, which was the original archives building). Both are misplaced architecturally but in front of the latter is a Captain Cook memorial tablet of minor interest, and a very interesting "ancient threshold rock of Liloa, an ancient king of Hawaii." This oblong lava stone used to mark the *kapu* (forbidden) entrance to Liloa's Big Island home and was said to have been shipped to Oahu by King Kalakaua.

Directly behind Iolani Palace is Hawaii's most recent center of power — the **State Capitol**, a $24.5 million building which has been both the pride and bane of Hawaii's lawmakers and taxpaying citizens. The massive structure's architectural lines and forms were designed to suggest Hawaii's volcanic and

Iolani Palace interior, main stairwell.

oceanic origins; and its high and flaring support pillars, it has been said, represent royal palms and the pompous and obvious symbolism they stand for. Paneling made of indigenous *Acacia koa* wood in offices and conference rooms gives the structure a Hawaiian touch, as do Hawaiian language greetings on the Governor's door (*E komo mai*—Please come in). But the building's greatest "local flavor" appears during regular February through May sessions of the State Legislature when you can hear Hawaii's lawmakers *hukihuki*, or argue island-style, in the State's most flawless and eloquent parliamentary-pidgin. It's one a da bes' free shows een town.

Dangling above the *makai* and *mauka* entrances are massive castings of the Great Seal of the State of Hawaii. This seal, an edited and embellished version of the original Royal Hawaiian Coat of Arms, includes images of Kamehameha I and the Goddess of Liberty (wearing a Phrygian cap and laurel wreath, but holding a partly unfurled Hawaiian flag in her right hand). Other symbols are a Phoenix bird with outstretched wings arising from flames; the State's motto; a rising sun surrounded by the words

"State of Hawaii, 1959," commemorating statehood; a quartered heraldic shield with parts of the Hawaiian flag, *kapu* sticks and a green escutcheon with a five-pointed yellow star in the center; and lower seal engravings of taro leaves, banana foliage and sprays of maidenhair fern.

On the *mauka* side of the capitol fly the American and Hawaiian flags and a blue, red and starred Governor's flag. First-time visitors to the islands, particularly those from British Commonwealth nations, are always surprised to see the British Union Jack in the upper left corner of Hawaii's red-white-and-blue State flag. It is thought that this flag—designed about 1816 for King Kamehameha I—includes the Union Jack out of consideration for the British sea Captain George Vancouver, who presented Hawaii its first flag when Kamehameha temporarily placed his islands under the protection of Great Britain. Some historians say Kamehameha adopted the Jack and Stripes flag so that Hawaiian ships at sea would look like both U.S. and British ships, thereby discouraging pirates from pillaging his Kingdom's vulnerable ships.

Roof of
Hawaii's
State
Capitol.

Fascinating artworks adorn halls, offices and the House and Senate chambers of the Capitol, but while you're on its *mauka* side spend a few quiet moments studying the black and squarish bronze sculpture of **Father Damien Joseph De Veuster**, the martyr-priest who lived and died among lepers at Kalawao on the island of Molokai. This blockish statue of Damien — by the Venezuelan sculptress Marisol Escobar — is a duplicate of one which stands in Statuary Hall in the U.S. Capitol at Washington, D.C. When it was unveiled in 1969 it caused much controversy in local art, political and church circles because Marisol's bold and tragic likeness of Damien was based on a photograph taken of him shortly before he died of leprosy in 1889. At the time, Damien was in great pain, and his former handsome features were grossly disfigured by leprosy. Controversy regarding the statue has waned, but in his spot on the Beretania Street side of the State Capitol, Marisol's Damien remains a powerful artistic statement and a telling memorial to that tough and loving priest.

Across Beretania Street, in the general direction of Damien's tortured gaze, is another memorial — the **War Memorial**, a 9-foot high copper and brass sculpture by Bumpei Akaji which houses an eternal flame in honor of Hawaii's men and women who served in World War II.

And to the left — or *Ewa* side — of that sculpture is a tidy white mansion, **Washington Place**, which is now the official residence of the Governor of Hawaii, but previously was the home of Lydia Kapaakea Dominis, the *alii* who ruled as Queen Liliuokalani when her brother King David Kalakaua died in 1891. This gracious structure, rendered in what was called a Greek Revival form of architecture, was built in 1846 for the American sea captain John Dominis who moved to Hawaii from New York in 1837. Dominis was lost at sea shortly after he finished building this grand home, but his widow and young son (John Owen Dominis, who later married the future Queen Liliuokalani) continued to live in his Honolulu mansion.

One of the first things Capt. Dominis' widow did was to rent, in 1847, several rooms in the house to Anthony TenEyck, then U.S. Commissioner to Hawaii. TenEyck established his United

Father Damien, sculpture by Marisol and actual photo taken a few weeks before Damien died in 1889.

States Legation in the House, and by late 1847 an American flag was fluttering over its front lawns. The following year, on February 22, 1848, Commissioner TenEyck issued a "semi-official" proclamation in which he "christened the beautiful, substantial & universally admired mansion of Mrs. Dominis, Washington Place," after George Washington, America's first president.

John Owen Dominis and the Hon. Lydia K.P. Kapaakea were married September 16, 1862, and took up residence at Washington Place with Dominis' mother. When Mrs. Dominis died in 1889, the property was willed to her son, so until Liliuokalani ascended the throne in 1891, moved into Iolani Palace and named her beloved husband the Prince Consort of Hawaii, she and Dominis continued to live here. When Prince Consort Dominis died on August 27, 1891, Washington Place became the Queen's property, but she didn't return there to live until her regime was overthrown in 1893. Until Queen Liliuokalani's death on November 11, 1917, at age 79, Washington Place remained a center of "royalty" and courtly social proceedings in Hawaii. Many were the

distinguished travelers who visited the Queen's Beretania Street home-salon; and not a few probably were treated to a private concert by the very musical Liliuokalani, who liked to sit and sing in her Music Room at a massive *koa* grand piano or strum the guitar she used to compose the song "Aloha 'Oe."

Because Washington Place is the private home of Hawaii's governor it is open to the public only on very special occasions. However, to maintain a sense of history and adventuresome spirit, a traveler who has strolled this far up North Beretania Street should proceed next door and peek in on **Saint Andrew's Cathedral**, an English-Norman structure built (slowly) between 1867 and 1958 of imported English sandstone. This headquarters of the Anglican faith in Hawaii was made possible by the bequests and political support of King Kamehameha IV and his Queen Emma, who became devout members of the Church of England during the early 1860s.

Only another block *Ewa* up Beretania Street — which, incidentally, is the Hawaiian word form of the English word "Brittania," in honor of a former British presence, both embassy and

Washington Place interior.

church, in this area—was the local Christian competition. These were the Roman Catholic missionaries who built the **Cathedral of Our Lady of Peace**. This coral building at the top of the **Fort Street Mall** was dedicated on August 15, 1843, by French priests of the order of the Congregation of the Sacred Hearts of Jesus and Mary.

Inside this church Father Damien, formerly Joseph De Veuster of Louvain, Belgium, was ordained on May 21, 1864; and it was also here, in 1846, that Hawaiians marveled to the awe-inspiring sounds of the first pipe organ they had ever heard. In a quiet courtyard at the rear of the cathedral is an unimpressive stump of the first *kiawe* tree ever planted in Hawaii. In 1827, Father Alexis Bachelot, leader of the first party of Catholic missionaries who came to Hawaii from France, planted several seeds of the algaroba tree, or mesquite, on the grounds of his Catholic mission. Seeds from the one *kiawe*, as they are known here, eventually spread throughout the islands, and are now one of the many introduced plants which have proved to be useful—as fuel, for honey-bee culture, as fodder for live-stock, and as a hardy forestation tree in dry regions. Their thorns, however, can be a hazard to barefoot hikers who accidentally step on them.

Hawaii's Gilded Conqueror

At this point in the Capitol District part of your stroll, head back down Richards Street—past the **Armed Services YMCA** (site of the original Hawaiian Hotel) and the **Richards Street YWCA** (with wrought-iron grilling, red-tiled terrazzo flooring and a courtyard swimming pool with a water-spout lion)—to King Street and the gilded statue of **King Kamehameha the Great** on the ocean side of Iolani Palace.

This heroic bronze bears little or no resemblance to Kamehameha the Great, but it's a grand Honolulu monument which is photographed dozens of times a day by tourists who want to be seen in the same Kodak frame with Hawaii's most famous warrior king. The statue is particularly impressive—and super-photographed—on June 11 and shortly thereafter when its neck, shoulders and arms are draped with 18-foot-long "Kamehameha Day" flower *lei* do-

Windows a Saint Andrew's Catedral.

nated and strung by local Hawaiian societies and schoolchildren.

The Kamehameha likeness, which was modeled for in the 1870s by a local fellow named John Timoteo Baker, who was mostly Anglo-Saxon but about a fourth Tahitian, shows the great king holding a barbed *pololu* (spear) in his left hand as a symbol of peace and his right arm outstretched in a gesture of *aloha*. Hanging from the king's shoulders is a huge feather cloak and on his head is a *mahiole*, or feather helmet. Around his loins and over his chest he wears a feather *malo*, loincloth, and sash.

When the Hawaiian Kingdom's Legislature of 1878 commissioned this statue, King Kalakaua selected Baker, a local businessman and close friend, to be the main model for the statue, because he was supposed to be the handsomest man in court circles. Photographs were taken of Baker and others wearing ancient clothing, and these pictures and copies of painted likenesses of Kamehameha were sent to Thomas B. Gould, an American sculptor whose studio was in Florence, Italy. Gould's first statue was cast in Paris in 1880 and shipped to Hawaii from Bremen, Germany, but off Port Stanley in the Falkland Islands the ship carrying it, the bark *G.F. Haendel*, caught fire and sank.

As a result, the statue now standing in front of Hawaii's old **Judiciary Building** — where it was unveiled during the week of Kalakaua's coronation in 1883 — is actually a copy of Gould's original. The original was recovered later during salvage operations off Port Stanley, brought to Hawaii for repairs, and now stands in front of the old courthouse at Kohala on the Big Island, near Kamehameha's birthplace.

Of secondary, but fascinating, interest are four bronze and gilt *bas-relief* plaques around the statue's white pedestal. These detailed plaques depict Kamehameha as he visits Captain James Cook, the "discoverer" of Hawaii, aboard his flag ship HMS *Resolution*; as he demonstrates his warrior's skills by warding off five spears hurled at him simultaneously; and as he reviews a fleet of war canoes from a bluff at Kohala, Hawaii. The last plaque represents a grand era of peace which followed Kamehameha's triumphant unification of the islands.

Baker, the model, and Kamehameha statue by Gould.

The old Judiciary Building just behind the Kamehameha Statue, known as Aliiolani Hale, also has a very royal history because it was originally designed by an Australian architect, Thomas Rowe, to be King Kamehameha V's palace. His Majesty's household plans changed, however, and by the time the building was complete in 1874 it was used instead as a courthouse-parliament building. The building now serves as the home of the State's supreme court. *Aliiolani*, one of Kamehameha V's formal Hawaiian names, means "a chief of heavenly repute." *Hale* means "house."

In a *Diamond Head* direction up King Street and across Punchbowl Street from the Judiciary Building and Kamehameha Statue is Hawaii's most famous religious structure, **Kawaiahao Church**.

On Sunday mornings, or when the church's Hawaiian choir is in rehearsal, the royal palms and *hala* trees on its hallowed Hawaiian-Christian grounds verily swell and sway with the lyrics of "*He A-kua he mo-le-le*—God is Holy" or with "*E Ha-wai-i e ku'u o-ne ha-nau e*," the opening words of Hawaii's most-

beloved song, "Hawaii Aloha," (by the Rev. Lorenzo "Laiana" Lyons 1807–1886), which in translation praise, "Oh, Hawaii, my own birthplace, my own land."

Indeed, if there is an active spiritual font in Hawaii for Hawaiians, it is probably this historic church which was constructed in the late 1830s and early 1840s of some 14,000 large coral blocks cut off nearby reefs and hauled to this site by members of the congregation. *Kawaiahao*, which literally means the "fresh water pool of Ha'o," was named after an ancient sacred spring which used to bubble up in this area near the **News Building** at the corner of South Street and Kapiolani Boulevard. *Ha'o*, according to oral traditions, was a one time queen of Oahu.

Designed by the Rev. Hiram Bingham, who led the first Congregationalist mission to Hawaii in 1820, "The Great Stone Church" at Kawaiahao has been the site of many historical incidents. It was here that Kamehameha III uttered his famous words—and now the State of Hawaii's motto—*Ua mau ke ea o ka aina i ka pono*—"the life of the land is preserved in righteousness"—following

Modern Kawaiahao Church and its pastor, The Reverend Abraham Akaka.

the restoration of Hawaiian sovereignty after a brief British takeover of the islands in 1843. This is also where Liholiho, Kamehameha IV, and Lunalilo (William Charles Lunalilo Kana-'ina) formally ascended the Hawaiian throne; where on June 19, 1856, Liholiho was married to Miss Emma Rooke; and where many sad, royal funerals began.

Even today, Kawaiahao, which has been administered for many years by the Rev. Abraham Akaka, often serves as a meeting place where matters of serious Hawaiian interest are discussed and acted upon. It is also a good place to hear some of the most inspired organ and choir music in the Hawaiian Islands, and a seat of worship favored by dignitaries and tourists who have been charmed for many years by Rev. Akaka's forceful words and an occasional "*ukulele* sermon," during which he accompanies his preaching with the joyful tinkles of that little instrument evolved by Hawaiians from the Portuguese *cavaquinho*.

Although the present Kawaiahao structure was dedicated on July 21, 1842, it was preceded by four thatched churches which were also built under Rev. Bingham's direction, the first in 1821. For many years this was the gathering place for missionaries and *alii* Christians.

The church's grounds also served as cemeteries for early missionary *haole* and native Hawaiians who were faithful members of its congregation. Several missionaries and some of their descendants are buried at the back of the church, while native Hawaiians and others were segregated in death on the harbor-side of Kawaiahao Church.

One Hawaiian, however, whose body received special treatment from Kawaiahao's administrators and congregation was King William Lunalilo, the popular "Prince Bill" whose Gothic tomb, the **Mausoleum of King Lunalilo**, stands just to the right side of the main entrance to the Kawaiahao churchyard. Lunalilo, who died in 1874 after a one-year reign, had requested that he be buried at Kawaiahao, away from the "clannish" Kamehameha kings and queens who rested in vaults in the Royal Mausoleum at Nuuanu. Lunalilo wanted to be "among his people," he said at his deathbed, so when he died his aging father, Charles Kanaina, respected his royal son's wishes. When the elder Kanaina died later, he was also placed in this impressive burial vault which says over its *mauka* entrance Lunalilo Ka Moi, Lunalilo the King.

Another edifice on Kawaiahao's grounds which merits closer study is **Likeke Hale**, an adobe schoolhouse, built about 1836, where early Congregationalist missionaries taught Hawaiian children the *palapala*, meaning the Bible and paper learning in general. This building made of mud, limestone, and coral fragments is the only survivor of many adobe structures built in Hawaii during the early 1800s, and it's still being used by Kawaiahao Church for Sunday School classes and smaller church meetings.

Just over a hedge and a narrow road from the schoolhouse is the yard where the missionaries lived, prayed and printed (in 1822) the first of their many 19th Century *palapala*, or writings, in the English and Hawaiian languages. These are the **Mission Houses**, now a museum complex, which are the oldest surviving Western-style structures in Hawaii. The main white **"Frame House"** still stands as prim, trim and true as the day it

An unused two-cent Hawaiian Missionary stamp, one of the world's rarest philatelic items (value is about $500,000).

was erected in 1821 of New England timbers which were cut and fitted in Boston and shipped around Cape Horn to Hawaii aboard the brig *Thaddeus*. She is the oldest wooden house in Hawaii, and for many years was home to several prominent missionaries, including Hiram Bingham, Gerrit Judd, and Elisha Loomis, Hawaii's first printer.

The complex's **"Coral House,"** where 20-year-old Loomis pressed and pulled sheets of the first printing in the North Pacific from an old iron and mahogany Ramage model press, was built in 1823; and a third building, the **"Chamberlain House,"** also constructed of coral blocks, was completed in 1831. Chamberlain House was used as a storehouse and home for Levi Chamberlain, the mission's purchasing agent. All three structures belong to the Hawaiian Mission Children's Society, an exclusive *kamaaina* club made up of missionary descendants. The society also maintains, in cooperation with the Hawaiian Historical Society, a small library behind the Mission Houses which is one of the finest repositories of rare and general Hawaiian history manuscripts and books in the world. It is open for use by private researchers during normal business hours.

"Western" Honolulu is just a little more than 150 years old, but she offers an odd mix of buildings to eyes interested in architecture. From the front entrance of Kawaiahao Church, a visual sweep of busy but pleasantly spaced King Street opens with the Greco-Roman **Library of Hawaii** (donated by philanthropist Andrew Carnegie and built between 1911 and 1912); continues *Diamond Head* past **Honolulu Hale**, Honolulu's "Mediterranean-Early Renaissance" City Hall (1928–1929); and ends in a burst of all-Americana at a red-brick structure with white pillars which locals facetiously call "Honolulu's Monticello," because it looks like Thomas Jefferson's historical home of that name. This structure, opposite the Mission Houses, was dedicated in 1916 as the **Mission Memorial Building** to honor the original New England missionaries and to serve as headquarters for the Hawaiian Evangelical Association. Since 1947 it's been used as a City Hall annex.

Back at the corner of Punchbowl and King, in front of Kawaiahao Church,

"Skygate," by Isamu Noguchi.

the tireless traveler can see, in a harbor direction down Punchbowl Street and just *Diamond Head* up Queen Street, another controversial downtown structure. But this one is controversial because its owners want to tear it down. It's the chalky red building (built about 1900) known locally as the **Royal Brewery**, or, according to the yellow sunburst sign above its entrance, THE — HONOLULU — BREW'G — & — MALT'G — CO. This gingerbread fantasy, at 533 S. Queen Street, was the original home of one of Hawaii's locally-produced brews, Primo Beer, and nostalgic drinking and non-drinking citizens have been lobbying for years to keep it from being destroyed. The 80-foot brewery's brick arches, corbels and wrought-iron fixtures reflect masonry craftsmanship and design concepts popular in America and Europe at the turn-of-the-century.

Indeed, curious and historic buildings abound throughout Honolulu, but perhaps the most interesting cluster of such structures outside of the Capitol District center are in a harbor area known as **Merchant Square**. This brick-rococo neighborhood is a pleasant four-block

walk down Merchant Street, Honolulu's old "Financial Boulevard," from the **Federal Post Office Building** (across the street from Iolani Palace). Many of the quaint bluestone, brick and stuccoed structures in that area have survived the demolition ball and construction crane and have been renovated into soulful little boutiques, pubs, restaurants, design studios and offices. One good example is the handsome, verandahed **Kamehameha V Post Office** built in 1871. This building, the first in Honolulu to be constructed entirely of concrete blocks, was used as a post office from 1884 to 1922, and since 1922 as a District Courts office building. Notice the old barrier cannon embedded in the sidewalk fronting this grand old hall.

Land of 'The Big Five'

But back in the urban and business open, a stroll up Bishop Street from the harbor carries a financier or funseeker past the graciously porticoed, sculpted and be-muraled suites and counting houses of the "Big Five" *kamaaina* corporations — all within 300 yards of each other. Big Five "men," as their

Dancers with the Honolulu City Ballet Company, prima ballerina Charlys Mirikitani Ing.

natty bosses are fond of referring to their employees, are proper as ever in tropical-weight suits, but if you're in the neighborhood on "Aloha Friday," which is every Friday, notice that nearly every man-on-the-street, Big Five type or not, is wearing a crisply pressed *aloha shirt*. And most *wahine* are draped in *muumuu* or *holoku* cut from this year's favored floral or geometric fabrics. Hawaii doesn't have "seasons" as such, so *aloha* clothing styles change according to new and approved tropical designs, even in male fashion circles.

There has been a longtime above-ground movement by Honolulu dress-code liberals to make every working day a bright "aloha wear" day, but apparently the dress-shirt-tie lobby is still strong enough to keep this rainbow-colored peril out of their *koa*-paneled board rooms. Except, of course, on Aloha Friday.

Honolulu's barons and burghers, however, have been very good about allowing "art" to proliferate in their conservative marketplaces. Murals, sculpture, tapestries and assorted other mind-benders abound throughout downtown and Honolulu in general. Art even

thrives underground, like in the Fort Street Mall's King Street underpass, where Oahu artist Edward Stasack has created a subterranean plaster-lava mural incised with several excellent copies of ancient Hawaiian petroglyphs. Another "downtown art" favorite, at least with children, is the 11-foot tall brushed bronze **Sun Disc** in front of the Financial Plaza of the Pacific at the corner of King and Bishop streets This solar sculpture by Bernard Rosenthal weighs about five tons, but can be made to rotate freely on its swivel base.

Move it, it's fun, even if you're an adult, but if you need to meditate on something less conceptual after accomplishing that mind-over-matter act, repair down Fort Street to Ala Moana Boulevard (where once stood the old "fort," *Ke Ku Nohu*, circa 1817 to 1857, which gave Fort Street its name). Cross Ala Moana, hop on the elevator to the top of the **Aloha Tower** and watch a fabled Hawaiian sunset disappear triumphantly into westside Pacific waters. This Aloha Tower vista sweeps from Diamond Head's stately profile and carries your eyes from left to right past Honolulu's southern waterfront and on

Kwan Yin Temple.

to the rugged northwest Waianae mountains. Behind you is Punchbowl Crater and the cloudy Koolaus, and before you — here and now — a wondrous Hawaiian sunset.

For the downtown wanderer seeking even more metaphysical forms of solace, there are many of those places too: on the *mauka* side of **Chinatown** — just past the confectioners, fish, flower and noodle mongers, and the lifesize statue of Dr. Sun Yat-sen at the entrance to the commercial **Cultural Plaza** — you'll find several Oriental temples where, as an ancient scholar once noted, *gold gods gathers light to themselves in the gloom.*

There's the Celestially appointed **Lam Sai Ho Tong** family temple above a market on the corner of River and Kukui streets, and on the opposite side of River Street and the sleepy Nuuanu Stream Canal (on the corner of Kukui Street and College Walk) sits a Japanese Shinto shrine. Both are opulent little sanctuaries, true to ancestral designs and redolent of the peculiar joss, incense and flowers favored in places thousands of miles west of Hawaii.

A more popular shrine is the **Kwan Yin Temple** a block *mauka* of here on Vineyard Boulevard, where both Buddhist and Taoist images gleam, but where a 10-foot tall statue of Kwan Yin, the Buddhist goddess of mercy, dominates.

Other solace seekers might prefer sitting quietly under a bo or walking in the shadows of other hardy tropical trees growing in the vast and verdant **Foster Botanic Gardens**, also on Vineyard Boulevard just beyond the Kwan Yin Temple. Several plants, such as the fragrant and ever-blossoming cannon ball tree indigenous to Guiana, are the only specimen of their genus and species in Hawaii.

Hidden *mauka* of the speedy Lunalilo Freeway and School Street are the serene **Liliuokalani Gardens**. In this little urban vale a deep natural stream and pool are fed by two entrancing waterfalls — **Makua and Waikahaluu ("rumbling water") Falls** — which erase any thoughts of the afternoon traffic jam you just left in Downtown Paradise. Swimming is allowed in these five acres of unspoiled nature which was Queen Liliuokalani's favorite town idyll and cooling-off spot.

Another central "town" place guaranteed to provide solace is **Thomas Square**, located between King and Beretania streets on the *Diamond Head* side of the Capitol District (alongside Ward Avenue). The square's high-spurting fountains, wildly adventitious banyans and bobbing monkeypod trees are an invitation to a noon nap.

Had enough rest? Then you're refreshed and ready for the **Honolulu Academy of Arts**, just across the street from Thomas Square (at 900 S. Beretania St.). "The Academy," as locals like to call the place, is Hawaii's most renowned fine arts center. Built in 1927 by the late Mrs. Charles Montague Cooke, the Academy's square block includes 29 galleries of Asian and Western art, plus five inner courts rich in flora and sculpture. Paintings by Modigliani, Diego Rivera, Picasso, Miro, Gauguin, Van Gogh, Mary Cassatt, Sargent and Camille Pissaro, and sculptures by Rodin, Bourdelle and Epstein, vie with contemporary masters and one of the finest Oriental collections in America for space in the Academy's permanent collection "on view." In addition, smaller antegalleries regularly host traveling exhibitions and shows by locally-renowned artists.

Torch ginger at the Foster Botanic Gardens.

IN AND ABOUT HONOLULU

From clouds-level, Oahu's populated coastal plains and lush interior valleys can be seen weaving in and out of steep central cliffs, or *pali*, and along narrow, sloping ridges which fan down from Oahu's two spinal mountain ranges — the **Koolaus** in the east and the **Waianaes** in the west. Honolulu proper and Waikiki are on the leeward, south side of the longer Koolau Range.

This zig-zaggy urban sprawl in and out of rimmed vales and along a curved seashore is most appreciated and spectacularly visible if you fly into Honolulu at night. In inky darkness, the island's white, ice blue and pink-amber street lights join commercial flashes of ruby, emerald and lapis neon to create a gigantic and scalloped lavaliere that glitters clearly for miles around.

At ground level, this flowing design — each scallop, curlicue and sparkling stone — evolves into a series of unexpected adventures. Indeed, one Oahu morning you can be groping through mist-shrouded rainforests dense with rainbows and jungle tangle, and that very noon, but a half-hour's drive and 25 miles away, your party of island-hoppers might find themselves chasing mongooses across jagged lava shelves.

In the greater Honolulu area alone there are more nature trail hikes than a hardy backpacker can negotiate in a few hurried months; and fringing Oahu are more than 130 sandy beaches, few of them ever seen by tourists (who like to offhandedly malign this populated place and seek sandy solitude on one of the more "in" neighbor islands).

Most first-time Oahu visitors hop onto a round-the-island tour bus complete with what local people call *hoomalimali*, *'ukulele* and *hula* dancers — *hoomalimali* being the Hawaiian word for flattering, but usually nonsensical small talk. That kind of ride can be fun, but it's also rushed, restricting and the driver usually drops his oohing and ahing charges at pre-arranged "tourist traps" where the *numbah one* — and only — prices include a percentage for the tour company.

Another, more personal alternative is the City's regular **TheBus** system, which completely circumnavigates the island for $1.00 (two 50 cent fares), usually in air-conditioned comfort. An Oahu TheBus traveler can laze along for miles, merely inhaling the scenery and marveling at local passengers. But when hunger or aesthetic curiosities beckon, he or she can hop off TheBus, muck around in some little cane town or fern forest, then reboard another TheBus going *your way*. It's a true "living on the easy" transportation bargain often overlooked by visitors. The best moving alternative to this style, of course, is to tour Oahu by private or rented motor car, but that is only if local friendships or your travel budget allow such convenience.

Meanwhile, pending one's choice of transport, breeze along on "Hawaiian time," meaning at no particular pace, on a few of the following suggested Oahu adventures. As a longtime traveler to Hawaii once noted, "You can drive around any island; the important thing is to get into the island itself and out of your car." Many of these unstructured visits can be covered by TheBus' numerous round and about the island routes (see Guide in Brief), but certain tucked-away spots will require a smaller vehicle or a bit of hiking to enjoy.

Preceding pages, the Koolaus from above Likelike Highway, Windward Oahu.

KALIHI-PALAMA

Auntie Mokihana suggests, for urban openers, that a tour of Kalihi-Palama, just up from downtown, would be a good Hawaiian way to start any Oahu day. But begin from the inside, she says, by first meeting for *ono* (delicious) Hawaiian *kaukau* (food) at one of Honolulu's many Hawaiian food cafes.

Eat up and then proceed up North King Street downtown to the venerable old **Kaumakapili Church** (at 766 N. King St. across Palama Street from the locally famous **Tamashiro's** fresh seafood market). *Kaumakapili*, the perch with eyes closed. This Congregational church originally was built in 1837 at the corner of Beretania and Smith streets downtown, but after that one burned down in 1900 during a big Chinatown fire, it was relocated at this busy Kalihi corner. Kaumakapili was the common man's counterpart to Kawaiahao Church. Commoner Hawaiians of the 19th Century disliked the long hike across town to ritzy Kawaiahao Church, and once

there they felt out-of-place alongside the wealthy *alii* who attended "the chiefs' church." So to solve both problems they built a more comfortable place of worship closer to their humbler Kalihi-Palama neighborhood.

A bit farther up N. King Street, then up Kalihi Street and across the Lunalilo Freeway, sits the world's greatest repository of Pacific and Polynesian researches and artifacts. This is the **Bernice Pauahi Bishop Museum**, established in 1889 by Charles Reed Bishop in **Kalihi-Waena** as a memorial to his wife Bernice, a princess and "the last of the Kamehamehas."

In academic centers, the Bishop Museum is known as one of the four most important multi-disciplinary museums in the United States, in a class with the Smithsonian Institution, the American Museum of Natural History and the Field Museum of Natural History. Besides housing the largest and most inclusive single collection of Hawaiian and other Polynesian curiosities on earth, the museum maintains natural history collections of more than 18,000,000 animal and plant specimens—including 420,000 prepared

Neon sign, Kalihi.

plants (the Herbarium Pacificum), 11,000,000 entomological specimens (insects and relatives), 20,000 lots of fish from the tropical Indo-Pacific region, some 6 million molluscs (shell animals) and a wide range of bird and mammal species.

However, the Bishop Museum is not just a dusty place favored by scholars; its public collections, both permanent and changing, are perhaps the most valuable briefing a first-time or many-times Hawaii visitor or resident can ever experience.

Available for viewing in the museum's *koa*-paneled halls and glass cases are carved and feathered gods, capes and other remnants of pre-contact Hawaii; brilliant regalia from the time of Kamehameha the Great; the monarchial crowns, thrones, royal orders and court costumes used in Iolani Palace by King Kalakaua and his sister, Queen Liliuokalani; and important pieces reflecting the sociocultural experiences of Hawaii's many immigrant groups.

The museum also manages and maintains a planetarium and astronomical observatory; and the *Falls of Clyde* four-masted sailing ship-museum in Hono-lulu harbor. All may be reached from Waikiki and downtown on board any of several red, double-decker London Transport buses which regularly shuttle visitors from the King's Alley shopping center via the *Falls of Clyde* to the museum. See the Guide in Brief section for details

Appropriately, the most *Hawaiian* center of learning in Hawaii sits just above the Bishop Museum in an area called **Kapalama Heights**. This is the **Kamehameha Schools**, a private complex of elementary and secondary schools supported by income earned by the vast estate of the Princess Bernice Pauahi Bishop (the largest private estate in Hawaii, with about 378,000 acres of land). The Bishop Estate's holdings— about a tenth of Hawaii—can be used solely to support and improve the Kamehameha Schools, which in turn can be attended only by students of Hawaiian or part-Hawaiian blood. This makes the school unique in the world, but a visit to its sprawling campus on the heights provides an observer with more than a high concentration of young Hawaiians. The view of the west side of Honolulu is quite spectacular.

Bishop Museum, interior gallery.

NUUANU VALLEY

Nuuanu, the cool height. More than a hundred years ago, the author of a guide book to Hawaii said Nuuanu was the "most beautiful among the valleys of Oahu." Though there are other valley residents who would differ, there was no doubt among early *haole* settlers that this valley was the best place to live. Nuuanu was the first suburb in which they built their Victorian mansions with broad *lanai*, and where they planted the monkeypods, banyans, Norfolk Island pines, bamboo, eucalyptus, African tulips and golden trees that now tower over the valley's indigenous ferns, hibiscus, *koa* and ginger (*awapuhi*). Many of these grand estates are still occupied and maintained by wealthy missionary descendants, but most have been sold or leased to institutions, churches or the resident consuls general of Asian nations. Nuuanu, where the "annexationists" drank Ceylon tea in their vast gardens, still has a *haole* elitist veneer in spots, but it's also rich in Hawaiian history.

In lower Nuuanu, at about the invisible point where Honolulu meets rainbows and mist, are the **Royal Mausoleum,** the **Queen Emma Summer Palace** and, among other points of interest, "The Western World's First Sake Brewery." And at Nuuanu's very top, on the windward edge of the cathedral-like Koolau mountains, is the **Nuuanu Pali,** perhaps the most windy precipice on Oahu.

But before stalking through the valley's lush, relax for a honky tonk moment at the creaky old **Pantheon Bar** at 1129 Nuuanu Avenue downtown. This pub near Nuuanu's sea-level source has known better days, but don't fret about its decor; instead, sit in the dust and funk and admire the massive mahogany bar and carved backbar which were shipped around Cape Horn to Hawaii in 1883. With those memories registered, leave "The Oldest Bar in the Newest State" and head *mauka* up Nuuanu Avenue to the "cool height" which gave this street its name.

Listen for the *oms* vibrating out of the **Soto Zen Mission of Hawaii** (at 1708 Nuuanu Avenue), a duplicate of a major Buddhist stupa at Bodhgaya, India, the

Nuuanu-style tea party, 1908.

holy place where Gautama Buddha gave his first sermon. This temple's Indianesque towers would appear most at home on a Himalayan crag, but a few Japanese influences — gardens of tinkling water, sand and *bonsai* plants — give its authenticity away, albeit in a charming and cosmopolitan way. This stupa, built in 1952, is somewhat similar to an even larger one, the **Honpa Hongwanji Mission** (nearby at 1727 Pali Highway), which was built here for the Shin Buddhist sect in 1918.

The "Father of Baseball"

Moments after one leaves the vibrational range of these two Honolulu centers of Buddhism, living force fields give way to the solemnity of old **Oahu Cemetery**. Half the names of local streets named after rich or famous *haole* residents can be seen on tombstones in this verdant memorial park. One in particular, though, has been receiving the meditative attention of serious sports fans from all parts of America. This is the layered, pink granite tomb of: "Alexander Joy Cartwright Jr. Born in New York City April 17, 1820. Died in Honolulu July 12, 1892."

This austere monument under a royal palm in the center of Oahu Cemetery (on the right side of its main entrance road) sits over the immortal remains of the man who invented America's grand old game, baseball. Though few people know Cartwright lived much of his life and died in Honolulu, millions in the baseball-crazy United States have heard of him as the man who dreamed up the baseball diamond concept, marked bases off at 90 feet apart, put nine players on a team, ruled that three outs and a team was through for an inning, and established nine innings as the length of a baseball game. The first baseball game ever played, under Cartwright's rules, took place on June 19, 1846, at Hoboken, New Jersey.

The "Father of Baseball" drifted west and eventually ended up in Hawaii while on a trip around the world. He liked Honolulu so much he stayed, and he became notable in local history not so much for teaching people here how to play baseball, which he did, but because he founded Honolulu's first volunteer fire department and served as its first fire chief from 1850 to 1859.

Only a few hundred yards farther up

Nuuanu Avenue on the opposite side of the street is the most important known burial spot in Hawaii — the **Royal Mausoleum**, where the bodies of Kings Kamehameha II, Kamehameha III, Kamehameha IV, Kamehameha V, Kalakaua, Queen Liliuokalani and other members or favored friends of those royal Hawaiian families were buried. The only two Hawaiian monarchs not buried here were King Lunalilo, who at his request was buried in a private tomb on the grounds of Kawaiahao Church, and Kamehameha the Great, whose bones were hidden away in a secret burial place to avoid defilement by potential power seekers.

The mausoleum, which lies on a 3.3 acre site chosen by Kamehameha V, was prepared in 1865 to replace an overcrowded royal burial tomb on the grounds of Iolani Palace. Its Gothic-revival chapel structure, built in the shape of a crucifix, was designed by Honolulu's first professional architect, Theodore Heuck, and originally contained 18 royal bodies. Later, the bodies were moved from this crowded chapel to separate crypts on these grounds.

This is a lovely, contemplative spot,

Swimming champion Duke Kahanamoku and baseball superstar Babe Ruth at Waikiki, 1939; and Baseball Hall of Fame plaque honoring Honolulu's "Father of Baseball."

and just below its stands of plumeria, *ti*, ginger, *kamani* and palms, you'll often hear the laughter of children swimming and diving into a deep pond at the base of Nuuanu Stream's **Kapena Falls**. On the mausoleum side of the falls, below the Pali Highway which curves and buzzes overhead, are also three important Oahu petroglyph sites, where ancient Hawaiian artists incised several primitive human and dog figures and other unexplained symbols into large stones alongside Nuuanu Stream. The popular dog figures are thought to be images of a ghost dog, *Kaupe*, who according to oral traditions used to haunt this valley. This petroglyph area is accessible through **Nuuanu Memorial Park**, another cemetery just *makai*, or on the sea side, of the mausoleum grounds.

On the opposite side of Nuuanu Avenue from these predominantly Christian burial sites and Polynesian wonders are two Buddhist complexes — the **Tenri Culture Center** (at 2236 Nuuanu Avenue) and the neighboring **Kyoto Gardens**, a serene little complex of gardens, *koi* ponds and a replica of a three-tiered **Sanji Pagoda** which stands at Nara in Japan.

Hot Sake and a Yellow Submarine

Nuuanu is a bit too spread out for walking browses, but while in the lower valley, Japan fanciers might enjoy crossing the Pali Highway to little **Pauoa Valley** and visiting "The Western World's First Sake Brewery" at 2150 Booth Road. **The Honolulu Sake Brewery and Ice Co., Ltd.**, founded 1908, is the first *sake* brewery in the United States and one of only four known *sake* breweries outside the Orient still actively producing that sweet rice wine (Brazil reportedly has three *sake* breweries).

The most fascinating thing about this clump of turn-of-the-century factory buildings and their *ichiban* (number one) product is that the brewery is operated traditionally, as *sake* breweries were during the last century. In Japan, nearly all *sake* breweries are highly automated and chemicalized, but this Honolulu brewery still makes *sake* by hand labor, and at last report, declined to add raw chemicals to speed up the brew's fermentation process. Prohibition and World War II (when the Japanese-owned brewery was shut down by martial law administrators following the Pearl Harbor attack) caused hardships for Honolulu Sake, but in 1970 its brewmaster, Takeo Nihei, received a special award from the Japanese Brewmasters' Association. The brewery also produces soy sauce and *kasu*, a *sake* by-product used for pickling and cooking.

From quiet Pauoa, a logical Nuuanu traffic flow will carry one back onto the swift Nuuanu Pali Highway (Route 61), which glides past the Royal Mausoleum, "Consulates Row" and mammoth umbrella trees to *Hanaiakamalama*, the "Foster Child of the Moon," known more commonly as the **Queen Emma Summer Palace**. This royal bower with a ginger and *ti*-lined driveway was built about 1847 and later sold to John Young II, an uncle of Queen Emma and son of Kamehameha the Great's chief *haole* adviser, the Britisher John Young. Queen Emma and Kamehameha IV in turn bought it from Young and named it *Hanaiakamalama* after a favorite Hawaiian demigoddess. Until Emma's death, the royal family used this home as a cool summer retreat, salon and courtly

Statue of Mary, Mother of Christ, St. Stephens Church on the Pali Highway, Nuuanu Valley.

social center. In 1890, the summer palace was purchased by the Hawaiian government and since 1911 has been part of a public park. The Daughters of Hawaii have maintained it as a museum since 1915.

In the palace's various grand rooms the Daughters of Hawaii have restored and tastefully displayed many of the royal family's personal belongings. Among enchanting items are a spectacular triple-tiered *koa* sideboard of Gothic design presented to Emma and Kamehameha IV by Britain's Prince Albert; a heavy gold necklace strung with tiger claws and pearls, which was given to Emma by a visiting maharajah; various opulent wedding and baby gifts given to the royal family by England's Queen Victoria, who was the Hawaiian Prince Albert's godmother; and numerous objects of purely Hawaiian design and royal purpose.

Among the most fascinating Hawaiian pieces are a stand of tall feather *kahili* (royal standards) in the Queen's master bedroom. These *kahili* are unusual because their tufts have been stripped, leaving the feathers' quills scraggy and nearly denuded. A palace guide explains that such tuftless *kahili* were used only in bedrooms, rooms used for meditation, and at funerals. They symbolize, she said, the fact that "life is often flying on another plane, stripped of its body," in such places.

At the back, mountain side of the palace is a long, grandly-appointed reception hall which Queen Emma had specially built to house a lavish party for the visiting Duke of Edinburgh (who for some unexplained reason didn't make it to the actual party). Meanwhile, outside the antique Hawaiian-Victorian interior are a proper rose garden, stands of *kukui* and *koa* trees, assorted Hawaiian flowers of seductively fragrant beauty, chattering Nuuanu birds and a sleepy little stream.

And behind and around the corner from the palace, off Puiwa Road, is a lovely little park, **Nuuanu Valley Park**, favored by lovers and daydreamers who like to lounge under its gigantic trees and play on its yellow submarine and old-fashioned playground swings.

A tour of lower Nuuanu Valley is pleasantly slow-going and preparatory for even more natural Nuuanu experiences. Continue with a drive (off the

A *hula* label localizes Honolulu's prize-winning sake.

NET 1.5 LITERS (50.7 FL. OZ.)   ALCOHOLIC CONTENT 15% TO 17% BY VOLUME

HAWAIIAN REFINED SAKE
TAKARA MUSUME

登録商標
REGISTERED   TRADE MARK

宝娘

PRODUCED AND BOTTLED BY
HONOLULU SAKE BREWERY & ICE CO., LTD.
HONOLULU, HAWAII 96813, U.S.A.

156

new Pali Highway) through the hanging vines, bamboo, wild ginger, jasmine and cool of Nuuanu's **Nuuanu Pali Drive**. Along this wending way through the forest you'll spot stately *kamaaina* mansions hidden away in the bush, a swimming and mud-sliding hole with the intriguing name **"Jackass Ginger,"** and, on rainy days, dozens of tiny waterfalls which run wherever wrinkled Koolau mountain ridges let them flow. One of the larger falls (on the left side of Nuuanu Valley just before you reach the Pali Lookout and two short tunnels which connect Nuuanu and Honolulu proper with Oahu's windward side) is called **"Upside Down Falls,"** real name **Waipuhia Valley Falls**, because its waters often are blown straight back up a cliff and turn into mist before they can reach a precipice below.

The **Nuuanu Pali Lookout** lies above a well-marked road spur just off the Pali Highway, and is perhaps the most written-about scenic spot on Oahu. Tour buses and assorted rental cars often clog the parking lot near this famous precipice, but it's still a magical spot worth visiting many times. During every season gale-force winds rush up this

Koolau palisade and literally stand one's hair on end. Also, the view of Oahu's windward side is magnificent: Alpine peaks rise behind and below like church spires, green and yellow banana groves ripple far below like breezy stands of wheat, flashy subdivisions are reduced to neat map grids, and tiny ship dots at sea seem to be steaming toward an unreachable horizon.

Since the early 19th Century guidebooks to Hawaii have named this gorgeous spot Oahu's number one tourist attraction. Verily, the 1,000-foot high Nuuanu Pali Lookout does rank among the best scenic points in Hawaii, and indeed in the world.

However, don't swallow an oft-repeated myth about the place which claims that this was the site of a huge battle in April, 1795—The Battle of Nuuanu—in which Kamehameha the Great and his legions drove hundreds or even thousands of Oahu warriors to their death over these palisades. Perhaps a few fleeing warriors met their ends here, by being pushed over or by committing suicide, but the usual story in its dramatized and touristic form is of great irritation to historians who know better.

PUNCHBOWL, PAPAKOLEA, AND TANTALUS

Another relaxing Honolulu tour is that of the three town heights areas commonly known as **Punchbowl, Papakolea** and **Tantalus-Round Top**.

Punchbowl Crater was known to Hawaiians as *Puowaina*, or "the hill for placing (of sacrifices)," because in olden times it was a site of human sacrifices. Like Diamond Head and Koko Head craters, Punchbowl (which looms just above downtown Honolulu at the top of Ward Avenue and just off circling Prospect Drive) emerged during Oahu's most recent eruption phase about 150,000 years ago. It and other similar tuff cones were pushed by volcanic action through a vast coral plain that had built up around this leeward side of the Koolau mountain range.

Today this sacrificial site is more famous as the location of the **National Memorial Cemetery of the Pacific** where more than 21,000 servicemen who served in World Wars I and II, and the Korean and Vietnam Wars, are buried.

The veterans' small flat white headstones, level with Punchbowl's expanse of grass, stretch like a computer design across the crater's 112-acre floor.

Regular Easter Sunrise, Veterans Day and Memorial Day services honor all 21,000 fighting men buried here and another 26,280 listed in a **"Courts of the Missing"** monument on Punchbowl's interior *Ewa* slope. But, ironically, the most famous person buried here was not a conventional war casualty or deceased veteran. Rather, he was a journalist whose ability to write about the average foot-slogging GI made him one of the most widely-read and beloved combat correspondents ever published.

This was **Ernest Taylor "Ernie" Pyle**, whose remains rest at gravesite number D109, surrounded by many of the very same GI's he wrote about and died with in one of World War II's last combat actions. Pyle was 44 when on April 18, 1945, he was hit and killed by Japanese machine gun fire on the small Pacific islet of Ie Shima west of Okinawa. Though he was originally buried in a wartime military cemetery at Okinawa, his remains were transferred along with those of other soldiers to Punchbowl in

Easter Sunday sunrise service at scenic Punchbowl, April 20, 1924.

158

1949 when the National Memorial Cemetery of the Pacific was officially opened.

At the spot where Pyle died on Ie Shima, a special tablet said: "At this spot the 77th Infantry Division lost a buddy." But in Punchbowl his marker is plain and simple, just like any other serviceman's (and his burial here was allowed not because he was a famous war writer, but because he had qualified by serving honorably with the U.S. Navy during World War I).

Fancy or not, shortly after Pyle was buried at Punchbowl, thousands of people a month began visiting his gravesite. Their numbers kept increasing as Pyle's posthumous fame was publicized, and in recent years, cemetery officials estimate, as many as 50,000 people a month visit his grave. To protect the grass around it the park eventually had to install special marble slabs on three sides of his plot.

Persons further interested in World War II history should study the several large and finely-detailed mosaic maps inside the memorial building. These ceramic panels chronologically recount famous Pacific battles fought during the past century. During World War II years this crater was honeycombed with storage tunnels dug into its inner harbor-side walls. The tunnels were used not for armaments, but to store U.S. currency. Understandably, Punchbowl was one of the most-guarded and off-limits places in Hawaii at that time.

From Punchbowl Crater's mountain side entrance, Puowaina Drive crosses a bridge over Prospect Street and drifts along a steep valley through one of Oahu's few Hawaiian Homes homestead communities. This is **Papakolea**, a neighborhood where persons of at least half-Hawaiian blood are allowed to lease homesites at a nominal fee established by Congress with the Hawaiian Homes Act of 1920. This complex, and others like it on all inhabited islands except Lanai and Niihau, are the Hawaiian equivalent of an American Indian reservation. But this particular neighborhood is doubly fascinating because it sits beside and below **Makiki Heights** and **Tantalus**, two of the island's most exclusive and pricey residential areas.

This side-by-side social contrast is most obvious when one leaves country-like Papakolea at the top of Puowaina Drive and turns right onto Tantalus Drive, a winding mountain road that twists below, around and above some of Oahu's largest *kamaaina* estates. Follow Tantalus Drive to its zig-zag conclusion and you will find yourself at some of the coolest and most panoramic vantage points on this side of the island. Dare to hike one of the many marked trails near the mountain's 2,013-foot peak, and you'll soon be thick into bamboo and fern beauty. There are at least a dozen knock-out viewpoints on this mount, but locals seem to agree that the best one—and perhaps the finest overall panorama of greater Honolulu from Diamond Head all the clear way to Pearl Harbor—is from **Puu Ualakaa State Park** on Tantalus' *makai-Diamond Head* flank.

A few hair-pin turns below this green garden peak is a straightaway stretch alongside a low lava rock wall which for decades has been a parking place much preferred by lovers and full moon watchers. Pause here for an unobstructed postcard view of Diamond Head and gaze into populated but still lush **Manoa**, a valley famous for its rainbows and unexpected curtains of cooling rain.

Memorial statuary in Punchbowl; and Ernie Pyle's former marker on Ie Shima Island.

THE SOLEMN PRIDE

MAKIKI, MANOA AND MOILIILI

Greater Honolulu's three M's—Makiki, Manoa and Moiliili—occupy areas just *mauka*, or mountain side, of Ala Moana and Waikiki. *Makiki*, named after a type of stone used as weights for octopus lures; *Manoa*, meaning "vast;" and *Moiliili*, the "pebble lizard" who was destroyed by Hiiaka, the goddess Pele's younger sister.

- **Makiki** today is largely a residential flats and heights just below Tantalus which some demographers say is the most highly concentrated part of Oahu after Waikiki. It's a prime example of what other parts of Honolulu may look like in a few years if property development keeps pace with the city's growing population. Condominia at its vertical best, and a nice warm up for the pleasant cool and neighborly charms of adjacent *Manoa*.
- **Manoa**, like Nuuanu, has long been preferred by discriminating islanders as a residential refuge from the heat and hassle of inner, commercial and concrete

Honolulu. Indeed, both Manoans and Nuuanans consider their places of residence the closest one can get to Eden and still be near shopping centers, TheBus lines and clear television reception.

Near the entrance to Manoa Valley, at the corner of Punahou and Beretania Streets, missionary descendants in 1924 built a new place of worship which, like Kawaiahao Church, is more Boston than Honolulu in its architecture. This is **Central Union Church**, the island's newest center of true *kamaaina* missionary social life. This grand stone structure would have pleased members of the first Congregationalist company.

Farther up Punahou Street, just as the street rises into Manoa proper, is the educational apple of every missionary descendant's eye: this is the private **Punahou School**, once called Oahu College, which the Reverend Hiram Bingham and his colleagues established in 1841 for the education of children of Congregational missionaries. The land on which the school stands was given to the mission for use as a school at the request of the powerful and christianized Queen Kaahumanu; and because it was the site

Hala and hala sculpture, Punahou School.

of a well-known freshwater spring, the school became known as *Punahou* which means "new spring."

That same spring which gave Punahou its name and which graces the school's seal (along with a *hala* tree and taro leaves) still bubbles fresh water into a pond which encircles the old campus' lovely new **Robert Shipman Thurston, Jr., Memorial Chapel**. The chapel's entrance doors, fashioned of honeygrained *koa* and embellished with copper repoussé panels created by artists Jean Charlot and Evelyn Giddings, lead solace seekers into a stained glass refuge which was inspired, according to stained glass artist Erica Karawina, by a Eugenia Sheppard poem that sings of "trumpeting rubies, redder than fire." In all, some 20 lancets, 10 to a side, play hot and cool colors upon the *koa*, lava and plaster of this circular chapel designed by architect Vladimir Ossipoff.

If you are among the fortunate few tourists who drive or walk by Punahou School's lava stone walls on the rare June through October evenings when the school's gigantic nightblooming cereus open like petaled moons, Punahou and these unusual Mexican cactus blossoms will remain indelibly stamped at the back of your traveling mind. This flower (*Hylocereus undatus*), a prickly climber brought from Acapulco by a visiting sea captain in the early 1800s, has foot-wide, many-petaled blossoms which open only at night — from about 8 p.m. and until Manoa's morning warm wilts them into a droopy daytime sleep.

Only about two blocks beyond Punahou is the junction of Manoa and East Manoa roads. From this point, the valley is a traveler's fancy. Some folks prefer to hike to the back of the valley — beyond the vast **Paradise Park** full of exotic birds. In those green reaches — where 160 to 200 inches of rain a year quench the wild thirsts of mountain apples, guavas, passion fruit and thimble berries — cool **Manoa Falls** bounces rainbow haloes off the happy heads of patient hikers who wallow like lost innocents in the headwaters of **Manoa Stream**.

Other Manoaphiles are partial to quiet strolls through the University of Hawaii's verdant **Lyon Arboretum** or through the **Manoa Chinese Cemetery** at the end of East Manoa Road. And yet others are partial to sit-down pastry at

Bird of Paradise Manoa.

the **Waioli Tea Room** (at 3016 Oahu Avenue), where the Salvation Army maintains a grass shack similar to the one in which Robert Louis Stevenson composed poems and short stories at Waikiki.

It was in Manoa Valley, at a favorite summer home, that Hawaii's powerful Queen Kaahumanu died just before dawn on June 5, 1832. According to accounts by missionaries of the time, when Kaahumanu was nearing death she asked to be taken to her favorite valley of Manoa. There, in a small cottage, a bed of fragrant *maile* and *awapuhi* (ginger) was prepared, over which was spread a coverlet of velvet. Upon this bed the Queen lay down to die, her hands clutching a newly-printed copy of the New Testament in Hawaiian given her by the Rev. Hiram Bingham.

Bare Feet, Books and Rainbows

At the sea side of this easy-going vale, where East Manoa Road runs into University Avenue, one can jog left onto University and back towards Waikiki into Lower Manoa. Here is the center of higher education in Hawaii, the expansive 300-acre **University of Hawaii at Manoa** campus attended by some 21,000 full-time students.

This institute has the usual academic and post-adolescent aura typical of any university, except that its student body — like Hawaii — is generally more colorful, casual and ethnically mixed than a university campus on the U.S. mainland or in Asia. T-shirts, walking shorts and bare feet are more common in classrooms than sweatshirts, Oxford cloth and wing-tipped shoes. Light, flower-patterned attire prevails in the UH's hallowed halls, and, appropriately, the school's athletic teams are known as the Rainbows.

At the **East-West Center**, a federally-funded institute designed to promote mutual understanding among the peoples of Asia, the Pacific and the United States, are numerous wonders of the East — including a Thai pavilion personally presented and dedicated by King Bhumibol Adulyadej of Thailand in 1967; a **Korean Studies Center** building hand-painted in the busy and intricate style of Seoul-area Yi Dynasty palaces; and the center's main hall, **Jefferson Hall**, which is fronted by large

The Mall, University of Hawaii, Manoa.

Chinese dog-faced lions and backed by a Japanese garden rich in sculptured grass, well-placed stones, *bonsai* trees and waterfalls which fall like music into a lily pond full of nibbling *koi*.

On either end of Jefferson Hall (designed by the renowned architect I.M.Pei)—above stairwells which descend and rise to the hall's dining and meeting rooms—are two complementary East-West murals, one, representing the West, by prolific local artist Jean Charlot, and another, reflecting Eastern philosophies, by Affandi of Jogjakarta, Central Java, Indonesia. (Another important Charlot mural may also be seen in **Bachman Hall**, the University's main administration building.)

Though the campus' architecture—which ranges from a battlefield bunker-with-gun slits look to wood-frame bungalow offices with broad, breezy verandahs—is distressingly eclectic and a planner's nightmare, the buildings are enhanced considerably by the 560 or more types of trees and plants which shade generous lawns and park benches.

Farther downhill from Manoa is what in most university towns would be called the local commercial area. This is **Moiliili**, where pubs, boutiques, moderately-priced cafes, bookstores, pool halls and other such student-preferred haunts proliferate.

Another area eminently worthy of afternoon poke-about strolls is a community about a half mile from Koko Head of Moiliili which has been known since ancient times as Kaimuki (properly pronounced Kah-eemoo-kee). *Kaimuki*, the *ti* oven, is mentioned in early Hawaiian chants as a place where mysterious *menehune* toasted *ti* leaves in ovens.

These days **Kaimuki** (which even oldtimer locals insist on mispronouncing Kye-moo-kee) is a wonderful urban spot rich in red dirt, mango trees, mutt dogs, saimin stands, porn theaters and always busy beauty parlors. Its character is frozen somewhere in the late 1940s or early Fifties. Indeed, Kaimuki is to Hawaii what Dayton is to Ohio.

Compared to other places in America, Hawaii maintains a slow, easy-going pace. And in Kaimuki, that pace — and life itself — gets even slower than you may ever want to be.

Affandi's "East mural Jefferson Hall East-West Center.

WINDWARD OAHU

Once your mental clock has wound itself down, and time no longer ticks away in readily perceived units of experience, and you are one with waving palms, falling coconuts and dancing surf, it is time to head for "the country." Curiously, though urban sprawl is creeping into her most vulnerable corners, Oahu's islanders still use this euphemism, "the country," to identify any place beyond **Ewa** or **Koko Head**. Everything between those two points is, by contrast, "in town."

Perhaps the best transitional way for a visitor to leave said *town* for said *country* is to glide out on the south coastal route from Waikiki to the Windward Side. This tour begins at the **Diamond Head Lighthouse** and continues in a broad five-mile coastal arc toward the next landmark, **Koko Head**. Enroute you will pass through the modern bedroom communities of **Waialae-Kahala**, **Waialae-Iki**, **Aina Haina**, **Niu Valley**, **Kuliouou**, **Hawaii Kai** and **Portlock**. These are all expansive and expensive suburbs where Honolulu's commuter *chic* thrive in poolside, dockside and tiki-torchlight splendor.

The drier side of the island came into living vogue during the past two decades since Statehood (in 1959) when Honolulu proper began running out of living space. Until then, now pricey Waialae-Kahala was notable for its vegetable gardens and piggeries, and the rest of this southern crescent was given over to dry scrub and sunburn. But a Sixties population splurge took care of that: Today, this part of Oahu is a sprawling sequence of roof-to-roof housing tracts and shopping centers — most of them on land parcels leased from large private estates which control this side of the island.

At **Kahala**, at the end of ritzy Kahala Avenue, is the **Kahala Hilton**, perhaps the nicest Hilton hotel in America, where wealthy guests nibble *pupus*, tipple martinis and ooh and ah as beachboys twice daily feed prancing porpoises and penguins in the hotel "fishpond." So much twinkling goes on in this hotel's starry, celebrity-occupied suites, that local newspaper columnists

Wilhelmina Rise, suburban heights and lights above Kaimuki.

refer to it as the Kahollywood Hilton. Every January, this gracious inn is *the* center of the sporting world when the Hawaiian Open PGA Golf Tournament is held on the manicured fairways and greens of the neighboring **Waialae Country Club**. Not bad, say oldtimers, for the site of a dusty old Hawaiian fishing village.

A Hot Pink Palace With Cool Poodles

At the other end of Kalanianaole Highway and Maunalua Bay, on the town side of Koko Head and Koko Crater, is a vast, self-contained community, **Hawaii Kai**, created by the late billionaire industrialist Henry J. Kaiser during the early 1960s. Kaiser's cluster of townhouses, condominiums, tract homes and a private inland waterway was formerly a parched expanse of *kiawe*, red earth and a shallow, neglected Hawaiian fishpond called *Kuapa*. Today, about 25,000 people call this dry valley home, and its projected future population is 50,000 to 60,000.

To be near his work, old man Kaiser built for him and his wife a pink home across the highway on Portlock Road below Koko Head. Not a usual little house, but a flamingo pink palace (pink was his wife's favorite color), complete with a principal mansion, guest houses, boathouse, greenhouse, trophy house, picnic house, servants' house, two swimming pools, tennis courts, yacht dock and a $20,000 air-conditioned poodle house and exercise yard. Kaiser's Texas buddy, President Lyndon Baines Johnson, stayed here in 1968 and exchanged war stories with fellow presidents Park Chung Hee of South Korea and Nguyen Van Thieu of the Republic of South Vietnam; and two years before that LBJ summit conference, in 1966, Jackie Kennedy and her kids were tenants during a frolic-filled summer. Those were the days, but even pink palaces fade into dreamland, and in 1971 the **Kaiser Estate** was bought by two millionaire bachelor brothers from Oklahoma.

From atop Koko Head rise, Hawaii Kai is a blazing, white-roofed flash of super-suburbia, but most of that eyestrain disappears as Kalanianaole Highway cuts over a saddle ridge and deposits you above the South Seas dream which is **Hanauma Bay**.

Hanauma Bay near Koko Head.

Hanauma Bay is an emerald blue *cul-de-sac* chock full of protected Hawaiian fishes which boldly swim up and kiss your face mask. *Hanauma*, "the curved bay," is an extinct volcanic crater or tuff cone which was eroded by the sea into a vast aquarium. From the cliffs above, it's easy to understand why Hollywood producers chose this State sealife refuge as a prime location for the filming of Elvis Presley's 1961 movie "Blue Hawaii." If you spend some breezy moments gamboling and snorkeling on that same palm fringed wink of sand and under those bluer than blue waters, chances are your dreams too will "come true in blue Hawaii."

Farther north along this jagged parkland's surf-pounded cliffs, other islands — Lanai, Molokai, and on clear days, Maui — loom out of the sea like blue ghosts. And at a next cliffside turn, packs of pink tourists wait at a parking lot lookout to hear the honking of the **Halona Blowhole**, a lava tube that does a brief geyser-like shtick at odd pressurized moments when the right incoming sea swell pushes through its underwater entrance. Appropriately, *halona* means "peering place."

Body-Whomping as Art

From that famous *puka*, or hole, this curving road makes a pleasant descent into **Sandy Beach**, and a quick rise to **Makapuu Point** and **Makapuu Beach Park**. Both Sandy and Makapuu are prized for the occasionally brutal but beautiful form of their bodysurfing waves. Lifeguards are almost always stationed near these body-whomping spots, but gremmie (inexperienced) bodysurfers are advised, no matter how strong at swimming they think they are, to play with caution in Sandy and Makapuu's top-to-bottom piledrivers. Indeed, the disconcerting sound of a neck snapping is not unknown in these fun but fickle waters.

At Makapuu — below a picture-pretty white lighthouse perched on a craggy black lava palisade — rough open seas, sheer black cliffs, hill-sized sand dunes and a great diving rock make for a grand playground and spectacular view. Offshore are two small islands — a small, greenish-black one in the foreground called **Kaohikaipu Island** and a larger, adze-shaped one properly named **Manana**, but more commonly known as

Snorkeling at Hanauma.

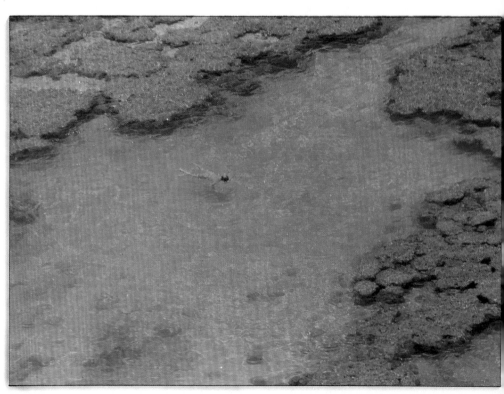

Rabbit Island (not because of its slight rabbit's head shape, but because it was formerly used as a rabbit-raising farm by a local plantation manager). A few desperate bunnies still hop about on this submerged tuff cone, but officially Manana is now a State-protected sanctuary for seabirds.

On Makapuu's inland side, if wind conditions are amenable, brilliantly colored bands of hang-glider enthusiasts may be seen floating like huge birds in thermal currents which sweep up the face of Makapuu's sheer 1,200-foot sea cliffs. Some kite fliers call this place "Hang Glider's Heaven" because of its ideal wind and take-off conditions. Ideal, yes, but also deadly: numerous hang gliders have died in Hawaii since the sport first soared to popularity in 1972. Glider accidents usually occur when freak winds or "technical problems" cause the aluminum and dacron kites to smash into the cliffs. However, like surfing cousins who ride monster-sized waves with few qualms, these 20th Century Icaruses continue to leap with increasing daring and regularity off Makapuu's *pali*.

Some kite-flyers have maneuvered their crafts all the way out to Rabbit Island on "inter-island flights." One chap, Mike Benson, who runs the Tradewinds Hang Gliding Center in Kailua, set Hawaii's out-and-back state record in late 1980 with a 35 mile flight from Makapuu to Waihee Valley and back. Benson also holds the state one-way record of 31 miles (flown in 1978 from Makapuu to the Brigham Young University-Hawaii campus in Laie). Another Hawaii aerialist, Jim Wills, in May of 1980 set a world record for time aloft by riding Makapuu thermals for 24 hours, 31 minutes and 7 seconds.

Below that neck-twisting focal point are other intelligent mammals who prefer a thicker medium for their daring antics. These are professional killer whales, porpoises, penguins, seals and other such aquatic creatures who pirouette, clap, and leap through hoops wearing *leis* for tourists who visit **Sea Life Park**, an arena-aquarium similar to such complexes in Florida and California. This park is the scene of fascinating aquanautics, but serious oceanographers might be more interested in the 700-foot pier and boathouse just north of here called the **Makai**

Body-whomping at Sandy Beach.

Undersea Test Range. This Makapuu facility is full of earnest Captain Nemos who, like that Jules Verne character, regularly conduct undersea explorations in futuristic submarines and little glass bubble marinemobiles. Their world, however, is not open to the general public.

The Koolaus: Green Spires Carved by God

For the next 30 miles or so, prepare to be dominated literally and psychologically by the peaks, *pali* and hypnotic lights and shadows which shift and play off Oahu's **Koolau Mountain Range.** Like a massive crenellated curtain ·which parts now and then to expose lone spires, fluted columns, crystal falls and little green valleys, these cliffs dwarf all other physical and social realities in their vicinity. The Koolaus, as the Hawaiians like to poetize, *lei i ka noe, wear mist as a lei,* rainbows like jewels, and rainfall like running tears. On and on they stretch — from Makapuu to Kahuku — like a chain of cathedrals designed by Gaudi, carved by God and painted by Gauguin.

Various windward towns, meanwhile

exist sleepily, and sometimes shockingly, beneath this awesome beauty.

Waimanalo, a tough little country town, has grazing livestock, cockfighting fans, native Hawaiians and esteemed backyard musicians (including Hawaii's most famous folksinger, Gabby Pahinui), thrashing through thorny *kiawe* and snoozing under seaside ironwoods. *E komo mai e na ho a aloha, welcome inside with love,* says a sign in front of the **Waimanalo Assembly of God Church**. Waimanalo still slumbers, but in 1977 a first stop light, the biggest traffic change in years, rudely began interrupting the central Waimanalo corner of Paolima Street and Kalanianaole Highway.

Beyond the dude ranches and reformatory school of upper Waimanalo rise the twin peaks of **Olomana**, a mount which might look more appropriate snow-covered and in the Swiss Alps. Olomana casts morning shadows at **Maunawili**, an emerald vale where two parting lovers inspired the good Queen Liliuokalani to write her timeless song "Aloha 'Oe." But just minutes past Olomana, Maunawili, and their fragrant cow pad-

Hanggliding, above Sea Life Park, Makapuu, and Rabbit Island.

docks and banana groves, are Oahu's second and third most-populated towns—**Kailua and Kaneohe**—which unfurl in a ticky-tacky, but somehow homey, snarl of tract houses, drive-on lawns, barking *poi* dogs (mongrels), screeching cats in heat and all the other suburban amenities middleclass and retired Americans have grown to expect.

Enter **Kailua town** on Kailua Road and pause for a quiet moment under the loud banyan tree on the corner of Oneawa Street and Kuulei Road. Your motor car's passengers will be charmed by the avant-garde symphony of mynah birds squawking in cacophonous stereo from that tree's every branch. But don't pause for too long or your car will soon be up to its hubcaps in mynah matter.

A fine, swimmable beach stretches the length of **Kailua Bay**, but the most convenient access to this wide swath of residential sand is at **Kailua Beach Park** (on Kalaheo Avenue) just before you enter the charming little community known as **Lanikai**. Sportsmen may be pleased to know that this windy area is also a favored place for catamaran sailing and windsurfing, and in 1978 was the site of the **World Cup Regatta** inter-

national windsurfing championships for men and women.

Nearby Kaneohe town, and the adjacent and large **Kaneohe Bay**, are notable for residential subdivisions which hug the bayshore, a large **Kaneohe Marine Corps Air Station** (on scenic **Mokapu Peninsula**), and a small island, **Coconut Island (Mokuo Lo'e)**, which is the site of a **University of Hawaii Marine Biology Laboratory**. But the bay itself, and beaches·which rim it, are very silty, much polluted and not worth considering for usual swimming and surfing purposes. Kaneohe area cultural attractions, however, include a masterly ceramic tile mural by senior island artist Juliette May Fraser at the **Benjamin Parker Elementary School** (on Waikalua Road), and a serene **Byodo-In Temple** that glows under 2,000-foot Koolau cliffs in **Ahuimanu Valley**. This temple (open from 9 a.m. to 5 p.m. daily) is a replica in termite-proof cement of Kyoto's famous Byodo-In Temple of Equality, and is the major structure in the **Valley of the Temples Memorial Park** off Kahekili Highway. Its duplicate beauties are greatly enhanced by its glorious Koolau backdrop, but the

Windsurfing regatta at Lanikai Beach.

seven-ton bronze bell, great golden Buddha of the Western Paradise, two-acre reflecting lake, peacocks, swans, ducks, meditation niches and dangling waterfalls also enhance its imported architecture.

Ancient Hawaiian Aquaculture

Very important culturally and historically are a series of ancient fishponds which rim Windward shores on the north side of Kaneohe town. Oahu once had some 97 such fishponds, which were used by Hawaiians to grow fresh seafood, but now only five are left intact. Four are on this windward coast, and a fifth is at Okiolilepe at Pearl Harbor. The windward four are at **Heeia** (just outside Kaneohe on Kamehameha Highway), **Kahaluu**, **Molii** (off **Kualoa Point**) and **Huilua** (at **Kahana Bay**). The splendid **Heeia Fishpond**, on the Kaneohe side of **Kealohi Point** near the **Trader Hall's** tourist attraction, is Oahu's biggest. It has a wall 12 feet wide and 5,000 feet long, and once enclosed a fish-raising area of 88 acres. In recent years land developers have proposed turning this classical example of Hawaiian engineering and biological production into a small-boat marina, but conservationists, historians, and archeologists are fighting those plans, so far with limited but encouraging success.

Onward and northward along Kamehameha Highway, the much sung about "living on the easy" concept comes to sleepy, believable life in the lap-lap of miniature waves against fishing boats docked under stilted homes, on panes of sunlight skipping·across taro paddies and the poetic sound of Hawaiian place names: Maeli`eli (mah-el-ee-el-ee), Kahaluu (kah-ha-loo-oo), Waiahole (Wai-ah-ho-lay) and Waikane (Wai-ka-nay).

In the last two places—the **Waiahole** and **Waikane** valleys—where taro, orchid, anthurium and vegetable truck farms still lend a tropical, country touch to the landscape, developers recently wanted to build a tract of 6,700 expensive homes and commercial facilities on the fertile heights and lowlands. But valley residents said no to such bulldozing and paving, and eventually—after much protest, poetry and fear—they managed to stop outright this urban

Kualoa, one of many playful beaches on Oahu's Windward side.

encroachment on their rural lifestyle. So today, you can still be charmed by the little Japanese lady selling backyard papayas and bananas from a shaded roadside stand, by horses grazing handsomely in quiet meadows, and by vast stretches of blood-red anthuriums and purple-pink vanda orchids glistening with morning dew.

To insure that the area remains this way, the State in 1976 bought 600 acres of the threatened Waiahole Valley and indicated that from then on the valley will be retained under a safe agricultural zoning designation to keep out speculative urban developments which might alter its rural character. Meanwhile, negotiations continue for the second valley, Waikane.

Symbolic of the struggle waged by area farmers during the mid-1970s is a mural on the north side of the old **Waiahole Poi Factory** building by Waiahole artist-resident Martin Charlot, one of the late Jean Charlot's four sons. This wall painting is of a shackled Hawaiian resembling Christ being led by an unidentified force out of the Eden he lives in. Local art in a smaller format may also be found inside the Waiahole

Poi Factory, which no longer makes *poi* but has gained local fame as a gallery where authentically wrought reproductions of ancient Hawaiian musical instruments and other artifacts can be commissioned and bought.

At **Kualoa Regional Park**, heads usually crane seaward for long, lingering looks at a cute little offshore island known to Hawaiians as *Mokoli'i* (the little *mo'o*, or lizard), but to everyone else as **Chinaman's Hat**. On low tide days, one can easily wade-hike on the reef to this coolie hat, bask on its palmshaded brim and photograph the graceful Hawaiian stilts (*ae'o*) and frigate birds (*iwa*) which soar overhead. Meanwhile, back on shore, on the south side of the park proper, is the aforementioned **Moli'i Fishpond** with a 4,000-foot-long retaining wall.

Kualoa has long been known as a part of Oahu which was exceedingly sacred to ancient Hawaiians and favored as a residential area by high chiefs. Today it is celebrated mainly for its fine beach, Chinaman's Hat, Moli'i Fishpond and sweeping **Kualoa Ranch**, the last good-sized working cattle spread on Oahu. Of lesser interest are the crumbling remains

aneohe rice elds and ne Koolau nountains, 920; and earby .aaawa 'alley, 1979.

up the road of an old sugar mill that was built in the 1860s by Dr. Gerrit P. Judd. Judd built this mill at a time when the sugar industry was beginning to experience tough financial times, so it was soon closed and hasn't been used in any way, save as a conveniently-placed tourist curiosity, since 1871.

A Lover Frozen In Place

A false front of another sort sits atop the green promontory, **Mahie Point**, which overlooks the *hala* groves, reedy lagoons and whistling ironwoods that rim the silent beauty of **Kahana Bay**. This is the **Crouching Lion**, a rock formation which was given that glamorous and commercial-sounding title by an entrepreneur who wanted to give his restaurant — the Crouching Lion Inn — a romantic name. From a certain prospect, the rock does look somewhat like a lion, but this geological landmark's real name is **Kauhi**. Kauhi, according to Hawaiian tradition, was a demigod from Tahiti who was imprisoned up there by followers of the fire goddess Pele. Legend says that Kauhi one day saw Pele's sister, Hiiaka, fell in love with her,

and tried to break out of his prison to get to her; but while he was doing so he was frozen in place, in his present crouching position. He has remained there ever since a prisoner of passion, and much misnamed.

Straw baskets bulging with plump papayas, "alligator pears" (avocadoes), and yellow hands of Chinese bananas hanging from twisted coat hangers inside weathered wooden fruit stands reinforce one's most optimistic vision of paradise. But windward Oahu visitors must be warned they will also see roadside examples of the most awful Hawaiian kitsch they can imagine. Foremost among these distateful objects of touristic commerce are once fine specimens of white reef coral which have been spray-painted in day-glo chartreuse, pink, orange and other such colors by shopkeepers of indiscriminate taste. One will also encounter, improbably, under coconut palm or fern bracken, mustached Palestinian rug merchants who sell machine-made velveteen tapestries and Filipino *puka* shell necklaces. Then, of course, there are overly romanticized sights — such as the aforementioned Crouching Lion —

Kitsch coral for sale, Swanzy Beach Park area.

which may be misleading. Another such misnamed locale is the **Sacred Falls** at **Hauula**, a waterfall one has to pay $1 per motorcar to visit and which is not really Sacred Falls, but **Kaliuwaa Falls**. *Kaliuwaa*, the *canoe leak*, was said to be an ancient hangout of the legendary pig god Kamapuaa, who in mythological times assumed the form of a man or pig, depending upon his intentions of the moment. The 30-minute hike to these falls along **Kaluanui Stream** is a bit dry and rocky at times, but does offer pleasant botanical moments when fragrances and fruits falling off Java plum, guava, *kukui* and mountain apple trees assault one's weary senses. The murmuring stream, trail and shockingly cool pool you can dive into at the end of the trail are a nice off-highway dose of rural refreshment.

Adventurers who prefer interior sights and comforts should continue due north to **Laie**, a predominantly Mormon community long known for its severely chaste temple — **The Mormon Temple** — built in 1919 by descendants of missionary Mormons who have been living in this area since 1864. Facetiously referred to as "The Taj Mahal of the Pacific," the interior of this temple of the Church of Jesus Christ of Latter-Day Saints (which has about 25,000 members in Hawaii) is generally closed to outsiders. Non-Mormons can walk about its beautifully landscaped grounds and outer courtyards, but sanctums are reserved for private religious ceremonies.

Other Mormon landmarks in Laie, where 95 per cent of the town's citizens are Mormons, are the Hawaii campus of **Brigham Young University** (formerly known as the Church College of Hawaii) and a vast "south seas modern" **Polynesian Cultural Center**. This extremely successful tourist complex has been staging and selling out tours, stage shows and pseudo *luau* dinners since 1964, and has been enviously recognized in show business circles as one of the longest-running, sold-out spectaculars in the United States. The center's main stage shows, performed nightly by young Mormon students from Fiji, Samoa, Tahiti, Tonga, Maori New Zealand and Hawaii, are designed, according to promo-brochures, to give visitors a "pure cultural view of Polynesia." That's a good idea, but the fast-paced show has many Hollywood moments, and re-

South Seas dreams at the Laie Polynesian Cultural Center.

constructed Polynesian villages on the center's grounds have a decidedly Disneyland veneer. However, visitors on package tour programs seem to heartily enjoy the Center's *Polynesien Nouveau* attractions. In keeping with Mormon precepts, no liquor is available anywhere unless, as tour bus drivers sometimes suggest, you bring along your own hip flask.

A totally non-commercial show, marvelously choreographed by the Pacific gods who sculpted this island, can be enjoyed just off Kamehameha Highway about a block north of the cultural center. This is scenic **Laie Point**, at the end of Anemoku and Naupaka Streets, where windward waters running hard from the north pound two little offshore isles, **Kukuihoolua Islet** (to the left) and **Mokualai Islet** (directly off the point's fingertip), with a force that is spectacular, frightening and beautiful. This performance is especially unnerving and wild when winter swells hit Oahu's North Shore with thunderous force and fury.

A "former tourist attraction" sits pretty and clean at the north side of Kahuku town. This is the **Kahuku Sugar Mill** which, until 1971, was an actual, operating mill where sugarcane was converted into molasses. For several years the mill was reopened as a 14-acre theme park. All the mill's former flywheels, gears, centrifuges, crusher rollers and steam gauges were color-coded and marked to show people how it was in the plantation days when Kahuku folk manned the machetes, tractors and vacuum pans. The park closed in 1982 but there is talk that someday it may reopen again. Meanwhile, the brightly painted mill sits as it did for decades, a reminder of the time when sugarcane was big business on the North Shore.

Even more interesting is the real Kahuku plantation village across the street, where quaint little workers' cafes, grocery stores, *karate dojo* and tiny homes survive much as they did when their residents responded to the mill's morning wake-and-work steam whistle, then trudged back to the village when the afternoon whistle signalled *pau hana*, or "work finished." A walk around this village, where ferns, orchids, air plants and succulent jades and donkey's tails hung out of cutaway bleach-bottle planters, is rewarding.

The Kahuku Sugar Mill.

Soldiers, Sunworshipers and Surfers

The country assumes some markedly different characters just north of Kahuku, where the auras of Mormon Laie and work-a-day Kahuku dissolve into military and nudist factors. To the left of Kamehameha Highway in the vicinity of **Kii** is a hilly military maneuvers area where camouflaged soldiers are often seen crashing through the dense *kiawe* overgrowth in full combat gear. And to the right, near an old deserted airplane landing strip, is Oahu's **Hawaii Nudist Park**, where island naturists swim, attempt volleyball, catch the sun's rays, play ping-pong and parade about in annual Mr. and Mrs. Nude Hawaii contests and Halloween costume balls. The GIs and nudists seem to coexist okay, but their neighborly detente has been threatened on occasion when curious Pacific Command Army helicopters have made one too many low buzzes over the nudists' private, "members only" nature park.

A few meadow-framed moments after one leaves Kahuku and swings from north towards the east and then slightly southwest, the feel of the land changes abruptly. The veil of the Koolaus ends here, and so does her wet, drippy coolness. An old sign warns: "Now Entering a High Surf Area. Oahu Civil Defense Agency." The North Shore's first major landmark is a huge hotel, the **Hyatt Kuilima Hotel and Country Club**, formerly the Del Webb Kuilima, where President Richard M. Nixon and Japanese Prime Minister Kakuei Tanaka held an ominous summit meeting in 1972 before Watergate and Lockheed political scandals expunged both as heads of state.

Facing the Kuilima complex from a tiny finger of land is **Kawela Bay**, a wonderfully idyllic crescent of shell-filled sand which developers recently earmarked for a mammoth hideaway hotel-townhouse resort complex. Already, many quaint wood frame houses that used to sit on Kawela's curves are being torn down and replaced with developable land and air.

A few miles farther, the world's finest surfing grounds crash onto offshore reefs and sandbars: **Velzyland, Sunset Point, Kammieland, Rocky Point, Gas Chambers, Pupukea, the Banzai Pipeline, Waimea Bay, Piddlies, Chun's Reef,**

Cane-hauling in the "old" days at Kahuku.

Laniakea, Himalayas, Haleiwa and Avalanche. Some wave riders talk about — only talk about — riding the 30 to 40-foot monsters that tube off **Kaena Point** on the extreme west end of the North Shore, but nobody's done it yet. For now, Sunset Point, the Pipeline and Waimea Bay will do just fine. The most jaded surfer will agree that a tubing, top-to-bottom spitter off one of those reefs generates enough adrenalin to keep anybody going through at least a few nervous lifetimes. Especially when Waimea Bay is breaking — so big, bruddah, that hundreds of people quietly and respectfully line the cliffs on the bay's point like spectators at gladiatorial finals; and City and County fire engines with revolving red and yellow lights don't wait for a rescue call; and the waves are so thunderous and crazy the ground trembles a little bit underfoot; and cars on the highway have to use their windshield wipers to take salt mists off the glass. That's when the dozen or so waveriders who are brave enough to do such things paddle out and begin to understand what it's all about when twenty to thirty-foot winter swells lift like glossy black holes on the blue-grey horizon. Once safely into "the lineup," the surfers wheel around and paddle frantically into scary thrills on pin-tailed surfboards called "elephant guns."

During spring, summer and fall months, Waimea Bay often is as placid as a lake, but when northern winter storms in the region of the Arctic's Aleutian Islands begin sending wave pulses across the blue Pacific, the bay and the North Shore in general can become unrideable and highly destructive fury. Like in December 1969, when more than 30 homes between Kawela Bay and Haleiwa were simply, awesomely, reduced to tinderwood as monstrous 50-foot waves pounded this coastline like cosmic jackhammers. People who survived that winter storm told reporters frightening stories about waves that swept property and lives into the sea. "A wave exploded over our house," said one trembling Sunset Beach man. "A wall collapsed on her," recalled another. "Imagine," said a fireman, "this wasn't even a tidal wave. They were just regular winter swells."

A good place to scan this disaster-prone area where men on fragile surfboards tease nature is above Waimea

Gerry Lopez, master surfing stylist, in an optimum-energy position at the Banzai Pipeline.

Bay and **Saint Peters & Paul Church** at the ancient but still patronized Hawaiian *heiau* known as **Pu'u o Mahuka**. This temple, is one of the largest on Oahu, and was once a site of human sacrifices. Historians are not sure, but they think that at this temple crew members of the British ship *Dedalus* were offered in sacrifice in 1794 after being captured as they tried to fill waterbarrels at the mouth of the **Waimea River**. At *Pu'u o Mahuka*, the hill of escape, Hawaiians still leave offerings for the old gods, usually stones wrapped in sacred *ti* leaves.

If you visit only one *heiau* on Oahu, this one off Pupukea Road (opposite the Sunset Beach Fire Station and above Waimea Bay) should be the one. It's about seven-tenths of a mile off upper Pupukea Road at the end of a bumpy, pot-holed dirt road, but the knock-out combination of eerie Hawaiian feelings and the spectacular North Shore panorama from up there are well worth vehicular hassle. This *heiau* has three distinct enclosures, with the two largest measuring about 520 feet long and 150 feet wide. An altar-like structure sits at the top of the main terraced enclosure,

and its stones often are flanked by modernistic *kapu* sticks topped with red and white cloth-covered balls. This temple was declared spiritually inoperative in 1819 when King Kamehameha II and the Queen Regent Kaahumanu ordered the overthrow of the ancient Hawaiian *kapu* system.

Shave Ice, Frigate Birds and Poi

Farther along the North Shore's surfing grounds, a small deco and rainbow-shaped cement bridge funnels traffic over a snug little stream into **Haleiwa**, an artsy little outpost (but the biggest town on this side of Oahu) where surfers, "hippies," Filipinos, Japanese and Hawaiians commingle and somehow create a sober, workable sense of tolerant, loving community. The Nasty Habits Boutique and Celestial Foods natural foods store look proper and probable across the street from a Filipino billiards hall that sells homemade *bagoong* fish sauce. And whether one is a Puerto Rican mechanic, California surfer girl with white sun screen on her nose, or a huge *blalah* Hawaiian from Leilehua town, every-

At Ehukai Beach Park, preparing for the world's finest waves.

body enjoys gnawing on state-of-the-art "rainbow" shave-ice cones (with ice cream and/or sweet red beans) available at the locally renowned **M. Matsumoto Store** on Kamehameha Highway.

Haleiwa means *home of the iwa*, or frigate bird, also called the man-o-war, a seafowl which likes to stretch its wings as much as seven feet when soaring across local waters in search of seafood.

A good time to visit Haleiwa is in the middle of summer, at the height of the O-Bon season, when the **Haleiwa Jodo Mission** climaxes its annual full-moon O-Bon Festival with a unique *Toro-nagashi* or *Floating Lanterns* ritual on the east side of Haleiwa's **Kaiaka Bay**. The sight of dozens of flickering lanterns floating upon the dark sea under a full moon, each a farewell light for a beloved ancestor's spirit, is moving in an ancient and very poetic Way.

During a walking tour of Haleiwa's cracker box streets, false-front buildings and Wild West wooden sidewalks, wander onto the grounds of the rebuilt **Queen Liliuokalani Church** (66-090 Kamehameha Highway). The church's old clock tells time not by the numbers, but by the 12 letters which make up Liliuokalani's name. The clock was a personal gift to the church from Hawaii's last monarch and only ruling queen.

Upon leaving Haleiwa, a traveler can either choose to continue south down Kamehameha Highway (99) through central Oahu and back to Honolulu, or continue farther east past taro and banana patches (and the **Haleiwa Poi Factory**, at 66-499 Paalaa Road) to the old plantation town of **Waialua**. Above

The Waialua sugar mill.

Waialua, atop 4,029 foot **Mount Kaala**, is the highest point on Oahu and the three white domes of a modern tracking station. And due west, just beyond Mokuleia on Farrington Highway (93), is the dead-end desolation and ruggedness of Kaena Point. This is country driving at its best, and for this Windward-North Shore tour, island's end.

On the *mauka* side of Farrington Highway at **Mokuleia** is the small **Gaylord Dillingham Air Field**, Hawaii's only soaring area, where glider pilots loop and dive in thermal air currents that rise alongside the 2,000-foot Waianae *pali* that dominates **Peacock Flats**. On the other side of Farrington Highway is the **Mokuleia Polo Farm**, Hawaii's most-exclusive athletic facility. It is here where visiting teams from the U.S. Mainland, Australia, England, and Ireland battle through gentlemanly chukkers of fiercely competitive polo (nearly every Sunday between late February and July) against local pony teams from Waikiki, Kahuku, Waimanalo and, of course, Mokuleia. Britain's Prince Charles has played in these matches, as have the Maharajah of Jaipur, the Marquis of Waterford and Lord Patrick Beresford. Such distinguished matches, however, manage to retain a tasteful, country character, whomever the competitors may be.

Polo fans like to arrive early with a picnic hamper, bottles of wine and other good cheer, then after eggs benedict and rissoles on the green, settle in for four chukkers of top-flight polo under rippling Hawaiian ironwoods. It's a very nice way to end a Sunday drive into *the country*.

CENTRAL OAHU

Persons who are so inclined or prefer to speed across islands will find the freeway and highway dash across Central Oahu and north to Haleiwa more to their liking, though at times it may remind them of the fast places they left on the Mainland and leave them wondering, breathlessly, what has happened to Hawaii.

At Honolulu proper, fasten your seat belts, race on to the **Lunalilo Freeway** and aim north along the abrupt frenzy which is a freeway in Paradise. Whizzing by, in order, will be:

• The **Moanalua Park and Gardens**, where huge umbrella-like monkeypod trees rock lazily, like gigantic and pliable mushrooms, just off the busy freeway. Behind this favored picnic place is an even more spectacular wilderness where three-story high white hibiscus trees shade a flashing stream, ancient Hawaiian petroglyph rocks and an old medicinal pool surrounded by morning glories, gardenias, ferns and fragrant vines. This is **Moanalua Valley**, a tranquil spot favored by Oahu nature-lovers. The valley is managed by a non-profit group called the Moanalua Valley Gardens Foundation, but free tours can be arranged by simply calling the foundation and stating your intentions. However, note that there are no restrooms or foods available once you leave the main road and head into the valley, so carry necessary fuel and amenities. As recently as 1976, the State planned to build a wide trans-Koolau highway through this verdant valley, but public pressure stopped the highway cold just outside the valley's entrance.

• Just *Ewa* of Moanalua Valley, on a ridge overlooking the freeway is the big **Tripler Army Hospital**, a pale pink structure that looks like a strawberry frosted layer cake. Tripler is the largest military hospital in the Pacific, and is responsible for serving the medical needs of personnel assigned to the huge CINCPAC (Commander-in-Chief Pacific) military region. The 14-story hospital was named after Gen. Charles Stuart Tripler, a brevet-brigadier general who served as medical director of the Army of the Potomac in the Civil War, and who wrote the Army's first standard manual on the medical examination of military recruits.

Hawaii's 'War Room'

• Central Oahu is thick with military sites, but perhaps the most potent of all is **Camp H.M. Smith** atop **Halawa Heights**. This former marine camp is one of the headquarters of the CINCPAC Commander, who oversees all U.S. military missions between California and the east coast of Africa. It was up here, in his curved "war room," where day-to-day activities of the Vietnam and Korean Wars were monitored by the Pentagon and President in Washington, D.C.

• On the sea side of the highway loom the west, middle and east lochs of **Pearl Harbor**, and the harbor-side towns of **Aiea** and **Pearl City**. In the foreground, looking like a rusting flying saucer, is Hawaii's new **Aloha Stadium**, where major athletic and other large crowd events are held throughout the year. The stadium seats 50,000 people.

Aloha Stadium, home of the Hawaii Islanders professional Triple-A baseball team, and site of an annual Hula Bowl

Queen Liliuokalani and U.S. Navy brass at dedication of Pearl Harbor, 1912.

football game between All-America collegiate football stars, is probably the only big athletic facility in the United States where vendors hawk Chinese crack seed and *saimin* noodles along with the usual Yankee hot dogs and hamburgers.

• Pearl Harbor and its environs have been an especially notorious geographical place since World War II when Japanese dive bombers nearly destroyed the U.S. Pacific fleet which was at anchor here on the morning of December 7, 1941. The most well-known monument to that "day of infamy," as President Franklin Delano Roosevelt called it, is a radiant memorial that straddles the hulk of the USS *Arizona* and the remains of 1,100 men who went down with her when a series of Japanese torpedoes and aerial bombs sank that battleship. This white **Arizona Memorial**, designed by Honolulu architect Alfred Preis, was made possible in part by a benefit concert staged on March 25, 1961, by the late rock-and-roll entertainer Elvis Presley. Presley's fundraiser, held at Pearl Harbor's Bloch Arena, raised some $62,000 for the USS *Arizona* Memorial's building fund.

Although the Arizona Memorial is the most-visited Pearl Harbor attraction, tourists may also pay their respects at a lesser-known, $141,000 monument to the dead which was built on **Ford Island** alongside the rusting hulk of the USS *Utah*. Civilian visitors, however, can visit the USS *Utah* site only if they are accompanied by a member or dependant of the U.S. Armed Forces. Authorities at neighboring Hickam Air Force Base also have not made a big thing about a plaque which marks the spot where America's *Apollo 11* astronauts first touched earth after their historic flight and walk on the moon in July, 1969; but there it sits, an obscure earthly tribute to that "one small step for a man and great leap for mankind."

• Another, low-key tourist attraction at Pearl Harbor is the **Pacific Submarine Museum** at the **Pearl Harbor Submarine Base** (open 9:30 a.m. to 5 p.m. Wednesday through Sunday). After getting a pass and instructions on how to get to the museum at Pearl Harbor's **Nimitz Gate** (off Nimitz Highway), would-be submariners and the intellectually curious can fondle defused torpedoes, twist dials and peer through the

Tourists inside the *USS Arizona* Memorial.

periscope of the ex-USS *Parche*, a World War II submarine, and study the interior of a Kaiten-class Japanese one-man suicide torpedo-submarine. Exhibits trace the exploits and hardware of "the silent service" from World War I through the nuclear submarine age.

• Weekend travelers might also want to get off the freeway at Aiea or Pearl City and head for the **Kam Drive-In**, next door to the **Pearl Ridge Shopping Center**, where from 8:30 a.m. to 3 p.m. every Wednesday, Saturday and Sunday a vast **Swap Meet** is held in this nighttime theater's empty parking lot. The Swap Meet, which advertises 99,999 bargains, is the closest thing to an Asian or Middle Eastern bazaar you'll find in Hawaii. It — and a similar one at the Aloha Stadium near Halawa Valley — haven't been publicized in tourist-related publications, so the hundreds of buyers and sellers who throng their makeshift stalls are almost exclusively local folks who deal in everything from homemade crochet-and-beercan hats to pickled green mango. Whether you want a "silky" aloha shirt or antique radio, you can bargain your heart away here, proving in every market minute that one man's trash is another's treasure. Admission for buyers is usually 50 cents.

Wahiawa: Home of Oahu's 'Healing' and 'Birthing' Stones

As one continues north on the H-2 Freeway towards Wahiawa, Oahu's central plateau (with the Koolau mountains to your right and Waianae mountains to the left) rises gradually until you reach the **Schofield Barracks Army Post** and **Wahiawa**, the highest residential community (in elevation) on Oahu.

Wahiawa can be by-passed altogether by staying on Highway 90 which separates the town from Schofield Barracks ("Home of the 'Tropic Lightning' 25th Army Division"), but backseat mystics might want to see:

• The **Healing Stones** which sit on a simple little altar inside a crude concrete building at 108 California Street in Wahiawa. During the late 1920s, pilgrims regularly visited these stones, which according to one legend were originally two Hawaiian sisters from the island of Kauai who flew here and were converted by greater powers into stone.

Aerial view of Aloha Stadium during football game.

Other myths attribute other origins to these phallic stones, but whatever the various legendary or geologic explanations, they have long been thought to emanate healing powers. Offerings, in the form of flowers, *ti* leaves and smaller stones, are regularly made by people who still feel that these stones exude hope, power and relief from physical misery.

• On the north side of Wahiawa, to the left side of Kamehameha Highway and just beyond Whitmore Avenue, are a group of sacred stones of a different spiritual sort. These are **The Birth Stones of Kukaniloko**, more commonly called the **Wahiawa Birthing Stones**, where wives of high-ranking chiefs bore their children in ancient Hawaii. According to oral traditions, Hawaiian chiefesses came here to bear their offspring on these stones' gently curved surfaces. Attendant chiefs, high priests and physicians would gather round an infant thus born, and during an impressive ceremony marked by the beating of great drums, chants, and tribute offerings, the high-born child would be named and his or her navel cord cut and ritually hidden away.

This eucalyptus-fringed spot has been venerated by Hawaiians since ancient times, but in recent years has been treated by most persons as little more than a clearing in a pineapple field. The result has been a desecration of an important cultural site by vandals and curiosity seekers. However, plans are being made by concerned Hawaiian organizations to restore and maintain this birthing shrine much as it must have been when chiefesses were brought here to endure the pains of labor in a consecrated setting.

From this open-air site, in the direction of the Waianae Range, you can look up the side of **Leilehua Plain** to the broad **Kolekole Pass** which was used by low-flying Japanese bombers as a convenient cover and western approach for their sneak attacks on Schofield Barracks and adjacent **Wheeler Air Force Base**. In 1969 when the Twentieth Century-Fox movie studio was engaged in filming the epic movie "Tora! Tora! Tora!," the sight of red-dotted Zeros, Kates and Vals roaring through Kolekole and raining simulated bombs and machine-gun fire on Schofield Barracks and Wheeler Air Force Base was strange indeed. Not a few Wahiawa residents

Pineapple fields and the infamous Kolekole Pass.

stood at this very site and relived memories of that morning of December 7, 1941 as they had actually seen it some 28 years earlier. As radio announcer Webley Edwards told them over the radio early that day: "This is not a maneuver, this is the real McCoy!"

Those pineapple fields stretching out on either side of Kamehameha Highway, often like row upon row of prickly yellow-green hand grenades, are also the "real McCoy," and Wahiawa is the growing center of that fruit which is so symbolic of Hawaii.

Pineapples were originally discovered by Westerners in South America and the West Indies, but were quickly spread throughout the world and some kinds were reported to be planted and thriving in Hawaii as early as 1813. However, the selling of pineapple on a commercial basis was not begun here until 1899 when Oahu entrepreneur James D. Dole planted 60 acres of Wahiawa land in this exotic fruit. Two years later Dole organized the Hawaiian Pineapple Company, Ltd., and by 1906 he began building a special cannery at Iwilei near Honolulu Harbor. The rest of this prickly story can be learned if you stop in at the nearby **Pineapple Variety Garden**, which was established at Kamananui Road and Kamehameha Highway in 1954 by Dole's number one competitor, the Del Monte Corporation. This garden outlines the history of pineapple-growing and has on display 29 living varieties of this fruit and other bromeliads which early Spanish explorers called the *pina*, because its fruit was shaped like a pine cone.

However, don't be misled like some first-time pineapple seekers by the fruit of the *hala*, or pandanus, tree. Because so many tourists have been heard exclaiming, "Oh look, pineapples," when they see the huge fruits in this tree's leafy branches, the *hala* is jokingly referred to by local people as the "tourist pineapple." From a distance it does indeed look like a pineapple, but it is not even closely related to "the king of fruits."

About four miles north of Wahiawa, low-lying pineapple plots give way to fields of waving sugarcane, and farther north up Highway 82 you will soon find yourself descending into Haleiwa town and the end of this speedy central route across Oahu.

Pineapple postcard, 1910.

Hawaiian Pineapples, District of Wahiawa, Island of Oahu.

HAWAIIAN PINEAPPLE

PICKED RIPE PACKED RIGHT

OAHU'S WEST SIDE

Oahu's West Side—or **Waianae Coast**—is perhaps the most maligned and misunderstood part of Oahu. It is true that this 20-mile coastline is dustier, drier and generally hotter than the rest of the island, but its rugged character has much natural and cultural beauty to offer the *akamai* (wise), tolerant and adventurous traveler, archeologist, sociologist and outdoorsman.

Because this side of the island is generally devoid of usual "commercial" tourist attractions, and because it is largely populated by poorer lower and lower-middle class working people, tourism promoters and package tour operators often avoid its more subtle attractions and tougher, country character.

However, question a longtime resident of **Nanakuli**, **Maili**, **Pokai**, **Waianae** or **Makaha** about the West Side, and they'll spend hours telling you why it's paradise as they perceive it. "It's the closest thing to an unspoiled Hawaiian place on this island," says a

Poinsettias and Ewa plantation home.

truckdriver from Lualualei. And a Nanakuli elder states flatly that, "You've never been to a real *luau* until you've been to a big one on this side." Indeed, big wedding and first birthday *luaus* hosted on this side of Oahu have achieved almost legendary fame, and often are remembered, like fine wines and historic events, according to the year in which they were celebrated, or—by modern Hawaiian estimation—by the number of *kalua* pigs and trucks full of beer which were consumed by friends and relatives.

As funky and island-style a place as any to prepare yourself for a West Side tour is the West-Central Oahu town of **Waipahu**, which is just *makai* of Pearl City and a quick freeway-ramp dash off the six-lane H-1 Highway. Waipahu is Oahu's last big town before you hook around the southern end of the Waianae mountain range into West Side scenes and stories.

Waipahu: Sugar Shack Flash And A Nameless Pool Hall

Waipahu, whose name means *bursting water*, is the improbable tract house and shanty town home of the Nameless Pool Hall, the creaky Marigold Bar, the casbahish Little Egypt's Cocktail Lounge, radio station **KDEO** (home of "Whodaguy" Ron Jacobs), one of Oahu's last two working sugar mills (the other is at Waialua on the North Shore), and what is probably the highest concentration of Filipino immigrant laborers on this island.

A Honolulu newspaper reporter once described Waipahu town as "an old Elia Kazan movie set run over by a truck. Or maybe two." Maybe, but when the red dust kicked up by cane hauling trucks settles, Waipahu also is one of the last places on this urban island where you can see, smell and feel old-time cane town living at its sweet and sleepy best. Consider the plantation camp homes that survive neatly, like adult toy houses, on the north side of town: old men on tilted front porches stroke their fighting chickens; old ladies trim orchid hedges and banana groves; and elders shake their fists at adolescent sons and grandsons who roar by in souped-up cars of chromium, candy-apple flash. Ah, but whatever the action, or wherever you go in Waipahu town, the cloying sweet and sour smell of processed sugarcane lingers in the air, explaining to your nose why this place exists.

Until the middle 1970s, Waipahu and the neighboring West Oahu townships of **Ewa** and **Honouliuli** and **Oneula** were devoted nearly exclusively to the growing and milling of sugarcane; but today these lands of green, waving and tassel-topped cane are being phased out, plowed under, paved over and carved into checkerboard subdivisions which by the 1980s will be housing several hundred thousand new Oahu residents. This planned **West Oahu City** will stretch from Pearl City all the way to **Makakilo** north of **Barbers Point** and west of Pearl Harbor. There will be a great concentrated need for recreational facilities and cooling-off places, and these will be provided by the nearby West Coast of broad sandy beaches, surfing and fishing grounds and quiet, aquamarine waters.

Each beach along this blazing coast has its devotees and character: **Ewa Beach Park**, for example, is famed for its abundance of *limu* (also called *ogo* in Japanese) or edible seaweed, and its shallow waters often are knee deep in Japanese, Hawaiian and Korean women busy plucking bags full of this green delicacy which is rich in natural salts and iodine. **Kahe** is another beach area, just north of Barbers Point and opposite a Hawaiian Electric Company power plant on Farrington Highway (93), favored by surfers. This spot is formally known as the **Hawaiian Electric Beach Park**, but locals call it **Tracks**, because remnants of the old Oahu Railway and Land Company's narrow gauge train tracks still run visibly between that beach and Farrington Highway.

Several reefs and points of land along this coast have been favored as west and north swell surfing spots since ancient times, but perhaps the most famous of all is **Kepuhi Point** at **Makaha** where for many years (since 1952) the annual Makaha International Surfing Championships were held. Because of more than 20 years of network television and film coverage of Makaha surfing contests, that beach has become quite famous in international sports circles. In recent years most major big wave surfing contests have been held on Oahu's vicious North Shore, particularly at the powerful Banzai Pipeline and Sunset Beach surf breaks, but most early armchair wave watchers got their first doses of

Rock formations, upper Makakilo.

surfing at its masterly and Hawaiian best by watching footage of spectacular male, female and tandem surfing meets at Makaha.

Slick and chic surfing attention has shifted to the North Shore from the West Side, but in recent years an "oldie-but-goodie" surfing event has caught the fancy of waveriding oldtimers. This is an annual surfing contest — "Buffalo's Longboard Contest" — which was organized in 1978 by Makaha Beach commander Buffalo Keaulana and other local bruddahs to renew interest in a cruisy style of surfing which was in vogue during the "hotdogging" Fifties and Sixties.

Meanwhile, to get into the properly Hawaiian mood one should be in to appreciate this side of Oahu, tune your car radio in to station KCCN (AM-1420), "the world's only all-Hawaiian music station," and sing along with island folksinger Liko Martin to his song titled "Nanakuli Blues." As Cousin Liko suggests, roll through surfside Nanakuli with thoughts of urban Honolulu far behind. Or as he expresses it in that very popular island song: "I gonna get in my *ka'a*/Gonna *hele* too fa-

ah/I'm never coming back again" and he's going to, like us, enjoy "Birds all along Sunlight at dawn/Singing Nanakuli blues."

Both 'Savage' and Civilized

Only about 27,000 people now live along these jagged shorelines and dry, rugged mountain slopes, but in ancient times the West Coast of Oahu was known as a major center of Hawaiian civilization, probably because of the rich fishing grounds that often thrash with silvery life in clear off-shore waters between Nanakuli and Kaena Point.

It was here, according to detailed oral traditions, that the important demigod Maui first lived and learned to make fire after he arrived in Hawaii from the land of his creators. And all along this coast, place name myths refer to the infamous man-pig Kamapuaa, who was renowned throughout Hawaii as a god who both charmed and harassed mortal worshipers with his capricious antics. Yet another Waianae story tells of an eel-man with supernatural powers who lived at Pokai Bay.

The stories are many, but so are the

physical remnants of these myths which one can still see, touch, explore and feel emotionally. A good seaside example is the important, but crumbling **Kuilioloa Heiau** on the extreme fingertip of **Kaneilio Point** on the south side of **Pokai Bay**. This *heiau* of coral and lava rock, which is surrounded by water on three sides, was built in the 15th or 16th Century in honor of 'Ilioloa, The Long Dog, who was the patron of travelers along this rugged coast. Hawaiian travelers no doubt appreciated such patronage, because this area reportedly was populated in ancient times by fierce cannibals who preyed on weak passersby. The name of the largest town on this coast, **Makaha**, which means fierce or savage, takes its name from these man-eating marauders. According to J. Gilbert McAllister, who wrote an important Bishop Museum survey entitled *Archaeology of Oahu* (1933), traditions indicate that these highwaymen hid behind high ridges and ambushed unwary victims who came their way.

"For many years these people preyed upon the traveler," McAllister writes, "until at one time men from Kauai, hairless men (*Olohe*) came to this beach. They were attacked by these cannibals, but defeated them, killing the entire colony. Since then the region has been safe for traveling."

Given that assurance of safety, you may want to wander into the back reaches of **Makaha Valley** and see the spectacular **Kaneaki Heiau** which was recently restored by the National Parks Service, Bishop Museum and the Makaha Historical Society. This 17th Century chiefs' *heiau*, one of the best-preserved on Oahu, was rebuilt entirely by hand, using *pili* grass, *ohia* timber and lava stones much as they were utilized by ancient craftsmen. Originally, this was an agricultural *heiau* dedicated to the god Lono, but archeologists speculate that Kaneaki may have been reconditioned in 1796 by Kamehameha the Great as a *luakini heiau*, or *heiau* of human sacrifice, in honor of his war god Kukailimoku. At the time, Kamehameha was amassing a huge fleet in the Makaha area in preparation for an invasion of the northwestern island of Kauai ruled by King Kaumualii. Perhaps, after that invasion fleet was forced back to Oahu by gale-force winds and raging seas, people were

Throwing fishnet on the Waianae Coast.

sacrificed near here to appease the angry and unhelpful gods.

This *heiau* is tucked away in a spectacular setting alongside **Makaha Stream** and is frequented by nearly tame flocks of peacocks, chukar partridges, and quail. Permission to visit the *heiau* (from 11 a.m. to 1 p.m. daily, except Monday) may be obtained by contacting the information desk at the **Makaha Inn**.

Another famous site you can walk into is located about three miles north of Makaha and just south of the scattered village of Makua. This is *Kaneana*, the **Cave of Kane**, more popularly called **Makua Cave**. Though this cave is 100 feet high in places and about 450 feet deep, it is not, as some people suspect, a lava tube. Rather, it was carved out by sea action some 150,000 years ago when its entrance was at or below sea level. According to an old Makua-area myth, this cave was occupied by a fierce character, Kamahoalii, who was able to alternate at will between being a human and a shark. Like most sharks, Kamahoalii had a fondness for human flesh, so in his/her guise as a mortal, he/she would periodically jump people and then drag them into this cave for dinner. Eventually, this human disguise was discovered and Kamahoalii had to flee into the sea, where he/she later was captured and destroyed by vengeful Makua residents. This cave has since been much vandalized by spray painters and beer drinkers, but it's still a cool refuge which will no doubt inspire further eerie and fanciful feelings about the human shark who used to lurk and lunch in its chilly shadows.

Yokohama and a Land Named Heat

A mile or so beyond this cave, on **Makua Beach**, is the photogenic area where much of the epic motion picture "Hawaii," based on James Michener's novel of the same name, was filmed during 1965. During that shooting, motion picture producers recreated on this beach an entire set representing the old Maui whaling town of Lahaina. That block-long set has long since been disassembled and carted away, but the same memorable backdrop of aqua waters, white surf and fawn sands remain for your West Side pleasure.

A few fleeting daydreams later, Farrington Highway ends and briefly

Sunbather at Nanakuli Beach Park.

becomes a road which, in turn, terminates at **Keawa'ula Beach**, a favorite board and body-surfing spot at land's end known to old-timers as **Yokohama Bay**. This wide sandy playground received that Japanese name because during turn-of-the-century days, when the Oahu Railway and Land Company was still operating, the train from Ewa to Haleiwa used to stop here to let off Japanese fishermen who favored the fishing at Keawa'ula. Nobody knows who actually coined the term Yokohama Bay, but the name stuck and later became well known in surfing circles because of popular left slide waves which leap off a shallow reef on the bay's south side. This surfing break is sometimes referred to as the "Poor Man's Pipeline," because its breaking style is sometimes similar to the hollow left-slide surfing spot on Oahu's North Shore known as the Banzai Pipeline.

Beyond Yokohama Bay, the landscape loses its sandy character and turns into a harsh jangle of black lava, thorny scrub brush and the rude desolation of **Kaena Point**. For good reason this place was called *Kaena*, or heat, and in ancient times Hawaiians were reluctant to cross its waste. Like a beak or arrow, Kaena points to the northwest. The point can be traversed, but only on a 4-wheel-drive vehicle, dirtbike, horse, or by foot. Attempt this journey in a conventional car or truck, and chances are you will lose your vehicle on a small lava crag or steep gully. Or maybe you'll simply destroy its mechanical underside on Kaena's dragon's teeth rocks. Consider Kaena *kapu* until further notice.

The end of this road is tough and foreboding, but it's a splendid Hawaiian place to complete one's tour of Oahu. Besides being Oahu's last frontier, Kaena Point, according to Hawaiian traditions, was the place from which souls departed from earth — the good to the right, and others to the left.

As you gaze out from this knifepoint of land named *heat*, consider this apt poem once chanted by the goddess Hiiaka, favorite and younger sister of the fire goddess Pele:

Kaena, salty and barren,
Now throbs with the blaze of the sun;
The rocks are consumed by the heat,
Dappled and changed in their color . . .

Fishing at Keawaula, "Yokohama Bay."

THE 'LEEWARD ISLANDS'

For practical touring purposes, the City and County of Honolulu ends at the sharp beaky tip of Kaena Point. However, unknown to most people, even to most Honolulu residents, the City and County of Honolulu is actually the most far-flung city in the world. Officially, Honolulu's jurisdiction includes 593 square miles of land on Oahu plus dozens of smaller points of land which stretch some 1,367 nautical miles to the northwest. These shoals, atolls and desert isles have names like **Nihoa, Necker, French Frigate Shoals, Gardiner Pinnacles, Maro Reef, Laysan, Lisianski, Pearl** and **Hermes Reef** and **Kure Atoll**. The better known **Midway Islands** are within this City and County zone, but they were put under the jurisdiction of the United States Navy in 1903. Some 2,000 Navy personnel and dependents and hundreds of thousands of goony birds live at Midway, but the other islets are uninhabited, save for **Tern Island** at French Frigate Shoals (which supports an airstrip and Loran navigation station maintained by the U.S. Coast Guard).

Now and then cruise yachts put into a protected lagoon on one of these islands, but except for periodic inspection visits by the Coast Guard and State wildlife officials, about the only landlife these islets see are millions of squawking seabirds, Hawaiian monk seals and occasional green sea turtles. Among interesting birds which populate these islands are Hawaiian noddy terns, sooty terns, red-footed and blue-faced boobies, Laysan albatrosses, shearwaters, frigate birds, wandering tattlers, Pacific golden plovers, Laysan honey eaters, bristle-thighed curlews and Laysan teals (said to be the rarest duck in the world).

These islands often are referred to as the **Leeward Islands**, but experts on the subject note that they should be properly called the **Northwestern Hawaiian Islands**. Eight of these islands and reefs—French Frigate Shoals, Pearl and Hermes Reef, Lisianski Island, Laysan Island, Maro Reef, Gardner Pinnacles, Necker and Nihoa — make up a region which is officially known as the **Hawaiian Islands Wildlife Refuge**.

The two closest of these islands, Nihoa and Necker, which are located about 250 miles northeast of Honolulu, once supported small groups of stone age Hawaiians. Agricultural and temple terraces and house platforms have been discovered on both, and archeologists from the Bishop Museum have found beautifully carved stone images, stone bowls, adzes, sinkers and other evidence of early human occupation on Necker. These objects may be seen in the Pacific Collection of the Bishop Museum at Honolulu. Though a shortage of drinking water would make living on these two islands very difficult at best, the proper harvesting of water and food sources would not make this an impossible desert isle fantasy. The two islands certainly are large enough: Nihoa is about a mile long, a quarter of a mile wide, covers about 156 acres and rises to a maximum elevation of about 900 feet; Necker is 1,300 yards long, covers about 41 acres, and has a maximum elevation of 276 feet.

Most of the Leeward Islands, however, are not so hospitable. Usually they are ankle or knee deep in exotic blends of guano, or are too flat or pointy to welcome a human existence.

Blue-faced Boobies on driftwood log at Lisianski Island.

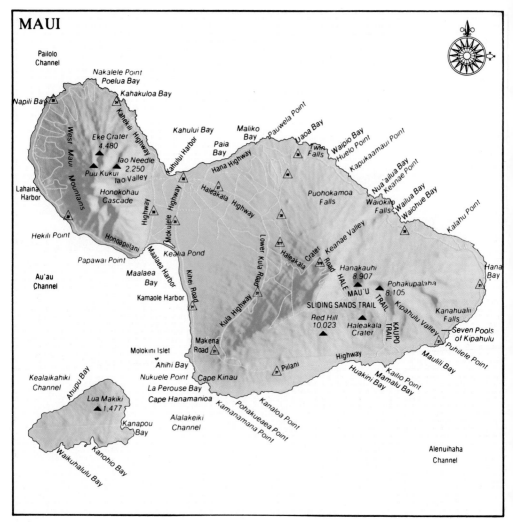

MAUI

Pailolo
Channel

Nakalele Point
Poelua Bay

Kahakuloa Bay

Napili Bay

West Maui Mountains

Eke Crater
4,480

Iao Needle
2,250

Puu Kukui

Iao Valley

Honokohau
Cascade

Lahaina
Harbor

Hekili Point

Honoapiilani

Papawai Point

Au'au
Channel

Maalaea
Bay

Maalaea Harbor

Kamaole Harbor

Molokini Islet

Kealaikahiki
Channel

Anupu Bay

Lua Makiki
1,477

Kanapou
Bay

Kanohio Bay

Waikuhalulu Bay

Alalakeiki
Channel

Kahului Bay

Kahului Harbor

Paia
Bay

Maliko
Bay

Pauwela Point

Uaoa Bay

Hana Highway

Haleakala Highway

Mokuele Highway

Kihei Road

Kealia Pond

Lower Kula Road

Kula Highway

Makena
Road

Ahihi Bay

Nukuele Point
La Perouse Bay

Cape Kinau

Cape Hanamanioa

Pohakueaea Point

Kanaloa Point

Kamanamana Point

Twin
Falls

Waipio Bay
Huelo Point

Kapukaamaui Point

Nua'ailua Bay
Keanae Point

Wailua Bay
Waiohue Bay

Puohokamoa
Falls

Waiokilo
Falls

Keanae Valley

Haleakala Crater Road

Hanakauhi
8,907

HALE

MAU'U TRAIL

Pohakupalaha
8,105

SLIDING SANDS TRAIL

Red Hill
10,023

Haleakala
Crater

Piilani

Highway

Kailio Point

Huakini Bay

Mamalu Bay

Maulili Bay

Kalahu Point

Hana
Bay

Kanahualii
Falls

Seven Pools
of Kipahulu

Puhilele Point

KAUPO TRAIL

Kipahulu Valley

Alenuihaha
Channel

Land Area:
728.2 square miles
48 miles long,
26 miles wide
Population:
Total: 60,300 (1977
  census estimate)
Makawao: 13,500
  (1977)
Kahului: 11,186 (1978)
Wailuku: 10,810 (1978)
Lahaina: 8,100 (1977)
Highest Elevation:
Red Hill (above
Haleakala Crater):
10,023 feet

Airports:
Hana: Hana Airport
Kahului: Kahului Airport
Kaanapali: Kaanapali
  Airport
Main Seaports:
Lahaina
Kahului Bay
Napili Bay
Hana Bay

Points of Interest

26 Ancient Paved Trail
41 Ancient Village Ruins
55 Bellstone
    (Pohakukaui)
27 Birthplace of
    Kaahumanu
56 Blowhole
31 Catholic Monument
35 Charles Lindbergh's
    Grave
 1 Haleakala National
    Park
10 Hale Ho'ike'ike
    Museum
38 Hale o Kane Heiau
23 Hana Airport
30 Hana-Maui Ranch
    Golf Course
29 Hasegawa General
    Store
54 Heakulani Heiau

 6 Holy Ghost Hall
    (1897)
39 Huialoha Church
    (1859)
 7 Iao Needle
11 Kaahumanu Church
    (1837)
53 Kaanapali Airport
13 Kahului Airport
46 Kaiwaloa War Heiau
    and Petroglyphs
 2 Kalahaku Overlook
12 Kanaha Bird
    Sanctuary
33 Kanekauila Heiau
 9 Kanda Gardens
17 Kaulanapueo Church
    (1853)
18 Kaumahina State
    Park
45 Kealawai Church (1838)

Preceding pages, Haleakala Crater, East Maui's
spectacular ''House of the Sun,'' at sunrise.

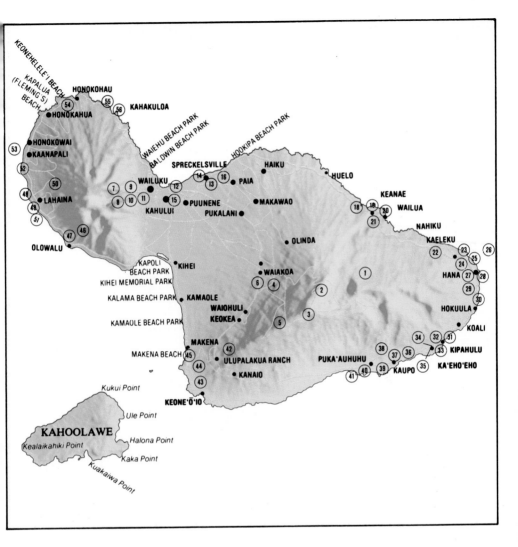

19	Keanae Church (1860)	
21	Keanae Valley Lookout	
8	Kepaniwai Heritage Gardens	
34	Kipahulu Hawaii Church (1857)	
40	Koa Heiau	
4	Kula Botanical Gardens	
51	Lahaina, Kaanapali & Pacific Railroad (1890 Vintage Cane Train Ride)	
50	Lahainaluna School	
43	Last Lava Flow on Maui (around 1790)	
37	Loaloa Heiau	
44	Makee Sugar Mill	
14	Maui Country Club	

25	Natural Arch	
47	Outer Island Vantage (Hawaii, Kahoolawe, Lanai, and Molokai)	
16	Paia Sugar Mill	
22	Pi'ilanihale Heiau (Largest Heiau in Hawaii)	
48	Pioneer Inn (1901)	
36	Popoiwi Heiau	
5	Public Hunting Ground	
15	Puunene Sugar Mill	
52	Royal Kaanapali Golf Club	
20	St. Augustine Shrine	
3	"Science City" Astronomical Observatories (Kolekole)	
32	Seven Pools of Kipahulu	

49	State Office Building	
42	Thompson Stables	
24	Waianapanapa State Park	
28	Wananalua Church (1838)	

Trails (Haleakala)

1	Halemau'u Trail
3	Kaupo Trail (private)
2	Sliding Sands Trail

KAHOOLAWE

Land Area:
45 square miles
11 miles long,
6 miles wide
Highest Elevation:
Lua Makika: 1,477 feet

MAUI

When Mark Twain visited Maui in 1866, he wore himself out tumbling boulders down the steep inner cliffs of **Haleakala Crater**.

At the time, Twain, 31, whose real name was Samuel Clemens, worked as a reporter for California's popular *Sacramento Union*. He was not yet the famous author of *Huckleberry Finn* and *Tom Sawyer*. But while he was roaming 'round Hawaii, Twain wrote a series of 25 humorous travel letters for the *Union*. These witty, subjective dispatches bore Oahu, Big Island and Maui datelines but the latter island, Maui, quickly became his favorite Hawaiian place.

The highlight of Twain's trip to Maui was his excursion to the top of Haleakala, an extinguished volcano on the eastern half of the island. "We climbed a thousand feet up the side of this isolated colossus one afternoon; then camped, and next day climbed the remaining nine thousand feet, and anchored on the summit, where we built a fire and froze and roasted by turns all night."

This "froze and roasted" quotation does not come from Twain's newspaper stories but from *Roughing It*, a semi-autobiographical travel book published in 1872. *Roughing It's* final chapters include about 30,000 words from the early Hawaii letters with the rest of it comprising new material expanded from his notebooks.

According to the book, Twain and his companions looked down on the inside of the "yawning dead crater, into which we now and then tumbled rocks, half as large as a barrel, from our perch, and saw them go careening down the almost perpendicular sides, bounding three hundred feet at a jump; kicking up dust clouds wherever they struck; diminishing to our view as they sped farther into distance; growing invisible, finally, and only betraying their course by faint little puffs of dust; and coming to a halt at last in the bottom of the abyss, two thousand five hundred feet down from where they started! It was magnificent sport. We wore ourselves out at it."

The next morning, Twain and his friends rolled out of their blankets and sat on the edge of the great mountain as the sun rose above the dangling clouds and threw a warm purple glow across the barren landscape of dead lava. "It was the sublimest spectacle I ever witnessed," Twain wrote, "and I think the memory of it will remain with me always."

'House of the Sun'

More than a century has passed since Twain journeyed to Maui, but travelers here continue to be awed by Haleakala, "House of the Sun." Today it is part of a U.S. National Park and visited by upwards of 600,000 people annually. A 30-mile trail system winds down into the crater and it is still possible to camp among the clouds overnight and wait for a morning sunrise.

Captain James Cook first sighted Maui on November 26, 1778 while sailing southwestward from the Aleutian Islands on his ill-fated final voyage. His simple description of Haleakala ("An elevated hill ... whose summit rose above the clouds.") is the earliest we have by a non-Hawaiian.

A group of New England missionaries were the first foreigners to climb to the peak in 1828, but it wasn't until 1841 that members of the U.S. Exploring

Sheltered lookout at Haleakala, sunset.

Expedition, led by Capt. John Wilkes, made reasonably accurate measurements and descended into the crater.

Modern surveys indicate that Haleakala Crater is 21 miles in circumference, 3000 feet deep and 19 square miles in area. The uppermost point is Red Hill, one of three prominent cinder cones. At 10,023 feet, this is the highest elevation on Maui.

In extreme contrast to the surrounding natural beauty, the summit of Haleakala has a space-age tennant. Here at **Science City** — a cluster of government buildings on the crater rim — scientists use huge telescopes to track foreign satellites across the sky and bombard the heavens with laser beams.

Haleakala has long been associated with the legendary demigod who gave the island its name. Maui was a magician and mythical figure in Polynesia even before the Hawaiian Islands were inhabited. He was cunning and full of tricks and ancient voyagers probably felt that this beautiful island possessed such a magical spirit it had to be his home.

According to Polynesian oral history, the island originally had only a few hours of daylight because the sun was fond of sleeping and liked to race across the sky. Due to these shortened days, Maui's mother, Hina, had troubled drying *kapa* cloth which she pounded from the bark of the paper mulberry.

Maui noticed that the sun appeared each morning over Haleakala and decided to capture the villain there. He first wove a rope of coconut fiber and one dark evening climbed up to the crater's edge to await dawn. When the sun awoke and began moving across the crater floor, he lassoed its rays, tied it up and prepared to kill the sun with a jawbone given to him by Hina. The sun, however, begged for mercy and explained to Maui that without its heat her *kapa* cloth would never get dry.

Sweet reason eventually prevailed and the sun's life was spared after it promised Maui that it would move slower across the sky in the future. The lasso was cut and Maui's fiery hostage released. Twain was to find out later that the top of Haleakala is still the best place to watch a Maui sunrise, probably, Hawaiians say, because the sun moves especially slow here — just in case its old enemy, Maui the trickster, is waiting in ambush.

Haleakala's outer slopes, heading toward Kaupo and Makena.

Maui No Ka Oi

Like voyagers of old, present day visitors to Maui might well believe that a magician has cast his spell over the island. It is not difficult to accept the local assertion that *Maui no ka oi* or "Maui is the best."

Maui, with its 728 square miles, is the second largest island in the Hawaiian archipelago and about 70 statute miles — or 30 air minutes — southeast of Oahu. Like Oahu, Maui began as two separate volcanic peaks that fused together thousands of centuries ago as lava bubbled and flowed down the slopes of their respective craters. West Maui broke first from the ocean floor and became serrated into several mountains. This dormant crater area is enveloped by the **Iao Valley** and **Puu Kukui**, a 5,788-foot summit which is the second rainiest peak in Hawaii (with about 400 inches of rainfall a year).

East Maui, the larger land mass, was formed during three distinct periods of volcanic activity centered at Haleakala. Gradually lava flowed westward from this side and cooled against the base of West Maui Volcano. The low-lying isthmus that joins the two peaks today gives Maui its nickname, the "Valley Island."

Fields of well-irrigated sugar cane cover this fertile plain and pineapple is grown in the surrounding foothills. **Wailuku** and **Kahului**, Maui's large twin-cities, blend together across the isthmus' northern end.

Wailuku, the Maui County Seat, also administers the islands of Molokai, Lanai and an uninhabited islet known as Kahoolawe. Three miles away is Kahului, Maui's deep-water port and the site of its major public airport.

It is at Kahului that most visitors to Maui (now over a million per year) arrive. Tourists don't usually tarry long here but nonetheless Kahului has become a busy commercial area with good shopping centers, a zoo, botanical gardens and **Maui Commuity College**, part of the University of Hawaii. Also, just off the highway between **Kahului Airport** and downtown is **Kahana Pond**, the state's most important waterfowl bird sanctuary and the home of several endangered species.

Kaahumanu Avenue, named after Kamehameha the Great's favorite wife and queen, leads directly into Wailuku's

Iao Valley and Iao Needle, West Maui.

Main Street. Wailuku is also a modern town but older than Kahului. In the **Wailuku Historic District**, on the west side of High Street in the central area, is **Kaahumanu Church**, Maui's earliest existing Christian church. Made of white-painted wood and plastered stone, it was built in 1837.

Off the Iao Valley Road is **Hale Hoikeike**, a small museum which originally was a home built in 1841 for Edward Bailey, headmaster of the former Wailuku Female Seminary. Bailey was an accomplished artist and some of his oil paintings are on display here. The museum is operated by the Maui Historical Society.

Iao Valley Road, a continuation of Kaahumanu Avenue and Main Street, is a three-mile drive from Wailuku into the Iao Valley. It follows Iao Stream all the way into **Iao Valley State Park**. Two miles down the road is **Kepaniwai Heritage Gardens**, a county park whose formal gardens and pavilions represent a cultural tribute to the many ethnic groups which have settled in Maui. The name of this park recalls a bloody 1790 battle waged by Kamehameha the Great's rival chieftans on Maui.

After he invaded the eastern end of Maui, Kamehameha decisively defeated enemy forces in Iao Valley with the help of two English advisers, John Young and Isaac Davis. It was a brilliant military victory for Kamehameha, but losses were heavy on both sides. After the battle, according to some accounts, Iao Stream was so full of dead bodies its waters would not flow. Appropriately, the name *Kepaniwai* commemorates this battle and means "the damming of the waters."

This scenic road ends in Iao Valley State Park, a lush mountain terrain dominated by **Iao Needle**, a 2,250-foot cinder cone pinnacle surrounded by the walls of **Puu Kukui**. Many climbers have attempted to climb this vertical rock formation but it is very hazardous. There is a parking lot at the end of the road and a path leads down to the stream and up to various sheltered spots for a view of the valley.

Backtracking the Iao Valley Road, Honoopiilani Highway hugs the lower mountain slopes and leads directly down the isthmus to **Maalaea**, a small coastal town with a splendid view of Haleakala across **Maalaea Bay**. This bay is well-known as a spawning ground for humpback whales (*Megaptera novaeangliae*) which are often seen off West Maui.

Maalaea Bay seems to be the first destination of the expectant whales as they swim in from Alaska and Arctic regions for the winter. They arrive here around November each year to give birth. Most births are singular but on rare occasions twins have been reported. From Maalaea Bay the humpbacks usually swim north along the coast past Lahaina, then turn west to visit the islands of Molokai and Lanai. Later they return south to Kahoolawe and then back to Maalaea Bay, a circular route which takes these mammals a distance of between 50 and 100 miles.

While it may take a whale about two days to swim and spout its way from Maalaea Bay to Lahaina, automobiles can make the trip in less than an hour, even allowing for a stop in between at **Olowalu** to see one of the island's best petrogylph sites. It is a beautiful drive, skidding atop seashore cliffs and down into plains full of waving sugar cane.

Cruise on as a whale cruises, then follow your nose into Lahaina town — Hawaii's much-touted hippie-jet-set capital of the Pacific.

Old Lahaina: Blubber, Bibles and Rum

Lahaina is the primary destination of most visitors to Maui. After the state capital of Honolulu, it is Hawaii's most widely-known town. Indeed, an increasing number of visitors bypass Oahu altogether as they head for the country-style, laid-back living that's become a trademark of this famous old whaling port.

Actually, though, Lahaina's roots go back much further than the days of big-time whaling. Following his victorious battle at Iao Valley, Kamehameha established a residence here along with Queen Kaahumanu. Kamehameha had another prominent wife and it was Queen Keopuolani who bore Kamehameha's three royal children, Princes Liholiho and Kauikeaouli (later to become Kamehameha II and III) and Princess Nahienaena. They were all born in Lahaina and thought of it as home.

When Kamehameha the Great died in 1819, the eldest son, Liholiho, inherited the throne as Kamehameha II. He made Lahaina the capital of his kingdom and it remained the center of Hawaiian government until 1845. It was also in 1819 that the first American whaleships visited the Hawaiian Islands. These were the *Equator* from Nantucket and the *Balaena* from New Bedford. Together, the crews of these two ships killed a large whale off the Big Island's Kealakekua Bay where Captain Cook had lost his life 40 years before.

The first whaleship to enter Honolulu was the *Mary* which arrived in 1820, the same year that Honolulu got its first Christian missionaries.

Whaleships and missionaries soon flocked to Maui and as early as 1823, the Revs. Charles Stewart and William Richards took residence in Lahaina under the sponsorship of Keopuolani, who helped them build a small grass church at Wainee.

Lahainaluna Seminary was opened by the missionaries in 1831 as a general academic school. Its initial classes were attended by adults but over the years it changed into a learning center for elementary and secondary students. The oldest American high school west of the Rockies, it continues to be one of the most respected educational institutions in Hawaii.

Old Lahaina,
circa 1873,

Liholiho and his wife, Queen Kamamalu, both contracted measles during a trip to London in 1824 and both died of the disease. Prince Kauikeaouli became the designated heir and in 1833, at the age of 18, took the title of Kamehameha III.

Kamehameha III had a great many lovers but he was closest to his own sister, Princess Nahienaena. Although the king spent much of his time in Honolulu on government matters, he returned frequently to Maui to entertain the pretty princess and their wild group of friends. Converted Christian chiefs eventually forced the couple apart and the two never married. Princess Nahienaena died at the age of 20, in 1836.

Later that same year, Rev. Richards became "Chaplain, Teacher and Translator" to the saddened king and thus was the first missionary to enter the field of Hawaiian politics. From him, Kamehameha III set about learning the American way of modern government. In time the young king instituted a policy of religious toleration and civil rights, proclaiming Hawaii's initial constitution in 1840. This constitution,

which provided for representational government and a national legislature, was drafted by a group of progressive Hawaiians on Maui. Among them was David Malo, one of the original adult students educated by missionaries at Lahainaluna Seminary.

Malo, often referred to as the first modern native-Hawaiian scholar, was torn between the ancient traditions of his people and changes being brought about by westernization. He was an active yet roughly-hewn writer whose seminal work, *Hawaiian Antiquities*, is still read over a century after his death.

He became an ordained minister and, after his government service, was pastor of a small church near the East Maui seaside village of Kalepolepo. When close to death, he requested that he be taken by canoe to Lahaina to pick out the proper spot for his grave. "It would," a biographer has written, "be above and secure from the rising tide of foreign invasion, which his imagination had pictured as destined to overwhelm the whole land."

Malo chose a hill called **Mount Ball**, overlooking his beloved Lahainaluna Seminary, and was buried there after his

Sailing through Lahaina Roads.

death. His reputation as an exemplary Hawaiian intellectual carries over to the present and each year the students of Lahainaluna High School — it became a public institution in 1923 — make "David Malo Day" one of Maui's most popular celebrations.

Malo wasn't wrong about the foreign invasion. By the 1840s, Hawaii had become the principal forward station of the American whaling fleet. Each year, thousands of seamen from Nantucket and New Bedford took liberty from their ships and prowled the waterfront streets of Honolulu and Lahaina.

Herman Melville, whose *Moby Dick* is the finest novel ever written about the whaling experience, visited Lahaina in 1843. He spent two weeks looking for a suitable job but found none to his liking.

King Kamehameha III was residing in Maui at this time and the town was relatively peaceful. Melville managed to visit the Lahainaluna Seminary before leaving for Honolulu where he remained for another four months, and at Honolulu he survived by working variously as a store clerk and as a pin setter in a downtown bowling alley. Melville originally wanted to remain longer in Hawaii but apparently changed his mind when the warship *United States* came into port. He enlisted as a common seaman and rode home to Boston on the vessel. Back in New England the whaler became a writer and never returned — except in his fiction — to the South Seas.

In 1844, the year after Melville departed, 326 whalers stopped at Lahaina and another 160 pulled into Honolulu. Over 400 ships came to Maui in 1846. The 1846 census showed that Lahaina had a total population of 3,557. There were 882 grass houses, 155 adobe houses and 59 of stone or wood. Local missionaries also reported that there were 528 dogs.

Lahaina was a favorite port-of-call because of its open roadstead. Offshore waters — commonly called **Lahaina Roads** — are sheltered by nearby Molokai and Lanai. Whalers discovered that their ships could safely anchor here and sail around West Maui in practically any kind of weather.

With the opening of whale-rich waters off the coast of Japan, the islands of Hawaii became even more of a replenishing base because Japanese shores were closed to all foreign trade.

Underwater whale watching, a new Lahaina sport.

Definite patterns began to emerge as these whaling ships began working the Orient and other areas of the Pacific. In the beginning, the ships sailed from New England around Cape Horn in the winter months and hunted the great whales until springtime when they stopped for supplies at Lahaina and Honolulu. Upon spending the summer months whaling, they would visit Hawaii again as they sailed back to New England.

The primary target of the Hawaiian whaling fleet was the sperm whale. It was not only the most numerous of the various species but also produced the best oil, which was found in the head cavity. The lower jaw of the sperm contained the large white teeth so prized by scrimshaw artists and used by the whalers for barter in more isolated island groups. In *Hawaiian Antiquities*, David Malo noted that the sperm whale was held to be the property of the king.

When the sperm whale could not be found, harpooners sought the toothless or baleen types. Among these were the right whale (the "right" one to catch), the bowhead, fin, gray and the acrobatic humpback which stayed close to Maui and Lanai. In the 1850s, as whaleships

got larger and voyages lengthened, their captains began spending summers on the northern flats and wintering along the equator. They then called at Hawaii during the spring and/or autumn and left their oil and whalebone ivory in storage. These products were usually trans-shipped back to New England in regular merchant vessels while the whalers once again took up the hunt.

Gold was discovered in California during 1849 and the rush to the West Coast there was of great benefit to Hawaii. Travel increased between the mainland and the islands and business prospered here. During these years, many new Californians sent their children to school at Lahainaluna Seminary because it was safer to send them overseas to Hawaii than back across wild Indian territory to the "real" New England.

An interesting description of Lahaina was published in 1851 — the same year that Melville's *Moby Dick* appeared. "Lahaina," wrote the Rev. Henry Cheever, "is one of those places which you like much better as you approach or recede from it, than when you are actually in it. A little way off it seems

"Pulling Teeth," late 1830s whaling sketch by Francis Allyn Olmsted.

Drawn by F.A. Olmsted

Lith of Endicott N.Y.

sweetly embosomed in breadfruit trees, and all fresh and lovely with sunshine and verdure, calmly enclosed seaward within a fence of foam, made by the sea breaking upon the coral reef. Ride over the rollers in a whale-boat or native canoe, get to the sun-burnt, dusty land, walk up a few rods, perhaps with pantaloons, to the mission houses, and make acquaintances on the way to your heart's content with Lahaina dust and caloric, and you will probably by that time be saying to yourself, 'Twas distance lent enchantment to the view.'"

The decline of the Pacific islands whale fishery began in 1859 when petroleum was discovered in Pennsylvania. Kerosene soon replaced the whale oil used in lamps, and wax did the same for the spermaceti in candles. Later, the American Civil War broke out and the Union purchased 40 whaleships in 1861, loaded them with stone and sank them to blockade the strategic southern harbors of Savannah and Charleston. This loss of tonnage cut deeply into the fleet and would never be replaced.

Confederate raiders such as the *Shenandoah* (which itself captured 39 Yankee whaleships in the Pacific) also inflicted great damage. After the war — Hawaii had been a neutral territory — the whalemen turned increasingly to Arctic waters for their catch. The final blow was thrown in 1871 when a group of 33 whaleships, including a few of Hawaiian registry, were caught in an ice floe off the northwest coast of Alaska. The ships had to be abandoned, and 1,200 rescued crew members, many of whom were native Hawaiians, were taken to Honolulu that October. From here most caught other ships back to New England. Overall, the fleet loss was put at about $2 million.

New Lahaina: Whaletown Chic

Although whaleships have long disappeared from Lahaina, this colorful waterfront town continues to preserve the spirit and architecture of the salty 1800s. This is where modern Hawaiian history began and where much of its drama now unfolds. Lahaina is also "where the action is" on Maui. The same narrow streets where Mark Twain and Herman Melville walked over a century ago are now brightly lined with dozens of gourmet restaurants, nightclubs and specialty shops with trendy names. But

Front Street of "New Lahaina," left and right.

despite its Hollywood, movie set veneer, Lahaina is a good walking town. It is almost level, only a few blocks deep, and pleasantly spread out for two miles along the coast. Weathered buildings hang out over the water. Though swimming is limited in the port proper, there are excellent beaches around, especially north towards Kaanapali where Maui's major resort hotels are located.

Get out of bed early and wander down to the sea-wall. The neighboring islands of Molokai and Lanai can be seen across the roadstead, sharply defined in the distance. Towards evening they become silhouetted against the fiery sky. Behind the town are sugar and pineapple fields leading up to the gently rounded, mile-high West Maui mountains. In the afternoon, softening light pops them into relief like cardboard cutouts against the clouds.

These green-covered fields and mountains serve notice that Lahaina hasn't always been a tourist mecca. Only as recently as the early 1960s, when **Front Street** was still largely cafes and grocery stores, a single tour bus downtown caused excitement among shopowners.

After the whalers left, West Maui belonged to the sugar plantation owners and in the late 1800s they imported thousands of immigrant laborers from China, Japan and Portugal. Many of these workmen stayed in the islands after their contracts had expired. Sugar remains an important part of Lahaina's economy—Maui produces one fourth of the state's annual crop—and a familiar local land-mark is the tall smokestack of the **Pioneer Mill**, built in 1860 by James Campbell.

Today a rebuilt 1890-vintage sugar cane train puffs over a six-mile route between Lahaina and Kaanapali, transporting tourists through canefields. Narrow-gauge tracks follow the haul line roadbed that was used by the Pioneer Mill until 1952, and Victorian-inspired train stations are located at both ends of this run by the **Lahaina, Kaanapali & Pacific Railroad**.

In 1962, the town was designated a National Historic District and since then the Maui County Historic Commission and the non-profit Lahaina Restoration Foundation have worked hard to encourage the preservation of distinctive older buildings and the construction of harmonious new ones. The

result is a fascinating blend of seaport nostalgia and contemporary living found nowhere else in Hawaii.

Center focus of Lahaina today is the **Pioneer Inn**, built in 1901. Although constructed over a quarter century after the Hawaiian fleet was lost in the ice off Alaska, it is a stylistic remnant of the whaling period.

This all-wood structure, wrapped around a large inner courtyard, fronts Wharf Street and overlooks the yacht harbor. On its walls are fading photographs of early ships and sailors, whaling equipment and other memorabilia. In the main entry way is a popular polychromatic sculpture (by island artist Reems Mitchell) of a weatherbeaten sea captain. This sly old salt has become the inn's trademark.

Inside the Pioneer Inn are posted the original house rules: "Women is not allow in you room; if you burn you bed you going out; only on Sunday you can sleep all day." Despite these stringent regulations, the quaint rooms enjoy close to a 100 percent occupancy throughout the year.

Downstairs there's a verandah restaurant called the Harpooner's Lanai, and also the Whaler's Bar, a popular hang-out for residents and visitors alike. The courtyard contains an outdoor restaurant featuring "broil-your-own" steak dinners.

Across Wharf Street from the Pioneer Inn, berthed in **Lahaina Harbor**, is the *Carthaginian II*. This 93-foot Swedish vessel replaced an earlier ship that was wrecked on a nearby reef in 1972. The floating museum contains a "World of the Whale" exhibit sponsored by the Lahaina Restoration Foundation.

Whale-watching has always been a popular pastime in Lahaina and a number of charter boats offer cruises designed strictly for that purpose. The humpback whale is now Hawaii's official state marine mammal.

The colorful Pioneer Inn dominates the **Town Square** but several other points of historical interest are within the block. A former court house, built in 1859, is now an art gallery, and cannons outside were taken from a Russian ship which sank offshore about 1816.

Ruins of an old fort are also found on the grounds. Or more correct, a reconstruction of what the ruins might look like. The original waterfront structure

Tourists at Pioneer Inn, 1979.

was pulled down in 1854 by order of the government. Its coral block stones were used to build the walls of **Hale Paahao**, a whaler's brig. This small prison — Hale Paahao means "Place of Confinement — is now open for visitors.

The town square's famous **Banyan Tree** was planted in 1873 by Sheriff William Smith to commemorate the 50th Anniversary of the first Protestant Christian Mission at Lahaina. It is the largest known in the islands and covers over two-thirds of an acre. At sundown it is a favorite roost for squawking mynah birds.

Most visitors confine themselves to the heart of Lahaina, a third of a mile long, between Shaw and Papalaua streets. Front Street runs perpendicular between the two and is the main shopping and entertainment strip. There's lots to do in that commercial stretch, and if you can't find it here, you can't find it. Wander in and out of the stores and browse as long as you like. The directory of business names — there's a Super Whale, a Whale's Tail and a Whaler's Market Place for a start — reads like nowhere else in Hawaii.

Lights go on when the sun goes down and music begins to blast from the town's many nightclubs. Quite a few top-name entertainers, from conservative ivory ticklers to heavy metal rockers, make Maui their vacation home and sometimes give surprise stage shows here.

Visitors can follow Front Street north until it merges with Honoopiilani Highway and continues with a smooth ride to **Kaanapali**, one of Maui's resort miracles. Twenty years ago this seaside area was primarily cane fields, but around 1960, the Amfac Corporation decided to develop a large hunk of land belonging to the Pioneer Mill Company into a resort complex of hotels, golf courses and condominiums. There are six hotels, the Whalers Village and Museum shopping complex and a local airport.

From Kaanapali the road passes through the beach villages of **Honokowai**, **Kahana** and **Napili**. There seem to be condominiums and apartment hotels springing up everywhere. Just beyond **Napili Bay** is **Kapalua**, meaning "arms embracing the sea." There is already a golf course here and a resort similiar to Kaanapali will eventually run along the coast.

The Kaanapali resort area.

The paved highway beyond Kapalua begins to round the northern end of the West Maui mountains, then stops at **Honokohau**. While the next dozen miles of cane haul roads offer spectacular coastline views, it's best to turn around unless you have a rough-riding jeep.

Upcountry Maui: Gentle Cowboys, Gourmet Onions and Pineapple Wine

From Kahului it is a pleasant drive along the Haleakala Highway to **Pukalani** and **Makawao**, upcountry villages which originally housed plantation workers and cowboys from nearby cattle ranches. They are now thriving again due to a renewed interest in rural living. The annual July 4th rodeo in Makawao is one of the island's most popular events.

Pukalani, the "Hole in the Heavens," lies at the geographical entrance to the Kula District. This is Upcountry Maui, where temperatures here in the salad bowl average in the low seventies and fall another ten degrees on higher slopes.

Agriculture at Kula is probably the most diversified in the state. Commercial farmers harvest a wide variety of vegetables, including lettuce, cabbage, turnips, tomatoes, cauliflower, cucumbers, carrots and peas. True gourmets believe that the extra-sweet Kula onions (forget about just plain Maui onions) are the best to be found anywhere, particularly after being baked and stuffed with butter.

During California Gold Rush days— while whalers were frequenting the bars of Lahaina—Irish potatoes, corn, and wheat were exported from Kula to the U.S. West Coast. Fruit, too, grows well in the rich volcanic soil here. Apples, peaches, plums and pears are planted in addition to pineapple, and half of all Hawaii's pineapples are grown on Maui.

At the 30,000 acre **Ulupalakua Ranch**, experiments are now underway to develop a grape suitable for a first-class sparkling wine. The vineyard, located five miles up the Haleakala ridge, hopes to be producing a red wine by the middle 1980s. It will be called La Perouse after the French explorer who anchored nearby in 1786. Already in production is a pineapple wine called **Maui Brut**.

Flowers are yet another part of the colorful Upcountry scene. Carnations

Ranch country, Kula.

head a long list of cut blossoms sent to Honolulu. Of particular interest is the protea, a new flower being raised here for world mrkets. The obscure protea — there are at least 60 varieties in assorted colors — is a tropical bloom biologically related to the macadamia nut. Hopes are high in Kula over this high-priced beauty.

Nearby is the Haleakala Crater Road which twists steeply up to a National Park headquarters. There are good over-looks of the crater itself and orientation panels at several spots along the way to the summit. On cold days the two visi-tors buildings will protect you from the sharp breezes.

At the **Kalahaku Overlook** you can see the famed Haleakala silversword, a re-markable plant with dagger-shaped sil-very leaves. The mature silversword (*Argyroxiphium sandwicense*) supports a central stem covered with yellow and reddish-purple florets. Flowering occurs from June through October and the entire plant dies after a single blooming season.

The crater below is a fragile wilder-ness area and hikers should keep to the marked trails. The National Park

Service maintains two campgrounds and three cabins for visitors.

Back down the road in Kula, near **Waiakoa**, is another often photographed building, the **Holy Ghost Hall of Our Lady Queen of Angels Church**. This octagonal church was built in 1897 by Portuguese laborers who were brought into the area to run farms.

Close to the **Ulupalakua Ranch**, the Upcountry road begins its descent, rounding the southern slope of Halea-kala and cutting across dry ranchlands. Piilani Highway continues on to **Kanaio**, **Puka'auhuhu** and **Kaupo**. The pavement ends at **Nu'u Bay**, about five miles before Kaupo, and from here to Kipahulu it's a narrow dirt road.

Despite a lack of moisture here, this is an exciting coastline drive. Cattle pas-tures are marked by old lava flows and the surf pounds away at the rocky vol-canic shore.

A pleasant place to stop is at **Kaupo** where a well-defined trail winds up the southern mountain slope from the village to **Haleakala National Park**. It crosses **Kaupo Gap** in the crater and ends at the **Paliku** cabin area, eight miles from park headquarters.

Bouquet of Haleakala silverswords and a *paniolo* in palaka jacket.

Little Kahoolawe Island: Red Dirt For Hot Bombs

Driving along the high Piilani Highway, it is impossible not to notice **Kahoolawe**, the smallest of Hawaii's eight major islands. Seven miles to the southwest, Maui County's uninhabited island has been the center of considerable controversy in recent years. This is because the U.S. Navy claims ownership of the island and regularly uses it for target practice. Since 1941 practically every type of conventional artillery—from guided missiles launched by F-4 Phantom jets to screaming 155 mm. howitzers—has been fired into its red soil. Shock waves from these explosions are sometimes felt on Maui as they reverberate across the narrow channel.

Many native Hawaiians feel that Kahoolawe and other sacred lands were taken illegally by the U.S. when Queen Liliuokalani and the monarchy were overthrown in 1893. They want the land returned to the state and the bombing stopped. A number of people have been arrested for trespassing on the island without the Navy's permission.

Prior to Captain Cook's visit, the residents of Kahoolawe were primarily fishermen. Most of them—it is unlikely the population ever got larger than 200—lived near the coast, although archaeologists have found a few inland settlements. David Malo wrote that the islanders planted yams and sugar cane on the island but the dryness of the soil prevented taro cultivation. The island was probably only used as a fishing base.

During the 1800's, the island was established as a penal colony by the monarchy. Queen Kaahumanu wanted to use it as a place to banish Catholics. Later it was briefly used for the exile of male prisoners who had committed serious crimes.

After this punishment was stopped—the last prisoner's sentence was terminated in 1851—the island was leased for sheep grazing and in 1910 was proclaimed a Territorial Forest Reserve. Efforts at reclamation progressed slowly until the start of World War II. The U.S. Navy was given full control of the island in 1953. In late 1980, the Navy released a report nominating 171 sites on the island to the National Register of Historic Places. Target areas near the sites have been abandoned.

A Toast to Monsieur La Perouse

It is doubtful that one could find a more romantic name for a Maui wine than La Perouse. From the future vineyards at Ulupalakua Ranch, a rugged jeep trail leads down to **La Perouse Bay**, a rock strewn anchorage near the southernmost tip of Maui. It's not a good spot for swimming but fishermen favor the area because of its isolation and lava-rock perches.

This lonely bay was named for the French explorer Jean Francois de Galaup, the Count de La Perouse, who stopped here in 1786. Two years later his two ships left for Australia and were never seen again.

Directly north of La Perouse Bay is **Cape Kinau**, an outcropping of land formed by the last eruption of Haleakala in 1790. It is now part of the **Ahihi-Kinau National Area Reserve**, a designation that will hopefully protect its unique environmental treasures.

Another jeep trail will take travelers from La Perouse Bay to **Makena** and a long stretch of beaches perfect for swimming. Its off-the-beaten-path location attracts a steady stream of backpackers

The late *kupuna,* Auntie Emma deFries in meditation on a beach at rugged Kahoolawe.

who often camp for a week or more at a time, discarding their clothes as they wear themselves out among the waves.

Farther up the coast is **Wailea**, as magical a piece of real estate as you'll ever find on Maui. A few years ago this area was a desert of briar patch, cactus and *kiawe* trees. Despite having five of the best beaches in Hawaii it only gets about ten inches of rain a year. Beginning in 1974, however, developers built two 18-hole golf courses, a tennis center, shopping facilities, two hotels and plenty of condominiums. Then they activited a sprinkler system and the desert turned green. Today, people literally stand in line to buy $100,000 condominiums and prices continue to skyrocket.

From the wonders of Wailea it's a pleasant drive past the roadside beach-parks of **Kamaole** and **Kalama**. It's another half-dozen miles from **Kihei**, on the eastern edge of Maalaea Bay, back into Kahului.

A Winding 'Highway to Heaven'

The two to three hour drive from Kahului to **Hana** takes a traveler over the most famous single road in Hawaii.

Indeed, there are parts of the **Hana Highway** that rival sightseeing anyplace else in the Pacific.

For the first half of the journey, by and past Haiku, the paved road is straight and wide. Later, around the 20-mile mark at **Twin Falls**, the road begins to twist and bend crazily along the cliffs. There are plenty of green-ferned valleys along the route with one-lane bridges that cross deep ravines and gushing stream beds. To the left is a drop-away coastline of jagged lava-rocks and pounding surf. On the right are cascading waterfalls, thickets of bamboo, paper-bark trees, ironwood and eucalyptus. Brightly-colored birds and flowers complete this Kahului to Haiku and on to Hana assault on the senses. As tourist brochures advertise, you are on Hawaii's "Highway to Heaven."

Because this "Heavenly Hana" side of Maui is discussed by another writer in the following article, we will leave you here, on Hawaii's Route 36, contemplating an upcoming, mind-bending course of 617 curves and 56 bridges which make navigating to Hana both a frustrating, fascinating and some say "ethereal," travel experience.

U.S. Navy detonates 500 tons of TNT on Kahoolawe, February, 1965.

THE HANA COAST

The "gateway" to the **Hana Coast** is the quiet community of **Huelo**. Huelo, with its little Congregational church, **Hakakaupueo**, the owl-resting perch, is one of those rural departure points where time seems to reverse itself. As with many pleasant Old Hawaii visions to be experienced along the winding Hana Highway, there is neither a geographic nor a historic explanation for the feeling of change, or of a beginning, one feels upon entering this village.

Where Land and People Change

From Huelo eastward to Hana the smell of flowers and dense foliage seems to reach further into the senses than before. The *aina*, the land, undergoes imperceptible but distinct changes which in some biological way drug a traveler and carry him or her into a more natural and less complicated past.

It has often been stated that the Hana Highway has more curves per mile than any other roadway on earth. Indeed, after spending the nearly two or three hours it takes to cover the 50 odd miles from Kahului to Hana you will no doubt agree with the above conjecture. However, stay alert, because this serpentining roadway is rich in constantly changing vistas, each seeming to challenge the last for spectacular combinations of color and grandeur. A missed glance could rob you of a scenic opportunity never again to be repeated.

One good place to unwind enroute to Hana is at the **Kaumahina State Park** near **Keanae**. Restrooms and picnic tables are provided, and the park's carefully tended grounds include samples of plants common to this coast. If you feel like a swim in a refreshing mountain pool, merely retrace your steps a few hundred yards to **Puohokamoa Falls**. Then from the Kaumahina parking lot hike to the upper left side of the park and experience a spectacular view of the **Keanae Peninsula**. If you are one of the fortunate few who see the moon come up over this rugged coastal beauty, you will understand why Hawaiians named this place *Kaumahina*, or rising moon.

Keanae legend has it that the god Kane thrust his spear into a rock here and that fresh water gushed forth. Once the site of many fish ponds, the Keanae Peninsula is now host to a community of taro farmers, nearly all of pure or part-Hawaiian ancestry.

A narrow road leaves the highway and curves a half-mile down to a scattering of houses, a tiny cemetery and a Congregationalist Church. The church was built in 1856, the year Abraham Lincoln was elected President, and was one in a "circuit" which Congregationalist ministers established around Maui.

In earlier times—when only a horse trail connected Keanae and Hana—there were two country-style grocery stores located here, and the field behind the church was a baseball diamond. The school building used to face in an opposite direction, but a big, 1946 tidal wave spun it around on its foundation. Sadly, a number of lives were lost along this coast during that disaster, but today's advanced *tsunami* warning systems are designed to prevent such tragedies in the future.

Crashing surf and jet-black lava offer a fine spot for wine-sipping and a seaside picnic, but Keanae folks ask that you leave nothing behind but fond

Along the Hana coast.

memories.

Wailua, the next Hana Highway community, is also blessed with an abundance of fresh water that is so necessary for the cultivation of taro. Its tiny Catholic Church — **St. Gabriel's** — was one of the first to be built on this coast. The lookout above Wailua is furnished with picnic benches, and fresh spring water is available free and cool for drinking just across the road.

Another and somewhat more popular roadside stop on the Hana side of Wailua is **Pua'aka'a State Park**, where restrooms, picnic tables, a rain shelter, natural waterfall and swimming pool all invite passersby to a refreshing rest and swim.

This coast, however, has not always been so idyllic. Hardy pioneers of turn-of-the-century Hawaii saw great economic opportunities along this fertile coast, and in their zeal they attempted to establish a boggling array of new cash crops here. These included both the usual sugar and pineapple, but also cotton, eucalyptus, vanilla beans and rubber. **Nahiku** not only produced rubber, but gained the distinction of being the first rubber-producing plantation in America. A drive down Nahiku Road belies the fact that there was once so much activity here, but the community used to buzz during its tapping season and was even serviced by a small railroad and barge-loading facility.

The most impressive agricultural accomplishment along this coast, however, was intended to benefit other parts of Maui. This is a fantastic array of ditches, pipelines and flumes which are considered by many agriculturists to be among Hawaii's greatest engineering accomplishments. While many Hana coast efforts were doomed to economic failure, this elaborate trans-island irrigation system literally transformed the island's arid central plain into a verdant and highly productive place. A century after it was built, this system is still in constant and efficient use. Most of the small concrete bridges you will cross on the Hana Highway were built in concert with this herculean effort, which is most appreciated when one considers the awesome logistics of transporting all construction materials by horse, mule and man power, which in turn were taken on to Honolulu by inter-island steamships.

'The Sky Comes Close to Hana'

After what seems to have been an eternity of road curves, fern grottoes, flower-studded rock walls and tinkling waterfalls, the Hana Highway unravels itself and your vehicle verily sails into the rolling hills and pastures of "Heavenly Hana." At the **Hana Airport**, you'll see propellor-set tourists buzzing in and out of Hana on the regularly scheduled small aircraft which commute to this corner of paradise; and perhaps a half-mile closer to Hana, persons who endured and enjoyed the road route to Hana often are found cooling their minds and heels inside waterfilled caves and tide-pools at **Waianapanapa State Park**. This seaside park built on a ragged but overgrown lava flow is a favorite East Maui campsite with good swimming, hiking trails and other appointments.

Old Hawaiians say that "the sky comes close to Hana," and they tell the area legend about a deity who once stood atop **Kauiki Hill** (the prominent cinder cone adjacent **Hana Bay**) and was able to throw his spear through the sky. Kauiki, which stands as an omnipresent guardian of Hana, once was the site of a large fortress where great battles were fought between residents of Maui and invaders from the Big Island of Hawaii. According to tradition, Kauiki was guarded by a large and fierce idol who kept invaders at bay. Big Island armies were able to establish strongholds on other parts of Maui, but Kauiki's strength remained intact, postponing for many years the complete conquest of Maui. *Kauiki*, the glimmer, also was the birthplace of Queen Kaahumanu, the favorite and most powerful of Kamehameha the Great's many wives. Kaahumanu, who in her later years adopted Christianity and encouraged Kamehameha II to overthrow the ancient *kapu* (tabu) system, allegedly was born in a cave at Kauiki. Her birthsite is duly acknowledged by a historic marker.

For a magnificent view of the Hana area, drive through a pasture to the top of nearby **"Lyon's Hill,"** where a large stone cross has been erected. This prominent crucifix is a memorial to Paul Fagan, the founder of **Hana Ranch**. Access to this memorial and viewpoint is permitted during daylight hours as long

Hana Bay and Kauiki Hill (right) from Lyon's Hill.

as the entrance gate is open, but go slowly — the road is steep and bumpy.

And before continuing either north or south of Hana, remember that Hana is the last stop for necessities such as gasoline, cold beer and food. There are two markets in town, but whichever you choose for shopping, be sure to stop in at the fabled **Hasegawa General Store**. This venerable establishment, made famous by the zany song "Hasegawa General Store," employs a "hall closet" system of stockage and inventory control. And if you don't believe Harry Hasegawa and family stock a little bit of everything, just think of something unlikely and ask for it. The Hasegawas are seldom stumped.

Directly across the street from Hasegawa's store is a famous battlefield where some of the bloodiest conflicts in Maui's history were fought. Hawaiian reports tell of more than a thousand war canoes being anchored here by invading forces from the Big Island.

On the upper side of Hana's main road you'll see many old buildings which were once part of an old **Hana Sugar Mill** complex. These remnants of Hana's plantation days reflect an era

Hukilau fishermen, Kipahulu.

when mostly Hawaiian Hana was transformed into a racial melting pot, with separate "cane camps" established for laborers of Filipino, Chinese, Japanese and Portuguese ancestry.

If you decide to go on past Hana, a few words of caution are in order. First, the road will get narrower, turning into a rutted, dirt byway that in places is little more than a trail. True, there are still more waterfalls and other such scenic beauty, but if you are road weary or faint of heart, this may be a good place to relax a while before returning to the other side of Maui. Also, driving the road past the Seven Pools area is prohibited by most car rental companies and is not recommended for standard passenger vehicles.

'Sacred' Pools, Bad Roads And a Sleeping Hero

Upon leaving Hana in a southern direction you will pass through several country road miles of scattered homes — some of them architecturally interesting, but most of them landscaped and "settled" in a comfortable Hawaiian style. The latter boast a happy abundance of children and puppies, two pleasant reminders to go slow and enjoy the view. You will also pass a number of beautiful waterfalls, most of them with chilly base pools excellent for swimming. The pools' rocks are slippery, but otherwise, Hawaiian legends not withstanding, you need not worry about other dangers or denizens. (Note: take a bag with you for your rubbish, or for the last person's, if he or she was so unkind as to leave any behind.)

The road soon carries you through the fourth and fifth pools of the so-called **Seven "Sacred" Pools**, properly known as the **Seven Pools of Kipahulu**, or, in ancient times, as *Oheo'o*. Because of these pools' prominence in ancient times, menstruating women were not allowed to bathe in these *kapu* waters. The pools are a beautiful part of this coast, but because of their well-publicized accessibility they are sometimes alarmingly congested with tourists. However, they are wonderful for swimming, and a knoll to the right of the last fall as it drops into the ocean is one of the most dramatic settings in Hawaii. It's a good place for a sip of wine and a line or two of impromptu poetry — but prepare not to be alone.

Just past the Seven Pools of Kipahulu is the abandoned **Kipahulu Sugar Mill**, distinguished by a smokestack. And just down from the mill, on the sea side of the road, is the entrance to tiny **Kipahulu Hawaiian Church**, a quiet place of worship which in recent years became famous when the renowned aviator Charles Lindbergh was buried, Hawaiian-style, in the church's small graveyard. Lindbergh, who in May, 1927 piloted himself and "The Spirit of St. Louis" from Mineola, New York, to Paris (and was greeted by Parisians as a great hero), died at his nearby home on August 24, 1974. The Hawaiian church here is quaint, and the graveyard is a poignant spot, but local people would appreciate it if you would remember the place and Lindbergh by driving on, thus giving him the peace and quiet he sought so desperately during life.

You now are headed for some *bad* roads. Also, heavy rains in this area can unexpectedly swell roadside and cross streams to river-like dimensions, and more than one motorist has spent worrisome hours stranded here, wondering how he would ever get home.

Cattle guards across the road mark the entrance to **Kaupo Ranch**, a large beef-raising operation that has been worked since before the turn-of-the-century. The picturesque church you'll see resting on the small surf-pounded peninsula below the ranch is **Huialoha** (a "Gathering of Love"), an old Congregational "circuit" church which was recently restored to its original condition by concerned residents and friends. The church was built in 1859, a time when Kaupo was almost totally landlocked, accessible only by sea and a primitive trail. There is an unlocked gate at the road leading down to the church, and you are welcome to visit the church-grounds (but please close the gate behind you).

This area's old place name is *Mokulau*, many islets, and was named for the gathering of lava rock islands which lie just offshore. The stone ruin behind the church was once a Hawaiian school.

If you're into photography, a great spot for a photo is the wide-angle vantage at the edge of **Mokulau Point** which includes the school, Huialoha Church and **Kaupo Gap** all in the same frame. The latter geological site is the "cut-out"

Huialoha Church at Kaupo.

in Haleakala's rim which in ancient times was the primary route taken by Hawaiians who traversed Maui on foot. This trail led through the awesome Haleakala Crater itself, and is thus extremely popular with modern-day hikers. Vegetation has hidden many historic sites in this area, but scores of carefully constructed walls of motarless lava stand as silent, crumbling reminders of a time when Kaupo hosted thousands of Hawaiian residents.

Kaupo Store, about a half-mile or so up the road towards Makena, once was the only local source of food and supplies, but is now open primarily to satisfy the thirst and hunger of tired hikers and overheated motorists. Bits of memorabilia abound in this little free enterprise, and if proprietor Al Soon is about, he will gladly show you some of the equipment his father assembled long ago to generate electricity and photographically record events of days past. The senior and late Soon was known throughout Maui for his inventive nature, and he once brought a disassembled Model T to this village by barge, thus introducing remote Kaupo to its first "gasoline buggy."

Just up the road, an abandoned Catholic church, **St. Joseph's**, begs for restorative favors which, hopefully, will be undertaken soon. The remains of a living site and Sunday school have almost disappeared into a tangle of brush here, but the grounds are a challenge to compulsive pokers-about, and the view of Kaupo Gap from St. Joseph's churchyard is unparalleled.

As the ocean comes back into clear view, one easily understands why the Hawaiian people found Kaupo an ideal place to settle: the sea is abundant with fish, the weather is dry enough to accommodate simple thatched structures, there are ample springs to provide fresh water, rain forests grow enough timber for construction purposes, and Haleakala contains all the hard basalt a Hawaiian ever needed to make adze heads and other tools of his trade. By simply moving from one elevation to the next, a person could completely vary his atmosphere and lifestyle, and provide for different earthly needs.

This part of Maui, desolate but strikingly and simply beautiful, is clearly a place apart, like all of Hawaii used to be.

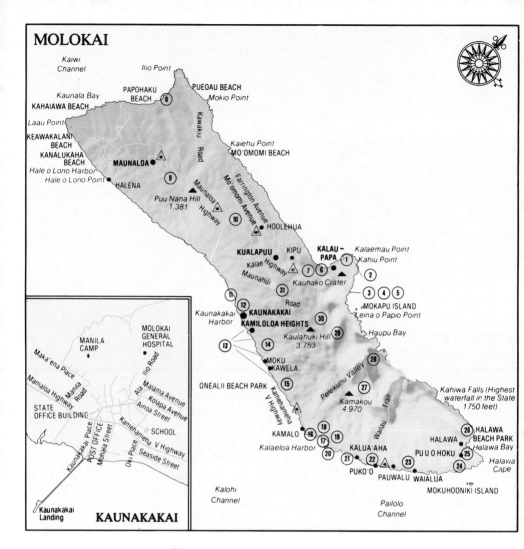

MOLOKAI

Kaiwi Channel

Ilio Point

PUEOAU BEACH
Mokio Point

PAPOHAKU BEACH ⑧

Kaunala Bay

KAHAIAWA BEACH

Laau Point

KEAWAKALANI BEACH
KANALUKAHA BEACH
Hale o Lono Harbor
Hale o Lono Point

HALENA

MAUNALOA △

⑨

Kaiehu Point
MO'OMOMI BEACH

Puu Nana Hill 1,381

Maunaloa Highway

Mo'omomi Avenue

Farrington Avenue

Kawakiu Road

⑩

HOOLEHUA

HOOLEHUA

KUALAPUU   KIPU

KALAU-PAPA ①

Kalaemau Point
Kahiu Point

Kalae Highway

⑦ ⑥

②

Maunahui

⑪   ⑤   ⑬

Road   Kauhako Crater

③ ④ ⑤

Kaunakakai Harbor
KAUNAKAKAI
KAMILOLOA HEIGHTS

⑫

⑤   ⑭

MOKAPU ISLAND
Leina o Papio Point

Kaulahuki Hill 3,753

③⓪

Haupu Bay

②⑨

MOKU KAWELA

⑤

ONEALII BEACH PARK

Pelekunu Valley

②⑧

Kahiwa Falls (Highest waterfall in the State 1750 feet)

Kamakou 4,970

②⑦

Wailau Trail

Kamehameha V Highway

KAMALO
Kalaeloa Harbor

⑯ ⑱
⑰   ⑲

②⓪   ②①   ②②   ②③

KALUA'AHA

PUKO'O
PAUWALU   WAIALUA

PUU O HOKU

HALAWA

②⑥ HALAWA BEACH PARK
Halawa Bay

②⑤

②④

Halava Cape

MOKUHOONIKI ISLAND

Kalohi Channel

Pailolo Channel

KAUNAKAKAI

MANILA CAMP

MOLOKAI GENERAL HOSPITAL

Maka'ena Place
Ilio Road

Mamaloa Highway   Manila Road

Malama Avenue
Kolapa Avenue
Ainoa Street

STATE OFFICE BUILDING

Ala

SCHOOL

Kaunakakai Place
POST OFFICE
Mohala Street
Oki Place
Kamehameha V Highway
Seaside Street

Kaunakakai Landing

Land Area:
260.9 square miles
38 miles long, 10 miles wide

Population:
Total: 6,300 (1977 census estimate)
Kaunakakai: 1,070 (1970 census)

Highest Elevation:
Kamakou Mountain: 4,970 feet

Airport:
Kaunakakai: Hoolehua Airport

Main Seaports:
Kaunakakai Harbor
Hale 'o Lono Harbor

Preceding two pages, Lanai, "The Pineapple Island" as seen from neighboring East Maui.

Points of Interest

3 Father Damien Monument
13 Fishponds, Ancient, Along the South Coast
19 Hokukano Heiau
10 Hoolehua Airport
22 Iliiliopae Heiau
31 Ironwood Hills Golf Course
28 Kaaiku Heiau
1 Kalaupapa Airfield
2 Kalaupapa Lighthouse
11 Kapuaiwa Coconut Grove
6 Kaule o nanahoa Phallic Rock
14 Kawela Place of Refuge
20 Kukui Heiau
18 Malae Heiau
27 Malahini Cave
9 Mauna Loa Golf Course
15 Pakuhiwa Battleground (1736)
7 Palaau State Park
26 Papa Heiau
24 Puu o Hoku Ranch
25 Sacred Kukui Grove
16 St. Joseph Church (1876)
4 St. Philomena Church (1872)
30 Sandalwood Boat
8 Sheraton Molokai Hotel
5 Siloama Church (1871)
17 Smith and Bronte Landing (1927)
21 Kalua'aha Church (1832)
12 Kamehameha V's Summer Home
29 Waikolu Lookout
23 Weloka Heiau

220

LANAI

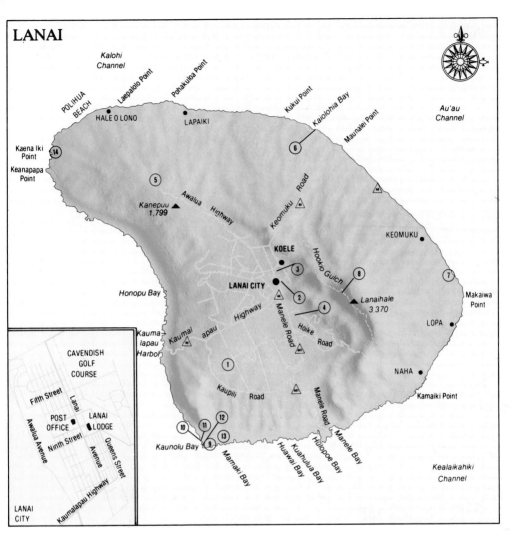

Land Area:
139.5 square miles
18 miles long, 13 miles wide
Population:
Total: 2,200 (1977 census estimate)
Lanai City: 2,122 (1970 census)
Highest Elevation:
Lanaihale: 3,370 feet
Airport:
Lanai City: Lanai Airport
Main Seaports:
Kaumalapau Harbor
Manele Bay

Points of Interest

3 Cavendish Golf Course
5 Garden of the Gods
12 Halulu Heiau and Petroglyphs
14 Kaenaiki Heiau
7 Kahe'a Heiau and Petroglyphs
10 Kahekili's Jump
9 Kaunolu Village
11 Kolokolo Cave
1 Lanai Airport
2 Lanai Lodge
6 Lighthouse Ruins
4 Luahiwa Petroyglyphs
13 Mamaki Heiau
8 Munro Trail

MOLOKAI

Nowhere in his travel letters did Mark Twain mention leprosy, until recently Molokai's chief claim to fame. Apparently he feared the subject would disturb some of his newspaper readers; especially any businessmen who might want to invest in the islands.

Two decades later, another celebrated author, the Scot Robert Louis Stevenson, was not so timid. In a public letter of his own, Stevenson defended a Catholic priest who had died of the disease in 1889 while helping the lepers. After his death, the priest had been attacked by a protestant minister in Honolulu as "a coarse, dirty man, headstrong and bigoted . . . not a pure man in his relations with women."

While it is not known when leprosy first came to Hawaii, it was identified here as early as 1830. In 1866, the year of Twain's visit, the *Warwick*, a government schooner, began transporting lepers to Molokai and dumping them on the isolated north coast peninsula called **Makanalua**, "The Given Grave."

The young Belgian priest, Father Damien Joseph De Veuster, arrived here in 1873 and remained until his death, 16 years later. During this period he organized the leper colony into a unified community. They built houses, a church and even a primitive hospital. Land was cleared, crops were grown and a modern water system installed.

Father Damien became a living legend in Hawaii, praised by his people and honored by his government for "efforts in alleviating the distresses and mitigating the sorrows of the unfortunate." By 1884 he had contracted leprosy himself and five years later he died at the age of 49.

Damien, a member of the Hawaiian mission of the Sacred Heart, entered into his "unclean" but spiritually strong life at a time when there was no known cure for leprosy, known to the Hawaiians as *ma'i Pake*, the Chinese disease. Leprosy was later renamed Hansen's Disease, after a Norwegian scientist, Armauer Hansen, who in 1868 identified it as *bacillus leprae*.

Stevenson's tribute to this saintly man was circulated worldwide and Father

The Rev. Elmer A. Wilson, pastor of Ierusalema Hou Church Halawa Valley; and interior of St. Joseph's Church (1876) near Kamalo.

Damien's reputation as the "Martyr of Molokai" has made him one of Hawaii's most beloved heros. Not until the late 1940s was leprosy brought under control by sulfone drugs. Today, less than a hundred lepers remain in the village of **Kalaupapa** although they are now legally free to leave the peninsula.

A Tough and 'Friendly' Island

Molokai certainly wasn't the "Friendly Island" in Father Damien's time. Its current nickname was a conscious public relations attempt to get rid of the leprosy image that had plagued Hawaii's fifth largest island since the mid 1800s. Still, there is no doubt that Molokai is as friendly as most rural areas tend to be. The land is primarily agricultural and development has been limited. And, best of all, the tourists are few.

On a map, Molokai is a slender slipper, 37 miles long and 10 miles wide. Its total area is 261 square miles.

The island has three geological entities, each created by volcanic activity millions of years ago. **Mauna Loa**, a tableland at the western end of the

island was formed first and rises to 1,381 feet. Later the **East Molokai Volcano** erupted and **Mauna Kamakou** was pushed up to 4,970 feet. This is the island's highest elevation.

Makanalua Peninsula, where the leper colony is located, was born even more recently, when **Kauhako Volcano** poured forth its lava to shape a flat tongue of land in the center of the northern coast. It is separated from the rest of the island by a fortress-like barrier of high cliffs.

The main **Hoolehua Airport** is eight miles from the principal town of **Kaunakakai**, across the island from **Kalaupapa Peninsula,** on the southern coast. This is the island's trading center although less than 1000 people live here. Ala Malama, the "main street," contains a quaint collection of wooden, false-front buildings that probably haven't changed much since the 1930s when pineapple production was in full swing.

A prominent feature of Kaunakakai is the dockside wharf which extends far out to sea. Until only recently this waterfront area was congested with pineapple barges being loaded for shipment to Honolulu canneries. Molokai's great

Kaunakakai town at sunset.

pineapple years, though, are over. Dole has closed down its operations here and Del Monte may do so as well. High labor and shipping costs make it almost impossible to compete with growers in the Philippines and Taiwan. In future years the island's agriculture will turn increasingly to other fruit crops, vegetables, grain, hay, and cattle raising.

Close to the Kaunakakai wharf are the remains of Kamehameha V's old summer home. Before Prince Lot became king in 1863, he lived on Molokai and, during his nine-year reign, spent his summers here. During this time he also planted the nearby **Kapuaiwa Grove**. Originally there were 1,000 coconut trees on ten acres of land.

Across the highway from the grove is Molokai's church row. These houses of worship are built on property provided by the Hawaiian Homes Commission. Churches with at least a partly native Hawaiian membership may get permission to locate here.

Fishponds, Battlefields and Gods

Travelers will find that only a few minor roads crisscross Molokai and these are quite rough on conventional vehicles. It's best to rent a jeep or stick to the pavement.

East from Kaunakakai, the Kamehameha Highway runs 30 miles to **Halawa**. The mileage doesn't seem like much until you drive it. However, there is much to see along this stretch and the second half is a narrow lane twisting along the coast. Remember, too, that unless you're camping out you'll have to turn around at Halawa and drive back.

Along the road are numerous fishponds built as far back as the 15th Century to supply food for families and retainers of chiefs. Such ponds were constructed on all of the Hawaiian islands but the largest concentration has been found on Molokai. The ponds were enclosed by walls of coral blocks and basalt stones, and rise up to six feet above water. Wooden gratings allowed small fish to enter from the sea but once full-grown and fattened they were too large to escape.

Many of these ponds have since been ruined by silt-buildup or tidal activity. A few of those that remain are either operated commercially or maintained by marine labs for aquaculture experi-

Halawa Bay from the road lookout above.

ments.

Hidden in the jungle valleys leading up the rugged slopes of Kamakou are enough old *heiau* and other historical sites to keep interested hikers busy for years. However, many of these sites are on private, locked properly, so check with the County Building in Kaunakakai before you violate a local *kapu*. Above **Kawela**, meaning "heat of (the battle)" is a battlefield where Kamehameha I won an early skirmish. It's written that his canoe fleet landed upon the beach in an assault wave four miles long.

In the same general area can be found the deteriorating walls of an old *puuhonua*, or place of refuge. Criminals who reached such a walled enclosure without being caught — and stayed there for a set number of days or hours — were eventually able to leave without fear of punishment.

Visitors should stop at **Kamalo** where Father Damien built the second of his two churches on this side of the island. He constructed this white, wood-frame structure in 1876 and dedicated it to St. Joseph. Nearby is also the **Smith and Bronte Landing**. It was on this spot that in 1927 Ernest Smith and Emory Bronte ended the first civilian transpacific flight from California by crashing into a *kiawe* thicket.

At **Kaluaaha** is **Our Lady of Sorrows Church**, built by Father Damien in 1874 and recently restored. The grounds are well kept and there is a wooden statue of the famous priest in the pavilion. Here, too, is **Kaluaaha Church**. It is the oldest standing church in the state, having been constructed by Congregationalist missionaries in 1832.

Three miles or so after passing Waialua, the road twists inland and begins winding up to **Puu-o-Hoku ("Hill of Stars") Ranch and Lodge**. Grazing on the green mountain slopes are a few thousand head of cattle.

Looking back down the mountain, the scenery is spectacular. Across the **Pailolo Channel** is Maui and the great bust of Mount Haleakala. Closer is tiny **Mokuhooniki Island**, used by the U.S. military for bombing practice during World War II.

Just past the ranch entrance is the sacred *kukui* tree grove of **Kalanikaula**. These gray-barked, silvery-leafed trees once encircled the home of Lanikaula, a local *kahuna* who dwelt there. Hawaiian

Ancient fishpond, near Moku on Molokai's south coast.

laborers once refused to help a Del Monte subsidiary company clear the area, and a Japanese grower who cut down some trees to plant pineapple there found that his crop merely wilted.

The road ends in **Halawa Valley**, a four-mile long and half-mile wide idyll. Hundreds of fishermen and farm families used to live here but only a couple still remain. Today this area of Molokai is popular with back-packers who must get permission from the ranch to camp in the valley.

In the rear of the valley are two waterfalls that feed a stream flowing into the sea. The longest is 250-foot **Moaula Falls**, legendary home of a giant sea dragon. Hikers who wish to swim in the pool beneath the falls should first find out if the dragon is home by tossing a *ti* leaf into the water. If the leaf sinks it might be better to come back another time. A floater indicates the dragon is away from his lair.

Beyond Halawa the **Pali Coast** to Makanalua is as beautiful — and as rugged — as you'll find anywhere in the world. There are meandering jeep trails through the interior, but unless you're a real adventurer it's best to see the Wailau and **Pelekunu Valley** areas by helicopter or from an offshore boat.

West End: Where Giraffes Roam

The central regions of Molokai are also excellent places to explore. Back through Kaunakakai and up past Hoolehua Airport the Maunaloa Highway runs through a dry landscape for about ten miles. **Maunaloa**, itself a former plantation town once operated by Dole, lies at the end of the road.

A number of secondary spurs branch off the main highway and wind down to the coastline. The **Sheraton-Molokai**, the island's only "luxury" hotel, is located at **Kepuhi Bay** near the northwestern tip. Other resort areas will follow. The beach is good and if you walk here on a clear night you can see the roller-coaster lights of Oahu and Diamond Head across the 25-mile wide **Kaiwi Channel**.

Molokai's biggest social event of the year takes place at **Hale-o-Lono**, a rocky harbor down from Maunaloa on the southwest coast. This cattle playground of red dust and *kiawe* trees is the starting site of the annual Molokai-to-Oahu outrigger canoe race held in October. The

Sand dunes and fresh water pool, Moomomi.

42-mile Aloha Week event ends at Magic Island in Honolulu's Ala Moana Park.

Much of this dry leeward side of the island is taken up by pasture land owned by **Molokai Ranch**, the largest local landowner. When Dole closed down its pineapple activities here in 1976 the company returned to the ranch almost 10,000 acres it had been leasing. Now much of this land has been planted with guinea and green panic grass for a commercial haying business.

So far, however, this is only a small part of the Molokai Ranch's operation. Cattle continue to be the mainstay of the company and its herd numbers around 3,000 head, some of which are pastured across the island at **Puu-o-Hoku Ranch**.

In addition to the cattle, Molokai Ranch has been keeping exotic animals in a high-fenced area below the former pineapple fields. Included are antelope, deer, giraffes, and other creatures that have brought a touch of the African Serengeti to this end of Molokai. These animals will be raised here for sale one day to zoos and game reserves. Tours to this Hawaiian nod to the Dark Continent are easily arranged.

The 'Topside' Land of Fragrant Wood

Another interesting Molokai sidetrip begins with a gravel-road turnoff a half-mile south of the Y-shaped junction of Maunaloa Highway and Route 46.

Nine miles ahead is the curious **Sandalwood Boat**, actually a hole in the ground roughly the size and shape of a 19th Century sailing ship's hold. Hawaiians used the depression to measure the amount of sandalwood that these ships could carry before releasing it to white traders who had commissioned them to do the work.

The fragrant wood was eventually shipped to the Orient. Sandalwood is no longer abundant on Molokai because, according to one story, the older laborers cut down all the young saplings so that later generations would be spared the slave conditions required to harvest the trees.

Farther along this road (off-limits to rental cars) is **Waikolu Lookout**, a sightseeing spot that gives a grand view down into a 3,000-foot deep valley ribboned with cascading waterfalls. This gorge is a watershed for the Makanalua Peninsula and there is a tunnel at the

The Kamakou mountains, East Molokai.

bottom that supplies irrigation water to the dry leeward plains. It is possible to hike into the valley but the foot trail ends at **Pelekunu Valley**.

Back out on the highway, Route 46 will take you through **Kualapuu** (the Del Monte company town) to **Palaau State Park**. The park road passes through an attractive forested area and there is an arboretum where native trees are displayed. From the parking lot it's a short walk and a slight climb to **Ka Ule o Nanahoa**, a phallic rock six-feet high that was visited in years gone by for the purpose of curing local ladies of infertility.

The park also has a **Kalaupapa Overlook** that offers a spectacular view over the 1,600-foot cliffs to the leper colony below. In his 1959 novel, *Hawaii*, James A. Michener described the peninsula as "a majestic spot, a poem of nature ... In the previous history of the world no such hellish spot had ever stood in such heavenly surroundings."

Kalaupapa — The 'Flat Plain'

The town of Kalaupapa is only a ghost of what it used to be during Father Damien's time. Once there were more than a thousand people here. Now there are less than 150.

Permission is required to visit Kalaupapa Peninsula but this is easily obtained through airlines or tour operators. If you're on your own, contact the Hawaii State Department of Health in either Honolulu or Molokai. Normally children under 16 are not permitted.

While there is a small airport on the peninsula, the Great Molokai Mule Train Ride is an unforgettable experience. Every day but Sunday, mule tours begin at a topside corral and wind down the same steep path that Father Damien took in the late 1800s.

Jack London followed this route in 1907 when he traced the priest's footsteps around Kalaupapa. Today, in his honor, some writers call it the **Jack London Trail**. He wrote a number of short stories relating to leprosy after his visit and devotes a chapter to the Kalaupapa residents in his *The Cruise of the "Snark,"* published in 1911.

The actual trail is about three miles long, with 26 switchbacks (and will require most of a day to negotiate round trip). Wear casual clothing—long pants

Ka-Ule-o-Nanahoa, the penis of Nanahoa, phallic stone near Puulua Hill, the Kalaupapa Overlook and Palaau State Park.

are recommended — and let the mules worry about where to put their feet. None has fallen down yet.

At the bottom of the cliffline it's only a short ride along the shore to the outskirts of Kalaupapa. No one is allowed to wander unattended here, however. Tours of the peninsula are given by the patients themselves and these guides are quite frank about their disease. They will answer any questions you might have about their isolated lifestyle. Patients may now leave the colony — leprosy is not highly contagious — but most remain because this historic peninsula has become their home. All of the houses are provided by the state.

Kalaupapa is a village town with an uncertain future. There are the small wooden houses, a few churches, a general store, and a social hall among the buildings. A weathered, termite-ridden hospital awaits a promised replacement. The meadows are full of neglected gravestones, rusting junk and bedspring fences. The area is overrun with dogs and cats but all are taken care of. Since the town is not allowed to have children — any new babies are taken "topside" to live — these pets have be-

come the "children" of Kalaupapa.

East across the peninsula is the abandoned settlement of **Kalawao**. This beautiful spot was the site of the original leper colony but after 1888, when a water pipeline was extended from **Waikolu Valley**, the residents moved to the less rainy and windy Kalaupapa side.

There are two well-known landmarks at Kalawao. One is **Siloama, the Church of the Healing Spring**. This Protestant structure was built in 1871. A year later construction began on **St. Philomena's Catholic Church** and it was completed after the arrival of Father Damien in 1873.

In the adjoining cemetery there is a fenced-in monument, but the priest's grave is empty: in 1936 Damien's remains were returned to Louvain, in his native Belgium.

The Kalaupapa Peninsula was designated a national historic monument in 1975 and in years to come it will likely become a national park. Nothing would delight the leprosy patients more. Such a park would be a fitting memorial to the saintly man who gave both his love and his life to the friendly people of Molokai.

Sandstone formation, near Moomomi.

LANAI

For almost a thousand years after the Polynesians arrived in Hawaii, Lanai remained uninhabited. It was considered a "ghost" island and a hangout for evil spirits.

The first settler, according to legend, was Kaululaau, son of an early Maui king named Kaalaneo. He was a strong but mischievous boy who delighted in pulling up breadfruit trees in the village of Lele, now known as Lahaina. This could not be tolerated long since the fruit of this tree was a necessary food to the people.

King Kaalaneo finally banished the young prince to Lanai, where he figured his son would either be killed by the ghosts or forced to grow up fast. If he ever wanted to return to Maui he could show his repentance by burning a fire that could be seen across the channel.

Kaululaau had no intentions of being killed so during the nights he hid in a cave and the ghosts were unable to find him. During the days he became a hunter and tracked down the spirits one by one. When the last was killed he built a fire on the beach and was welcomed back to Maui as a great hero.

Now that the evil was disposed of, the people from the neighboring islands of Maui and Molokai began migrating to Lanai. This is believed to have happened sometime after 1400. The original inhabitants were probably fishermen who lived along the coast but in later years they discovered that the fertile interior lands were ideal for raising crops.

A 'High and Craggy' Isle 'That Abounds in Roots'

While there have always been stories that a Spanish galleon was wrecked off the island in the 1500s, the first known Europeans to sight Lanai were members of Captain Cook's third Pacific voyage. Cook, however, never saw it himself.

That opportunity fell instead to his successor, Capt. Charles Clerke. It was Clerke who commanded the expedition after Cook was murdered at Kealakekua Bay on February 14, 1779. Just over a week after Cook's death on the Big Island the *Resolution* and *Discovery*

Lanai, red earth and blue sky.

230

sailed along Lanai's southern and western coastlines.

"The country to the south," one of Clerke's officers recorded, "is high and craggy; but the other parts of the island had a better aspect and appeared to be well inhabited. We were told that it produced very few plantains and breadfruit trees; but that it abounds in roots such as yams, sweet potatoes and tarrow."

Even today there are few breadfruit trees on the island. Oldtimers say that this is because the exiled Kaululaau pulled up all the trees here just as he'd done earlier in Lahaina.

After Clerke departed, European visits were sporadic. La Perouse passed nearby in 1786 and George Vancouver circled around the island, but did not land, in 1792. Vancouver's surgeon noted the "naked appearance of the island, which seemed thinly covered with shrivelled grass in a scorched state. No hamlets or plantations were to be seen, no trees or bushes adorned the face of the country . . ."

This desolate description of Lanai is clear evidence that the island was fought over frequently by warring chieftains.

Not until 1795, three years after Vancouver's visit, did Kamehameha I emerge from the pack victorious, uniting all of the Hawaiian islands except Kauai and Niihau. It took him another 15 years to obtain sovereignty over these two holdouts and in 1810 — by diplomacy, rather than by war — he became the first absolute ruler of Hawaii.

King Kamehameha I was extremely fond of Lanai and during his reign kept a summer home at **Kaunolu Bay** on the southwestern cape. During this time there was a small village here and the king enjoyed fishing in the area. Athletic tournaments were also held at Kaunolu in his honor.

The periodic residence of the king on Lanai was the beginning of the island's modern history.

Pineapples and Norfolk Pines

Eight miles west of Maui and seven miles south of Molokai, Lanai is the sixth largest of the Hawaiian islands. Kahoolawe, pockmarked since World War II by artillery fire, lies 15 miles to the southeast.

Lanai is rocky and pear-shaped, 17

Pineapple fields and Norfolk pine outside Lanai City.

miles long and 13 miles wide. The total area is 141 square miles. Observed from Maui, the land buckles upward from its southern base to a height of 3,370 feet at **Lanaihale**. From there it tapers downward, sloping gradually to the sea. This characteristic topography gives the island its name, Lanai — the "hump."

Like all the other islands in the chain, Lanai is a volcanic land mass. It consists of a lone crater, **Palawai**, now extinct. The **Palawai Basin** makes up Lanai's best farmland.

There is a single airport on the island, five miles from the only town, **Lanai City**. Visitors also have the choice of but one hotel, the **Lanai Lodge**. This is a white-painted, wooden structure, built in 1927.

Lanai City was laid out in 1924 to house the original 150 foreign laborers that Jim Dole brought in to work in his pineapple fields. Two years earlier Dole's Hawaiian Pineapple Company had purchased nearly the entire island from Harry and Frank Baldwin for $1.1 million.

Jim Dole, a persevering businessman from Boston, changed the face of Lanai. More than 15,000 acres of the island were eventually turned over to pineapple cultivation. He spent another $2 million on building his plantation town and in creating a harbor at **Kaumalapau**.

Dole paid good wages for his day and he had no trouble attracting Chinese, Japanese and Filipino workers. Lanai City became a model town with individual family homes on nicely landscaped lots. Today there are about 2,500 residents, mostly Filipinos, on Lanai.

'World's Largest Pineapple Plantation'

Castle and Cook is owner of approximately 98 percent of Lanai. It acquired the island in 1961 when it bought the assets of Dole Corporation, formerly the Hawaiian Pineapple Co. Oceanic Properties is a wholly-owned subsidiary of Castle and Cook which conducts the bulk of the company's real estate activities and which was responsible for the development of the Lanai Plan.

The "Lanai Plan" has since been approved by the State and it will serve as a guide for the island's future growth. Under the plan, tourism will be limited and the population kept to 15,000. Low-rise resorts will be allowed in designated

Dockworkers, Kaumalapau Harbor.

areas, but nearly 80 percent of the island will be left to agriculture or open forest and meadowland.

Unlike Molokai, where pineapple fields are quickly disappearing, Lanai will remain the home of Hawaii's favorite fruit for many years to come. It's truly "The World's Largest Pineapple Plantation."

Criss-crossing 'The Hump' And 'Kahekili's Jump'

There are only about 25 miles of paved roads on Lanai but a good jeep will allow you to explore countless more. If you're not afraid to eat dust, discovering Lanai can be a great adventure.

It should be repeatedly stressed that Lanai is not an island for the package tour traveler intent on seeing sights at a glance, then moving on in air-conditioned comfort to another island. Lanai is for the hardy traveler who doesn't mind rugged hiking, brambles, rough underbrush, and dusty red earth which eventually stains your exposed parts and clothes a chalky rust.

An excellent source of information if you'd like to do some serious hiking on Lanai — or indeed if you'd like to hump into any of Hawaii's more obscure areas — is Craig Chisholm's splendid manual, *Hawaiian Hiking Trails* (The Touchstone Press, Beaverton, Oregon, 1977).

Beginning at Lanai City, there are three paved primary roads that connect with the coast. The best and busiest is the southwestern highway that leads down to **Kaumalapau Harbor**. Here, as Jim Dole envisioned a half-century ago, over a million pineapples a day are unloaded from company trucks during the summer harvest season and taken by barge to the Honolulu cannery, 60 nautical miles away on Oahu.

A very rough jeep road off the highway will take you down to **Kaunolu Bay**, but plan to drive over three miles of rocky trails. Your reward will be the ruins of **Kaunolu Village**, King Kamehameha's summer residence and the most complete archaelogical site of its type in Hawaii.

Dr. Kenneth Emory of the Bishop Museum spent half of 1921 doing research on the island, camping alone for five weeks at Kaunolu. By then the village had been abandoned for 50 years.

He found the remains of 86 house

Fisherman at Hulopoe Beach near Manele Bay.

platforms, 35 stone shelters, grave-stones, and detached garden plots. The *heiau* of **Halulu** is located on the west bank overlooking the stream bed, while the king's home is thought to have been on the eastern ridge.

From here the noblest of all Hawaiians could watch as his warriors proved their bravery by darting along a narrow path and leaping 62 feet into the sea from Kahekili's Jump. The object was to clear a 15-foot ledge at the base of the cliff.

A Touch of the Antipodes

It is possible to walk east along the shoreline to **Hulopo'e Bay** but only the hardiest hikers should try it. A much easier route is down Manele Road from Lanai City. Hulopo'e Bay has an attractive coastal park and is the best place to swim on the island.

Just around an easterly point from Hulopo'e Bay and its beach is **Manele Bay** and another smaller beach where sailboats can often be seen bobbing at anchor during stopovers between Maui and Oahu. Camping is allowed in this area, but get permission and instructions

from the Koele Company in Lanai City before setting up tents and other such camping paraphernalia.

Lanai's most unique touring route is surely the **Munro Trail**. This can be reached from Manele Road (4-wheel drive is recommended) by taking the Hoike turnoff up to the ridge and circling around to **Lanaihale**, the highest elevation on Lanai. On a clear day you can see all the major Hawaiian islands except Kauai and Niihau.

George C. Munro was a New Zealander who was hired around 1910 to manage the Lanai Ranch. He was also an amateur naturalist and had the habit of riding horseback through the mountains, sowing seeds from his saddlebags wherever he went.

Among his successful plantings were the Norfolk Island pines that have become an island trademark. Besides adding a touch of the antipodes to the landscape the pines collect moisture from the air and increase the island's supply of ground water.

The Munro Trail continues down past **Hookio Gulch**, scene of a 1778 battle in which Kamehameha I participated, to **Koele** and back to Lanai City. Here, too

Shipwreck Beach.

are more Norfolk Island pines. Munro later transplanted small trees from the hills for Jim Dole and their presence in Lanai City made his town a much cooler place to live.

Windward Lanai: Shipwreck Beach And Hawaii's 'Garden of the Gods'

Another popular excursion area is the island's convex northeast coast. It can be reached by following Keomuku Road until it forks near the shoreline. To the left is a trail to **Shipwreck Beach**; to the right is a better road that leads to the abandoned village of **Keomuku**. Both require at least an hour of travel time.

Shipwreck Beach is so described because the trade winds roaring between Maui and Molokai often get powerful enough to drive boats up on the reef. Although there is a rusting World War II hulk offshore, most of the wrecks occurred during the days when wooden sailing ships and steamers anchored regularly in Lahaina.

Keomuku Village was abandoned after the collapse of the Maunalei Sugar Company in 1901. Parts of the plantation offices and company store were subsequently dismantled and shipped to Maui. Most of the remaining buildings have been torn down in recent years but there are plans to restore an old wooden church that has miraculously survived the fickle fates of man and weather. A jeep trail continues around the eastern coast to the former Hawaiian village site at **Naha** but it's a rough ride and almost impossible to make on a rainy day.

Sometimes neglected by visitors is a geologic curiosity known locally as the **Garden of the Gods**. It can be reached by driving northwest along the Awalua Highway, which at this point is a dirt road through pineapple fields. Here, seven miles from Lanai City, is a strange playground of strewn boulders and disfigured lava formations. These rocks seem to have been dropped from the sky. Nowhere else on Lanai is quite like this and unusual photographs of the area can be taken at sunrise or sunset.

Despite its other-worldly appearance, the Garden of the Gods makes an interesting camp site for a night under the stars. Don't worry about ghosts. The name of this windswept sand canyon is proof enough that the evil spirits of ancient Lanai are never coming back.

Garden of the Gods.

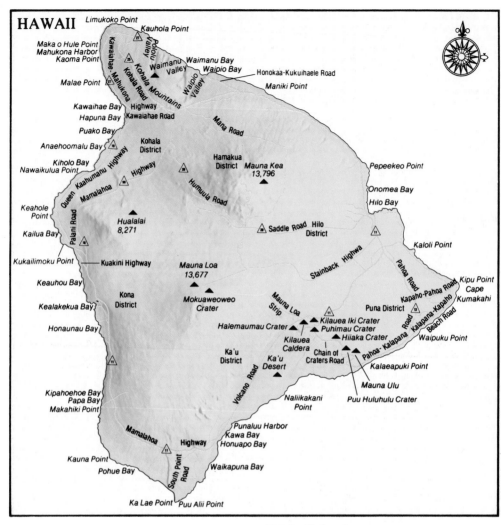

HAWAII

Limukoko Point
Kauhola Point
Maka o Hule Point
Mahukona Harbor
Kaoma Point
Kawaihae
Kohala Road
Malae Point
Mahukona
Pololu Valley
Waimanu Valley
Waimanu Bay
Waipio Bay
Honokaa-Kukuihaele Road
Maniki Point
Waimea
Kohala Mountains
Waipio Valley
Kawaihae Bay
Hapuna Bay
Puako Bay
Highway
Kawaihae Road
Anaehoomalu Bay
Kohala District
Kiholo Bay
Nawaikulua Point
Queen Kaahumanu Highway
Mamalahoa
Highway
Hamakua District
Mauna Kea
13,796
Pepeekeo Point
Keahole Point
Palani Road
Humuula Road
Mana Road
Onomea Bay
Hilo Bay
Kailua Bay
Hualalai
8,271
Saddle Road
Hilo District
Kukailimoku Point
Kuakini Highway
Kaloli Point
Keauhou Bay
Mauna Loa
13,677
Stainback Highway
Pahoa Road
Kipu Point
Cape
Kumakahi
Kealakekua Bay
Kona District
Mokuaweoweo Crater
Mauna Loa Strip
Kapaho-Pahoa Road
Puna District
Kalapana-Kapaho Beach Road
Honaunau Bay
Halemaumau Crater
Kilauea Iki Crater
Puhimau Crater
Hiiaka Crater
Pahoa-Kalapana Road
Waipuku Point
Kilauea Caldera
Chain of Craters Road
Kalaeapuki Point
Ka'u District
Ka'u Desert
Mauna Ulu
Puu Huluhulu Crater
Kipahoehoe Bay
Papa Bay
Makahiki Point
Volcano Road
Naliikakani Point
Mamalahoa
Highway
Punaluu Harbor
Kawa Bay
Honuapo Bay
Kauna Point
South Point Road
Waikapuna Bay
Pohue Bay
Ka Lae Point
Puu Alii Point

Land Area:
4,037 square miles
93 miles long,
76 miles wide

Population:
Total: 79,200 (1977
        census estimate)
Hilo: 42,699 (1977)
Kona: 12,600 (1977)
Puna: 8,100 (1977)
Kohala: 6,800 (1977)
Hamakua: 5,200 (1977)
Ka'u: 3,900 (1977)

Highest Elevation:
Mauna Kea: 13,796 feet

Preceding pages, the summit area and a moon
rise at Mauna Kea; cattle country above Pa'auilo,
the Big Island; and a fern forest at Volcano, the Big
Island.

Airports:
Hilo: Hilo International
        Airport
Kona: Ke-ahole Airport
Kamuela:
        Waimea-Kohala Airport

Main Seaports:
Hilo Bay
Kawaihae
Kailua, Kona

Points of Interest

33 Ahu-a-Umi (16th
   century heiau)
9 Akaka Falls State
   Park
   Ancient Canoe Moorings
47 Ka Lae
72 Kalamanu
69 Kalapana
55 Ancient Footprints
   in Lava
62 Anthuriums of
   Hawaii Garden
7 Boiling Pots
38 City of Refuge
   National Historical
   Park
35 Coffee Farms
12 Douglas, David,
   Historical
   Monument
56 Fern Jungle
   (Kilauea Iki Crater)

61 Glenwood Park
54 Hawaii Volcanoes
   National Park
48 Heiau o Kalalea
46 Heiau o Molilele
37 Hikiau Heiau State
   Monument
6 Hilo Country Club
1 Hilo International
   Airport
2 Hilo Zoo
34 Holua Slide
42 Hoopuloa Church
   Monument
30 Hulihee Palace
   (Kailua-Kona)
16 Kalahikiola Church
59 Kalani Botanical
   Garden
28 Kaloko Fishpond
20 Kamehameha I
   Birthstone

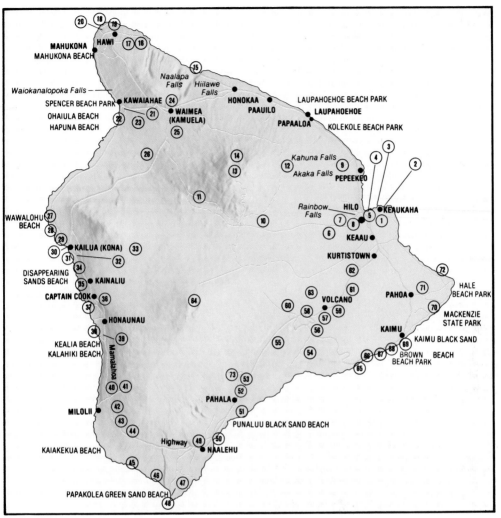

THE BIG ISLAND, HAWAII

So complex is the island of Hawaii that no nickname embraces all of it at once.

Call it the "Orchid Island" for the wild purple blossoms that grace the roadsides of Puna and Hilo. Call it the "Volcano Island" for half of it is alive, with myriad fissures steaming and two mountains eager to erupt. But also call it the "Big Island" for it is so huge that each of its five districts is larger than any other island in the Hawaiian chain. Big indeed, but no one here boasts or brags.

A rough diamond in shape, Hawaii thrusts four capes to the tradewinds a hundred miles apart. If time permits, the island should be explored counter-clockwise starting from Hilo. Then a meaningful sequence of its varied climates, landscapes, peoples and adventures can unfold: humble flowers in Hilo, plantation towns in Hamakua, giant valleys in North Kohala, cattle ranches in Kamuela, deserts and oasis beaches in South Kohala, coastal resorts and coffee hills in Kona, startling green sand in Ka'u, and, finally, active Kilauea volcano in Puna — epitome of Hawaii's past and future.

Hilo: 'The Crescent City'

Hilo was always a trading place. Hawaiian tribes came to the **Wailuku River** that separated Hilo from Hamakua, shouted their bargains across the rapids, and gingerly made exchanges. Foreign ships found deep anchorages between the coral heads of its wide bay, and eventually a channel was dredged so steamships could put in.

Horse-shoers, missionaries, farmers, jewelers, tailors, teachers and dentists dropped anchor in Hilo; mothers and fathers opened shops. By respecting their own and their neighbors' traditions, Hilo families grew peaceful and prosperous. The late Aunty Edith Kanakaole, who spoke and sang the language of *Hawaii nei*, composed chants when a volcano erupted and now her daughters teach *hula* to men and women. The Lyman family restored their missionary forbears' house as a museum, then built a full-size museum complex —

Tidal wave memorial, Kaikoo Center, Hilo.

SHINMACHI TSUNAMI MEMORIAL

IN MEMORY OF
THOSE WHO LOST THEIR LIVES
IN TIDAL WAVES ON THIS ISLAND.

DONATED BY
SHINMACHI CLUB

the **Lyman Mission House and Museum** — on their land. Built in 1839, it is the oldest frame building in Hilo and is furnished with effects of the missionary era. Adjacent to the mission home is the new museum complex which features ethnic history exhibits, volcanic and scientific displays and other curious artifacts.

Touches of Japan

The Japanese, especially, embody Hilo's American Dream. Those who came as peasants to sweat sugar out of the soil raised English-speaking children who flocked into civil service and free enterprise; many have been elected to the County Council and the office of mayor. Respectful of their parents, they have run the island with particular sensitivity to the needs of older people. And the Japanese influence is undeniable: non-Japanese join neighborhood funeral associations called *kumiai*, businessmen of all races join the Japanese Chamber of Commerce and Industry, and a weekly Japanese newspaper, *The Hilo Times*, is still published here. Every summer a full-rigged sailing ship docks from Japan; its sailors parade in colorful costumes alongside local children bearing lanterns in an International Festival of the Pacific.

Hilo's people are soft-spoken and humble. "Progress" has, in many ways, passed them by; an easy pace here mitigates against rapid changes. Hilo faces the dawn: it is a daylight city. Many shops open at sunrise, and restaurants do most of their business — and serve their best food — at lunchtime.

Hilo is, simply, old-fashioned. Impatient tourists grumble when they don't find endless beaches or brassy nightclubs. The island is too young, geologically, to have evolved many coral beaches, so "beach parks" in Hilo are just shallow places along the shore good for swimming. Local entertainers still have to work at daytime jobs to feed their families. Serious travelers will find attractions that are — like the town itself — quiet and contemplative places. The **Rainbow Falls** in the **Wailuku River Park** sport prismatic trim in early mornings and late afternoons when the sun is oblique to its cascade. At **Liliuokalani Gardens**, near Banyan Drive hotels, is a Japanese garden of stone bridges, lions and lanterns, and a

Off-loading tuna, Suisan Dock, Hilo.

tea ceremony house. Early risers can watch Hilo's fleet of high-prowed fishing "sampans" bring their catch to auction at the **Suisan Dock**. On Highway 11, the new **Panaewa Zoo** displays rainforest plants and animals, and **Nani Mau Gardens** has probably the largest collection of orchid varieties in the state. An arboretum operated by the State Division of Forestry on Kilauea Avenue is a park on weekdays, where fruit in season may be sampled off the trees. Hilo's downtown buildings are old, and many are quite beautiful; wooden awnings overhang the sidewalks as shelter from the rain. Horses were once tethered to iron rings that are still imbedded in the curb along Waianuenue Avenue.

Located 5½ miles south of Hilo on Highway II is the **Mauna Loa Macadamia Nut Mill** and Visitor Center. Mauna Loa, a subsidary of C. Brewer and Co., is the world's largest grower, processor and marketer of macadamia nuts.

Battered Into Rubble

Downtown once stretched the length of the bayfront, and so Hilo was nicknamed the "Crescent City." But on April 1, 1946 a cruel tidal wave swept half the town inland, then dragged the debris seaward. Hilo rebuilt and recovered, stretching a stone breakwater across the bay to shield the harbor. But in 1960 another *tsunami* broke over the shore, swirling in the bay like tea in a shallow cup. This time there was no rebuilding. Civic leaders resolved that no more homes or businesses should ever again be battered into rubble, no more lives should be lost. They drained the lowland crescent and raised a new hill 26 feet above sea level. There they mounted a new government and commercial center and called it **Kaiko'o**, rough seas.

From the roof of the Hilo Lagoon Hotel, if weather is clear, **Mauna Kea** dominates the northwest. Dark forests circle the mountain above the bright green sugarcane, thinning out as the altitude rises, finally vanishing — along with shrubs, grasses and birdlife at the alpine heights where snow in winter gives the "white mountain" its name. A windy plateau named for its saddle shape serves as a bridge between Mauna Kea and the "long moutain," **Mauna Loa**.

The old Hamakua Coast railway, about 1920.

The Hamakua Coast:
A Journey Through Old Hawaii

Hawaii's people came here to work and a great wave of laborers was Japanese. From the end of the 19th Century until the 1930s, they brought their faiths and family-based life to the islands. Although many of the "camps" in which they lived are now occupied by newer immigrants, the plantation lifestyle along the Hilo and Hamakua Coasts was molded by this Japanese experience. To go back in time, to see what the quiet, agricultural world of prewar Hawaii might have looked like, travel along this coastal road into the past.

Once a railway carried sugar and freight, commuters and weekend excursion passengers between the mills of Hamakua and Hilo. Cars and horse-drawn carts followed a simple winding road between the workers' camps, with palm trees for fenceposts along the sea cliffs. After the 1946 *tsunami* undercut most of the railway bridges, they and their tracks were demolished. Trucks took over, clogging the old road until a new highway was laid bypassing the camps.

A traveler can return to the plantation era and enjoy an old-fashioned part of Hawaii by driving along the quiet Mamalahoa Highway, as the old road is called, and using the main Highway 19 to bridge its gaps. Wainaku Street, in Hilo, is the start of the Mamalahoa route. A right turnoff leads to **Honolii**, a river estuary with the only reliable, year-round surfing waves in the Hilo vicinity. After picking up the highway again, a right turn past **Papaikou** is marked "Scenic Drive 4 miles long." That beautiful stretch follows the coast past **Onomea Bay**, once a major sugar port.

There once was a sea-sculpted arch on its northern side but one day in the late 1940s, according to an artist who was painting it at that moment, it suddenly collapsed after a mild earthquake; now it is just a notch in the ridge. The old road rumbles over many one-lane wooden bridges covered with bright red African Tulip flowers in spring and squashed guavas in autumn. Plantation workers have, by and large, left the camps to buy fee-simple homes on company land far below the current market prices. At **Kulaimanu**, near **Pepeekeo**,

Hamakua Coast, 1979.

their fine gardens and flower beds are turning old cane fields into lush, warm neighborhoods. **Kolekole Park** is on another stretch of the old road, as is the town of **Honomu** where a spur (route 220) leads to the high (420 feet) and thin **Akaka** and **Kahuna Falls**.

Shielded From Poverty

Change comes so slowly to **Hamakua** that few people see it. A new house, a new car, a new storefront, perhaps, but never anything startling. Towns like **Laupahoehoe, Papaaloa, Paauilo** and **Paauhau** look and feel much as they have for generations. On weekends Filipino families secretly pit and wager on the fighting chickens they proudly rear. Fathers and sons take their dogs into the muddy forests on pig hunting expeditions. Children and old men play softball in the parks. The paternal mills and the fraternal labor unions have shielded them from poverty — they are the highest-paid agricultural workers in the world. A cloying smell of freshly-fertilized fields and an overpowering mist of sweet cane juice being boiled into molasses drifts over parks and banana patches, clings to gardens and rose-apple trees, and wafts into the three great gulches of **Maulua, Laupahoehoe** and **Kaawaloa**.

The rivers that cut through those volcanic channels have their sources far uphill where few visitors or residents ever go. With permission from neighboring ranchers to unlock their gates, occasional hunters and foresters ride their jeeps and horses up into the high lands of the **Laupahoehoe Forest Reserve**. It is a landscape misty in summer and frosty in winter. Here the tall *koa* and *ohia* trees stand; some are selectively logged, then trucked to Hilo, sawn and kiln-dried to become furniture and veneer. Many others are being slowly choked by aggressive vines which the foresters desperately fight to cut back. Bluegum eucalyptus, planted as a windbreak earlier in the century, has also grown too thick, so many stands are chipped and sold to Japan by the boatload to become stiff paper and wallboard.

Hidden in the forest reserve are some cold-weather trees which were planted in the 1920s by the farsighted foresters: spruce, cypress, maple, redwood.... When the current blight has extermi-

Sugar mill artifacts on Hamakua Coast.

nated all the elms in North America, perhaps scions for new breeding stock may be taken from the handful of elms untouched here at **Keanakolu**. The reserve was established to protect the watershed of the island's windward side, so rainfall can soak into the rich earth and not run off, pooling underground to be tapped for irrigating sugarcane fields far downhill.

King Cane Is Dying

The sugar industry, however, is slowly declining in local importance. Hawaii's agribusinessmen are already hedging their bets by planting macadamia nuts (Queensland nuts, as they are called in their native Australia). The trees mature late but bear for decades, annually dropping hundreds of incredibly hard shells enclosing sweet white meats. The **Hawaiian Holiday Macadamia Nut factory** in **Honokaa** has a wide assortment of tasty products for sale. Its store is open daily from 8:30 a.m. to 5 p.m. Candy-coated macadamia nuts are a forgettable luxury, but the plain nuts, roasted or raw, are a healthy, wholesome snack while driving.

Waipio Valley, a few miles north of Honokaa, is broad and deep, and was almost certainly the center of the island's cultural and political life in the century before the European arrivals. It was home to thousands of farmers who drained garden terraces and irrigated taro patches. Its twin waterfalls, called **Hiilawe**, feed a broad river that was stocked with fish that skilled men and women could catch with their bare hands. The black alluvial beach knew the keels of dozens of canoes that crossed its treacherous currents to trade with neighboring valleys. By the early 20th Century Waipio's young people had moved away to work on the plantations, and rice replaced taro in the wet ponds. After World War II, two *tsunami* flooded the valley floor and the remaining families lost nearly all their possessions. Gradually, fiercely independent farmers returned to the fertile places.

In the 1960s the American Peace Corps trained volunteers here, preparing them for life in rural Asia by building Borneo-style longhouses and Filipino-style huts. Today, the little village is abandoned, but visitors may pitch a tent

Waipio Valley and her twin falls of Hiilawe.

there, a short hike away from a swimming pool below **Hiilawe Falls**. Many hikers cross the beach and scale the Z-trail on the far side enroute to **Waimanu Valley** seven miles north over irregular terrain. There a traveler may find the perfect stillness of a valley totally unoccupied by permanent residents.

Paniolo Cowboy in the 'Poo-Y-U'

Early European visitors were proud to offer Kamehameha domesticated animals to raise and eat. But the low stone walls of the Hawaiians were unable to contain goats, sheep or cattle. After ten years feral herds were ravaging cultivated farmlands and gnawing young trees to death from coast to coast. In 1809 a vigorous New England American named John Palmer Parker offered to round up the *haole* animals in exchange for a homestead. Kamehameha gave him two acres, and Parker's ranch and dynasty began. Today, **Parker Ranch** cowboys run some 50,000 head of cattle over 224,000 acres of pasturelands which often are referred to as "the largest privately owned ranch in America." During the early 19th Century, however,

Parker had to bring Spanish-American cowboys to Hawaii to help him rope and brand the wild cattle. These *vaqueros* were called *paniolo* (after *Espanol*) by the Hawaiians, and to this day all Hawaiian cowboys are referred to as *paniolo*, and their grazing areas as *paniolo* country. In later years some Portuguese joined them, playing an Iberian guitar and a miniature guitar the Hawaiians called *ukulele*, or jumping flea. Locally-born boys were trained as ranch hands too, and today there are Oriental, Hawaiian and Caucasian *paniolo* riding the Parker Ranch range.

Rodeos are as popular here as in the American West, and several are staged every summer. There is even a unique-to-Hawaii event: the "Poo-Y-U" which recalls that earlier era when Parker and his men had to round up wild cattle alone. A man would lasso the giant animal and run his horse around a forked tree, looping his rope through the "Y" as a pulley and dragging the beast up against it.

In the late 19th Century, the family business became the largest cattle ranch under individual ownership. Colonel Samuel Parker supplied most of the

Paniolo action at Kamuela.

locally-produced beef in Hawaii through his own slaughterhouse in Honolulu. Until a port was constructed, his cattle were herded to the ocean at **Kawaihae** and forced to swim through the surf to waiting ships which hauled them aboard in slings onto open decks. Nowadays they are driven through gates into enclosed barges, practically unaware that they are going to sea. In the 1960s, Parker's heir Richard Smart sold large unproductive and coastal tracts in South Kohala to resort developers and turned over the day-to-day management of the ranch to professionals. He has since opened a museum about his family's history, displaying their possessions and old ranching equipment, in the **Parker Ranch Shopping Center** in **Waimea**. That town, also called **Kamuela** (Hawaiian for Samuel), grew up with the family's fortune. Proud of the past, a neighbor, Anna Lindsey Perry-Fiske, stages an authentic and sincere pageant called "Old Hawaii on Horseback" every two years. At the western edge of town, where the road to Kohala branches off, is the **Kamuela Museum**, an independent and eclectic collection of ancient Hawaiian tools, antique American and Chinese furniture, and a rare lava stone — quite heavy — that actually floats in water.

In Lush Kohala:
Fan Tan, Opium and Agriculture

Incessant winds funnel through the channel between Maui and Kohala, yet, in the 1880s, **Kohala** led the island in sugar production. An enterprising planter named Samuel G. Wilder hired Chinese laborers to construct a narrow-gauge railway (from **Niulii**, at the tip of the island, to the port of **Mahukona**) that was formally opened by King Kalakaua himself. Within fifty years trucks replaced trains and the railroad was abandoned and dismantled — just as it was in Hamakua, Puna and everywhere else in Hawaii.

But the men who had laid the tracks found new work in the sugar mills and fields. Until World War II, immigrant Chinese were linked to their traditional culture through numerous Societies of Men which served their communities' social needs. One of these, Tong Wo ("together in harmony"), was one of the secret cliques which emerged in 16th

Rangeland, near Paauilo.

Century China to overthrow the Manchus, and flourished overseas wherever Chinese settled. Members identified one another by passwords, special gestures and manipulations of chopsticks. Sun Yat-Sen came to Hawaii in the 1880s, and again in the first decade of the 20th Century seeking help from the societies to finance his revolution in China.

Bachelor laborers and family men founded Tong Wo a hundred years ago to serve Hakka dialect speakers at **Halawa**, Kohala. Weekdays it served as a language school. There was a kitchen for festival days. At night the men gambled at *fan tan*; there was an opium loft reached only by a rope ladder. Elderly pensioners, unable to maintain a home alone, took rooms, and as a man neared death he moved to the "death house" on the Society grounds, for it was bad luck to die at home. The hillside sloping down into **Halawa Valley** is dotted with antique headstones.

The main building was restored and rededicated in 1971. Ornate, but not elaborate, it has scrollwork linking the beams and posts, and plaques engraved with proverbs and phrases surrounding the doors and windows. Archeologists

and residents have mapped the grounds, replacing and restoring several outbuildings. After a century of existence, Tong Wo sparkles with renewed life.

A Wealth of Nature

Dense forests cover the round, eroded hilltops of Kohala, a mile above its deep-cleft valleys and ravines. Along their ocean faces, streams seep out of cracks in the cliffs and plunge a thousand feet to the sea; at the heads of the valleys the falls are nearly twice that high. At the turn of the century a technique for tapping mountains for water was established, and engineers came to do it. The **Kohala Ditch** was christened in 1906—a water-course eighteen miles long that drew out the headwaters of **Waimanu Valley** and carried them to **Honokane**, terminating in an 850-foot man-made waterfall. Immigrant Japanese workmen bored and blasted 44 tunnels eight feet wide and seven feet high—the longest nearly half a mile. At least six men died and countless others suffered from exposure and chills in the icy darkness of the flooded tunnels.

Along Kohala's Highway 27, ar-

Queen Kaahumanu Highway, North Kona.

cheologists have partially restored a Hawaiian fishing village. **Lapakahi State Historical Park** is open daily, with self-guided tour maps and well-developed exhibits of early life in an era of subsistence. Inside its stone enclosures fishermen and their families prayed for good catches, shaped and maintained their canoes, raised a few vegetables, and led simple lives. Unlike a *heiau* (temple) of the royalty and priests, Lapakahi is the legacy of working people.

For War Gods and the Very Rich

Hot, dusty and very dry, **South Kohala** looks like the western United States—but with a seacoast. **Kawaihae** is its harbor, exporting sugar and eucalyptus wood chips from Hamakua. Above it stands the largest restored *heiau* in Hawaii: **Pu'u Kohola**, built by Kamehameha I for his war god, Kukailimoku, and inspired by his vision of military conquest. He invited his chief rival to its dedication, then had him killed as its last and greatest sacrificial offering.

The road south is lined with *kiawe*

Coconut palms, North Kona Coast.

(mesquite) trees and prickly-pear cacti, both of whose thorns are pests—yet the tree is burned into first-rate charcoal and the cactus blooms develop into sweet blood-red fruit. On land the Parker Ranch found too dry for cattle, Laurence Rockefeller commissioned a luxury resort, piping water for its grounds and golf course all the way from Waimea, and filling its halls and public areas with artifacts from Asia. Although the **Mauna Kea Beach Hotel** had to truck in sand to widen its beach, half a mile south lies **Hapuna Beach**, the largest beach on the island and a State Park with picnic areas and some small cabins.

Four miles south of the Mauna Kea Beach Hotel, and 25 miles north of Kailua-Kona, is the new **Mauna Lani Bay Hotel**. This, too, is a luxury resort with a dramatic six-story arrow-head design that points toward the sea. Ocean views are available from 92 percent of its rooms. Located at the foot of Mt. Hualali and along a beautiful sandy beach, the **Kona Village Resort** at Kanupulehu recreates the kind of Polynesian settlement visitors to the Big Island may have seen a couple centuries back.

The Kona Coast: Sunshine, Lava, Gourmet Coffee and Pakalolo

In the past, the only way to drive from Kohala to **Kona** was along a narrow road (190) far uphill from the ocean. Today, however, a highway (19) named for the gigantic Queen Kaahumanu connects Kawaihae with **Kailua**. Tall and heavy, the queen was Kamehameha's favorite wife. Widely respected as his widow, she formally broke the *kapu* (taboo) system and moved against the old animistic religion in favor of Christianity, welcoming the first missionaries to Kona. The highway passes through some of the driest land in Hawaii, where tiny beaches and historical curiosities are strung along the coast like beads.

At **Puako**, a broad reef provides shallow-water snorkelers with fish. Here too, a mile walk inland, are some of the finest Hawaiian rock carvings. Petroglyphs are among the earliest human artifacts: by pecking and chipping at stones, man has everywhere left pictures and ideographs of himself and his ideas for generations to come. Most Hawaiian petroglyphs are chiseled into smooth *pahoehoe* lava shelves along major trails. Some, here, are three and four feet long, typically human or animal shaped. Circles with a dot inside are *piko* holes, receptacles for umbilical cords of newborn children, from which fortunetellers could divine the child's name and future. At **Anaehoomalu**, a few miles to the south, a similar field lies along the "King's Highway" footpath marked with stone cairns. There, some 19th Century influences can be seen, including English letter initials, horses, and figures bearing rifles. A modern form of writing in stone has begun to appear along the sides of the new highway. White coral rocks have been arranged on the black lava into graffiti honoring high school teams and clubs, and hearts enclosing sweethearts' initials and names.

Many times along its route, the road crosses 19th Century lava flows. Some swallowed up beaches and trees at the oceanside, but others were naturally diverted and left these oases untouched. At **Anaehoomalu Bay**, a perfect crescent of golden coral sand separates the ocean from an ancient fishpond, and a triple row of coconut palms stretches like a

Boat day, old Kailua Town, Kona, about 1885.

tree-lined boulevard along the shore. There is a desert-island feeling here, for the delicate vegetation ends abruptly at the sharp black lava just inland. South of Anaehoomalu, **Keawaiki**, **Kiholo** and **Makalawena Bays** are similar gems, but they are not open to public roads. Boaters with small, shallow craft, however, can anchor in them. By State law the land between the sea and the vegetation is open to all. Here in the dry silence lie tiny beaches and brackish lagoons: such stuff as dreams are made of.

Bougainvillea Blurs, Luaus and Discotheques

Besides sailing and hiking, the most exciting way to see West Hawaii is on a horse. This open country has been ridden by *paniolo* and their animals for over a century. It is a gritty, broad and breezy stretch of land that is best experienced from a saddle. Farther south, the 8,000-foot summit of **Hualalai** dominates **North Kona**, and is visible all along the coast. Game birds flock to it, and sheep and goats wander over its dormant heights, foraging on dry shrubs and grasses, and drawing photographers

and hunters to them. Safaris are available, led by experienced guides who provide transportation, lunch and shooting equipment. Many residents prefer to hunt with bow and arrow, and several areas on Hualalai and in the **Saddle** are reserved for that sport.

The lava that covers West Hawaii presents a perpetual challenge to landscapers, so the highway section between Kona's **Keahole Airport** and **Kailua** is lined with exotic bougainvillea that flash by as irridescent blurs of purple, red and pink. Almost all the plants on the Kona coast are imported and cultivated, and the *makai* side of Kona has become an enclave of newly-arrived people as well. Alii Drive and Kuakini Highway are filling up with new condominium apartments that are gradually replacing family homes. The narrow coastal strip is secured at either end by resort and budget hotels in Kailua and Keauhou that offer the only "night life" for a hundred miles, including commercial *luaus* and discotheque dancing. Kona is a place where visiting *haole* can be loud without offending local residents, since so few now live near the oceanside hotels.

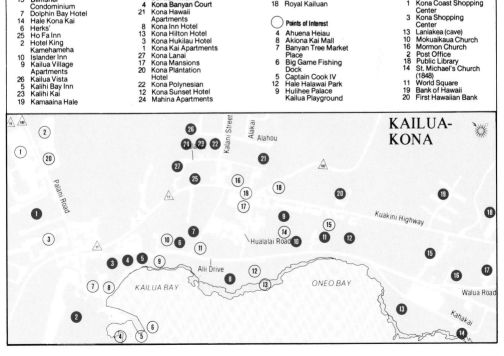

Hotels & Apartments
15 Billfisher Condominium
7 Dolphin Bay Hotel
14 Hale Kona Kai
6 Herks'
25 Ho Fa Inn
2 Hotel King Kamehameha
10 Islander Inn
9 Kailua Village Apartments
26 Kailua Vista
5 Kalihi Bay Inn
23 Kalihi Kai
19 Kamaaina Hale

11 Kona Alii Condominiums
4 Kona Banyan Court
21 Kona Hawaii Apartments
8 Kona Inn Hotel
13 Kona Hilton Hotel
3 Kona Hukilau Hotel
1 Kona Kai Apartments
27 Kona Lanai
17 Kona Mansions
20 Kona Plantation Hotel
22 Kona Polynesian
12 Kona Sunset Hotel
24 Mahina Apartments

16 Malia Kai Apartment Hotel
18 Royal Kailuan

Points of Interest
4 Ahuena Heiau
8 Akiona Kai Mall
7 Banyan Tree Market Place
6 Big Game Fishing Dock
5 Captain Cook IV
12 Hale Halawai Park Kailua Playground
9 Hulihee Palace

17 Kona Chamber of Commerce
1 Kona Coast Shopping Center
3 Kona Shopping Center
13 Laniakea (cave)
10 Mokuaikaua Church
16 Mormon Church
2 Post Office
18 Public Library
14 St. Michael's Church (1848)
11 World Square
19 Bank of Hawaii
20 First Hawaiian Bank

The first Christian church in Hawaii, **Mokuaikaua Church** on Alii Drive, was built in Kailua in 1823, and even now young and "born-again" Christians are making Kona their home. Many of them are ex-"hippies" who say they have abandoned drugs for Jesus' sake. Crusaders and revivalists form congregations—one operates a restaurant, another a wholesale food cooperative. These young people have been received by local people with more *aloha* than they gave to long-haired drifters in the 1960s, many of whom were beaten and terrorized. Because so many youths were accused of stealing fruit, and slept in Kona's beach parks without permits, no camping at all is now permitted anywhere in this district.

Catching Ahi for Sashimi

For the shore-bound, Kailua has some charm. The priceless **Hulihee Palace** is a tiny museum of memories, recalling an era when the royal families' lifestyle was centered here. The harbor has a tiny beach that is safe for swimming, and, next to it, a *heiau*, **Ahuena**, that was for years covered by a hotel.

When it was demolished and replaced, the new hotel was set back from the bay and the owners restored the *heiau*. The site was **Kamakahonu**, the "turtle eye" home, in his old age, of Kamehameha the Great. When he died here, in 1819, loyal attendants hid his bones, lest they be defiled by his enemies. Occasionally, amateur archeologists claim to have found the burial site—caves were traditional—but it has remained undiscovered: possibly it was sealed by a lava flow, or it may even be under water.

Kailua's greatest attraction is its fabled deepsea fishing. More than a dozen Pacfiic Blue Marlin, each weighing over 1,000 pounds, have been boated within an hour's run from the pier. Hawaii's leeward side, sheltered from the prevailing winds, draws fish and fishermen from great distances. *Ahi* (tuna), *ono* (bonefish), *ulua* (jack crevalle), *mahimahi* and swordfish are caught daily by anglers from Europe, America, Australia and Japan. Each summer in late July or August, the Hawaiian International Billfish Tournament is staged here. The dockside price of *ahi* for *sashimi* falls to only a dollar or two a pound, and ice machines work overtime,

Kona anglers with 252-pound *ahi* (yellow fin tuna).

keeping fish and chilling drinks.

The mild climate grows cooler uphill. *Mauka* **Kona** towns are filled with industrious people who remember when coffee was the mainstay of their lives. Moist air, clear sunshine and porous volcanic soil produce one of the world's gourmet coffees. Until recently, schools in Kona closed during the harvest seasons because families depended for their livelihoods on the number of burlap sacks of bright red "cherries" they could deliver to the mill. Only one mill remains in operation. At **Napoopoo**, where visitors are always welcome, the beans are fermented, dried in the sun, sorted, roasted and packaged. Where once wholesalers outbid each other for the privilege, today only one Chicago company buys the entire crop of Kona coffee; and there is never enough to meet coffee addicts' demand.

Harvesting 'Kona Gold,' The Connoisseur's Pakalolo

Recent portrait of a "Kona Gold" bud and dock-side *hapa-haole* and friend.

Deep in the hills, off the jeep roads, tiny, stooped coffee farmers live out their last years alone. Widowers and bachelors, many of the lonely old men are now cared for through government help, providing them with hot meals and medical attention. Young people have now settled here to become farmers, leasing acres from large estates for a pittance and buying up the fee-simple farmlands that come on the market. They are raising — not coffee — but vegetables, citrus fruits and, especially, hemp. The so-called "Kona Gold" marijuana — known locally as *pakalolo*, or crazy tobacco — is a cash crop far surpassing coffee (and approaching sugar) in net worth. It is illegal, but even though police regularly confiscate plants after helicopter surveillance, and hardened criminals have infiltrated the marketing of it, marijuana cultivation will probably continue to be part of Kona's agricultural future.

Above elevations where coffee will grow rises a forest of native trees. Around their trunks twined the wild *maile*, a fragrant vine that is prized for *leis*, braided for brides and grooms, and unraveled ceremoniously when new public works are unveiled. As the population swelled, and construction abounded, *maile* became scarce; today it is rare and expensive. But a retired County Councilman, whose family has

ranched in *mauka* Kona for a hundred years, recently developed a technique for cultivating *maile* alongside his orchids. Further uphill, in what is now cattle country, a few scrawny sandalwood trees stand out alone. Whole forests of the creamy, aromatic wood were sold by the early Hawaiian kings to merchants bound for China, thereby enriching the kings and traders but denuding the hills.

The Mysterious Mounds of Umi

The Hilo and Kona sides of Hawaii have never been linked directly. The "King's Highway" of foot trails circumscribed the island since prehistoric times. It was later widened for horses and eventually motor vehicles. The shoreline segments of the trail can be hiked, and many travelers have urged the County and State to preserve them as parks. The only road between the mountains, the **Saddle Road**, bypasses Kona, and connects the cattle and former sheep ranges of the Parker Ranch on the flanks of Mauna Kea. In 1849 a prominent *haole* doctor persuaded King Kamehameha III to let him survey and build a road over Crown lands directly from Kona, the seat of government, to Hilo, the only deepwater port. Convict laborers began at the edge of the forest and followed the nearly straight line Dr. Judd drew on the map. In ten years they had gone about halfway to Hilo when Mauna Loa suddenly erupted. A broad river of lava poured down the mountain wall and covered a part of the road. It was never completed.

By sheer luck the most desolate and mysterious historical place on the island was not inundated. A scant quarter-mile from the edge of the flow stands the remains of a monument to a 15th Century king. Umi was his name, and he is the first known leader of the people of the Big Island. Conquering district after district, he completed his military unification of Hawaii here, on a desolate plateau where — in a curious optical illusion — Mauna Kea, Mauna Loa and Hualalai appear nearly the same size. Umi, according to some vague traditions, ordered a census taken, and stones were brought up from the provinces representing numbers of people and animals and units of land. These heaps (*ahu*) of stones were fashioned into a place of worship, probably decorated with artifacts and offerings. But the

Nene geese, Volcano area.

plateau, cold and waterless, proved a distant and unpleasant seat from which to govern so vast an empire. The **Ahu a Umi** was abandoned long before new immigrants came up from the South Pacific. Herdsmen in the 19th Century built corrals with the stones, dismembering the original walls which have never been rebuilt. Archeologists have been slow to arrive, and the mounds of Umi are today overrun by wild goats. It has been 500 years since ancient armies bivouacked on the plain in the geographical center of the island. The echo of Umi's warriors, dueling and shouting, is now silent. But, only a few miles away in the Saddle at **Pohakuloa**, American armed forces practice war games. The concussions of their ordnance punctuates the still silence at the mounds of Umi.

Mauna Kea towers over the Saddle; its trails have been hiked for generations by bird-watchers and game hunters, but in the past ten years astronomers have set one telescope after another on its summit. Their presence irks hunters and conservationists alike, for they are perceived as desecrations. To the astronomers — who were encouraged to build here by the State, which welcomes "clean" industry — no site in the Northern Hemisphere is so high, so clear, so free from light and heat, and so easily accessible. The University of Hawaii and the governments of Canada and France, the United States and the United Kingdom have built or are constructing giant reflecting telescopes on neighboring cinder cones. Their staffs maintain an all-night vigil in the thin cold air while computers and cameras record the infrared images of stars and planets.

Snow-skiing in the Tropics

Permafrost beneath the summit is all that remains of a glacier that surmounted Mauna Kea in the last ice age. Most years, from December through March, skiers can whisk down the snow that blankets the peak. The altitude takes some people's breath and appetite away, while the ferocious sunlight sears unprotected eyes and lips. As there is no lift, four-wheel drive vehicles must be used to reach the snow fields. Slalom races are scheduled each Presidents' Day holiday weekend in February. Skiers have

Summit of the "White Mountain," Mauna Kea.

their choice of several fine runs, some over a mile long. Beginners, for example, can ski the wide and shallow **Poi Bowl**, or the larger **Pele's Parlor**. Intermediate skiers, meanwhile, prefer the **Prince Kuhio Run**, a mile-and-a-half from cinder cone to cinder cone, and experts like to slide down the east side of the summit on the **King Kamehameha Run** that drops 1,000 feet in the first six-tenths of a mile. Cross-country skiers can, with a little walking, cover even more ground. But no matter how cold the ice is up there, it is comforting to remember that an hour's drive takes a skier to the warm Pacific Ocean.

Captain James Cook met his untimely death on a beach at **Kealakekua Bay**, where almost a hundred years later a white obelisk was erected to mark the spot where he was overwhelmed by angry natives. Visitors can ride a day cruise ship to this bay from Kailua-Kona, or they can drive to it through rugged brush and lava fields. Farther along this jagged Kona shore, the people of **Keei** and **Milolii** still fish for a living from their tiny·villages. True, they use outboard motors to power their canoes, but they haul their boats onto stony shores by hand, and salt and dry their catch in the sun. Nowhere is a feeling of neighborliness so strong as in these little villages of handbuilt stone walls topped with nightblooming cereus.

A stranger riding along the coast from Napoopoo and emerging at **Honaunau** will be startled to see full-sized primitive idols and an immense stone platform with walls six feet thick topped by thatched huts. In this ancient *puuhonua*, or place of refuge — now known as the **Pu'uhonua 'O Honaunau National Historical Park** — ancient Hawaiians pardoned sinners and war criminals who reached sanctuary there, committed themselves to the mercy of priests, and did proper penance.

Ka'u: Green Sands, a Desert and Fiery Madame Pele

South along Route 11 lush greens are more and more frequently interrupted by lava flows. Where there is enough rain they are quickly covered with lichens, grass and *ohia*, the first tree that will return to new land. Where the climate dries out, and the lava stays barren, that is **Ka'u** — the first-settled but

Seaside idol, Puuhonua 'O Honaunau; and detail from Martin Charlot mural, Konawaena High School Gymnasium, Kealakekua, South Kona.

now least-populated place in Hawaii. In the 1950s and 1960s, unscrupulous real estate salesmen trafficked in these raw lava acres, hawking them sight-unseen to Americans who thought they would one day retire to a tropical paradise. Nonetheless, some hardy pioneers built homesteads by hauling in crushed cinders, manure, sugarcane wastes, topsoil and seeds.

Next to an old redwood water tank is the turnoff to **South Point**, an 11-mile road that traverses unfenced range lands where cattle cross the road at will. The cliff at the end of the road is the southernmost place in the United States, and it is studded with holes and iron rings where boats have moored to it for generations. The nearby shore was the first landfall ever made by the Polynesian voyagers who called it **Ka Lae**, the Point. This cape has been whipped by ceaseless winds for eons. Ancient lava flows broke open veins of olivine—a clear green mineral—that has tinted the brown earth with its green streaks. The old flows have been severely eroded by winds and storms, revealing their successive layers in the sculpted cliffs.

A three-mile hike east from South Point through the dry, grassy plain, leads to the unique **Green Sand Beach**. Here an entire cinder cone of olivine collapsed into a little bay. The olivines can be set in jewelery, but none has ever been found much larger than buckshot. The beach is safe for swimming on a calm day, but can be reached only by scampering down the face of the cinders.

At Kilauea Volcano:
Ti, Taro and Gin for Pele

The entire island, but particularly the coastline of Ka'u and Puna, is unstable. In 1868, and again in 1975, major earthquakes drowned what few beaches had clung to the rocks, and deprived fishermen of safe, familiar landings. Minor earthquakes are common events.

At **Kilauea**, almost every year, there is some eruption, beginning in the National Park which encloses Hawaii's active volcanoes. Far from being dangerous—as are explosive volcanoes in the Mediterranean or around the Pacific rim—Hawaii's volcanoes are major attractions, and roadsigns are always set out at the park rangers' discretion, advising the best vantage points

Collecting fresh lava specimens, Volcanoes National Park.

from which to view their activity.

When Kilauea erupts at the summit, the crater of **Halemaumau** has been known to fill with lava. A typical eruption begins with a change in the pressure of the underground "plumbing," then a crack or rift opens in the caldera on top. Fountains dozens or hundreds of feet high squirt flaming rock into the air and puddles collect and form a lake. Heat greater than a million camp-fires blast from the surface, sucking up the colder air which flings stinging cinders and sharp ashes into a whirlwind. The lava reverberates with explosions of liquid rock, spewing yellow and white hot. Waves, like surf, beat against the cooler edges of the crater, and hard plates of dark crust crack, split and sink like foundering ships into a burning lake.

At these times, respectful Hawaiians make pilgrimages to the volcano, carrying offerings of *ti*, taro and gin for the goddess Pele. Madame Pele is said to have made her home on every island, always moving southeast toward hotter and newer firepits. Geologists have essentially agreed with that scenario, for it is consistent with their theories that the islands are drifting northwestward,

after having been made by lava issuing from a standing vent under the ocean. Eventually Pele will depart from her home at Kilauea for a new island that is being built up even now and that some day will emerge off the coast of Puna, southeast of the Big Island.

Perhaps once in a generation the giant Mauna Loa will erupt. In 1975, after a quarter-century of silence, it sent a thin stream down to the northeast into the Saddle. What might have made that eruption dangerous, however, was the fact that Hilo lay downstream. In 1888, Mauna Loa produced a flow that oozed perilously close to the city, stopping—it is said—only when Pele heard pleas and prayers from a high princess. In 1942, American aircraft dropped water and explosives on the leading edge of a similar flow with the same result, but there is no evidence of cause-and-effect in either method. The 18-mile trail through the National Park to the summit of Mauna Loa is a difficult and unforgettable hike. It takes a day just to reach the **Red Hill** cabin at 10,000 feet, and most of the next day to attain the summit cabin. There, from sunrise through dusk the unspoiled colors of the lava

New plant life at the edge of Devastation Trail.

262

gleam, unmelted snow glints from cracks in the rock—it is the only source of water—and the high cold air makes sturdy travelers light-headed and mystical. But well-prepared-for and calmly undertaken, no place in Hawaii is so rewarding to experience.

Curtains of Fire, Footprints Under Glass

The earliest visitors to Kilauea stayed in a thatched hut. In 1877 a master carpenter was hired by Samuel Wilder's steamship company to build them a real hotel. That original **Volcano House** was eventually moved back from the crater's edge and restored. Renamed the **Volcano Art Center** it is no gift shop; it is a first-class gallery of paintings, photographs and sculpture inspired by the Volcano, and serves as a focal point for artists who have settled nearby. The lounge, dining room and library of the latest hotel to be called Volcano House overlook the giant crater of **Halemaumau** and offer a soft seat from which to watch a summit eruption. Lunchtimes the dining room is very crowded with bus tourists enroute to Hilo or Kona, so the leisurely traveller is advised to ex-plore the park all day, perhaps carrying a picnic lunch. In the town called **Volcano**, just beyond the park boundary, two local stores sell the components of a fine picnic: cold, cooked fishcakes, packets of dried shrimp or squid, fresh greenhouse tomatoes, hardboiléd eggs, and *sushi*—seasoned rice wrapped in fried soybean curd or seaweed. In season there are tangy *poha* (groundcherries) and plums and papaya. The less-adventurous may sample from a conventional take-out food counter.

Kilauea is famous for its "curtain of fire," a wall of flaming, tree-shaped fountains which break-out—almost annually—along well-known rift zones. To the southwest is the **Ka'u Desert**, downwind from the summit, where noxious gases and dehydrated breezes inhibit vegetation. Here too, in 1790, a freak eruption of gas and dust suffocated a phalanx of warriors opposing Kamehameha. Those who were able to flee left foot prints in the clay-like mud that fell from the heavens. Kamehameha interpreted this event as one of divine assistance. Today, all that can be seen of the tragedy are a few footprints, preserved under glass.

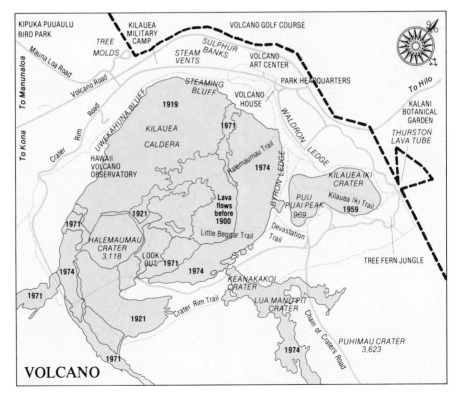

VOLCANO

Puna: Where Astronauts
Walk 'On the Moon'

If an eruption moves southeast, it may burn part of the *ohia* forests that have grown up on the old flows in **Puna**. All of Puna is young, and volcanically active. There have been hot, spring-fed bathing pools near the sea for centuries; one was buried under a flow in 1955 but another opened up at **Pohoiki**. A hole was drilled near **Pahoa** and enough heat was discovered to persuade the U.S. government to invest in the island's geothermal energy potential. But the volcano is not always so benign. **Kalapana** village and nearby subdivisions were nearly burned by a week-long eruption in 1977 that drove lava to within half a mile of them. But they were spared the fate of Kapoho where, in 1960, fountains of lava suddenly broke out of a cane field and released a carpet of slow, crumbly *a'a* lava which gradually swamped the town and added a few hundred acres to the island as it tumbled to the sea. It left only the high, wooded hills to stand green above the new black plain. All the people fled to safety, but their homes, farms and shops were turned into rock — sharp and uninhabitable. A science-fiction movie of an asteroid landscape could be filmed at Kapoho; indeed, American astronauts actually trained for moonwalking on Kapoho's moon-like lava.

Ten years ago, eruptions along the south-east rift closed the **Chain of Craters Road** that connected the upland Volcano area with Kalapana by the sea. Hawaii County and the National Park have built a new road, so a traveler can now make a single circular tour, take a drive down the rift zone, and witness the entire life cycle of Kilauea in a day. When the fiery streams leave their fissures they pick up speed pouring over the *pali*. Slipping through underground tunnels, the lava extrudes like paint from a tube and rolls toward the sea. Undulating, with a "whummp" and a "whoossh" it covers the forests and ferns, molding weird shapes around charred tree trunks that can be seen at **Lava Tree State Park** in Pahoa.

New, uncooled lava glistens with a silvery, prismatic sheen like the scales of freshly-caught fish. It, too, turns dull as its heat dies away. When it crosses a road the asphalt catches fire, and oily

Blood-red anthuriums grow like wildfire near the sea, and along the Chain of Craters Road, a fern emerges from *pahoehoe* lava.

black smoke clouds rise, visible for a dozen miles. White puffs of trapped gases escape from bubbles in the fudgy lava, and heat waves warp and twist lines of sight along its rippling hot surface.

Black sand is the exploded debris left when hot lava touches cold seawater. Waves push dunes of it up against the hard rocks, filling the crevasses and the ledges with crystalline chips until they look like a beach. But they are temporary, and their erosion is inevitable. A few may last only a day or so; many remain for years, but eventually the earth shakes, the waves and tides drag them off, and the black sands fall to the base of the cliffs far below the surface. At **Kaimu**, in Puna, the most famous and picturesque black sand beach is slowly disappearing. Palms that are undermined now were a quarter-mile inland at the turn of the century; many have already toppled. Only strong swimmers and surfers should tackle the swift currents that are at work in Kaimu.

Further along the red-paved road (137) is a smaller beach called **Kaena**, and past the lighthouse at **Cape Kumukahi** is another black sand beach at **Honolulu Landing**. That one grew dramatically after the 1955 and 1960 eruptions, yet it is washed away entirely some winters, leaving only smooth wet stones behind. When the sand does return, waves break exactly on the offshore ledge dragging poor swimmers under. In truth, no part of the Puna coast is safe, and even skilled local fishermen who pluck *opihi* (limpets) off the rocks are occasionally killed by the unpredictable sea.

When hot lava touches the cold ocean a hiss of steam sweeps over the cliff tops. Griddle-hot black rock ruptures, displaying its red heart. Wash of wave. Black. Wash. Break. Red. Hiss. Wet. This is the way the Hawaiian Islands were made. It is an impermanent landscape that blossoms in fire, is etched by wind and rain, and sinks demolished into the constant sea. The island of Hawaii is a reminder that nature never rests, never has rested since the earth was everywhere a sea of molten lava. We inhabitants, dwelling on her cooler crusts, are but travelers ourselves, and no more fixed in our places than are the tiny volcanic crystals which rest on her fragile shores.

A sunbather worships on disappearing black sands at Kalapana.

265

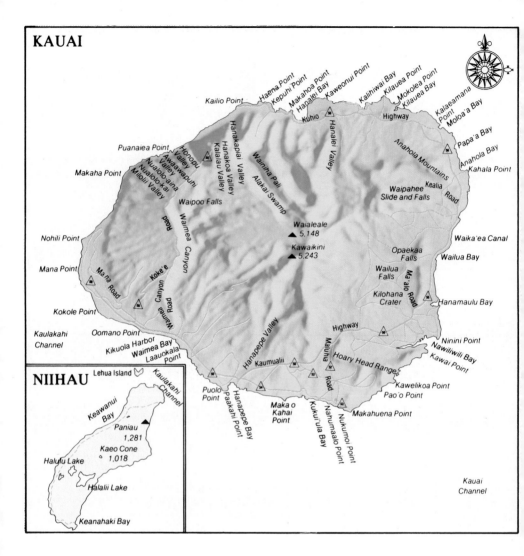

KAUAI

Haena Point
Kepuhi Point
Makahoa Point
Kailio Point
Kaweonui Point
Hanalei Bay
Kalihiwai Bay
Kilauea Point
Mokolea Point
Kilauea Bay
Kalaeamana Point
Moloa'a Bay
Kuhio
Hanalei Valley
Highway
Papa'a Bay
Anahola Bay
Anahola Mountains
Anahola Bay
Kahala Point
Puanaiea Point
Hanakapiai Valley
Kalalau Valley
Hanakoa Valley
Honopu Valley
Awaawapuhi Valley
Nualolo-aina
Nualolo-kai
Miloli'i Valley
Wainiha Pali
Alakai Swamp
Waipahee Slide and Falls
Kealia Road
Makaha Point
Waipoo Falls
Waika'ea Canal
Nohili Point
Waia.leale ▲ 5,148
Kawaikini ▲ 5,243
Opaekaa Falls
Wailua Bay
Mana Point
Ma'na Road
Koke'e Road
Waimea Canyon
Wailua Falls
Ma'alo Road
Kilohana Crater
Hanamaulu Bay
Kokole Point
Kaulakahi Channel
Oomano Point
Kikuola Harbor
Waimea Bay
Laauokala Point
Hanapepe Valley
Kaumualii
Highway
Mauna Road
Hoary Head Ranges
Ninini Point
Nawiliwili Bay
Kawai Point
Kawelikoa Point
Pao'o Point
Makahuena Point
Puolo Point
Hanapepe Bay
Paakahi Point
Maka o Kahai Point
Kukui'ula Bay
Nahumaalo Point
Nukumoi Point

Kauai Channel

NIIHAU
Lehua Island
Kaulakahi Channel
Keawanui Bay
Paniau 1,281
Kaeo Cone 1,018
Halulu Lake
Halalii Lake
Keanahaki Bay

Land Area:
548.7 square miles
33 miles long, 25 miles wide

Population:
Total: 34,400 (1977 census estimate)
Kawaihau District: 8,800 (1977)
Waimea: 8,300 (1977)
Koloa: 8,000 (1977)
Lihue: 7,700 (1977)
Hanalei: 1,700 (1977)

Highest Elevation:
Kawaikini: 5,243 feet

Airports:
Lihue: Lihue Airport
Princeville: Princeville Airport

Main Seaports:
Hanalei Bay
Nawiliwili Harbor
Port Allen

Points of Interest
1 Alakai Swamp
33 Coconut Plantation Market place (Waipouli)
44 Dry Cave (Haena)
28 Fern Grotto (Near Wailua)
13 Fishing Shrines (South Coast)
42 Hanalei Plantation Museum
32 Hauola Place of Refuge (Wailua)
31 Hiikina o Kala Heiau (Wailua)
16 Ho'ai Heiau (Near Kukui'ula)
36 Hole-in-the-Mountain (Near Anahola)
29 Holoholoku Heiau (Wailua)
3 Kalalau Valley Lookout

Preceding pages, Sunset amber on the roseate walls of Waimea Canyon, West Kauai.

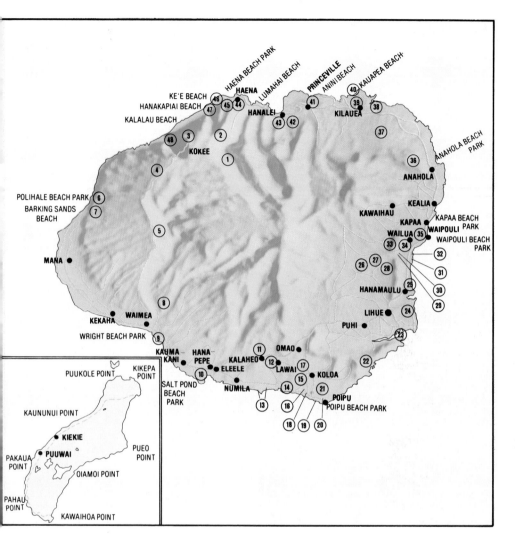

KAUAI:

At the heart of the island of Kauai, at its center, is a wonderland of vegetation and fauna unique in the world. Here, a mile high, a long, narrow depression lies suspended amid the mountains. From its sides fall thin, jagged ridges and deep verdant valleys and canyons. The bowl, the depression, is the **Alakai Swamp**. At its eastern end is **Waialeale**, the wettest spot on earth, where almost 500 inches of rain fall annually. At the other end are the precipitous ridges and valleys called **Na Pali**, the cliffs.

Between them is Alakai, a calabash filled with rare plants and birds that exist nowhere else. The *'olapa* grows here, a tree whose leaves flutter in the slightest breeze, when all else is still. And the *'ohi'a*, shrouded in mists, its deep green leaves and bright red blossoms providing shelter and food for the honeycreepers and other birds of Alakai. There are ferns here, great, tall tree ferns and tiny fragile ones with fronds so delicate one needs a magnifying glass to

pick out their parts. The environment is even more fragile than the ferns.

Many of the Alakai's birds are endangered today. For some of them, civilization has made most of the island uninhabitable, and only the Alakai remains sufficiently untouched for them to survive.

And even here their survival is threatened. The *akialoa*, a small bird with a long, curved beak almost as long as its body, has not been seen in more than a decade, and may be extinct. The *'o'o 'a'a*, with its haunting, whistling call, has only been seen by man in one limited area, nesting in a single *'ohi'a* tree, in the past few decades. The bird is the size of a mynah, but more slender. It has a slate-grey body with small patches of yellow feathers under its wings and on its thighs. The feathers were used in the days before the coming of white men to make the colorful cloaks and helmets of Hawaiian royalty. The birds would be caught on sticks coated with gum, relieved of their yellow plumage, and released. The feathers, along with red ones from other birds, were worked onto a net-like backing, each carefully tied in place.

A variety of *'o'o* once existed on each of the major islands, but today only the Kauai *'o'o 'a'a* exists. Other bird species have declined similarly. Of all the Hawaiian islands, Kauai has lost the fewest of its native feathered creatures. Today, the final refuge of Kauai is also changing with the advance of civilization. A Federal program is seeking solutions to the problem of declining native bird populations in the forests of Hawaii, but few solutions appear to be forthcoming.

The Alakai is a dense jungle for the most part. It is cut occasionally by the beginnings of streams, which splash through the vegetation. The water is the color of tea, for it is stained by pigmentation in leaves that have been steeping in Alakai's water for centuries. There are open spaces in the jungle: bogs. Here there is virtually always standing water. A hiker sinks, sometimes to his ankles and sometimes to his waist, in the black mud. It is so wet in the bogs that plants would drown if they sent their roots too deep, so the root systems stay on the surface and the plants are stunted. A full-grown, flowering and seeding *'ohi'a* will be a foot high in a bog, while a few yards away another will grow to 50 feet.

MOHO NOBILIS, GREEN & KO.

Wilderness, Kokee, Kalalau, and Incredible Waimea Canyon

Outside the Alakai, the island changes dramatically. Tradewinds, warm and wet, gather moisture from the vast Pacific, and when they breeze across Kauai are caught in a funnel formed by the **Anahola** mountain range on the north and the **Haupu** range to the east. The breezes are carried to Waialeale, 5,150 feet high, where the altitude and the temperature make them give up their moisture. The rains fall all along the slopes leading to Waialeale and then over the Alakai, which is 10 miles long and two miles wide. By the time the winds reach the north and west side of the island, they are dry. Thus, while Waialeale is drenched, Kekaha, on the far west side of the island, gets little more than a dozen inches of rain annually.

The only populated place in the uplands is **Kokee**, at the western end of the swamp. A road runs up from **Waimea** and **Kekaha** into the area, where residents from all over the state have vacation cabins on leased State land. Also inhabitable are a dozen State-owned cabins that anyone can rent, as long as reservations are made several months in advance. The cabins are operated from the **Kokee Lodge**, a restaurant, tourist shop, bar, convenience shopping spot and information center. It's the only commercial operation in the mountains. Next door is the **Kokee Museum** with displays depicting the natural history of Kauai and the other islands. There are pictures and live examples of important native plants. There are the birds to be found in the wild, a three-dimensional map of Kauai, a wild boar's head, and more. The lodge and museum are located in the State Park, and on its grounds strut *moa*, wild Hawaiian chickens (*Gallus gallus gallus*) which enjoy special legal protection.

There's great hiking in the Kokee area, such as the **Iliau Nature Loop** for strolling, and, for the real hiker, the **Kukui Trail**, which drops a steep, zigzag course down the side of the remarkable **Waimea Canyon**. But if you're in the mood for less strenuous serenity, simply drive to the top of Kokee's beauty to the **Kalalau Valley Lookout** and, on a clear day, meditate on one of the world's most wonderful views. The panorama from that 4,000 foot high lookout will more than reward the trials of your zig-zaggy ascent to Kokee.

Also very much worth the effort are a series of dream-like views of the Waimea Canyon. This roseate canyon's headwaters are in Alakai. Waterfalls tumble from this green, cool and wet swamp into deep valleys carpeted in greenery. As the plum and

guava-rich valleys converge into gorges, a change quickly occurs. Wetness of the swamp is left behind and the vegetation becomes more sparse. The *'ohi'a* gives way to the *kukui*, the candlenut tree. The gorges meet the main canyon, and the *kukui* yields to dry country trees, the native *wiliwili* and introduced *kiawe* and lantana. The weather here is hot and dry, and the stream bed holds the only moisture. Reddish dust blows from barren hillsides. By the time the **Waimea River** meets the sea, its currents carry a heavy suspension of earth. From the sky, one can see the river pour into the blue Pacific, like blood oozing from a wound.

The Kalalau Valley as seen from Kokee.

A Russian Fort and Barking Sands

The people of old Hawaii took advantage of the island's climate changes. The chiefs moved their courts sometimes from the warmth of Waimea to the cooler Wailua on the east side. When Capt. James Cook arrived at **Waimea** in January, 1778, there were no chiefs there. Historians suggest the royalty were holding court at Wailua. Cook had left before the *ali'i*, the chiefs, could return to greet him.

Cook's journal speaks of collections of grass structures all along the southern coast of Kauai. They indicated the closeness of the island's people to the sea. Kauai provided its residents many ways to the sea. The island is ringed with sandy beaches. The largest is the stretch of nearly unbroken sand from Waimea to **Polihale**, a distance of more than 15 miles. Today, there is a state park at Polihale. Farther along the beach is the **Pacific Missile Range Facility** at **Barking Sands**, followed by sugar plantations, privately-owned property fronting the shore, and Waimea.

On the south bank of the Waimea River is the Russian **Fort Elizabeth**. In 1816, an agent of the Imperial Russian government came to Kauai seeking the cargo of a ship that broke up on the island's shore. The man, Dr. Anton Sheffer, convinced Kauai's King Kaumualii that they could conquer the rest of the islands together. Kaumualii helped Sheffer build a fort along the river. He used Russian design and Hawaiian construction techniques. Thus, you find today a star-shaped Russian-designed fort built of traditional Kauai stonework. Sheffer's Machiavellian bid for Hawaiian power failed miserably, but ruins of the fort he named after Russian Tzar Nicholas' queen remain as a testimonial to his adventurism. The state has begun clearing brush and developing a visitor information center there.

Just a few miles east of Waimea, on the oceanside of sleepy **Hanapepe** town, are a group of prehistoric **salt ponds** which have been worked by local Hawaiian salt gatherers since time immemorial. There, along the seaside just off Highway 543, members of the Hui Hana Pa'akai 'O Hanapepe (The Hanapepe Salt Makers Group) still manufacture salt in the old Hawaiian way during

Waimea, Kauai, 1873. Note walls of old Fort Elizabeth in foreground.

Waiméa, dans l'île de Kauaï. — Dessin de J. Moynet, d'après un croquis communiqué par l'auteur.

spring and summer months. These traditional saltmakers fill small, mud-lined ponds with sea water, and let the sun evaporate the water away, leaving behind heavy salt crystals. Many of these Hawaiians work ponds which have been passed down through his or her family for several generations.

Also on Kauai's west side is the prestigious **Pacific Tropical Botanical Garden** in **Lawai Valley**. This is a congressionally-chartered botanical garden whose aims include saving endangered plants of the tropics, locating and growing plants of medicinal and economic importance and informing the public of significant findings. Tours of the gardens are available on certain days, but one should call ahead to make a reservation because walking space is limited.

The tours normally include a visit through **Lawai Kai**, the verdant estate of John Gregg Allerton, who has willed his gardens to the Pacific Tropical Botanical Garden on his death. Lawai Kai is a wonderland of vegetation and statuary at the base of **Lawai**, where it meets the sea in a clean, white sand beach.

As one moves further east and then north to the wet and windward sides of the island, Hawaiian names of other Kauai beaches roll off the tongue like a staccato poem: **Poipu, Mahaulepu, Kalapaki, Hanamaulu, Wailua, Kealia, Moloaa, Kilauea, Hanalei, Wainiha, Haena, Hanakapiai, Kalalau, Honopu, Nualolo, Milolii**. And these are only a few of the better-known ones. Some of Kauai's beaches are easily accessible, some require hiking, some can be reached only by boat or helicopter, and to get to some of them requires the permission of the owner of an adjacent property.

The 'Little People'

Theories differ as to how and when Kauai, Hawaii's oldest populated island, was first inhabited, but popular are fables regarding the *menehune*, a group of lower class Polynesian people discussed in this book's historical section. Modern legend describes the *menehune* as a race of little people, like leprechauns. They were seldom seen and worked only at night. In a single night, they would perform prodigious works, and accept in payment only a single shrimp per worker. Among the construction projects attributed to them are the **Menehune Ditch** in Waimea, which indicates a knowledge of stonework not seen elsewhere in Hawaii, and the **Alakoko Fishpond**, also called the **Menehune Fishpond,** outside Lihue and near **Nawiliwili Harbor**.

Kauai folklore is rich in place name romance. The volcano goddess, Pele, for example, was associated with Kauai long before she made her home at Kilauea Crater on the Big Island. One famous story about Pele places her at beautiful **Haena** on Kauai's North Shore during a big *hula* festival. In order to join the dancing, Pele takes the form of a beautiful young woman, and though she is a goddess with supernatural powers, she has human desires and falls in love with a young, handsome Kauai chief named Lohiau. The remnants of **Lohiau's hula platform** and house can still be found at the Western side of **Ke'e Beach** in the Haena area.

Other Kauai legends, or oral traditions, concern the activities of *kahuna*, the Hawaiian class of trained professionals or wise men. In the realm of superstition are many visible remnants of ancient Hawaiian culture which in recent years have become popular tour-

ather
nd son,
anapepe.

ist attractions. One such attraction is a large bank of rock at **Wailua**, just up the road toward the mountains from the **Coco Palms Hotel**. It is a birthstone, a place where persons of high rank were born. **Pohaku-ho'o-hanau**, it is called, or more commonly, *piko* stone, *piko* being the Hawaiian word for navel.

According to this stone's legend, the umbilical cords of the newly-born were wrapped in cloth and hidden in cracks of the stone. They were carefully hidden, because ancient chants indicate that if a rat were to steal the cord, the child would grow up to be a thief.

Such superstitions — not too unlike Western fears of walking under ladders or breaking mirrors — imbued Hawaiian culture with yet other layers of respect and fantasy.

Kauai's Hawaiianness is still very obvious, but since 1835, when Hawaii's first commercial sugar plantation was started at Koloa, the island's ethnic character has gone through many radical and charming changes. As in other parts of Hawaii, sugar attracted a diverse lot of people willing to work in its dusty, itchy fields and pungent mills. First, in the 1850s, came the Chinese.

Then the Japanese, and later Portuguese, Puerto Ricans, Norwegians, Germans, Koreans, Spaniards, others, and last the Filipinos

Thus many of Kauai's communities developed as plantation towns, often with the different races separated into camps within the towns. The camp towns were spread around the island, generally as they are found now, along the sea, so sugar could easily be transported to ships for export. Today, many of the sugar firms that started the towns are gone or have been merged with other companies, but the communities themselves persist. **Waimea, Numila** (the Hawaiian pronunciation of New Mill), **Puhi, Kealia** and **Kilauea** are some of the towns that have lost the plantations that helped start them.

There are only four sugar mills now, and five sugar-growing companies. Gay & Robinson grinds its cane at Olokele Sugar Co.'s **Kaumakani** mill, Kekaha Sugar Co. has its mill in **Kekaha**, McBryde Sugar Co. has the **Koloa** mill, and Lihue Plantation Co. has its mill in the County seat, **Lihue**.

Two museums in Lihue are highly recommended. First, in the center of town,

Modern sugarcane workers spraying herbicide, Kaumakani.

on Rice Street, is the **Kauai Museum**. Open weekdays and Saturday morning. Located off Nawiliwili Road (Hwy 58) in Lihue is the **Grove Farm Homestead**, a historical museum of plantation life in Kauai. Reservations (245-3202) are required.

The Good Life at Taylor Camp

The island has a substantial transient population. While the term "transient" can be used to refer to tourists, on Kauai it is more frequently used to identify people called "hippies." They are wanderers who generally come with little money to a place they consider paradise. Some work at odd jobs, some collect public welfare, some have personal incomes, and some make their living selling marijuana they grow in the hills and in canefields.

In the early 1970s, there were several communities of transients on the island. The best known was **Taylor Camp**, on the far north side of the island at Haena. There, the mostly-young visitors constructed houses in the trees. The structures were made of cast-off wood, bamboo and clear plastic. Sixty or more people lived there at a time. Their homes were shaded by Java plum trees and flanked by the small, clear **Limahuli Stream**. In the front yard was a magnificent white sand beach.

Taylor Camp took its name from its owner in the late 1960s and early 1970s, Howard Taylor, the brother of actress Elizabeth Taylor. In the mid-70s, the State bought the land for part of the planned **Haena State Beach Park**, but it took years of legal wrangling to move the transients, who claimed squatters' rights. Finally, the court actions complete, the State burned the tree houses.

Many of the Taylor campers found other abodes, taking their bamboo and plastic with them to more desolate parts of Kauai. One of the most popular new places was in the deep valleys of Kauai's **Na Pali Coast**.

The road system that circles most of the island stops at the ends of this coastline. Here are 13 miles of jagged shoreline beauty, flanked by **Polihale Beach Park** on the west and the proposed **Haena Beach Park** on the north. Most of the Na Pali area itself is under State Parks jurisdiction.

Waniha Bay, north shore, near Haena.

On their northern end, the valleys are deep and green, but toward the vast, sandy beach at Polihale, they become dry. A foot trail starts at Haena — there is no vehicular access to Na Pali — then rises on a ridge and drops into lush **Hanakapiai**, two miles in, which has a lovely pool and waterfall at its back and a crescent of white sand at its mouth. The ocean here is often treacherous, but the sunbathing is generally superior. And although public nudity is illegal, many visitors brown themselves in the buff when park rangers aren't around.

Zigzagging above the Sea

From Hanakapiai, the Na Pali trail zigzags a heart-thumping course upwards and scurries in and out of small valleys and across a sheer cliff face to **Hanakoa**, a hanging valley. Like several other valleys here, Hanakoa sweeps from the heights in a flourish of vegetation and ends abruptly, hanging over the ocean, its stream turning into a misty waterfall that falls on the rocks and sea below.

There is a rangers' cabin at Hanakoa, and from it the jungle-shaded trail wanders out and along the shallow valleys and cliffs until it drops, and ends, in **Kalalau**, which is the largest of Na Pali's valleys. You can camp at Kalalau with a permit from the State Parks office in Lihue. Parks officials maintain portable toilets in the valley, but there's no safe drinking water. You should boil or use purification tablets if you use stream water. There are no cabins or shelters and only an occasional uninhabited cave.

There is a stream at one end of the valley mouth, and a waterfall at the other. A beach joins them. And at the back of Kalalau are fruit trees, brooks and the remains of ancient house sites and stone lined taro patches used by Hawaiians who lived there until the early years of this century.

A hardy hiker can reach **Kalalau Valley** from Haena in six to eight grueling hours, but you need a boat or helicopter to get to most of the rest of Na Pali's valleys and beaches. The major attractions are **Honopu, Awaawapuhi, Nualolo-aina, Nualolo-kai** and **Milolii**. The people who lived here in centuries past had trails, but they are impassable today. The tree trunk that spanned a

The Na Pali coastline.

section of cliff between Honopu and Awaawapuhi is rotted and the ladder that connected the upper and lower sections of the Nualolo-aina and Nualolo-kai trail is gone. Landslides have done their work on the rest. But in the valleys, the remnants of the old civilization remain.

The extensive stonework survives that formed the taro paddies of Nualolo-aina (*aina* means land), a hanging valley, and the remains of the fishing village at Nualolo-kai (*kai* means sea). The people of the former had no good access to the sea, and the people of the latter had little land or fresh water, so each group worked what it had, and they formed a trading relationship, a single community built of necessity in two valleys.

Aquaculture and Agronomics

Today's Kauai is a little more complicated, but the farmers and fishermen are still there. Farmers are growing taro at Hanalei, Waimea and a few other places. They're growing papayas at the State-sponsored Moloaa cooperative, which can be seen along the main highway between Anahola and Kilauea.

Sugar is grown over most of the island and truck crops are grown on acreage scattered about in small farms.

There are still a few commercial fishermen, but the majority of Kauai's fishing is done by individuals with their own small boats, who fish on days off from their regular jobs. Some of the commercial fishing docks have been taken over by sport fishing boats that take visitors out for prizes like marlin, *aku*, *kawakawa* and *mahimahi*.

But the newest form of fishing on Kauai is a modern version of the traditional Hawaiian fishponds. In old Hawaii, large ponds were built along the shoreline to form enclosures in which fish for eating were raised and harvested. On Kauai, the best example of such a fishpond is a rare one built in a river instead of on the shore. The aforementioned Alakoko, or Menehune Fishpond at Lihue was constructed by cutting off an elbow in the **Huleia River**. It is no longer in regular use, but is a scenic spot much visited and admired by both residents and visitors. The modern fishponds are built inland on Kauai, and used not primarily for fish, but prawns. The process is called aquaculture.

Barking Sands Beach, Polihale State Park, northwest Kauai.

In **Kilauea**, where the closing of the Kilauea Sugar Co. made both land and an irrigation system available, is the largest prawn farm in the world. Acres of land have been graded and turned into shallow, rectangular ponds. Kilauea Agronomics hatches the prawns in dry, warm Hanapepe and transports them to the main ponds in Kilauea to grow to market size. There are two smaller aquaculture ventures on the north shore, and more are expected.

As a result of the increased interest in aquaculture here and of the research that has been going on into prawn culture and other forms of aquaculture, Hawaii has become the pond farming capital of the world. Much of the attention is focused on Kauai, as others wait to see how the pioneer ventures here handle the problems of this developing industry.

Kilauea is also the site of a huge guava industry, being developed by Kilauea Agronomics. The firm plans to work 600 acres of guava orchards, build a processing plant and develop markets for products that can be made from guava.

While at Kilauea, however, don't just get lost in prawn-filled ponds and guava orchards. If you've brought your bathing suit along, seek out Kilauea's famous **Slippery Slide**, a man-made water slide and falls which was created by Hollywood entrepreneurs for a setting in the movie "South Pacific."

Public access was recently cut off by the landowners due to a liability question, but reopening is expected. It's worth stopping by to check, just 200 yards back of Kilauea's little St. Sylvester's Church.

Where Jet and Yacht Sets Frolic

Kauai people are very low key and guarded about their more private and special beautiful places, but that does not mean that tourism is shunted aside on the Garden Island. Indeed, Kauai is visited by more than half a million people annually. Many arrive in the morning to climb into tour buses and visit scenic areas, and leave in the evening of the same day. But many others spend several days becoming acquainted with the island. Mostly, the visitors come from the mainland United States,

Bodysurfing, "Brennecke's Beach," Poipu, West Kauai.

from Japan, and from Canada, but the lure of the islands is worldwide, and tourists come from around the globe.

They usually stay in hotels and condominiums at four major tourist destination areas, each providing something different. The big four are **Poipu, Lihue, Waipouli-Wailua** and **Hanalei.**

Poipu, on Kauai's southernmost point, is the sunniest of the island's resort districts. It has several hotels and condominiums, all fronting the shoreline. There are hot, sandy beaches, generally calm, light blue water and several scenic spots, such as the **Spouting Horn**, a water spout in the shoreline rocks of an old lava flow, and "**Brennecke's Beach**," a spot renowned for its sometimes perfect bodysurfing waves.

The Lihue area sports Kauai's biggest and only high-rise hotel, the **Kauai Surf Hotel**, on **Kalapaki Beach**. Lihue is the seat of county government, the island's major business district and shopping area, and the site of Kauai's only airport capable of handling commercial jet traffic. Nearby are the Menehune Fishpond, Nawiliwili Harbor, the island's major port, and most amenities you might crave while on this slow-paced island.

A string of resort hotels and condominiums runs along the shore from Wailua to Kapaa, with most of them in between, at Waipouli. Here are the **Wailua Golf Course**, a municipal 18-hole facility, **Wailua Beach**, the **Wailua River**, which carries tour boats to the **Fern Grotto** (a favorite wedding site), and the modern **Coconut Plantation Marketplace**, a resort shopping center.

On the north shore, meanwhile, is **Princeville at Hanalei**, a 1,000-acre resort community with a 27-hole golf course, shopping center, homes, several luxurious condominium projects and a hotel or two in the offering. Hanalei is the wettest, and correspondingly the greenest part of the island. When rains drop upon the mountains, countless waterfalls hang like strands of silk thread upon the dark green cliffs.

Beginning at Princeville, to the end of the road at Haena, there are several valleys, each fronted by a curved sandy beach. **Hanalei Bay**, the largest on Kauai, is a favorite spot for yachtsmen in summer, and there are frequently more than two dozen yachts at anchor there. In winter, when big surf from the

Catching rays at Lumahai Beach

north makes anchorage there unsafe, the bay is a challenge for the island's best surfers. Waves generated by storms in the North Pacific can reach 30 feet in height on the reefs of the north shore.

Further north along this coastline is a jewel-like spot called **Lumahai**, a cuticle of sand whose brightness is offset by black lava rock that protects it on both sides. There is the blue of sea beyond the sand and the green of *hala* trees behind it. Access to the beach down a dirt trail is across privately-owned property, but no one has been arrested for tresspassing on this paradise in recent years. This is the beach where many parts of the movie "South Pacific" were filmed, where Mitzi Gaynor sang to the world that she'd wash that man right out of her hair.

Tough Little Niihau, A 'Forbidden' Neighbor

The resort areas, however, haven't cornered the market on Kauai's best places. Indeed, one part of Kauai County is completely *kapu*, or off limits, to even longtime residents of Kauai. This is the privately owned island of **Niihau**, referred to by some people as "the forbidden island."

Across the **Kaulakahi Channel** from Kauai's west side, about 17 miles distant, Niihau rises dimly through sea mists like a huge prehistoric creature. It is a dry island, denied rain because it falls in the lee of Kauai, whose mountains collect most of the moisture. Niihau was bought from King Kamehameha V in 1864 and remains in the hands of Kauai's wealthy Robinson family.

Fewer than 300 people live on the island, and virtually all who do work for the Robinsons, running cattle and sheep, making charcoal from *kiawe* trees and gathering honey. Niihau is the only island in Hawaii where Hawaiian is the primary language. In Niihau's only village, **Pu'uwai**, there is a grammar school run by three Niihau residents, and children learn English along with the other academic pursuits recommended by the State Board of Education. The children go to Kauai or to Oahu (usually to the Kamehameha Schools for Hawaiians) for high school and further education.

State education officials and tax officers are allowed on the island, and a couple of doctors make infrequent trips to check on the populace, but otherwise, access is limited to residents and members of the Robinson family. The residents move freely from Niihau to Kauai on the somewhat limited transportation facility, a World War II landing craft, because there is no airfield on Niihau.

The island is politically a part of Kauai County, but the relationship is little more than a paper one. There are virtually no County services, no County roads, no sewers or garbage collection, indeed, no county employes. But Niihau residents do vote. They voted Republican long after the Democratic Party gained control of the State government, and while the rest of "modern" Hawaii voted 17–1 in favor of statehood, Niihau's Hawaiian voters cast the one dissenting district vote against it.

Niihau is a small, arid island—it contains just 73 square miles compared to Kauai's 553 — but in the center of its desolation is **Lake Halalii**, the largest (182 acres) natural lake in the Hawaiian Islands.

The toughness of Niihau's people is best described with the story of the island's major contact with World War II, a story that has become a legend in Hawaii.

When a Japanese pilot's plane was damaged over Pearl Harbor on December 7, 1941, he was unable to fly it back to his carrier. He landed on Niihau and a Niihau Hawaiian, Benehakaka Kanahele, took the pilot's papers. The pilot convinced a Japanese man living on Niihau to get him a gun, and the two of them went to further arm themselves by taking the machine guns off the wrecked plane. Trouble was, Kanahele had already confiscated the ammunition.

The next day, the pilot and the other man captured Kanahele and his wife. While holding his wife hostage, they sent Kanahele to find the pilot's papers. He returned empty-handed. The Japanese pilot was angry, and prepared to shoot the Hawaiian and his wife.

Kanahele decided it was time to act. As he moved, the pilot fired a shot into Kanahele's mid-section, then a second, and then a third. Kanahele, 51, didn't stop. He picked the pilot up and smashed him on a stone wall. The Japanese man from Niihau shot himself to death on seeing Japan's invasion of the island so quickly overcome.

Rid Your Property of Unsightly Brush Piles...

Turn them into beautiful FREE mulch!

Mail This Card Today for Free Details

3 13

Dept. A240

YES! I want to know more

Name

The Revolutionary
SUPER TOMAHAWK
turns unsightly brush
piles into FREE mulch!

Another Niihau claim to fame comes in the form of precious garlands which Niihau *lei*-makers make of tiny shells which wash onto the island's shores. A good Niihau shell *lei* is highly prized in Hawaii and fetches high prices in off-Niihau jewelry stores and museum shops. The island's women pick up the little white, burgundy, spotted or brown shells along the beach, prick a hole in the ends of each shell and string them straight or in complicated designs. It takes hundreds of shells to make one strand, and several strands to make a proper Niihau shell *lei*.

The *leis* are worn with pride by Hawaii's women to special social gatherings, to be displayed and to be admired. Indeed, at any Kauai gathering worthy of proper *kamaaina* patronage, the only adornment of stature equivalent to that of the Niihau shell *lei* is another *lei* native to Kauai County: a wreath of *maile* and *mokihana*.

Maile and Mokihana: Whiffs of Old Kauai

While the fragrant *maile* vine grows on several of the islands, it is Kauai's small-leaved *Maile lauli'i* that is most fragrant. And the anise-scented *mokihana* (*Pelea anisata*) is found only on Kauai.

Maile is a vine that normally grows on the sides of other plants, in the wet areas of the island's mountains. Given a twist, its bark comes loose from the stem and can be pulled free, leaving a supple strand with the leaves still attached. These strands are tied together into lengths of six or more feet. Six or eight lengths are then braided together. The aroma comes some time after the stripping, from the bruised bark.

Maile alone can be draped around the neck, or used in place of ribbon-cutting for dedications. Instead of being cut, the *maile* is untied. But for wearing, even more prized than *maile* alone is a wreath intertwined with a *lei* of *mokihana* berries. These berries, too, are gathered in the mountains of Kauai. They grow on gangly shrubs with waxy leaves that also give off the pleasant scent of anise. The berries are light green and shaped somewhat like small, rounded dice. The *maile-mokihana lei* is most frequently given to honored visitors, graduates and the bride and groom at weddings.

Lehua islet (foreground) and the island of Niihau as seen from the north.

HAWAIIAN CREATIONS, MOVES WITHIN NATURE

'Auhea 'o Kumukahi?
Aia i Hau'ula, ua noho ia, puni ana o ke
ki'i.

Where is Kumukahi?
He is at Hau'ula, He has settled down,
  enraptured by a statue.
— *From* The Legend of Halemano.

Pre-contact Hawaiian art has long been recognized as one of the finest in the Pacific and indeed the world. Hawaiian art is particularly valuable today because the artist working with his material provides a concentrated image of the Hawaiian working with his environment.

Most human beings have developed two types of culture or approaches to living. In the one, we impose ourselves on our surroundings, laying down roads, flattening mountains, erecting monuments. In the second, we move within nature, drawing on its forces without disturbing them.

Cultures of the first type have been studied more thoroughly. Their remains make them more accessible, and we Westerners recognize in them kindred aspirations, in fact, early stages of ourselves.

But there is a growing interest in cultures of the second type, especially as we become more conscious of environmental problems. We begin to feel the need to study the attitudes and techniques by which whole populations were able to support themselves on lands which they left virtually intact. Art is perhaps the deepest expression of an attitude toward the world.

Pre-contact Hawaiian art is valuable, not only in itself, but because we are aided in understanding it by Hawaiian literature, Western reports of early Hawaiian life, and the traditions and life-styles of contemporary Hawaiians. The unusually complete reconstruction possible can help us in our interpretations of cultures which have left fewer remains.

Chants of Cosmic Origin

Hawaiians were close observers of their environment. Their extensive vocabulary reveals their attention to minute details of plants, bodies, weather, light, and so on. Winds and rains were given names and their characteristics carefully noted. Similarity of form was one criterion by which objects were grouped and interrelated. Composed around 1700, the *Kumulipo* chant of the origin of the universe arranged natural scientific traditions in a sequential development of elements, plants, animals and humans, whose history was continued into the time of the composer.

This close observation was naturally practical. Hawaiians were and continue to be expert users of their environment. Hawaiian medicine, for instance, was superior to Western at the time of first contact and for years afterward.

But utility in Hawaiian thinking was inseparable from beauty. The octopus lure worked because it was attractive. A rock was sacred because of its power to elicit a response from the person who viewed it. The Hawaiian interpreted his deep esthetic response to his environment as the result of a power inherent in it, a power as important as the forces of winds and waves.

Emotions and reactions were therefore not unconnected to thought. Just as similarity of form was considered a revelation of affinities between objects, so feelings and responses were to be researched as indications of the cosmic order. Such responses were formulated into names, epithets, and sayings and then taught and passed down in the oral tradition as carefully as methods of farming and fishing.

At times, procedures and ceremonies were established to trigger the traditional reaction. The pilgrim to the narrow valley of Kaliuwa'a on Oahu's windward side would be told to cleanse his mind of all negative thoughts — all pettiness, rancor, and complaining — before entering. Then he would be led up the valley, reciting the prescribed prayers, making the prescribed offerings, and listening to each episode of the saga of the violent, local god as he passed the site where it had occurred. Finally, the pilgrim would arrive at the mountain end of the valley with its waterfall and pool. Prepared now, he would plunge in, and the shock of the ice-cold water would cleanse his mind blank.

A class of experts specializing in the choice of house and temple sites interpreted landscapes through traditional, codified principles. Standing at a temple, we can be sure that the landscape we view was meaningful. At the temple of Kū'ilioloa at Kāne'ilio Point, Pōka'ī Bay, Oahu, we seem to be at the center of a circle traced by the horizon of the ocean on one side and the line of the mountains on the other. A near ridge seems to push the peninsula out against the waves which crash against it. Was the site chosen because it made visible the Hawaiian concept of a unified cosmos of balanced forces?

Clearly, the Western term "art" and the ideas associated with it can be used only with great caution in discussing Hawaiian culture. The Hawaiian lived in a universe he found beautiful and meaningful. The many sectors of his culture were designed to extend and deepen his appreciation of that universe and

throwaways, as some could be in Samoan culture. Fishhooks and carrying sticks were sculpted and polished with the greatest care and passed down as heirlooms. Even leaves for temporary plates were gathered with religious ceremony and disposed of with thanks.

Because the environment was appreciated, it was disturbed as little as possible. The snarer was careful not to injure the bird as he caught it, plucked its few colored feathers, and then released it into its forest home. The builders of a house or temple were careful

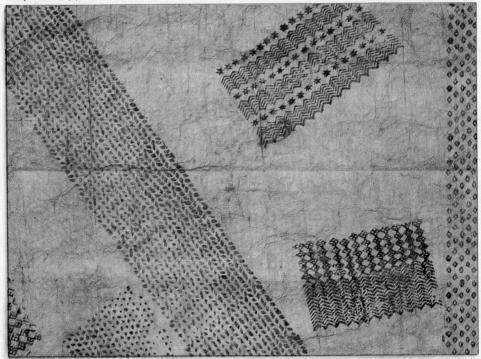

to enable him to live more fully his course and portion within it. The serious life was *ka 'imi loa*, the great search.

Unobtrusiveness Expressed

Because every dimension of life was involved, none was considered insignificant or unesthetic. Tools were not merely utilitarian

Preceding pages, Ancient Hawaiian petroglyph cave, Ka'u, the Big Island of Hawaii; and above, a fine specimen of 19th Century Hawaiian *kapa*.

not to displace or destroy the elements of a site which made it appropriate.

Because natural objects have an inherent beauty and power, the expert needed only to recognize them and do that minimal working and arranging which would render them useful and perceptible to all. The shell needed only as much polishing as would reveal its shine. The yellow feathers needed only the faintest scattering of red to release their full glow. Calabashes were rubbed and oiled until the grain of the wood itself became the surface decoration. A little chipping, and the shark shape of a rock was even clearer.

The artist could even let natural forces do most of the work. He bound twine around the gourd when it was young and let it grow into the desired shape. He cut away sections of the bark and let the sun print the pattern.

The humility of the artist before his material was that of the Hawaiian within his world. When he portrayed himself in petroglyphs, he chose sites and scales which expressed his unobtrusiveness: rocks hidden in the forest or covered by the ocean at high tide. Natural furrows and depressions were

Concentrations of Power
Gleaming in the Firelight

Indeed, the Hawaiian artist reached a peak of sensitivity to the effect of his own actions on his material. He saw how the stone adze compressed the grain of the wood as it struck, pounding as well as cutting. He then added to this effect by rubbing and polishing until he created images of wood made so dense that they seem as much pressed and molded as carved. Unwrapped and gleaming in the firelight, the images seem concen-

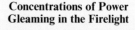

incorporated into the image as if they had prefigured it. When the image needed to be used, perhaps in telling the story of the forebear depicted, it could be daubed with moist red earth which the rain would later wash away.

The attitude of the Hawaiian artist enabled him to search deeply into the qualities of his materials. The *kapa* maker handled the fibers of her bark cloth so suavely that she achieved an unparalleled gauziness and transparency.

trations of powers beyond their size.

Given iron tools, the temple-statue carvers explored the new sizes and splintery surfaces possible and how multiplied faceting could catch the sunlight and take the weathering.

The Hawaiian's consciousness of all the elements in his world, his technical inventiveness, and ideal of deep, esthetic exploration, form the basis for his accomplishments in

Kukailimoku war god images wrought of wood, feathers, wicker and dogs' teeth; from the collection of the Bernice Pauahi Bishop Museum.

featherwork. Throughout Polynesia, feathers have been used and treasured, and religious speculations have been formulated about man's relationship to birds and the firmament. Yet Hawaiian featherwork is unrivaled for range, quantity, and esthetic achievement.

From the earlier, very limited use of small tufts of feathers, the artist had to envision the possibility of large objects covered over their whole surfaces. Techniques of snaring had to be invented; adepts found and trained. Generations passed in the gathering of the necessary quantities of feathers for large pieces. Methods of preservation had to be developed for the treasured stores. Vines were plaited into bases, and strong, thin twine was used to attach the feathers singly or by small tufts.

The Hawaiian artists elaborated whole new forms for feather-work: large and small capes, helmets and helmet bands, of various shapes and combinations of feathers; breastplates, fans, flywhisks, standards, wands, god images, and shrines. In literature, legendary houses were described which were entirely thatched with precious yellow feathers. This restless inventiveness continued into postcontact times, when feathers were applied to skirts, hatbands, ties, toques, and dresses.

Just Before the End, A Great Efflorescence

This same creative search is evident in the history of Hawaiian design. Their Polynesian heritage included a highly developed sense for geometric surface decoration. Early stone god images resemble Marquesan art with simplified details applied like ornaments to the surface of the statue. This geometric tradition continued in many types of art work. But beside it, Hawaiian artists developed a new esthetic in which form produced the dominant impression.

That finished form was in turn largely determined by the shape of the natural object used as material. The shape of the tree trunk was retained in the post image, just as it was in the canoe. The main emphasis then was not on working the natural object, but on choosing it. This new esthetic suggests, therefore, a deepening realization of the consequences of the view that natural objects have inherent beauty and power and that man's search is to recognize them.

In turn, this new esthetic seems to have influenced surface decoration. Certain shapes on feather capes are simple, yet unlike the traditional geometric ones. They seem to be based on natural sights which the artist simplified into silhouettes appropriate to his medium. The artist's training in the geometric tradition is indicated by the simplicity of the silhouettes, but their untraditional character suggests that he wanted to preserve something of the natural sight itself. This same procedure can be found in petroglyph figures and has a utilitarian parallel in *poi* pounder forms which have been reduced to the minimum functionally necessary.

Hawaiian cultural history is marked by such innovations, stages in a creative search as far reaching as any in human history and which continues in various forms among Hawaiians today. The monuments of that search have inspired artists who came to Hawaii from all over the world and provide the basis for a contemporary movement of native artists centering around the Hale Naua III led by sculptor Rocky Jensen. But the classical visual arts, attached as they were to the native technology and religion, suffered more than most aspects from the arrival of Westerners and Christianity. Hawaiian artists turned to Western forms, and much classical art was lost or destroyed.

But just before the end, there was a great efflorescence. The Hawaii Island chief, Kamehameha, was preparing to launch the campaign which would eventually unite all the islands under his rule. He gathered all the great men of his domain, organized armies, built fleets, and collected supplies. He allied himself with the powerful priesthood of the war god Ku and began to repair and extend the major temples, having them furnished with an unprecedented quantity of god images carved on a new, heavily monumental scale and in a new, marvelously intricate style. Sculpturesque, muscular bodies in the clenched fist crouch of a boxer were crowned by slab-like heads with grimacing mouths, enormous eyes, and elaborately faceted hairpieces.

Living among the great men of his exciting time, feeling within himself the last surge of classical art, the Hawaiian sculptor left us, in his image of the god, a portrait of the human being—all courage, strength, and aural shimmer—at the fearful point of the great search.

SOUVENIR.

ALOHA OE

(My love to you.)

MARCH.

The Queen Kapiolani.　　The Princess Liliuokalani.

Composed and arranged by

J. THOMAS BALDWIN.

Incorporating the popular Song "Aloha Oe"

BY THE

Princess Liliuokalani

And performed by

BALDWIN'S BOSTON CADET BAND

AT THE

Grand Reception given by the City of Boston to

Queen Kapiolani and Princess Liliuokalani

May 12th 1887.

HAWAIIAN MUSIC AND DANCE

No music has girdled the earth more smoothly, more often and more completely than Hawaiian music and none has remained so popular with so many for so long. Say "Hawaiian music" to a banker in Bangkok, an army captain in Amsterdam, a housewife in Minneapolis and all get the same romantic, dreamy look. They're thinking of swaying palms and hips ... the *hula* ... the sultry slack key guitar ... a chilling, tremulous falsetto voice ... the dazzling plunky-plunkiness of an *ukulele* ... the keening accents of a steel guitar. Titles and phrases

pot, historically quick to accept and absorb whatever comes to its golden shores. Nowhere is this phenomenal rate and degree of cultural assimilation more apparent than in the music. Listening to Hawaiian music today is like listening to the islands' history.

In ancient times, the sounds of Hawaiian music were primitive, consisting of long, monotonous chants recited either without accompaniment or against a background of drums made from coconut trees, gourds, bamboo rattles and pipes, sticks and pebble castanets.

from the old songs float by: "I wanna go back to my little grass shack ..." "Tiny bubbles, in the wine ..." "Dreams come true, in blue Hawaii ..." "To you, sweetheart, aloha ..." "Lovely *hula* hands ..." "Oh, we're going to a *hukilau* ..." "*Aloha 'oe* ..."

Hawaii has been described as a melting

Hula halau (longhouse), above, on Oahu, circa 1852, drawn by the Swiss artist Paul Emmert.

The ritualistic aspects of the music were quite complex, on the other hand, playing a vital part of daily life and a significant role in all religious beliefs and services. The chant was the means of establishing contact between man and god. Entering a *hula* school in those days was equivalent to entering a monastery.

The *hula* is Hawaiian folk dance. Legends say that goddesses of the dance were Laka and Hiʻiaka. (If not actually worshipped, both are still well respected today.) At first, it was performed by men and women, but only men could perform the *hula* during temple worship services. It was believed that by pantomiming an action, that action could be controlled in the future. Thus there were many dances for wished-for events, such as a successful hunt or fertility.

The *hula* later engulfed all of Hawaiian society and became many things—a teaching tool, a popular entertainment, and a basic foundation for the *lua*, an art of self-defense known only to ancient Hawaiians. As the *hula* became widespread, wars and governing duties kept the men too busy for the years of rigid training required to be a

nations of sound. Thinking that the quickest way to a Hawaiian's soul might be through his ears, the missionaries enrolled the natives in church choirs.

Progress was slow. The broader tones required by church hymns were new to Hawaiians, so the songs were learned by rote as the missionaries sang the hymns—called *himeni* by the natives—over and over and over again, and the natives copied as best they could. Finally, choirs were formed. The *himeni* remain a strong influence today. Choirs are most popular and so are several Hawaiian songs with religious themes and messages.

Hawaiian music's other most dominant influence reflected a Hawaiian king's wish to

Royal Hawaiian Band, H

hula performer. Thus the women began to share equally in the performance of the *hula*.

Then an odd thing happened. After uncounted hundreds of years, in 1819 King Kamehameha II overthrew the *kapu* (taboo) system and with it the ancient religion. This left the Hawaiian people spiritually disoriented—and ripe for what arrived the following year, Christian missionaries from New England.

These devout and dedicated settlers built churches amid the Hawaiian huts, held services and sang hymns. The Hawaiians had never heard melody and four-part harmony before and they collected by the hundreds outside the small lava rock and clapboard churches to listen to these exotic combi-

be westernized and came in the form of a single man. King Kamehameha V decided that he wanted a royal band (like those in Europe) and the brisk, mustachio'd Heinrich Berger was imported from Germany (in 1868) to be bandmaster.

Berger, who is known today as the Father of Hawaiian Music, served as director of the Royal Hawaiian Band from 1872 until 1915. During this time he conducted more than 32,000 band concerts, arranged more than 1,000 Hawaiian songs, composed 75 original

Bandmaster Heinrich Berger and his Royal Hawaiian Band (above) in circa 1910 postcard; and *ukulele* player (right) photographed by Theodore Kelsey at Palolo Valley, Oahu.

292

Hawaiian songs (including several still popular today), while reversing the traditional order of the *mele*, or song—composing the music before the words. Soon after that, the Hawaiians were doing the same and before the 1870s ran out, they were composing lyrics and music simultaneously. Berger also served as personal inspiration and teacher for two generations of Hawaiian musicians, some of whom later went on to stardom.

'The Jumping Flea,' Slack Key

From other lands came other influences. The guitar, for instance, was brought by early whalers or more likely by traders from Mexico and California. (And not, as is popularly believed, by Mexican cowboys, who arrived later, in 1832.) In time the traditional

Some believe it was named for a small Englishman who came to Hawaii and, once mastering the instrument, happened to jump about while playing it. Others insist that the player's fingers merely looked like jumping fleas when strumming.

Scholars are also arguing about who actually invented the steel guitar, and how he did it. Some say a Hawaiian student discovered the sound when he dropped his pocket knife upon the strings of a guitar and holding it there with one hand, plucked the strings with the other, moving the steel knife to "slide" the sound. Others think the inventor of the steel guitar had been in India, where he could've seen an Indian stringed instrument, the *gottuvadyam*, played similarly. While the steel guitar has been much identified with

style of playing was changed as the Hawaiian musicians loosened the strings and tunings became whatever the player wished them to be. This style of playing was called *ki ho'alu*, or slack key, and is as uniquely Hawaiian as flamenco is Spanish.

From Madeira, Portugal, in 1878, with laborers imported to work in the sugar cane fields, came a small, four-stringed instrument called the *braquino*, or *cavaquinho*. As with so much else in Hawaiian musical history, there is disagreement as to how the *braquino* became *'ukulele*, Hawaiian for "jumping flea."

Country and Western music in recent years, it remains the single most identifiable part of the Hawaiian instrumental sound.

The descendants of the ancient *ali'i* ruling Hawaii in the final years before annexation to the United States in 1898 were among the most talented and prolific composers of song that the island culture ever produced. The

Above, court *hula* master Ioane (John) Ukeke, "The Hawaiian Dandy," and his troupe, about 1880; and (right) *hula* stereoscopic, about 1920, by the Keystone View Company, New York.

294

best known of these was King David Kalakaua, a plump and jovial man whose "champagne dynasty" is recognized also as an inspiration for a genuine musical renaissance.

Kalakaua was a gifted politician, world traveler and patron of the arts. He promoted the 'ukulele and steel guitar and formed his own musical group, entering into competitions with relatives and friends. He collected the legends and myths of Hawaii into a definitive, and literate, book and co-wrote (with Henri Berger) Hawaii's national anthem, "Hawaii Pono'i," a song that's still sung at ball games and public assemblies. The hula, long suppressed by the missionaries and near death, was revived under his personal direction. Much music is played

best (most adaptable) Tin Pan Alley songwriters were writing "Hawaiian" music, too.

'Yaaka Hula Hickey Dula?'

If most of those new songs had little to do with true Hawaiian musical tradition—and often doubletalk served as Hawaiian, as in "Yaaka Hula Hickey Dula" (a hit for Al Jolson)—the influence was immediate and significant. The craze took many authentic Hawaiian groups across America for many years, where they, in turn, accepted the phoney Hawaiian songs (to satisfy requests), eventually turning them into Hawaiian "classics." At the same time, they began arranging older, more authentic Hawaiian songs with the newly popular jazz beat that they heard

10156 T   Native Hula Girls in Characteristic Attire near Honolulu, Territory of Hawaii.

today on the birthday (November 16) of this bewhiskered king.

His sister, Liliuokalani, probably came even closer than he to understanding and synthesizing ancient Hawaiian and Western music traditions and form. Probably the most gifted Hawaiian of her class and time, she composed a song that's appeared in at least half the Hawaiian movies ever made (even Elvis sang it) and has been a certifiable "hit" for more than 70 years: "Aloha 'Oe."

The sound of Hawaiian music changed again after Liliuokalani's kingdom was wrenched away by aggressive sugar growers and Hawaii became a territory of the United States. This directed great interest toward Hawaii and in 1915 a group of Hawaiian musicians, singers and dancers were the runaway sensation of the Panama-Pacific International Exposition in San Francisco, sparking a craze that swept North America and soon spread to Europe. Soon after, the

everywhere they went.

Hula dancers became all the rage in vaudeville, even in circus sideshows. Sometimes they were called "cootch" dancers, because many of the performers—few of whom were actually Hawaiian—adapted the movements freely and lasciviously.

Back in Hawaii, the first hotels were going up on Waikiki and dance bands were being formed for the growing number of tourists. Ragtime, jazz, blues, Latin and foxtrot rhythms were interposed with Hawaiian themes and, horrors!—English lyrics. The purists were appalled, as always, but by 1930 the hapa haole (half Caucasian) song was an entrenched and accepted part of Hawaiian music and a staple on what was to become the most widely heard radio program in all the world, "Hawaii Calls."

Then Hollywood called. And when Bing Crosby introduced two hapa-haole classics, "Sweet Leilani" and "Blue Hawaii," in a single film (*Waikiki Wedding*) in 1937 and "Sweet Leilani" won the Oscar for the best song, movie companies began churning out languid musical romances by the score.

Again the *hula* was revived, and—for Hollywood—cleaned up a bit as authentic island practitioners like Hilo Hattie were featured in many films. Now and forever more the swaying hips and limbs of the grass-skirted dancer would be the foremost symbol of Hawaii's widespread image of carefree sensuality.

When one songwriter urged visitors to Hawaii to keep their eyes on the hands, in one sense it was good advice, for when the singer says, "Lovely hula hands/graceful as the birds in motion," the arms are extended and the hands move gracefully to simulate

dominated and middle-of-the-road singers like Kúi Lee and Don Ho emerged as the only Hawaiian stars.

In the 1970s there came another Hawaiian renaissance, as persons with Hawaiian blood discovered an ethnic awareness and pride (like so many other Third Worlders). So pervasive and energetic was this second cultural rebirth that all the traditional Hawaiian arts experienced a rich revival.

Down Home Cha-lang-a-lang

The music became more "contemporary" (a word used by the musicians themselves). Politically relevant lyrics were added along with new rhythms, new instruments and greater amplification, thus attracting the at-

swooping birds. In "The Hukilau Song," which is about fishing, the hands throw out and pull in the net.

The 30-year period from 1930 to 1960 is regarded as Hawaiian music's "golden age," as the music of Hawaii circled the world again and again, on television as well as in radio and film. Wherever the traveling *hula* dancers and musicians went, they found enthusiastic audiences.

Then came the Beatles, changing Hawaiian music just as they changed so many things. In fact, they nearly killed it. For 10 years, young Hawaiians were disinterested in the traditional island sound. Hawaiian music on local radio dropped to a low five per cent. Rock

tention of the young Hawaiian who'd turned away from his heritage for so long. At the same time, there was renewed, fervent interest in the older, more traditional Hawaiian sounds. And some of the young composers appealed to everyone by writing new songs (and chants!) about the kings and ancient gods. In the 1970s, Hawaii acknowledged its roots.

Young Hawaiians also began dancing in the ancient style. Not since the early 1800s,

Right, Hawaii's well-known folksinger, the late Gabby Pahinui. Above, the Makaha Sons of Niihau, jamming at Makua Beach, Oahu, 1979.

when missionaries labeled many *hula* obscene and banned them, have such powerful and erotic movements been seen in Hawaii. Indeed, suppression of *hula* had been so complete, that by the 1850s it had nearly disappeared, and when 40 years after that King Kalakaua saved the *hula*, much had been lost forever.

Today, though, the *hula* retains much of its serious heritage. Contemporary students heed ancient ritual religiously. (Although none are asked to give up sex to be a *hula* performer, as was true in ancient times.) Different *hula halau* (schools) compete fiercely to out-do one another. *Hula* masters, or *kumu hula*, are revered figures. And with the male *hula* now in a period of rich revival, the dance has become a symbol of the islander's

as much a part of dinner with friends as the predictable *laulau* and *poi* — and has, in fact, given birth to a raucous, good-timey backyard style of playing called *cha-lang-a-lang*.

Hawaiians believe that music is not just a means of communicating with god, but also a gift from god, so they in turn give it freely — while walking along the street, lazing at the bus stop, or wherevah. Professional performers give their music freely at dozens of benefits every week.

The visitor to Hawaii cannot possibly avoid the music; it is everywhere. Young men collect in twos and threes in the parks with their guitars. Children have performed the *hula* every Sunday morning at the Ala

newly rediscovered sense of Hawaiianness.

Still, the *hula* remains basically an entertainment, and as such it is also a symbol of Hawaii's widespread image of carefree sensuality. Thus it's become almost a cultural trademark, one which has been used to great advantage to attract visitors.

A Hawaiian scholar has noted that no other Hawaiian art form has been so westernized and yet has so retained its Hawaiianness. It's clear that one reason is that, despite all the changes, music and dance remain a vital part of daily Hawaiian life, just as in pre-European times.

For every special day (honoring Prince Kuhio, or Kamehameha the Great, etc.) and for all the ordinary days in between, music is played. Songs have been written about even the most mundane subject — for example, "The Hasegawa General Store," "Bottles and Cans (a song about Maui's Makawao dump)" and "The Runny Nose Hula." The sound of the slack key guitar (or *'ukulele*) is

Moana Shopping Center for over 10 years, adults at the Kodak Hula Show for 25. The Royal Hawaiian Band, still performing after all these years, appears in several public concerts each week, notably at noon nearly every Friday at the Iolani Palace Coronation Bandstand. Right in Waikiki there are more than 25 clubs and showrooms offering traditional Hawaiian music at least one and often every night of the week. Many hotels offer their guests free hula lessons. And radio Station KCCN (at 1420 on the AM dial) calls itself "the world's only all-Hawaiian music station."

A guide to the "most Hawaiian" music currently being played in Hawaii is included in each issue of the Hawaiian Music Foundation's monthly magazine, *Ha'ilono Mele* (Music News), available at selected record stores and hotels on Oahu or from P.O. Box 10293, Honolulu, HI 96816, USA. Cost is $1.25 per issue.

LEIS

Remember the last time you were in Baghdad, Firenze or Keokuk and the only airport greeting you received was noise, chaos, and lost luggage? There's no guarantee you won't get the same in Honolulu — but somehow, when a friend greets you with a flower *lei*, you know you're no stranger in a strange land and even a grueling, sleepless 10-hour trip can seem very far away.

When you receive a lei, it's more than a circle of flowers and fragrance accompanied with a kiss. In the old days it was an offering to the gods. Today the custom belongs to everyone and, if done in authentic Hawaiian tradition, it begins with an attitude ... a spirit of thankfulness as each blossom is picked from the earth, then strung one by one so each will shine at its most brilliant. It may take a thousand blossoms to fill a lei; when presented to a friend, stranger, or beloved, it is a symbol of beauty, made with care and given with love. With a real Hawaiian lei, no blossom, leaf or recipient is insignificant.

Of course, some leis have humbler beginnings. Today's mass airport arrivals and greetings with hastily bought leis can depersonalize and commercialize the custom, but only if you think so. At its lowest, a lei is a souvenir; at its noblest, a work of art and offering of *aloha* that comes in as many different styles and forms as there are reasons for giving them.

Lei-giving on the kitsch side ranges from lifesavers and Chinese crack seeds strung end to end, to miniature bottles of liquor, some alternating vermouth and gin to create a "martini lei." The real heretics indulge in plastic flowers that never wilt. Even the Hawaii Visitors Bureau attempted giving

plastic leis years ago, but that artificial aloha soured to outrage and the effort was soon pooh-poohed into abandon. In the old Matson steamship days, tossing a lei overboard was a custom introduced by the West: if a tossed lei returned to shore, it was thought, the visitor would return to Hawaii.

Today, if you don't have an occasion, you make one up. If you have no flowers, there are seeds, leaves, pods, shells, nuts, berries, twigs. The tradition is as old as Hawaii itself, and from the time the volcano goddess Pele's sister Hiiaka is said to have presented the first *lehua* leis to her sisters on a beach in Puna, these garlands have become art, custom, and ornament.

To Honor Pele, Laka and Love

In ancient times, leis took the form of head wreaths and necklets as well as the long circular or open-ended strands we know as leis today. They were used originally as offerings to deities in the sacred dances and chants of Hawaii. A lei worn in a dance was never given away; it belonged to the goddess of the dance.

There were six types of leis used in traditional religious dances, and they are being

Left, "Hula Girl," wearing *maile lei*, about 1908, by Ray Jerome Baker; and above, Mrs. Ray Jerome Baker on "Boat Day" in the 1920s.

revived today. The *palapalai* and *pala'a* are two ferns that still grow on island mountains; the *pukeawe*, a little red berry; the *lehua*, blossom of the *ohia* tree, often called the flower of Pele; and the *a'ali'i*, a small, leaf-like flower in greens and oranges, depending on which island and location it came from. *Maile*, a fragrant leaf and vine dedicated to Laka, the goddess of dance, decorated every altar and is the best known today of the six traditional leis. It is said among some Hawaiian elders that the spicy fragrance of *maile* still lingers at ancient *heiau*, and the

authority Mary Kawena Pukui recalls how leis for *alii* were given to the attendant or presented with a bow, for no hands of a commoner were to rise above the head of royalty.

Today even horses in parades wear leis, and parades for the many Island holidays are showcases for floral fantasies that have only grown with time. The "May Day is Lei Day" tradition, initiated by Islander Don Blanding in 1928 to attract tourists to the Islands, brought us the renowned and annual pag-

elegant, open-ended braided strands are among the most popular today for personal use and official Island ceremonies.

Fortunately, the legends have lingered through the evolution of different customs and Western influences. The Hawaiians have always been affectionate, but the lei-cum-kiss tradition had its unlikely beginnings with a World War II entertainer. When dared to kiss an officer publicly, she was embarrassed and gave an excuse. As she kissed him and presented her lei, she claimed it was a Hawaiian custom, and it immediately became one.

It's a far cry from the original custom, which was formidably formal. Hawaiiana

eantry of May 1 and leis characterizing each island. To this day, each island has its own special lei; shells for Niihau, *mokihana* for Kauai, *ilima* for Oahu, *kaunaoa* for Lanai, *hinahina* for Kahoolawe, *kukui* flowers for Molokai, *lokelani* for Maui, and *lehua* for the Big Island. Exotic princesses wearing *holokus* in the colors of each island wear the lei of their island in the floats, pageants and ceremonies of Hawaiian holidays.

In the meantime, some leis and customs have vanished with time, among them a seaweed lei called *limu kala*, used in ancient Hawaii in rituals for the ocean deities. Nor do we see nursing mothers today wearing leis of sweet potato vines, worn in the old days to increase lactation.

Fragrance, Form and Spirit

Leis today are less superstition and more sentiment and ornamentation, made of flowers, shells, paper, rainbow colors and multitudes of textures of anything that can be fashioned by the five basic techniques. If your local lei-maker is retreating to *wili paukuku*, it means she is winding roses and begonias in a certain style. *Humuhumu* is a lei sewn onto a backing; *wili*, a lei that is wound; *hili*, braided with greens; *haku*, braided with flowers; and *kui*, strung.

banana bark as string. For the more elaborate feather leis reserved for the royalty of old Hawaii, strips of *olona* bark were twisted into a fine cord, flexible and strong enough to secure myriads of feathers invisibly.

For the artists of lei-making, no detail is insignificant, not even the simple tying or packaging of the lei. Most people finish their leis with ribbons and toss them in a plastic bag for freshness. Lei-makers like Barbara Meheula aren't quite so casual. For the finishing, called the *po*, she makes flower and fern corsages to replace the standard ribbon.

In the *kui* method alone there are countless variations, from the pristine beauty of a plumeria lei to the more structured *maunaloa*-style vanda. *Kui* leis are the *pikake*, ginger, carnation, and other popular flower leis sold by the hundreds daily by airport and Maunakea Street vendors. Some flowers, such as *pakalana* and tuberose, are seasonal; others, like the magical *pikake*, are available year-round for $2 to $2.50 per strand.

Before needle and thread were introduced to Hawaii, stiff grass blades from Nuuanu Valley were used as needles and strands of

Left, *hula* girls, Kapiolani Park *hula* competition, 1978; and above, postcard showing *lei* sellers at Honolulu Harbor on a 1930s "Boat Day".

Instead of a plastic bag (which she claims will cause flowers to droop sooner when removed from the bag), she goes strictly Hawaiian. One day it might be a woven basket, another day a bamboo carrier or banana leaf wrapper. This day it's the magical, healing coolness of *ti* leaves, stalks bundled with authority at one end, then leaves gently unfolded around them like a banana peel. The *ola'a* lei, amethyst in color and made of more than 1,000 blossoms, is exquisite, and its packaging must equal it. It is wound softly around the *ti* leaf stalks, sprayed with a mist of water, wrapped up again with the leaves. The stalks quickly fold into a handle; the soft, cool bundle is hung in the cooler, complete.

In the traditional Hawaiian way, the same kind of care and consciousness is exercised when materials are taken from the land. It is a harvest, and the gatherers come with thanks and respect. A mountain or valley is never stripped. Plants are never taken whole, and in any one area, enough is left growing to allow regeneration. They are clipped, not pulled from stalk or root. Mature leaves are taken and the young are left to grow while old cuttings with seeds and spores are scattered on the ground to germinate. "Traditional Hawaiian leis are coming back

because of the hula revival," notes Barbara Meheula. "The mountains are being scoured for leis, and we must take care of them.

"If it looks like a tree is struggling, I'll walk five miles to another tree."

Perhaps the biggest challenge to the survival of native plants, she notes, is not the *hula* dancers who are making leis, but rather the introduced flora that run rampant throughout the mountains. When plants such as lantana, guava, and blackberry were introduced to Hawaii's wilderness, little was it realized that they would become a threat to the more fragile plants indigenous to Hawaii.

"In the old days, all the plants were pampered." Mrs. Meheula explained. "When the introduced plants came in, they were just like diseases."

Above, Hawaiian Pa'u rider and her horse, both wearing lei, circa 1920s; and right, the late Iolani Luahine, much treasured for herself and her inimitable dancing of the ancient *hula*.

Because of this delicate balance in the island wilderness, the *hula-halau* are meticulous in educating their students on the ethics of picking flowers and plants for leis. Even the humble, ubiquitous plumeria blossom (or frangipani) is treated like a jewel.

Hawaii's native birds have been less fortunate. Only occasional travelers through remote areas such as Haleakala Crater still glimpse the *i'iwi* and *apapane*, noted for their bright crimson feathers used in the leis, capes and ornaments reserved for the *alii* of old Hawaii. The *mamo* and *o'o*, prized for their yellow feathers, are extinct. There were other reasons for their disappearance: land development, the introduction of new wild-life, and disease.

Now the *kapu* on wearing feather leis is long gone and the birds used are less exotic. But along with Niihau shells, these leis are the rarest and most expensive. Mary Louise Kekuewa, who teaches feather lei-making at the Bishop Museum, points out one rare specimen, a blue neck pheasant lei that would devastate ecologists. "It takes 90 to 125 birds for this one and five hours to sew one inch of the lei," she explains. No wonder it can cost up to a thousand dollars!

There are infinite colors and patterns from just two basic styles, round and flat. Popularly worn as headbands and hatbands as well, they're made from the feathers of peacocks, pheasants, ducks and geese bought from local hunters (who are given a hunting quota by law) and Mainland outlets. It is a far cry from the old days, when feathers were gathered for years and bundled and stored in banana leaves. In those days, feathers were tied and bundled with *olona* cord, for sewing came with the missionaries in the 1820s.

The styles of Niihau shell leis, considered museum pieces today, have evolved as well, but not quite so dramatically. The popular three-strand pikake style is a later development, and like all Niihau shell leis it is rare and prohibitively expensive. The tiny, fragile leis, called *pupu Niihau* or *momo* by the people of this privately owned island, cost hundreds of dollars and are not easily available.

Unlike flower leis, they last forever. But one thing is important in this priceless Hawaiian custom: Time matters not in the giving of a lei.

Fragrance and form may fade in a breath, but the spirit of a lei remains.

SURFING

Ina aohe nalu, alaila kahea aku i kai, penei
  e hea ai:
  Ku mai! Ku mai! Ka nalu nui mai Kahiki
  mai,
  Alo poi pu! Ku mai ka pohuehue,
  Hu! Kaikoo loa.

If there is no surf, invoke seaward in
  the following manner:
Arise, arise ye great surfs from Kahiki,
The powerful curling waves. Arise with
  the *pohuehue.*
Well up, long raging surf.
— *a* pohuehue, *or surf coaxing chant,*
  collected by the historian Abraham
  Fornander.

We now call it surfing, but the ancient
Hawaiian name for this sport was *he'enalu,* a
term rich in oceanic and poetic nuance. The
word's first half, *he'e,* for example, can mean
"to change from a solid to a liquid substance;
to run, as a liquid; to flow, as blood or water;
to slip or glide along; to melt away; or to flee
through fear." And *nalu,* the second half,
implies the roaring, surging and rolling motion of a wave as it glides toward a beach; the
forming of a wave; and the slimy liquid or
the face of a newborn infant.

Piece those word parts together and wha'
emerges is a simple definition — "wave
sliding" — or a semi-poetic interpretation
which allows surfers from the earliest of
surfing times to be as newborn babes fleeing
in a slippery, flowing form through a terrify-
ing, roaring and surging saltwater womb.
Such Freudian presumptions sound a bit
fanciful and idealistic, but ask any person
who's ever been locked into a thick tubing
wave what he thinks about that rebirth concept and chances are he or she will heartily
and humbly endorse it.

Nobody's sure when Polynesians first engaged in this subtle and spectacular water-
sport, but Hawaiian chants which date to the
15th Century recount surfing exploits and
indicate that surfing by then was so refined
that special contests were held between
famous surfers. These were widely heralded
affairs, sometimes pitting high-ranking chiefs
against each other, and on shore crowds of
supporters would indulge in heavy-stakes
gambling by placing property bets on a
favored waverider.

Left, in the tube, Banzai Pipeline, Oahu.

Not unlike modern-day surf cultists who
drop everything they are doing to heed the
siren call of good waves, Hawaiians also were
easily tempted and distracted from drudgery.
One particularly slack month, according to
a noted Hawaiian scholar, Kepelino
Keauokalani, was the one we call November,
which in the Hawaiian nature calendar was
known as *Ikuwa. Ikuwa,* Kepelino wrote,
means "deafening" because it "is the season
of the worst storms." Or, as he recalls in his
manuscript *Traditions of Hawaii:*

"It is a month of rough seas and high surf
that lure men to the seacoast. For expert
surfers going upland to farm, if part way
up perhaps they look back and see the
rollers combing the beach, will leave their
work, pluck ripe banana leaves, ti leaves
and ginger, strip them, fasten them about
their necks and stand facing the sea and
holding sugar-cane in their hand, then
hurrying away home, they will pick up the
board and go. All thought of work is at
an end, only that of sport is left. The wife
may go hungry, the children, the whole
family, but the head of the house does not
care. He is all for sport, that is his food."

'A Most Supreme Pleasure'

And so *he'enalu* flowed on for several
centuries before the white man, the *haole,*
began putting into Polynesian shores. The
first known Western observer and writer of
surfing was Britain's esteemed Captain James
Cook, who in December 1777, saw a Tahitian
native paddling a small outrigger canoe into
long rolling waves off Matavai Point. "I
could not help concluding," Cook wrote in
his log, "that this man felt the most supreme
pleasure while he was driven so fast and so
smoothly by the sea."

Later, in Hawaii, in 1778, Cook and his
men marveled at the agility of men who were
riding across crystal combers on short or long
wooden planks we know now as surfboards.
Cook's Lieutanant James King of HMS
Resolution said of Hawaiian surfing: "The
boldness and address, with which we saw
them perform these difficult and dangerous
maneuvers, was altogether astonishing and is
scarce to be credited."

Indeed, and nearly every other writer who
spent time in Hawaii during the next cen-
tury-and-a-half after Cook and King was

astonished by this uniquely Polynesian entertainment. "It did not seem that a lightning express train could shoot along at a more hair-lifting speed," was Mark Twain's reaction in 1866. And much later, in 1907, author Jack London spun grand rococo lines about a surfer — a brown Mercury — who emerged from an "invincible roar ... not struggling frantically in that wild movement, not buried and crushed and buffeted by those mighty monsters, but standing above them all, calm and superb, poised on the giddy summit, his feet buried in the churning foam, the salt smoke rising to hs knees ..."

By the turn of the 20th Century, however, surfing, like the race which had for so long enjoyed and refined its movements, was dying, partially because Christian mis-

is credited with renewing local and national interest in surfing, but it was probably the promotion of Hawaii tourism in general which brought wave-riding back into vogue. The sport was further promoted in 1908 when a group of *haole* sportsmen leased land at Waikiki Beach and started a private beach-club called the Outrigger Canoe Club, dedicated to the perpetuation and preservation of Hawaiian outrigger canoeing and board surfing. Another, older club, *Hui Nalu* (Surfing Club), was formally chartered in 1911 by a group of Hawaiian surfers, and thus was the glamorous Hawaiian sport of surfing officially organized in modern times. Both the Outrigger and Hui Nalu clubs are now more actively involved in outrigger canoe competitions than surfing, but since the

sionaries discouraged it, charging it was a decadent distraction, but also because Hawaiians were becoming more and more preoccupied with a newly Western lifestyle. A few so-called "beachboys" still rode the mellow swells that curl over Waikiki's broad reefs, but in the flurry of civilization and commercialization of Hawaii many surfing traditions and favored surfing grounds were forgotten.

London's gushy piece on surfing, entitled "A Royal Sport: Surfing at Waikiki," often

Left, early 1900s surfer on the beach at Waikiki; and above, "Jeux Haviens," an 1873 engraving by the French artist E. Riou, showing women surfers at an unidentified Hawaiian beach.

founding of those premier clubs the sport has spread quickly throughout the wet world — first to California and Australia, and eventually to distant places such as New Zealand, Bali, Java, Japan, the Seychelles and-Mauritius in the Indian Ocean, South Africa, France, Spain, the Carribean, Mexico and Peru. There is no way of gauging the sport's economic impact in general, but related revenues have been estimated to be in the millions of dollars annually, particularly if one includes surfing-related fashions in an economic review.

As for the sport's technical purity, not a summer or winter surfing season passes without some new hydrodynamic wave-riding theory being field and market tested. Gone are the days when *alii* Hawaiians stood with statuesque poise on 18-foot *koa* boards which weighed a hundred and fifty pounds. Also gone are early 1900s Waikiki-style surfboards made of California redwood. And just as extinct are balsa "pig boards" of the early 1950s. All have given way to futuristic potato chips, boogie boards, knee machines, lightning bolts, fish, pin and swallow tails, convoluted rails, bungie cords, stinger fins and other such surfing esoterica. Certain rubber-bodied waveriders now think nothing of banking hard off the bottom of a wave like an erratic rocket and carving a full 360-degree trail across a wave's glassy, fast-breaking face. Others prefer late straight-up-and-down takeoffs over shallow coral reefs. Dangerous, yes, but it places them in better

position for that saltwater rebirth. Hopefully, as adrenalin sends a rush up their crouched spine, they will be spit out of an exploding tube of water before it sucks them and their glossy craft "over the falls" and into an awful body-grinding garden of jagged coral heads and purple-spiked sea urchins.

Such encounters with the nervous deep require a certain sporting spirit that is two parts clean fun and perhaps one part death wish; but to prepare himself better for varying wave conditions, however calm or violent, the modern and complete Hawaiian

waverider now maintains not just one surfboard, but an all-purpose "quiver" of boards. One board is specially shaped for country waves of medium but solid wall intensity, another is for "hotdog"-sized town waves on sleepy south, swell summer days. Others, depending on just how specialized his riding has become, are dartlike "guns," the largest of which are called "elephant guns," designed for big wave breaks such as the deadly Banzai Pipeline, Sunset Beach and Waimea Bay on Oahu's North Shore.

In recent years, surfing also has entered a brave and new professional era which features as much as $150,000 in contest money up for grabs annually in a worldwide International Pro Surfing (IPS) contest tour. Much like touring PGA golfers, surfers who are into waves for money now pack their salty trunks and quivers and make the rounds of professional surf meets held in Hawaii, California, Australia, South Africa, Brazil, New Jersey and Florida. And at the end of each competition year, this pro circuit's top-ranked surfers don tuxedoes and receive singular honors at an International Surfing Grand Prix awards banquet held at some luxury hotel in Hawaii. "We're trying to do away forever with the image of surfers as beach bums," explained an IPS official.

Because Mother Nature and Sister Sea are fickle, it is difficult to predict when surfing will be best in Hawaii, but most major big wave surfing competitions are held during November and December when Oahu's North Shore surfing grounds are thundering loud with the world's most famous surfing waves. During the summer, when swells are being generated from the then wintry Southern Hemisphere, surfing and surf-watching are best on Hawaii's south shores.

Among the more famous professional surf-outs (usually held at a North Shore beach on Oahu) are the Smirnoff Pro Hawaii meet, usually held during the second half of November; the Pipeline and Women's Masters meet, first two weeks in December; the Duke Kahanamoku Classic, also during the first two weeks in December; and the World Cup Hawaii, held during the second half of December. For further information about annual surfing competitions, see Honolulu's daily newspapers or *Surfer* and *Surfing* magazines. Or scan the bulletin board in any good surf shop.

Left, the split and splintered surfing remains of a "wipeout," North Shore, Oahu; and right, a surfer "kicks out" of a steep Sunset wave, Oahu.

A 16-shot motordrive camera sequence of surfer Reno Abellira
going into and out of a tubing wave three times on the same wave-ride at 'Pipeline Right'.

ISLAND FOOD

What, indeed, is Island food?

Is it Hawaiian food, Oriental food, Polynesian food, Cosmopolitan food, *chop suey*, *saimin*, mango, *opakapaka provencale*, or *teriyaki* hamburger? Ask any islander and you'll get a different answer; consult any island menu and you might choke on your chichis and nachos. Lesson number one in island gastronomy is that the only singular characteristic of contemporary Hawaiian food is its own inability to be characterized.

Let's start with the place itself. To Americans, Hawaii is technically a state but intrinsically a foreign country. To the swelling waves of immigrants from the East, Hawaii is the first outpost of the Western frontier, the proverbial promised land. And to everyone tapping into the inimitable diversity of this polyglot paradise, Hawaii is sights, sounds, smells, tastes and infinite imaginings from everywhere. Just everywhere.

It isn't surprising, then, that the gastronomical offerings of this tiny Pacific state range from the most sophisticated Continental cuisine to humble but exquisite peasant dishes of Vietnam, Northern China, and Japan. Although Oriental restaurants have always been abundant here, recent waves of immigrants have brought new Korean, Thai, Vietnamese and Filipino restaurants offering ethnic foods with a new twist: mango-squid salad ... chicken with papaya ... shrimp paste on sugar cane ... fish with bitter melon ... At Thai restaurants like the Mekong, Thai House and Khun Mariam, exotic concoctions combine island seafood and produce seasoned with rare Eastern spices and condiments, pickled, sauteed, steamed ... Shops like The Asian Store (on S. Beretania Street) sell occasional specialties such as bananas steamed in *mochi* rice and wrapped in *ti* leaves, while shelves of fungus, seaweeds, canned kumquats and unlikely ingredients from foreign cuisines beckon the palates of at-home diners and restaurant chefs alike.

Mango Bread and Opakapaka Diablo

Even elegant Continental dining rooms can't escape the ubiquitous local influence. Where else but in Honolulu would you find *mahimahi* in a Moroccan restaurant or veddy veddy kosher Italian and French waiters announcing their Pacific specialities: *opakapaka diablo*, prosciutto with papaya or mango, Maui onion salad, fresh *ono* macadamia.

Some restaurants, like Matteo's, serve no fish unless it's freshly caught in island waters. Others express the ethnic influence in *teriyaki* and sweet-sour sauces that, alas, often fall appallingly short of the real thing.

Among the best-known of the exquisite eateries are the Third Floor at the Hawaiian Regent, Michel's at the Colony Surf, John Dominis surfside at Kewalo Basin, Canlis, Bagwells 2424 and Marrakech, a Moroccan restaurant where you can make like Hollywood over couscous, pastilla and the gyrating navels of gorgeous belly dancers. If you could

do without the dance or dress but prefer gourmet fare just the same, restaurants like the Bistro, Robert's Cafe Kapahulu and Chez Michel (in Eaton Square) provide quality continental cuisine with a charming and less formal ambience. Garcons and bona fide French accents parade before you with a small but choice selection of palate pleasers, ranging from crepes Florentine to endives gratinee, followed by delectable French coffees and pastries you'd write home about. Even more casual are Horatio's in Ward Warehouse, the Good Earth. T.G.I. Fridays, the Willows

"Eating Poi," circa 1847, from the voyage of the Swedish corvette *Galathea*.

(especially in the Kamaaina Room) and Laulima, Honolulu's best-known vegetarian restaurant, where gourmet mushroom stroganoff meets vegetarian moussaka with a lassi chaser and the best date bars in town.

The real education in island offerings comes with Oahu's weekly open markets, where local farmers and backyard growers sell fresh vegetables and exotic fruit with a family feeling and at reasonable prices. Here, among a staggering array of island specialties, seasoned shoppers will sniff out the best: Kahuku watermelon, Waimanalo corn, Maui

If you really tune in to the offerings of Hawaii's open markets, you can sense the wonderful fecundity of the tropical elements. Here the seasons and weather are generous, giving expression to a natural rhythm that fills island life with bountiful mangoes now, passion fruit then, wild pomelos, guavas, and mountain apples, with papayas, pineapples and bananas all year round. In Hawaii, the state of everlasting summer, the seasons are marked by flowers and fruit.

A casual promenade through any island supermarket provides another glimpse of the

onions, local sweet potatoes, assorted fresh seafood and seaweeds, Manoa bib lettuce, fern shoots, burdock ... You may not find neighbor island specialties like Maui's custard apples, called cherimoya, or Kona oranges and avocados, but by divine intervention you might uncover a Chinese mama-san with homemade mango bread or *manapua*, steamed dumplings with various fillings. For many travelers and Islanders alike, the pristine beauty of the neighbor islands is nearly matched by its down-home specialties: Kilauea corn from Kauai, Maui potato chips, Puna papayas, and Maui *manju*, a Japanese pastry of sweet black beans enveloped in a flaky or steamed crust.

abundance here. Everything from kiwi fruit to fresh *tofu* (soybean curd), lotus root, *on choi* (a Chinese green vegetable), *daikon*, *sashimi* (raw fish, an island delicacy), and fresh soybeans line the shelves and counters in an infinite expression of culinary potentials. Most supermarket clerks are ready with a simple tip or two in the preparation of the more obscure ingredients, so all that's needed is an open mind and palate.

Laulau at a Luau

One thing you won't find at an open market, or any Waikiki restaurant, is authen-

Luau at the Dillinghams, 1888.

tic Hawaiian food. Restaurants like the People's Cafe, Helena's in Kalihi and Kapahulu's Ono Hawaiian Food still serve the real thing, but Hawaii's only indigenous cuisine is fast becoming an anomaly in its own land. Catered *luau* for tourists often lack the most distinctive feature of Hawaiian cookery: the use of an *imu*, an earthen pit lined with *kiawe* wood and lava rock that steams and smokes as no other oven can.

The *imu* imparts a distinctive flavor that can't be duplicated with the standard ovens and liquid smoke (heresy to the purists!) used

sizzling rocks, is wrapped in leaves and wire and placed in the *imu* along with any available fish, taro, yams or breadfruit (called *ulu*). The *imu* is then covered with layers of burlap ... leaves ... canvas ... and soil until only a large mound appears. When the pig is removed hours later, it is called *kalua* pork.

In ancient times, Hawaiians drank and ate stronger stuff—such as *'awa* (a numbing narcotic drink wrung from roots of the *Piper methysticum*), vegetarian-fed dogs baked in the *imu*, and chicken wings boiled in blood.

by some hotels and catering services. But the culinary function is only a part of it; this remarkable Hawaiian device is actually a unifying family experience, drawing uncles and cousins to assist in the digging and preparation. Like the feasting at the *luau*, called *paina* in the old days, the work was to be shared too.

The custom is still observed today as relatives fish, harvest and cook in preparation for the smaller family *luau*. The pit is dug a day ahead, *kiawe* wood and lava rocks gathered and heated, banana stumps cut and prepared for lining the *imu*. The moisture of the stumps prevents burning and creates steam for cooking. The pig, stuffed with

But these days their feasts are considerably milder and eminently adaptable' to Euro-Asian tastes. Indeed, what gourmet would not appreciate a properly prepared *laulau*, that Hawaiian concoction of pork, beef, salted fish and taro tops which is baked, steamed or broiled to tender taste in a green wrapping of *ti* or banana leaves? Very tasty, but like true *kalua* pig, difficult to prepare.

"Nowadays, it seems to be getting harder," says David Kailio, wiping his brow after burying three pigs in the family *imu* in Kahaluu. "That's why we all help each other. We want the younger ones to know how so

Native *luau*, 1910.

they can take over." The Kailios have managed for 25 years to retain an intimate, authentic Hawaiian quality in even their catered *luau*, a rarity in an increasingly commercialized market.

At traditional family gatherings such as baby *luau* or birthdays, people would bring or send gifts, called *hookupu*. A family from Kauai might have sent taro. Relatives from the Big Island might have offered *opihi*, raw shellfish that sell today for at least $80 a gallon. Part of the tradition is acknowledgement, family style: "The *opae* (baby shrimp)

was called *pa'i'ai,* a hard, purple paste to which they added water for the desired consistency. The thicker the *poi*, the fewer fingers were needed to eat it with; thus were born "three-finger" and "two-finger" *poi*, epithets still used today.

If you don't get to a real family *luau*, there are countless other appeasements, from the very grand to the small and simple. *Saimin* and *sushi* are two Japanese dishes that have become hamburgers of the Island set. Some *luau* tables today even include *sushi*—

came from Hamakua," the emcee might announce appreciatively. "The taro is from Waiahole, and the *haupia* (coconut pudding) came from Auntie Honey." Applause.

The other ethnic influences came early, in the 1800s, when missionaries began bringing cake to the local *luau* or the Chinese, chicken *luau*. These are standard fare at some *luau* today, along with *lomi* salmon, salmon marinated with onions and tomatoes, introduced by early whalers.

Poi, the paste still used as a staple in some Hawaiian homes, was prepared from taro, baked in the family *imu* and pounded into a thick concentrate that could last a month. It

seasoned rice, fish and vegetables rolled in seaweed—while *saimin*, a delicate noodle soup, is served in virtually every diner and neighborhood restaurant. If you really want to do what the locals do, it's *de rigeur* to try both—but beware of the MSG (*monosodium glutamate*).

No matter how long your stay in Hawaii, by the time you leave you would have just scratched the surface of Island food. *Poi* might have been nothing to write home about and you might have missed your neighborhood deli, but wouldn't you have traded ANYTHING for just one fresh lichee?

Waikiki tourist buffet, 1979.

KE KUMU HAWAII.

HE PEPA HOIKEIKE I NA MEA E PONO AI KO HAWAII NEI.

"O ka pono ka mea e pomaikai ai ka lahuikanaka; aka, o ka hewa ka mea e hoinoin'i na aina."

Buke 1.   HONOLULU, OAHU, MEI 13, 1835.   Pepa 14.

HE ZEBERA.

Ua like kekahi ano o ka Zebera me ko ka Lio. Ua like ka heluna o kona mau niho, a ua poepoe ka maiiuu o kona mau wawae, aole hoi i maheleia, ua like no me ko ka lio.

O ka Zebera, o ka lio, ua nui ka lio. O ka Zebera, o ka hoki, ua nui ka Zebera. Ua olenalena ke oho o ka Zebera, a he onionio eleele nae. Ua kaawale ka olenalena, a me ka eleele. Nolaila ua like me ka mea i penaia. Ua like kekahi mau helehelena ona me ko ka lio, a me ko ka hoki kekahi. O kona kino a me kona uha, ua like me ko ka lio, a o ka ai, a me ke poo, ua like me ko ka hoki. He poepoe maikai kona kino, a ikaika maikai kona mau wawae e like me ko ka lio.

Aole holoholona i oi aku kona maikai mamua o ko ka Zebera, ke nana aku. O ka onionio, oia ka maikai loa.

Pokole makalii loa kona oho, a ua hinuhinu. Ua onionio kona kino a pau, he eleele, a he olenalena, o ke kino, o ka ai, o ke poo, o ka maka, o na pepeiao, nolaila, i ka ike ana aku, ua like ia me ka mea i hoonacaiia i ka ribine.

Ua loaa ia holoholona ma na ululaau nui ma Aferika; aole i loaa ma Asia, a ma Europa, a ma Amerika.

Ma na ululaau, kahi o ia lio e noho ai, ua hihiu loa ia, a no kona mama, loaa ole ia e na lio Arabia a pau.

Makemake loa lakou e noho pu a hele pu, he ohana nui, nolaila, ua nui loa lakou i ikeia ma kahi hookahi.

I ka wa e ai ai kekahi mau mea, kiai no kekahi mau mea, o hiki mai auanei ka enemi, he kanaka paha, o ka ilio paha. Ina i ike mai ka poe kiai i ke kanaka, a i ka ilio huhu paha, alaila, hoike koke aku la lakou, i ka poe e ai ana; alaila, holo nui lakou, a no ko lakou mama, aole loaa iki lakou i kekahi holoholona.

No ka hihiu o ka Zebera aole ia i hoolaka loa ia, no ka mea, ina i paa i kona wa uuku, hoowalawaha no ia i ka mea e hoohana mai ia ia.

Ina i malama pio ia oia i na makahiki he nui loa, a hanai mau ia i ka lima o ke kanaka hookahi, aole ia e oluolu ke noho ke kanaka ma kona kua. A ina hele mai ka malihini, alaila, moe koke no kona mau pepeiao ilalo, a hoomakaukau e nahu mai, a i ole ia, e huli no a keehi mai.

Ma kona wahi ua hakalia loa ka loaa ana o keia lio. No kona hihiu a me kona akamai, aole ia e loaa i ka hoowalewale, a no kona mama aole loaa i ka hahai ana. Nolaila aole i loaa pinepine ka Zebera nui. I ka wa uuku, hahai ka poe hahai, a hoomanawanui loa, a pomaikai ke loaa, no ka mea, he lio kuai nui loa ia lio.

A e kuai nui loa no hoi kona ili, no ka maikai, a no ka mea, aole i loaa pinepine. Ua manao nui loa ia ia lio, i mea hoike; a nolaila ke kuai nui, i mea hoike aku i kanaka.

O ka onionio o ka Zebera, oia kona mea like ole loa me ka lio. A he okoa no kekahi helehelena ona, okoa ko ka lio. Ua nui ka lio, a ua oi aku ka maikai o kona ai, a me kona poo, a me kona mau pepeiao mamua o ko ka Zebera.

He mama ka Zebera, he lohi ka lio. He lokomaikai nae ka lio, a oluolu ia ke lawe i ke kanaka ma kona kua. Ina i ee ke kanaka maluna o ka Zebera, o kona pii no ia, a holo ino, i haule ke kanaka.

E hoomanawanui no ka lio ma na hana a pau a ke kahu e haawi aku ai ia ia. Aka, o ka Zebera, aole hiki ke hoolaka ia ia, no kona huhu loa. Ma ka onionio maikai o kona ili, ua oi aku ka maikai o ka Zebera mamua o na holoholona a pau. He onionio like, a maikai wale no.

I noonoo kakou i ka mooolelo no na holoholona a pau, maopopo no ko ko Akua lokomaikai. Ua hooneleia kekahi holoholona i ka mea i loaa mai i kekahi. O ka Elepani, ina kiiia mai oia, aole ia i mama, aole hiki ke holo a pakele, nolaila, ua haawiia mai kona nuku i mea e pale aku ai i ka hewa. He pepeiaohao ko ka Lachaokela a me ka Bufalo a me ka Bipi, i mea e pale aku ai i ka hewa.

He maiuu oioi ko ka Liona, a me ke Tiga, a he mau kui kekahi. Oia ko laua mau mea eha, e pale aku ai i ka hewa, a oia no hoi na mea e loaa ai ka laua ai.

O ka Zebera, aole ona pepeiaohao, aole kui, aole oioi kona maiuu, i mea e pale aku ai i ka hewa, aka, no kona mama, o hiki ia ia ke holo, a pakele, aole loa e loaa e kekahi i lio hae.

Nolaila, e mahalo kakou i ka lokomaikai o ke Akua, i kona haawi ana i na holoholona a pau ana i hana'i i na mea e pono ai, i mea hoi e pakele ai lakou i ka hewa.

THE HAWAIIAN LANGUAGE

I ka 'olelo no ke ola a me ka make.
In the language is life and death.
— *an ancient Hawaiian proverb.*

To describe the Hawaiian language in an English fashion is difficult because it is very much a language of emotions, poetry and nature-related sounds and nuance.

Indeed, for hundreds of years the alphabet of the Hawaiian language was and still is nature in its many animate and inanimate forms. And probably because the language in its oral form proved satisfactory for so long, it was never given a written, literate form until after the coming of Westerners to Hawaii in the late 18th and early 19th Centuries. Instead, the Hawaiian language thrived expressively and melodically as the exclusively spoken language of a Polynesian people who were rich in unwritten literature — including complicated poetry and songs, histories, genealogies and mythologies — which were never recorded outside Hawaiian minds. All that we know of the Hawaiian language and ancient Hawaiians was memorized long ago, and passed on verbally, from mouth to ear, and generation to generation, from the earliest of Hawaiian times.

Today, through accidents of history over which the present generation of Hawaiians had no control, few people speak the Hawaiian language. However, certain Hawaiian words and names are still an important part of an islander's daily vocabulary, and the Hawaiian language is of great symbolic importance to the Hawaiian people. At its very least, the language of the Hawaiian people is their most ancient possession.

Historical linguists have not determined all the intricacies of the development of the Hawaiian language, but a fairly clear picture has emerged regarding its relationship to other languages. It is known, for example, that Hawaiian belongs to the Austronesian (formerly termed Malayopolynesian) language family. These were languages spoken by seafaring peoples who spread over an area of the globe larger than that covered by any other people until the 18th and 19th

Centuries, when Europeans began exploring various parts of the then known world.

Hawai'i is the farthest point of Austronesian expansion to the north, Easter Island to the east, and New Zealand to the south. From these points westward, Austronesian tongues are spoken throughout the Pacific to Indonesia, Malaysia, the Philippines and Taiwan, with the farthest western point being the island of Madagascar which lies in the south Indian Ocean off the east coast of Africa.

Hawaiian is classified more specifically as a Polynesian language most closely related to languages spoken in Tahiti, the Marquesas and surrounding island groups of the South Pacific. According to historical linguists, it was from these islands that persons destined to be the ancestors of Hawai'i's people originated. They had reached the South Pacific, and later Hawai'i in the Central Pacific, by slowly following a travel route which began in Southeast or Indo-Malay Asia, then coursed around the north coast of New Guinea through the islands of Melanesia and, finally, into Polynesia.

The various Indo-Malay peoples continued to develop along their own linguistic paths, but their distant relationship to the Hawaiian people is still reflected in certain words and verbal inflections. Instead of the Hawaiian term *i'a*, for fish, people of Southeast Asia say *ika* or *ikan*; instead of *hale*, for house, they say *fare*, *'are* and *vale*; and instead of *maka*, for eye, they say *mata*.

A Pathway to the Soul

By 1819, when the first Calvinist-Christian missionaries began sailing to Hawai'i from Boston, they had already heard the Hawaiian language being spoken by Hawaiians who had traveled to the East Coast of America as seamen on various ships. The missionaries had succeeded in converting some of these adventurous Hawaiians to Christianity, and it was due to the devotion of one ardent Hawaiian Christian, who was known by the name 'Opukaha'ia, that the first missionaries were inspired to sail to Hawai'i and establish a mission here. They knew the Hawaiian language was only a spoken language, but they were eager to set it to writing, to enable them to translate their Bible, hymns and Christian teachings, and ultimately gain converts in the Hawaiian Islands.

Page (left) from the early Hawaiian newspaper *Ke Kumu Hawaii*, issue of May 13, 1835.

Upon arriving in Hawai'i in 1820, the missionaries immersed themselves in their work of saving souls and attempted to communicate their teachings in a faltering form of Hawaiian. By 1823, after studying the Hawaiian language and putting it on paper in a somewhat phonetic form, the missionaries arbitrarily established a Hawaiian alphabet. They did this by voting, because various missionaries throughout the Hawaiian islands differed upon certain sounds to be represented by their respective phonetic letters. For example, some missionaries argued that the K sound should be a T sound, or that the flapped R sound was really an L sound. But when a final vote was taken, the K sound was adopted over the T, and the L over the flapped R. And in the end, missionary linguistic concensus established the consonants of the Hawaiian language as H, K, L, M, N, P and W. And it was agreed that the Hawaiian vowel sounds would be the five distinctive A, E, I, O and U of Western language forms. Thus these twelve letters have functioned as the accepted Hawaiian alphabet to this day.

The Hawaiian language continued to be the spoken and later written language of the land in government, business and social circles of the Hawaiian Kingdom, and over the years it was used almost exclusively in some seventy Hawaiian language newspapers. Gradually, however, this rich and expressive language has nearly become extinct.

Aloha Hawaiian Language

The last Hawaiian language newspaper, *Ka Hoku O Hawai'i, The Star of Hawaii*, printed at Hilo on the Big Island, stopped its presses in 1948. And though Hawaiian was still the language in general use on the floor of the Territorial Legislature at the beginning of this century, it quickly was replaced by English. Today, Hawaiian is rarely spoken at home or heard on the streets, and the only place where Hawaiian still exists as a daily spoken language is on the privately owned island of Niihau, which has a mostly Hawaiian population of about 250 residents.

Today there is little hope, except on Niihau, that a child will learn Hawaiian as his mother tongue. It has been estimated that there are approximately 2,000 native speakers of Hawaiian left today, and of this number approximately 250 are on Niihau, with the remaining 1,750 scattered throughout the islands and a few on the West Coast of America. Most of these 1,750 persons are senior citizens, and they rarely speak Hawaiian to their children, so the language

will probably die with them sometime during the next 20 to 25 years.

A small dedicated group of people regularly lobby for the continued welfare of the Hawaiian language, but except for recent State legislation which recognized Hawaiian as the State of Hawaii's official language, little has been done to insure the language's continued life. Hawaiian language courses are taught in a few private and public schools and at the University of Hawaii, but the kind of public funding which would insure that the language remains strong and alive has never been allocated by the State's lawmakers, who tend to regard Hawaii's native tongue as a linguistic curiosity or quaint, nostalgic reminder of Hawaiian times past. It has never been accorded the educational status of foreign languages such as German, French and Russian.

Mahalo for Your Kokua

Nonetheless, Hawai'i still is special if only for her language, and it is one of the few states which can claim such linguistic distinction. However, where does the fast-fading state of the Hawaiian language leave you, the visitor, in Hawaii?

If you are like most first-time visitors, you'll probably find yourself tripping over the pronunciation of Hawaiian place names. And to make matters worse, the first local, or *kama'aina* (oldtimer), you speak to will more likely than not compound your problems by advising you incorrectly.

As a visitor, however, you should realize that you do help to preserve the Hawaiian language in indirect ways, such as paying dollars to listen to and see Hawaiian music and dance (which of course are done with Hawaiian words and lyrics). Also, a curious sort of tourist Hawaiian has evolved in recent years, which combines snatches of Hawaiian, pidgin and English at their provocative and sing-songy best. No doubt you'll hear the song lyrics, *"Honi kaua wikiwiki* (kiss me quickly), a sweet brown maiden said to me, as she gave me language lessons on the beach at Waikiki," and your waitress will say *"mahalo"* and *"aloha"* at your cafe table (though at home she'll prefer to use "thanks" and "bye").

Persons who would like to learn more about the Hawaiian language should see the language guide and index-glossary in the Guide in Brief section.

Advertising page from the later Hawaiian newspaper, *Ke Au Hou,* this issue published at Honolulu on September 28, 1910.

319

TALKING LOCAL

Eh, brah. You guys teenk we local folks talk funny kine, eh? Well, chry wait. I going learn you why you no understan'. I like educate you 'bout da kine; dat way you folks not going experience one communication gap in Hawaii nei.

Da kine communication gap indeed. The first time visitor to Hawaii may well be multilingual and worldly-wise, but he will find to his bemusement and astonishment that the most common "ethnic" language spoken in Hawaii is not Japanese, Chinese, Korean, Filipino, Samoan or even Hawaiian. Rather, local folks will be heard carrying on in pidgin English, a bastard language form which flits in and out of social and cultural circles like a haughty, invisible mynah bird.

Pidgin, also called "summer English," is an international catch-all term used to describe any *creole* tongue which borrows freely from two or more languages. Originally, the word "pidgin" referred to the way in which Cantonese merchants involved in the early China trade with Europeans spoke English. Somehow, "business" came out sounding like "pidgin," and probably because most conversations in those days had to do with business, 18th and 19th Century traders began referring to the curious way in which Chinese spoke all English as "pidgin," or "pidgin English."

Da Kine

Many of those same early Chinese migrated to Hawaii beginning in the early 1800s and they, of course, continued to "talkie-talkie same-same." However, in Hawaii they had to contend not just with English, but also with the melodious Hawaiian language, and later with Japanese, Korean, Portuguese, Filipino and other immigrant dialects which began to cross-pollinate Hawaii. This, of course, caused problems.

Oh, vat to do. Eventually, Hawaiian and English became the generally accepted languages of daily usage, but in the meantime—and ever since—plantation immigrants who had to learn to communicate and coexist on these small islands created the complicated *lingua franca* now generally known as pidgin. However, there was pidgin and there was pidgin, and even today there are extreme differences between pidgin spoken at Hana and Waianae, or at Kona and Hanapepe.

Certain terms such as *da kine*, an island-wide catch-all which refers to anything and everything, are understood everywhere in Hawaii, but subtle forms of *paniolo* (cowboy) Big Island pidgin are nearly unintelligible to speakers of Kauai fishermen's pidgin.

Chry Not to Make Ass

It's a phenomenon which has driven language scholars mad. Every year or so some visiting linguist composes an academic treatise on Hawaiian pidgin forms, but all that does is make *da kine* more complicated and less understandable to outsiders. Da truth of da matter is dat dere are no structural or pronunication rules for Hawaiian-style pidgin. And the only way to become fluent in one or many of its forms is to live in Hawaii all your life and absorb the language's nuances, much as a child absorbs mother's milk or a lover love. After being here a few years you may feel comfortable with a few well-timed pidgin grunts, words or maybe even a complete four-word phrase, but try to carry on a properly-inflected conversation and you will probably, as locals express it in pidgin, *make ass.*

The best advice this book can offer to the newcomer and would-be longtimer is to simply listen to pidgin, enjoy it and smile a lot when you are confronted by something you don't quite understand.

Gavan Daws, a self-described "*haole* historian" and author of the sensitive and very readable Hawaii history book *Shoal of Time*, once wrote that local pidgin is more than just a simplified way of talking. It is also, he said, an almost secretive "resistance movement against English" and "the great mark of the local boy, whatever his genes." Daws, an Australian well-versed in "Strine," that equally peculiar mutation of the Queen's English spoken Down Under, sees pidgin as a very effective, sort of underground verbal weapon.

"The consummate pidgin speaker, in fact," wrote Daws in a book called *The Hawaiians*, "is likely to be taking a continual subtle revenge upon haole condescension. There are piercingly witty men and genial philosophers among the pidgin speakers, and many a haole loose among them never learns, even with experience, whether he is being skewered and spitted for roasting or, alternatively, graciously pardoned for existing."

Gorgonian Coral

Regal Slipper Lobster

Fried Egg Nudibranch

Pacific Spotted Dolphin

Hawaiian Lobster

Flat Worm

Lionfish

Cup Coral

Eggs of Nudibranch

Yellow Head Eel

Longnose Hawkfish

Flat Worm

GUIDE IN BRIEF

Traveling to Hawaii

By Air:

Hawaii is regularly serviced by six American airline companies (American, Continental, Northwest Orient, Pan American, United and Western); three charter airlines (Overseas National, Trans International and World Airways); and several foreign air carriers (Air Micronesia, Air New Zealand, Qantas Airways, British Airways, Canadian Pacific Air, China Airlines, Japan Air Lines, Air Nauru, Korean Air Lines and Singapore Airlines, among others). Most aircraft that land at Honolulu International Airport touch down on the Reef Runway which was completed in 1977 on a shallow reef-lagoon between Honolulu Harbor and Pearl Harbor.

Inside the ultra-modern airport complex are murals, sculptures, paintings, weavings, stitcheries and batiks in Hawaiian themes created by top local artists. This airport art display, which breathes cultural life and color onto the terminal's walls and stretching corridors, is a tangible result of a 1967 Hawaii legislative act which designated that one per cent of all appropriated public works funds is to be used for the purchase of works of art for State buildings throughout Hawaii. Japanese, Hawaiian and Chinese gardens also enhance the terminal's promenade areas.

By Sea:

Calling by ship at Honolulu Harbor in the downtown district of Oahu is still a gracious and romantic way to arrive in the islands. Only a few passenger liners, however, regularly put in at Honolulu these days. Some of these liners are of foreign registry and people cannot legally travel between two U.S. ports on them. Some of the shipping lines and their ships which regularly stopover in Hawaii are:

P & O Lines: The *Oriana* sails in the spring and in the autumn around Europe, the Caribbean, North America, the South Pacific, New Zealand and Australia, stopping in Hawaii along the way. Also, P & O's *Canberra* makes a round-the-world cruise which runs from Southampton via the Panama Canal and the West Coast U.S.A. to Hawaii and Fiji before returning to Southampton.

Princess Cruises Line (represented by P & O): The *Island Princess* traverses the South Pacific from various North American ports via Hawaii annually in the fall on various routes.

Royal Viking: Liners run four to five times annually on round-the-world and Pacific cruises via Honolulu.

A more economical alternative for those with a flexible schedule is to sail by passenger-freighters. The **States Line**, based in California, has cargo ships with a 12-passenger capacity, such as the *Idaho*, which circles the Pacific twice a month from Yokohama, Japan, to San Francisco, stopping over in Hawaii. The States Lines' booking agent in Tokyo and Yokohama is PTL Kaigai K.K.

Inter-Island Hopping:

Four domestic airlines—Continental, Northwest Orient, United and Western—also fly directly into and out of Hilo on the Big Island. If you are traveling on a full-fare roundtrip ticket from

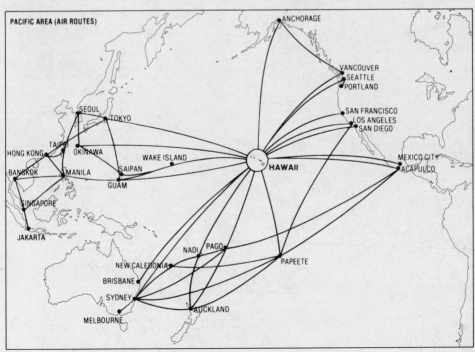

PACIFIC AREA (AIR ROUTES)

the U.S. Mainland or Canada inquire about "Common Fare" discount ticket which allow you to travel from Oahu to any of the neighboring islands at a low fare of about $17 per island stopover. This bargain, designed to serve as an island-hopping incentive, is available in cooperation with Aloha Airlines, Hawaiian Airlines and Mid-Pacific, Hawaii's three inter-island carriers.

There also are a number of small commuter airlines which propellor passengers at lower altitudes and along more scenic inter-island routes.

S.S. Oceanic Independence
S.S. Constitution

These large passenger liners, operated by American Hawaii Cruises, provide extended cruises between the Hawaiian Islands. The *Oceanic Independence* and her sister ship, the *Constitution*, sail weekly in opposite directions to and from Honolulu. Seven-day voyages as well as three and four-day trips are available. All of the amenities of full-service cruise ships are standard aboard. Bus shore excursions are optional and rental cars are also offered in each port of call for those passengers who want a more leisurely pace. Contact a travel agent for current schedules and prices.

Travel Formalities

Immigration:

Visitors from foreign countries need to show a valid passport with a USA visa and a current health certificate with a non-expired small-pox vaccination.

Animal Quarantine:

Hawaii is rabies-free. All incoming animals are placed in a quarantine station for 120 days at the owner's expense and responsibility.

Agricultural Regulations:

Baggage is inspected coming and going through the airport. It is forbidden to import and take out many fresh fruits and plants, except for coconuts and pineapples. Avocadoes, bananas, and papayas must first be fumigated at the Plant Quarantine Division at 701 Ilalo Street, and mangoes and lichees must be pitted and peeled before they can be taken to the Mainland. Fumigated fruits bound for foreign countries may be purchased at the airport.

Most flowers strung in leis may be worn to the Mainland. Those restricted outside Hawaii are the rose, gardenia, jade flower, *maunaloa* and all plants in soil.

Exchanging Currency:

Currency conversion is readily possible at the International Airport terminal's cashier counter in the Customs area and at Hawaii bank branches located at the airport. This service is also provided at certain hotels. Refer to **Island Resources** for a directory of banks and currency exchange companies.

Getting Acquainted

Direction-telling:

Hawaiian islanders share a common vernacular for directions, which has nothing to do with cardinal directions or where the sun rises and sets. Rather, it deals with *local* geographical features.

The two most common directional terms are *mauka* and *makai*. *Mauka* means upland or towards the mountains, and *makai* means towards the sea. In the Honolulu area, directions also are given in relation to *Ewa*, a plantation town just west of Pearl Harbor, and to *Diamond Head*, the famous volcanic crater-landmark to the east side of Waikiki. Those four orientations — *mauka, makai, Ewa* and *Diamond Head* — make eminent sense to local people. Say north, south, east or west and you'll receive looks of bewilderment.

Weather:

There are no seasons in Hawaii. Most of Hawaii experiences balmy 73° F–88° F weather from April through October, and cooler, wetter 65° F–83° F weather during other months. Rarely does the mercury drop below 60° F. The surrounding sea and northeasterly tradewinds are a natural air conditioning system. Once in a long while, rare southerly or westerly winds cause a sticky-humid weather situation popularly called a "Kona condition." This mugginess, however, is usually temporary and before long prevailing Pacific tradewinds resume as usual.

Certain areas on each island — usually on the windward side of mountains — receive more rainfall than others. The wettest spot on earth is Mount Waialeale on Kauai which has been drenched by as much as 486 inches of rain a year.

In higher altitude places such as Kula and Haleakala on Maui, and Kokee on Kauai, temperatures range from 48° F to 72° F, and in mountainous parts of the Big Island the average temperature drops down to 31°F to 58°F during the winter and at night. Snow falls on Mauna Kea in the winter, so be prepared with warm clothing if you intend to tour these areas.

Sometimes, when there is a volcanic eruption on the Big Island, a smoky pall lingers over the islands for a few days. Islanders call this volcanic haze "vog."

Severe Weather:

Hurricanes rarely strike Hawaii. Earthquakes, however, occur more often and sometimes forebode a *tsunami*, the proper term for a seismic or tidal wave. Check the green pages of local telephone directories for Civil Defense tsunami inundation maps and related emergency information regarding such hazards.

Civil Defense Warning:

Civil Defense sirens which warn of natural disasters or an impending nuclear holocaust are tested at 11:45 a.m. on the first working day of every month. Related instructions are broadcasted on all commercial radio stations by the Emergency Broadcast System.

Time Zones:

National time differences are staggered as follows:

Hawaii Standard Time:	12 noon
Pacific Standard Time:	2 p.m.
Mountain Standard Time:	3 p.m.
Central Standard Time	4 p.m.
Eastern Standard Time:	5 p.m.
Atlantic Standard Time:	6 p.m.

When the mainland United States sets its clocks forward for Daylight Savings Time, usually from May thru October, add an hour to all the above time zones except Hawaii's.

International time differences are as follows:

Hawaii Standard Time 12 noon	
Japan:	7 a.m. tomorrow
Bangkok:	5 a.m. tomorrow
Paris:	11 p.m. tonight
London:	10 p.m. tonight

Clothing:

Dress is cool and casual in Honolulu and even more so beyond the city proper. Light and loose garments are most suitable for the summer months. Hawaii has seen just about every imaginable fashion — from string bikinis to high fashion and ethnic chic — so wear what makes you comfortable. Local Hawaiian print *muumuu* and aloha shirts are practical all-around garments and are considered an acceptable substitute for continental wear on most occasions. A few exclusive restaurants and nightclubs still require a coat, tie and shoes, but they are rare exceptions. Rubber or mat-and-velvet *zoris* (Japanese slippers) are ideal for pacing the pavement and easy to slip off and on at the beach and before entering private homes where people usually go barefoot. Leather sandals and shoes are most appropriate for nightlifing, particularly in slippery-floored disco parlors.

For the cooler, wetter months, pack a sweater and an umbrella. A parka and heavy jacket are advised for hiking in mountainous areas on Maui, Kauai and particularly on the Big Island.

Sunburn Prevention:

Not just "mad dogs and Englishmen" choose to go out in Hawaii's mid-day sun. Sun-bathing is a common sport here. To prevent sunburning, however, be sure to liberally rub on a lotion containing a sunscreen (e.g PABA) while exposing yourself to the intense ultra-violet rays found in these latitudes. Also, tan slowly: take no more than about 30 minutes of direct sun exposure the first day out, 40 minutes, the second day, and 50 minutes the third day, slowly creating a tolerance for tropical sunlight.

For treatment of sunburn, various commercial remedies are available, but locals often rub on the gooey juice of a freshly cut aloe vera cactus plant. Liquid vitamin E also soothes sunburn when applied topically.

On Being Cautious:

Hawaii is a lovely place with a reputation for hospitality and all the good cheer that the word *aloha* implies. However, travelers should be warned that she can also be a dangerous place. All types of crime — including burglary, robberies, assaults, rapes, and other criminal forms — are occurring more and more as the islands become populated and begin to experience the same economic and social pressures other "civilized" places take for granted. When traveling, always lock room and car doors, and exercise caution when you are approached by strangers. Be particularly careful in areas far from population centers. Car break-ins and beachside thefts of personal property are, unfortunately, becoming a quite common occurrence in Hawaii, even at popular tourist sites. Hitchhiking is never advised. If you have any emergency problems that require the assistance of police, ambulance or firefighting personnel, go to the nearest telephone and dial 911 or 0 and ask for the emergency services assistance you need.

Getting to Town

By TheBus:

A #8 yellow-brown-and-orange striped **TheBus** departs every 10 minutes from Honolulu Airport to Waikiki via downtown and Ala Moana Shopping Center. Fare is 50 cents and exact change is required. Passengers are limited to one carry-on bag compact enough to be held on the lap or placed under the seat.

By Tour Bus, Limousine, Taxi:

The next best transportation bets are tour buses and car-pool limousine-taxis that transport passengers directly to any hotel in Waikiki for a modest fare. The biggest such company is called Gray Line. There are also metered taxis that will take you anywhere provided you pay the metered price and tip the driver for baggage handling and general services.

Car Rentals:

Arrangements for car rentals can be made either at several U-Drive counters located at all the airports or at resort area hotels. There are numerous vehicle rental agencies listed in the yellow pages of the Honolulu Telephone Directory.

On Oahu, the minimum age for renting a car is 21. On the neighbor islands, the age requirement is 25. An international driving license is required of foreigners, and a valid state license of Americans.

Campers and 4-Wheel Drives:

Campers are available on all the islands except Lanai. Four-wheel drive vehicles are rarely available. It is advisable to make reservations for them. Check local telephone directories for current listings for these specialized rental firms.

Camping Out:

Campgrounds are run by the National Park Service, the State of Hawaii, the four island counties and private organizations. Plan camp outings ahead of time (State parks require a seven-day advance application for permits, plus a shelter fee). Conditions and rates vary, so refer to current maps, brochures and proper agencies for information. To make reservations, call or write to the following agencies:

Federal Parks

National Park Service
300 Ala Moana Blvd.
Suite 6305, Box 50165
Honolulu, Hawaii 96813
Phone: 546-7584

Pu'u-kohola Heiau
National Historic Site
P.O. Box 4963
Kawaihae, Hawaii 96743
Phone: 882-7218

Superintendent
Haleakala National Park
P.O. Box 537
Makawao, Maui, Hawaii 96768
Phone: 572-9306

Superintendent of Parks, Hawaii
Volcanoes National Park
Hawaii National Park, Hawaii 96718
Phone: 967-7311

Superintendent of Parks
City of Refuge National Historical Monument
Honaunau, Kona, Hawaii 96726
Phone: 523-4525

State Parks

(Address letters to the District Office of the Hawaii Department of Land and Natural Resources, Division of State Parks)

Island of Hawaii
P.O. Box 936
Hilo, Hawaii 96720
Phone: 961-7200

Island of Kauai
P.O. Box 1671
Lihue, Kauai, Hawaii 96766
Phone: 245-4444

Kokee Lodge
Manager, Kokee Lodge
P.O. Box 518
Kekaha, Kauai, Hawaii 96752
Phone: 335-6061

Island of Maui
P.O. Box 1049

Wailuku, Maui, Hawaii 96793
Phone: 244-4354

Island of Molokai
P.O. Box 153
Kaunakakai, Molokai, Hawaii 96748
Phone: 533-5415

Island of Oahu
1151 Punchbowl Street, Rm 310
Honolulu, Hawaii 96813
Phone: 548-7455

City and County Parks

County of Hawaii
25 Aupuni Street
Hilo, Hawaii 96720
Phone: 961-8311

City and County of Honolulu
650 South King Street
Honolulu, Hawaii 96813
Phone: 523-4525

County of Kauai
4396 Rice Street
Lihue, Kauai 96766
Phone: 245-4982

County of Maui
1580 Kaahumanu Avenue
Wailuki, Maui, Hawaii 96793
Phone: 244-5414

Molokai
Dept. of Parks Recreation
Kaunakakai
Molokai 96784
Phone:

Koele Company
Lanai City
Island of Lanai, Hawaii 96763
Phone: 565-7125

Customs, Lifestyle, Media

Aloha Friday:

Friday is usually greeted in the islands with aloha attire. On this day, even businessmen doff coats and ties and don aloha shirts of bright and cheerful Hawaiian floral, *kapa* and other island prints. Ladies often tuck a fragrant plumeria behind their ear or drape a gracious *kukui* nut or flower *lei* on their shoulders. These are appropriate accessories for their *muumuu*. This is a unique Friday custom that has become *de rigeur* here, even in State, Federal and business offices and at public schools.

Hawaiian Time:

Time in the islands is not noticeably defined by the four seasons and Hawaii's balmy tropical climate tends to warp any rigid schedule. Islanders are lax about time, especially when going on dates and to meetings outside of strictly commercial business circles. Some even consider it rather brash or inconvenient to be too early or punctual to a casual affair. This tendency of being "fashionably late" by 10 minutes or so is commonly referred to as being on "Hawaiian time."

Tipping:

Tipping for service is expected in Hawaii. Generally, airport porter's baggage handling fees run about 50 cents per bag, and taxi drivers get tipped 15% plus about 25 cents per bag. A 15% tip at an exclusive restaurant is usual, and at coffee shops you should tip whatever you feel is fair for services gratefully received.

Television:

There are five commercial television channels which originate in Honolulu. These are Channels 2 (KHON-NBC); 4 (KITV-ABC); 9 (KGMB-CBS); 11 (KHET-educational); and 13 (KIKU, a Japanese language station). Satellite transmitters serve the neighbor islands, and several private cable television companies provide uninterrupted and special television programming by subscription.

Radio:

Honolulu's listeners tune in to some 25 commercial radio stations — 17 on the standard AM band and 8 on the FM band. Selections range from progressive rock and jazz music stations — to an all Hawaiian music station (KCCN) and all news station (KHVH).

The Press:

Six daily newspapers are circulated in Honolulu—two in English, two in Japanese, and two in Chinese. The state-wide circulated English dailies are *The Honolulu Advertiser*, a locally-owned morning newspaper, and *The Honolulu Star-Bulletin*, an afternoon newspaper owned by the Gannett chain of newspapers. The bi-lingual English-Japanese newspapers are *The Hawaii Hochi* and *The Hawaii Times*. The two Chinese language dailies are *The New China Press* and *The United Chinese Press*. Several other newspapers are published by ethnic groups, the military, religious organizations, and the tourism and business industries.

On the Big Island, Hilo town has its own daily, *The Hawaii Tribune-Herald*. Lihue, Kauai, and Wailuku, Maui, have their own bi-weekly papers, *The Garden Island*, and *The Maui Daily News* and *Maui Sun*, respectively.

The foremost monthly magazines published in Honolulu are *Honolulu*, a general city news-features magazine, and *Hawaii Business*.

Cinema:

Current movies are shown in some 35 theaters and drive-ins on Oahu alone. Foreign and more *avant garde* type films are shown regularly at the University of Hawaii at Manoa campus on smaller screens at a lower fee (check the daily events columns in *The Advertiser* and *Star-Bulletin* for current showings), and assorted samurai, kung-fu and erotic porno films are screened at specialty theatres on all islands.

Communications

Mail:

Normal American postal rates apply. It usually takes a 30 cent aerogram about five days to get to Japan and about three days to get to the U.S. mainland. Airmail postcards are 13 cents to the Mainland and 28 cents to all foreign countries. The main post office is located in the old Federal Building on King Street downtown, telephone 546-5625.

Telephone:

From the middle of the Pacific, you can dial directly to almost anywhere in the world. A multi-lingual staff of operators will assist you with your calls. Long-distance telephone call rates are listed in the green pages of the Honolulu Telephone Directory, or just dial "O" and an operator will assist you. Coin box telephone calls are 15 cents.

Emergency Calls

Fire, Police	911
Ambulance (accident)	911
Ambulance (maternity, other)	538-9011
Coast Guard Search/Rescue Center	536-4336
FBI	521-1411

Other Vital Service Agencies (Oahu)

American Red Cross	734-2101
Armed Forces Police	543-2641
Honolulu County Dental Emergency Service	536-2135
Honolulu County Medical Society	536-6988
Life Guard Service	922-3888
Poison Information Center	537-1831
Police Department	955-8111
Sex Abuse Treatment Center	533-2200
Suicide & Crisis Center	521-4555
Waikiki Drug Clinic	922-4787

Telephone Services

Free Interpreting	595-7267
Operator Assistance	0
Oahu Directory Assistance	1411
Inter-island Directory	
Assistance	1 + 555-1212
Mainland Directory	1 + Area
Assistance	Code +
	555-1212
Time of Day	543-3211
Military Telephone Information	
Operator	471-7411
Mailgrams	521-1818
Inter-island Radiograms	546-3890
(from Coin Telephones only)	0

Telegraph Companies:

ITT World Communications Inc.	531-0561
1164 Bishop Street	
RCA Global Communications Inc.	536-2521
223 S. King Street	
Western Union International Inc.	537-6311
333 Queen Street	

Post Offices:

Main Branch, Federal Building,   546-5625
Downtown
General delivery open Monday–Friday, 7:30
a.m.–4 p.m.; 7:30 a.m.–11:30 a.m., Saturday.
Other services open 8 a.m.–4:30 p.m.
Monday–Friday; 8 a.m.–noon, Saturday.

Ala Moana Center Branch   946-2020
Open 8:30–5 p.m., Monday–
Friday; 8:30 a.m.–12:30 p.m., Saturday

Waikiki Branch, Saratoga Road   941-1062
Open 8 a.m.–4:30 p.m., Monday–
Friday; 8 a.m.–noon, Saturday

American Express Clients' Mail   922-5547
2222 Kalakaua Avenue
Open 8:30 a.m.–4:30 p.m., Monday–
Friday; 9:30–12:30 p.m., Saturday

Information Board

Airport Information	847-9433
Aloha Stadium (ticket office)	487-3877
Animal Quarantine Station	841-6228
Blaisdell Memorial Center (ticket	
office)	
Arena (10 a.m.–6 p.m.)	521-2911
Arena (after hours)	536-7334
Concert Hall	536-7334
Customs	546-5181
Dept. of Parks & Recreation,	
marathon clinics, physical fitness	531-2865
Hawaii State Library, Main Branch	548-4775
Waikiki-Kapahulu Library	732-2777
Hawaii Visitors Bureau	923-1811
Hawaii Trail & Mountain Club	247-3922
Immigration Office	546-8920

Permit Section	523-4525
Plant Quarantine Division	548-7175
Surf Report	847-1952
U.S. Govt. Passport Agency	546-2131
Waikiki Child Service (babysitting)	922-5575
Weather Forecast for Honolulu	847-0234
Waikiki Shell (ticket office)	521-2911

Transportation

Campers & Coaches

Beach Boy Campers (Oahu, Kauai,
  Maui, Hawaii)   955-1849
Suite B2-A, 1720 Ala Moana Blvd.
Honolulu 96815

Holo Holo Campers (Oahu,   836-2202
  Maui, Hawaii)
28 Lagoon Drive
Honolulu 96819

Taxi

Aloha State Cab	847-3566
Charley's Taxi	531-1333
Sida Taxi	841-0171
Sunset Taxi	537-9760
Waikiki Charley's Taxi	955-2211

Bus Information

The Mass Transit Line bus station office located
at 1140 Alapai Street near downtown publishes a
good bus map and guide to Oahu (purchasable at
bookstores and shops around town). Free information and printed schedules are also available at
their Ala Moana Center information booth at the
Kona Street entrance. For information by telephone, call 531-1611 between 5:30 a.m. and 10
p.m. daily.

Circle Oahu via City Bus for $1.00

Part 1:

Waikiki-Central Oahu-North Shore-East Coast-
Waikiki; bus #8 Ala Moana Center. Request a
transfer. Transfer at Ala Moana Center onto bus
#52 Kaneohe/Wahiawa or Wahiawa/Kaneohe
(depending on which direction you prefer to
travel). The bus returns to Ala Moana; pay another 50 cents on board the #8 bus back to Waikiki;
$1.00 for complete trip; students up to grade 12,20
cents; youths under six, free.

Part 2:

Waikiki-Downtown-Kailua-Makapuu Point-Hawaii
Kai-Waikiki (southeast Oahu); take bus #57
Hawaii Kai.

Others

MTL City Bus Schedule & Info	531-1611
Open-Air Pedicab Co., Waikiki	923-3106
Double-decker London Bus Schedule	
(for service between the King's Alley,	
Falls of Clyde and the	
Bishop Museum).	847-3511

Airlines

(Serving Honolulu International Airport)

Air Micronesia	955-1155
Waikiki Outrigger Hotel	
2335 Kalakaua Avenue	
Air New Zealand	923-7638
2354 Kalakaua Avenue	
American Airlines	526-0044
733 Bishop Street	
Suite 1970	
Braniff International	922-3311
Surf Rider Hotel	
2353 Kalakaua Avenue	
British Airways	955-1155
Ala Moana Bldg., Suite 1517	
Canadian Pacific Air	845-9324
2222 Kalakaua Avenue,	
Suite 212	
China Airlines	536-6951
Pacific Trade Center	
190 South King Street	
Continental Airlines	
Waikiki Outrigger Hotel	955-1155
2335 Kalakaua Avenue	
1059 Bishop Street	
Japan Air Lines	533-6241
2272 Kalakaua Avenue	
Korean Air Lines	923-1896
2350 Kalakaua Avenue	
Northwest Orient Airlines	955-2255
Ilikai Hotel Lobby	
2360 Kalakaua Avenue	
Pan American	
2342 Kalakaua Avenue	955-9111
1021 Bishop Street	
Philippine Airlines	923-2066
2356 Kalakaua Avenue	
Qantas Airways	922-5341
2200 Kalakaua Avenue	
United Airlines	
2316 Kalakaua Avenue	547-2211
1077 Bishop Street	
Western Airlines	
2301 Kalakaua Avenue	946-7711
1965 Bishop Street	

Inter-Island Airline Commuter Services

Air Hawaii	848-2011
3049 Ualena	
Air Molokai	536-6611
216 Lagoon Drive	
All Hawaii Air	847-2321

38 Lagoon Drive

Aloha Airlines	836-1111
2222 Kalakaua Avenue	
Hawaiian Airlines	
Waikiki Business Plaza	525-5511
1040 Bishop Street	537-5100
Maui Commuter	523-1109
Honolulu Intern'l Airport	
Gate 4	
Mid Pacific Airlines	836-3313
550 Paiea Street	
Oahu & Kauai (O.K.) Airlines	847-3947
218 Lagoon Drive	
Royal Hawaiian Air Service	847-3504
Honolulu Intern'l Airport	
Gate 4	

Island Resources

Banks & Foreign Currency Exchange Companies

American Express	946-7741
1600 Kapiolani Blvd.	
American Security Bank	923-2011
2270 Kalakaua Avenue	
Bank of Hawaii	
2220 Kalakaua Avenue	923-2911
Financial Plaza of the Pacific	537-8111
Ward Plaza (opposite Fisherman's	
Wharf)	521-1011
Bank of Tokyo Ltd.	521-9811
Davies Pacific Center	
841 Bishop Street, Suite 2110	
Central Pacific Bank	923-3176
2400 Kalakaua Avenue	
City Bank	546-2411
810 Richards St.	
Deak-Perera Hawaii Inc.	
Davies Pacific Center	537-4928
841 Bishop Street	
Airport Branch	836-3603
2335 Kalakaua Avenue	922-1916
First Hawaiian Bank	923-0745
2181 Kalakaua Avenue	
Hawaii National Bank	923-3802
2280 Kalakaua Avenue	
Liberty Bank	548-5000
99 N. King St.	
Philippine National Bank	521-1493
Suite 312, 1000 Bishop Street	

Churches and Temples

Central Union (United Church of Christ)
1660 Beretania at Punahou Street, Makiki
Tel: 941-0957
Worship: 8:40 a.m., Sunday

Church of Jesus Christ of the Latter Day Saints
(Mormon)
1560 Beretania Street, Waikiki
Tel: 941-5693
Sunday School: 11:30 a.m.

Daijingu Temple (Shinto)
61 Puiwa Road
Tel: 595-3102

First Church of Christ (Scientist)
1508 Punahou Street, Makiki
Tel: 949-8403
Services: 9:30 & 11 a.m., Sunday
Reading room: 1988 Kalakaua Avenue
Tel: 949-1421

First Presbyterian Church
1822 Keeaumoku at Nehoa Street, Makiki
Worship: 9 & 10:30 a.m., Sunday
Special bus from Waikiki provided

Friends, Religious Society of (Quakers)
2426 Oahu Avenue, Manoa Valley
Tel: 988-2714

Greek Eastern Orthodox Church
17 Old Pali Place, Nuuanu
Tel: 595-7088
Services: 10 a.m., Sunday

Honpa Hongwanji Mission (Buddhist)
1727 Pali Highway, Nuuanu
Tel: 536-7044
Services: English: Youth   9 a.m.
                     Adults   10 a.m.
             Japanese: 7:30 a.m. & 1:15 p.m.

Jehovah's Witnesses
1228 Pensacola Avenue, Makiki
Tel: 531-2990
Meeting: 9:30–1:30 p.m. & 4:30 p.m., Sunday

Kawaiahao Church (Congregational)
957 Punchbowl at King Street, downtown
Tel: 538-6267
Services: 10:30–Noon, Sunday
            In Hawaiian and English

Korean Buddhist Temple
2334 S. King Street, near University Avenue
Tel: 947-7117

Nichiren Shoshu Academy
2729 Pali Highway, Nuuanu
Tel: 595-6324

Our Lady of Peace Cathedral (Roman Catholic)
Fort Street Mall at Beretania Street, Downtown
Tel: 536-7036
Services: 5, 6, 7, 8, 9, 10, 11, noon & 6–7 p.m.,
Sunday; 6 p.m., Saturday; 6–7–noon,
weekdays

Prince of Peace Church (Lutheran)
333 Lewers Street, Waikiki
Tel: 923-3835
Services 9 & 11 a.m. & 7 p.m., Sunday

St. Andrew's Cathedral (U.S. Episcopalian)
Corner of Queen Emma and Beretania Streets,
    Downtown
Tel: 524-2822
Services: 7, 8, 10 a.m., 5 p.m., Sunday; 7:30 a.m.
    weekdays; 10 a.m., Wednesday

St. Augustine's Church (Catholic)
130 Ohua Avenue, Waikiki
Tel: 923-7024
Services: 6, 7, 8:30, 10, 11:30 a.m. & 6 p.m.,
    Sunday; 6 p.m., Saturday; 7:30, 8:30
    a.m., noon, first Friday

Seventh Day Adventist Church
2313 Nuuanu Avenue
Tel: 524-1352
Worship: 11 a.m.
Sabbath School: 9:30 a.m.
Mid-week service: 7:30 p.m., Wednesday

Temple Emanu-el (Jewish)
2550 Pali Highway, Nuuanu
Tel: 595-2120
Services: Reform: 8 p.m., Friday
            Traditional: 10 a.m., Saturday

Todaiji Hawaii Bekkaku Honzan (Buddhist)
426 Luakini Street, Nuuanu
Tel: 595-2083

United Methodist
Wesley Foundation
1918 University Avenue, Manoa Valley
Tel: 949-1210
Services: Sunday

Waikiki Baptist Church
424 Kuamoo Street (across Ambassador Hotel)
Tel: 955-3525
Services: 9:45 a.m., Sunday
Worship: 11 a.m., 7 p.m., Sunday

Hare Krishna Temple
51 Coelho Way, Nuuanu
Tel: 595-3947

International (Transcendental) Meditation Society
227 S. King Street, Room 201
Tel: 537-3339

Consulates & Legations

Australian Consulate   524-5050
Penthouse, 1000 Bishop Street

Belgian Consulate   524-1191
Financial Plaza of the Pacific

Chinese Consulate   595-6347
2746 Pali Highway

Consulate General of Japan 1742 Nuuanu Avenue	536-2226
Consulate General of the Republic of Panama 1568 Uluhaku Place	262-4949
Consulate of Austria 2895 Kalakaua Avenue	923-8585
Consulate of Denmark Suite 311, 444 Hobron Lane	955-1001
Consulate of Finland 605 Kapiolani Blvd.	525-8000
Consulate of Monaco 45 S. King Street	538-7876
Consulate of Portugal 20th Floor, 1441 Kapiolani Blvd.	946-8080
Consulate of Republic of Nauru Mr. Kenneth Char, Consul Aloha Airlines Administration Bldg.	842-4201
Consulate of Sweden 1856 Kalakaua Avenue	941-1477
Consulate of Switzerland 1060 Kealaolu Avenue	737-5297
Consulate of the Netherlands Suite 1100, 2222 Kalakaua Avenue	923-3344
French Consulate Room 706, 130 Merchant Street	533-7378
Honorary German Consul 916 Kaaahi Place	847-4411
Indonesian Consulate Suite 924, Davies Pacific Center	524-4300
Italian Vice Consul 11 Hanapepe Place	523-3622
Korean Consulate 2756 Pali Highway	595-6109, 595-6274
New Zealand Government Trade Correspondent Suite 1707, 2270 Kalakaua Avenue	922-3853
Norwegian Consulate 536 Ulukou	732-6009
Philippine Consulate 2433 Pali Highway	595-6316
Royal Thai Consulate Suite 305, 735 Bishop Street	524-3888
Samoan Consulate 1720 Ala Moana Blvd.	941-9418

The Island Economy

Hawaii's Military Presence:
War Rooms and Vast Commands

Since the U.S. military participated in the 1893 overthrow of Queen Liliuokalani, its primary importance in Hawaii's social, political and commercial development has been undeniable. Besides turning Hawaii into what one radical chic writer called "a sugar-coated fortress," its payrolls have poured billions of dollars into island pockets. In 1976 alone, Hawaii-based military expenditures were about $2 billion, much of that going to about 19,000 civilian employes and 56,000 active duty personnel (with about 67,000 dependents). If you add servicemen and their dependents to military civilian workers and their dependents, the number of people who directly owe their livelihoods to the armed forces is more than 170,000, or about a fifth of the State's population (of about 886,000 in mid-1976). Until 1976, when tourism revenues nosed ahead, defense spending was the number one "industry" in Hawaii.

When wars or "armed incursions" were being waged by the United States in the Pacific—beginning with the Spanish-American War and continuing through World War II, the Korean War and, most recently, the war in Vietnam—these figures reached enormously disproportionate heights. Indeed, during World War II, when the military literally ran Hawaii (under Martial Law, from Dec. 7, 1941, the day Pearl Harbor was attacked by Japan, until Oct. 24, 1944), the islands' military population often outnumbered Hawaii's civilian residents.

Today, the Oahu-based Commander-in-Chief Pacific (CINCPAC) manages the largest command force in the world. He is responsible for all American units in the Pacific, Indian and Arctic Oceans, Southeast Asia and the Aleutian Islands, or about half of the world's land and sea area. From his "war room" and headquarters at Camp H.M. Smith and Pearl Harbor, he coordinates the routine and emergency actions of about 240 ships, 1,100 aircraft and 233,000 Navy and Marine Corps personnel. And on the island of Oahu alone, his four Army posts (Fort Shafter, Schofield Barracks, Tripler Medical Center and Fort DeRussy), two Air Force bases (Hickam and Wheeler), two Marine Corps bases (Kaneohe Marine Corps Air Station and Camp H.M. Smith) and two Navy bases (Pearl Harbor Naval Base and Barbers Point Naval Air Station) utilize 93,000 acres of land, or about a fourth of that highly populated island.

Agricultural Features
Sweet Exports: Sugar and Pine

Agriculture—which has traditionally meant sugar and to a lesser extent pineapple—doesn't wield the economic clout it did when Cane was King, but it is still an important industry. In 1976, cash receipts from sugar ($252 million), pineapple ($125 million) and other diversified agriculture ($107.9 million) added up to about $485 million, and the industry employed about 16 per cent of Hawaii's labor force.

But after Annexation and before World War II, Hawaii's planters had replaced Hawaii's kings and queens as the recognized island aristocracy. Trade reciprocity, annexation, and a quietly successful monopolization of all aspects of Hawaii's economy—including banking, retail and wholesale commerce, transportation, insurance and major utility companies—had created an awesomely powerful "plantation elite" which ran the islands in a neo-colonial, paternalistic fashion for the entire first half of this century. From about 1910 until just after World War II, a handful of firms known as the Big Five (Castle and Cooke, Alexander and Baldwin, C. Brewer, Theo H. Davies and American Factors) virtually owned Hawaii's economy and key political figures. As oldtimers are fond and not-so-fond of recalling, "Not a nickel could be earned or spent in the islands unless at least one of the Big Five had a part in the transaction." Most of the chief executives of these *kamaaina* (long-time resident) cartels were descended either from early missionaries or from annexationist-businessmen who were "active" during Hawaii's not-so-gay 1890s. By capitalizing on vast land and political bases acquired by their ancestors, these ruling families were so good at commercial exploitation that by 1931 they controlled 95 per cent of the sugar industry. With the coming of World War II and martial law, and the post-War years and the growth of workers' unions as Hawaii's chief political force, this era ended.

The Success of Labor, An American Dream Realized

Ironically, the greatest and still-emerging powers in Modern Hawaii are the sons and daughters of immigrant plantation laborers who were brought to Hawaii to earn pennies a day picking pineapples and cutting sugarcane for the Big Five. Following World War II, Hawaii's formerly docile workers began making more and more demands on their *haole* employers. They were no longer satisfied with the paternalism and low wages of seasons past, and almost immediately after martial law was lifted in the mid-1940s, labor unions began delivering ultimatums to their employers. Particularly active was the International Longshoremen's and Warehousemen's Union (the ILWU), a militant labor organization known for being extremely tough and inflexible in California's labor-management disputes.

Because of the ILWU's socialistic style, many business leaders attacked it as a Communist organization bent on anarchy. That didn't ruffle its negotiators at all. Nor was its popularity decreased. Between 1944 and 1947, Hawaii's ILWU membership swelled from 900 to about 20,000. And in 1946, to show their force to skeptical and critical plantation managers, the ILWU's leaders called a strike of every field and mill worker in the sugar industry. That 77-day strike resulted in wage increases, other employee benefits, a decidedly positive victory for unionized labor, and a new political era in the Hawaiian Islands. Three years later, in 1949, labor's might again was conclusively proven when the ILWU sponsored a 178-day strike of 2,000 Hawaii longshoremen. By then, Hawaii had become almost completely dependent upon shipping for most of its foodstuffs and basic commodities, so the strike by dockworkers effectively crippled the Territory's economy and demonstrated the strength now held by its working class. Under the brilliant and tenacious leadership of ILWU labor organizer-negotiators, notably Jack Hall and Harry Bridges, Hawaii's immigrant laborers entered the 1950s in a place of conspicuous political prominence.

Probably because the plantation bosses who ran things were staunch Republicans, the workers chose the opposite national political party—the Democratic Party—as a vehicle for waging political battles. In 1954, labor factions and Hawaii's "Japanese vote" combined forces to nearly destroy Hawaii's Republican Party—and to end 52 years of conservative *haole* rule—by sweeping both houses of Hawaii's Territorial Legislature. Since then, the Japanese and labor-based Democratic Party has been unchallenged as Hawaii's major political force.

A high point of sorts was reached in November 1974, when George Ariyoshi, the son of a former *sumo* wrestler and *tofu* maker, was elected Hawaii's governor and thus became the first Oriental person ever to hold such a high post in the United States. Ariyoshi's election marked what one Honolulu newspaper reporter called "The American Dream realized."

The Flocking of Tourists to Everyman's Vision of Paradise

Hawaii's "number one industry" is the product of an ongoing tropical dream which continues to feed on itself and become more fanciful, more lucrative and more believable to more potential visitors with every click of a visitor's camera shutter. Since 1778 when Captain James Cook and his Lieutenant James King began gathering notes for the first detailed guidebook to Hawaii, ever-increasing waves of curious travelers have put into these islands. But it was no wonder, given the splendid reports they had received from distinguished writers of the times. John Boit, a logkeeper on board the *Columbia*, the first American ship ever to visit Hawaii (in 1789), recounted to his countrymen that Hawaii's inhabitants "appear'd to me to be the happiest people in the world. Indeed there was some thing in them so frank and cheerfull that you could not help feeling prepossess'd in their favour."

During the next two centuries after Boit, Hawaii's mystique grew with every story written, every *hula* dancer and surfer sketched or photographed, and every lilting Hawaiian melody broadcast. This Polynesian picture was always framed by arching coconut palms, bathed in the light of a big butter moon, and lapped by gently rolling surf. By 1976, Hawaii's appeal was so tantalizing that more than 3.2 million people passed through her tourist turnstiles. That's more than 200 times the 15,000 who visited in 1946, four times the number who arrived in 1966, but only about 59 percent of the 5.4 million tourists who are expected to visit during the year 1985. Aloha!

Fun under the Sun

Listing a detailed shopping and tour guide to Oahu alone would be almost as exhausting as actually shopping and traveling to each and every one of those stores and attractions. Waikiki itself is flooded with shops, arcades, market places and other amusements running up and down streets and narrow lanes and rising some 30 stories above street level. Tours and attractions around Oahu and outside Waikiki are regularly advertised in local media.

Free weekly publications such as the *Waikiki Beach Press,* the *Island News* and *This Week on Oahu* advertise some of the myriad shopping and tour options available under the Hawaiian sun. Also, the Hawaii Visitors Bureau at 2270 Kalakaua Avenue, Suite 801, has all the brochures and information about the Aloha State you may want.

Shopping

A Fine Selection:

Cosmopolitan residents and visitors shop for a variety of international goods and domestic creations in shops throughout the Islands, but Hawaii has its own distinct goods to add to the market place. Items range from Polynesian kitsch lavastone tiki gods with olivine stone eyes to fine Niihau shell leis which may cost as much as $2,500 for four strands. A selection of things which capture a true *local* essence include the following:

Shells: A modest, simple gift from the Pacific seafloor. The large conch shell was used to call people to meetings in old Hawaii. The pure white cowrie is a rarer variety of shell, and the teenie-tiny white, pink and red Niihau shells, which look like miniature conches, are patiently gathered on only a few secret or generally inaccessible Hawaiian beaches and strung into long finite leis. They are pricey, but of exquisite Hawaiian taste.

Coral Jewelry: Brittle branches of black, pink and rarer gold coral are plucked from the deep blue by island divers. (Red coral usually comes from Japan and the Mediterranean.) These veinous coral branches are then cut and set by jewelers into pins, clips, rings, pendents and necklaces. Prices vary.

Wood: Monkeypod, *koa* and *milo* are three popular island woods used for making furniture, calabashes (large ceremonial bowls) and other fine wood creations. *Koa* and rosewood also are used to make quality guitars and ukuleles.

Plants: Exotic hibiscus, anthurium, bamboo, orchid, *ti* and bird of paradise plants (and their seeds) are potted in sterile peat moss and agriculturally inspected. (Warning: Be sure they were inspected by the Agricultural Inspection Board before attempting to take them to the mainland.)

Kukui nut and seed leis: The tradition of stringing and wearing the brown and black-and-white *kukui* nuts, commonly called candlenuts, is still very popular. *Koa* seed leis are also appealing, but most

of those are strung in the Philippines.

Macadamia nuts: Delicious roasted and eaten plain or chocolate-covered, this rich nut is true gourmet fare. Macadamia nut products are grown and packaged on the Big Island.

Kona coffee: Hawaii's own homegrown and roasted coffee beans are produced at Kona on the only commercial coffee plantations in the United States. This Big Island product is accorded a gourmet status in international coffee-drinking circles.

Jellies, jams and preserves: Local tropical fruits such as guava, *poha*, mango, *lilikoi* passion fruit, papaya and coconut are made into luscious spreads unlike any you'll taste anywhere else on earth.

Chinese preserves: Introduced by the Chinese, these preserves have become a favorite snack treat in Hawaii and are craved by those truly accustomed to local tastes. Plums, cherries, mangoes, olives, apricots, lemons and limes are dried and salted or preserved in sweet-sour sauces. One famous variety of sweet-sour pickled plums known as "crack seed" comes with its seed cracked, thereby allowing its aromatic kernel to enhance the flavor. Shops specializing in these pickled seeds can be found in most major suburban shopping areas and downtown.

Dried gourds: Called *ipu* in Hawaiian, the large tan bottle gourd is hollowed-out and dried and used as a drum and as a receptacle for food, water, and paraphernalia. A smaller dark gourd is used to make *hula* instruments. The *ipu* also serves as a hanging flower pot.

Hawaiian instruments: Popular Hawaiian *hula* instruments include the *ipu* drum, *puili* (slashed percussive bamboo sticks), *uliuli* (a feather-topped gourd rattle filled with seeds) and *iliili* (small smooth stones used like castanets in a set of four). There are also the *hano* (nose flute) and *ukulele*. All are available at island *hula* supply shops and some music stores.

Woven goods: *Lauhala* (pandanus) and coconut frond and fiber baskets and hats are popular. Rattan baskets of a finer weave are used to carry school books as well as *hula* instruments.

Tapa: *Tapa* (barkcloth), properly called *kapa*, is made into popular items—wallhangings, placemats, bags, hats, etc.—but the *tapa* for sale is not actually Hawaiian *kapa*, but a related fabric made in Samoa and Tonga. Real Hawaiian *kapa* was last made during the 19th Century.

Clothes, Hawaiian print textiles, patterns: Honolulu has its own fashions, the *muumuu* and aloha shirt. The first *muumuu*, designed and introduced by the early missionaries, was a loose, lengthy, high-necked, long-sleeved shroud. Because of variations in its style, *muumuu* has come to refer to just about any casual smock, long or short, made of Hawaiian print fabric. The aloha shirt was first marketed in the 1930s by a Chinese tailor in Honolulu. It is a simple button-front shirt with short sleeves made of Hawaiian print textiles. *Muumuus* and aloha shirts are sold and worn everywhere. Some island occasions, such as wedding receptions and dinner parties, specify "aloha attire" as the preferred dressing mode. Hawaiian clothes patterns are available for seamstresses in dry goods stores.

Photographs of old Hawaii: Peer into Hawaii's past. Leaf through the photo albums at the State of Hawaii Archives, downtown off South King Street on the Iolani Palace grounds. The Archives is open from 7:45 a.m. thru 4:30 p.m., Monday through Friday. Photocopies and xeroxes are available for a dollar and up and take a few days for printing. Tel: 548-2355

Feather hatbands: The irridescent hues of the feathers of birds such as the pheasant and peacock today are worn as hat bands by properly attired local folk.

Perfumes and colognes: Select from a line of bottled tropical flower fragrances such as gardenia, *pikake*, ginger and others.

Surfboards: Custom-made fiberglass surfboards can be shaped to adapt to one's height, weight and personal taste in design by some of the world's finest shapers.

Cockroaches and maile leaves: Don't go home without your own gold-dipped maile leaves or a cute little cockroach, jokingly referred to as Hawaii's "state insect."

Where to Shop

Highlighted below are several popular off-beat shopping spots on Oahu:

In Waikiki:

Weekend Art Mart

the Honolulu Zoo alongside the Monsarrat Street fence; 10 a.m. to 4 p.m. Saturday and Sunday.

International Market Place

2330 Kalakaua Avenue, in the heart of Waikiki; 9 a.m. to 11 p.m. daily.

King's Village

131 Kaiulani Avenue, a block *mauka* of Kalakaua Avenue; 9 a.m. to 11 p.m. daily.

Hemmeter Center

Fronting Kalakaua Avenue between Uluniu and Kaiulani Avenues; 9 a.m. to 11 p.m. daily.

Kuhio Mall

Behind the International Market Place on Kuhio Avenue, between Seaside and Kaiulani Avenues. 10 a.m. to 10 p.m. daily.

Royal Hawaiian Center

On Kalakaua Avenue, between Lewers Street and the Outrigger Hotel; 9 a.m. to 9 p.m. daily.

Rainbow Bazaar

2005 Kalia Road, on the grounds of the Hilton Hawaiian Village Hotel; 9 a.m. to 11 p.m. daily.

Waikiki Shopping Plaza

on Kalakaua Avenue at Royal Hawaiian and Seaside Avenues; 6 a.m. to 1 a.m. daily.

Eaton Square

444 Hobron Lane, about two blocks *mauka* of the Ilikai Hotel; 10 a.m. to 6 p.m. daily.

Ewa of Waikiki:

(Bus instructions from Waikiki provided)

Ala Moana Shopping Center

Walking distance or bus # 8 from Waikiki; 9:30 a.m. to 9 p.m. Monday thru Friday; 9:30 a.m. to 5:30 p.m. Saturday; and 10 a.m. to 4 p.m. Sunday.

Ward Warehouse

1050 Ala Moana Boulevard at Ward Avenue; take bus # 8 Airport/Hickam; 10 a.m. to 9 p.m. Monday thru Friday; 10 a.m. to 5 p.m. Saturday; and 11 a.m. to 4 p.m. Sunday.

Downtown Honolulu and Chinatown

Shopping at the Union and Fort Street Malls, Maunakea Street open market, Hotel Street, Nuuanu Avenue and at Merchant Square; take bus # 2 or # 8 marked Airport or Airport/Hickam from Waikiki or Ala Moana Center.

Kukui Market Place

1200 College Walk; take bus # 2 Liliha or School Street to downtown corner of Hotel and River Streets and walk two blocks *mauka*.

New China Cultural Plaza

100 North Beretania Street, walking distance from downtown, *mauka* side of Maunakea Street and Chinatown; regular business hours; take bus # 2 or # 8 Airport or Airport/Hickam.

Pearl Ridge Shopping Center

98-211 Pali Momi; 10 a.m. to 9 p.m. Monday to Friday; 10 a.m. to 5:30 p.m., Saturday; 11 a.m. to 4 p.m., Sunday; bus #8 to Ala Moana Center Request a transfer. Transfer onto bus # 50 Ewa Beach, # 52 Wahiawa Heights, Waipahu, Barbers Point, or Makaha. Buses stop one block from the Pearl Ridge Shopping Center

Kam Drive-In Theatre Swap Meet

98–850 Moanalua Road, opposite Pearl Ridge Shopping Center; 7 a.m. to 3 p.m., Wednesday, Saturday and (big day) Sunday; 50 cents per buyer. (See Pearl Ridge Shopping Center for bus information.)

**Honolulu Academy of Arts, Bishop
Museum and Mission Houses Museum Gift Shops**

check under *Tours* for addresses and hours.

Other shopping spots on Oahu:

University Business District

Around the University Avenue and South King
Street intersection; Puck's Alley shopping arcade,
goods store, *hula* supply shop, theatre, bike shop,
"crack seed" center, health food stores, cafes, bars,
etc.; bus #6 Woodlawn/Ala Moana Center/
Pauoa.

Kaimuki Business District

Waialae Avenue; features surfshops, health food
stores, night clubs, several excellent Korean restaurants established by recent immigrants, and
sundry neighborhood shops and cafes; cinemas;
bus #2 to King Street; transfer onto any #1 bus.

Kapahulu Business District

Kapahulu Avenue, *mauka* side of Waikiki, features Kilohana Square shopping area, local surf-
shop, health food store-cafe, athletic gear shop,
records and tape cassettes, boutique, cinema, etc.,
bus #8 Waikiki to the end of the line; transfer onto #14 St. Louis Heights.

Koko Marina Shopping Center

In Hawaii Kai on a man-made marina; 10 a.m. to 9
p.m., Monday thru Friday; 10 a.m. to 5 p.m.
Saturday and Sunday; bus #2 to King Street;
transfer onto bus #57 bound *Diamond Head* on
King Street.

Annual Holidays and Special Events

January

The Hula Bowl Football Game: An annual football
classic featuring East and West College all-stars in
a head-on tumble at the Aloha Stadium at
Halawa, Oahu; first Saturday of the month.
State Legislature Opening: Annual Legislative session is initiated on the third Wednesday of January
with a colorful ceremony: *lei* presentations and
Hawaiian music, *hula* and informal speeches.
Chinese New Year: Celebrated on the day of the
second new moon after the winter solstice (around
mid to late January) for 15 days. Clanging cym-
bals, pounding drums, rounds of fire-crackers and
traditional lion dances chase bad spirits out of
homes and shops in Chinatown, downtown
Honolulu, clearing the way for a *Kung Hee Fat
Choi* (Prosperous New Year).
Narcissus Festival: Five weeks of various Chinese

shows, displays and events coinciding with
Chinese New Year; topped with the coronation of
the New Year's Chinese Narcissus Queen.
Hawaiian Open Golf Tournament: Hawaii's big-
gest annual golfing event; a four-day event at
Waialae Country Club, Oahu; televised live on the
U.S. Mainland.

February

Punahou Carnival: Largest and most popular
school carnival in the State in early February.
Fruit jams, jellies and other homemade local foods
on sale; Manoa Valley, Honolulu.
Haleiwa Sea Spree: In the Haleiwa-Waialua vicinity on Oahu's North Shore; in honor of Queen
Liliuokalani's reign; surf contests, canoe races,
torchlight pageant and fair. Check newspapers for
announcements.
**Hang Ten American Professional Surfing
Championships:** At an undetermined location depending on where the surf is up during the contest
week.
Mauna Kea Ski Meet: A four-day ski competition
between members of the Ski Association of
Hawaii; on Mauna Kea's slopes, Big Island;
around mid-February.
Cherry Blossom Festival: An eleven-week Japanese
festival of cultural demonstrations including flower arrangement, tea ceremony, martial arts, and
the selection of an annual Cherry Blossom Queen;
late February, early March.

March

Kite-Flying Contest: Held in March at Kapiolani
Park. Contestants of all ages make and enter kites
in four divisions: largest, smallest, most beautiful
and furthest flying kite.

3rd: Girls' Day (Hinamatsuri) Dolls Festival:
Japanese customarily honor young girls on this day
with a gift of a doll for their heirloom collections.
Japanese department stores usually host intricate
doll displays.

Polo Season Opens: Early March; matches are
held at 2 p.m. on Sundays at the Mokuleia Polo
Field on Oahu's North Shore.

Kamehameha Schools Song Festival: A Friday
evening in the month; a Hawaiian choral singing
competition between classes of this school for
Hawaiian and part-Hawaiian youths is staged at
the Blaisdell International Center; admission free.

17th: Saint Patrick's Day: A green parade and long
day of local Irish fanfare along Kalakaua Avenue
through Waikiki.

26th: Kuhio Day: State holiday honoring the
birthday of Prince Jonah Kuhio Kalanianaole; cel-

ebrated with parades, memorial services at the Nuuanu Royal Mausoleum, and ceremonies at Kawaiahao Church downtown. A special Prince Kuhio festival takes place on the weekend closest to his birthday on the island of Kauai, his birth-place.

Kona Stampede: Two days of hooting *paniolo*, Hawaiian cowboy, rodeo events; in the Honaunau Arena, Honaunau, Big Island.

April

Merry Monarch Festival: Four to five days of fun and pageantry—costume, mustache and side-burns contest, parade, pageant and flower show; in early April; at Hilo on the Big Island.

Miss Aloha Hawaii Pageant: Beauty pageant held at Hilo, Big Island; date announced in newspapers.

Bishop Museum Festival: A Sunday day-long festival on the museum grounds; Kalihi, Honolulu.

8th: Buddha's Birthday (Wesak): Celebrated largely by Japanese Buddhists with tea ceremonies and traditional singing and dancing on the Sunday closet to this day: Blaisdell International Concert Hall. Honolulu.

Flora Pacifica: Show of specially nurtured island flowers and plants, especially orchids; usually on the grounds of the H. Alexander Walker estate, 2616 Pali Highway, Honolulu; around late April to early May.

Easter: Sunrise services held at the leper colony of Kalaupapa, Molokai; and at the National Memorial Cemetery of the Pacific, Punchbowl Crater, Honolulu.

Easter Hat Parade and Egg Contest: Sponsored by the Department of Parks and Recreation in each district; check newspapers for exact date and location or call the DPR office. Some of the most unique and imaginative Easter bonnets are created of island materials such as raw coconut fiber, palm fronds and *koa* seeds.

May

1st: Lei Day: "May Day is Lei Day in Hawaii Garlands of flowers everywhere . . ." goes a popular *hula* melody. . . . On this day every spring, people celebrate May Day island style—dressed in cheerful, printed *muumuu* and aloha shirts, lots of leis and smiles. Students (particularly in the elementary level) at most schools throughout the islands perform multi-ethnic dances and songs in full costume (usually on the first workday of the month) and welcome all visitors to attend their special shows. Much pageantry happens throughout the day at the Waikiki Shell at Kapiolani Park, Waikiki, including a *lei* making contest, sunset *hula* show and the coronation of a Lei Day Queen.

5th: Boy's Day: Long colourful paper or cloth carp fish are strung up outside Japanese homes to honor boys in the family — so that they may pursue their goals like the strong-spirited carp that fights upstream current.

Honokaa Rodeo: Mid-May; sponsored by the Hawaii Saddle Club; Honokaa, Big Island.

Fiesta Filipina: Month-long series of Filipino music and dance performances, handicraft exhibitions, and the selection of a Miss Filipiniana Hawaii; Honolulu.

Memorial Day: Last Monday of this month; school children place flower leis on the 22,000 — plus grave markers at the National Memorial Cemetery of the Pacific, Punchbowl Crater, Honolulu.

"Old Hawaii on Horseback": Happens at Waimea, Big Island, during May in odd-number years.

June

11th: Kamehameha Day: In commemmoration of Kamehameha I, the great king who united the Islands; Kamehameha's gold statue in front of the Judiciary Building downtown is draped with 40-foot long leis. Then there is a formidable, gala parade down Kalakaua Avenue, complete with floats and elegant *pa'u* horseback riders wearing colors and flowers representative of their home islands.

Mission Houses Museum Annual Fancy Fair and Hawaiian Quilt Display. A part of the Kamehameha Day Celebration. This fair includes over 50 of Hawaii's finest crafts-people demonstrating and selling handcrafted items. The Hawaiian Quilt display is in the 1831 Chamberlain House and features over 25 Hawaiian quilts from private collections.

July

4th: Walter F. Macfarland Canoe Regatta: At Waikiki Beach.

Canoe Races: Hilo Bay, Big Island; announced locally.

Transpacific Yacht Races: Single hullcraft race on odd-number years; multi-hulls on even-number years; setting off from San Pedro, California on July 4th and racing until they cross a Diamond Head finish line some 9 to 25 days later. Conventional yachts also race from Victoria, B.C., to Lahaina, Maui on even number years. Also, two other competitions—the "Around-the-State Yacht Race" and "Little Transpac"—follow the above Transpacific Yacht Race.

Windward Oahu Fair: State's grandest agricultural show during July includes orchid, anthurium and *bonsai* displays, plus a home show, handicraft exhibitions, livestock and poultry shows.

Moku o Hawaii Championship Canoe Regatta: Held at Kailua-Kona, Big Island; date to be announced.

Japanese O-Bon Dance Festival: Japanese Buddhists dressed in simple cotton *kimono* and *yukata* honor deceased ancestors in this lively dance under *shoji* paper lanterns and around a tower supporting a spirited drumbeater and vocalists. Temples throughout the islands advertise these dances. O-Bon festivals (around 7:30 p.m. to midnight) are held throughout July and August; outsiders are invited to join in the merry dancing. O-Bon Season ends on a full moon evening with the *Floating Lanterns Festival* at the Haleiwa Jodo Mission where candlelit hexagonal lanterns on a lotus base are set afloat at a nearby beach.

Hawaii Okinawa Jubilee: Music, dance, martial arts and other arts of the Ryuku Islands are sponsored for several days; see local newspapers for times and locations in Honolulu.

Samoan Flag Raising Day: Lots of Samoan singing, dancing and athletic competitions and a *kava* root drinking ceremony; Honolulu. Check newspapers for date.

August

Japanese O-Bon Festival: See July.

Ukulele and Hula Festivals: Occur on two different Sundays at the Kapiolani Park Bandstand, Waikiki.

Water Week: Board of Water Supply takes visitors on a guided tour by underground cable car into the Halawa fresh mountain water reserve; check newspapers for exact date.

50th State Fair: Hawaiian quilt-making contests, local musicians, and a rainbow of ethnic dances, produce and livestock shows, food booths, carnival rides and booths, commercial displays and specially scheduled entertainment; usually at the Blaisdell International Center; advertised in Honolulu newspapers.

Kauai Open Invitational Golf Tournament: Three consecutive days at the Wailua Golf Course, Kauai. See newspapers for details.

Queen Liliuokalani Canoe Regatta: From Honaunau to Kailua-Kona. See newspapers for details.

Hawaiian International Billfish Tournament: Around July through August; giant marlin are caught during this 10 day tourney at Kailua-Kona on the Big Island.

September

1st: Waikiki Rough Water Swim: From Sans Souci Beach two miles *Ewa* to Duke Kahanamoku Beach; open to all ages in several swimming division.

Labor Day Rodeo: Kauai; check newspapers for details.

Labor Day Fishing Tournament: Maui; check newspapers for details.

Seniors Tennis Tournament: Early September at the Mauna Kea Beach Hotel; Kawaihae, Kona, the Big Island.

Na Mele o Maui: Five-day festival of Hawaiian music, dance, arts, crafts, cultural displays, canoe races and luaus; Maui.

October

Aloha Week: Third or last week of October; at Honolulu and on the Neighbor Islands; Hawaiian-style festivities, including coronation of a Hawaiian Royal Court at Iolani Palace, flower parade from downtown to Waïkiki, Aloha and Monarchy Ball, and an exhibit of shells from international shores sponsored by the Hawaiian Malacological Society.

Maui County Fair: Early October at Kahului. Check local newspapers for announcements.

Shinto Thanksgiving Festival: Celebrated in early October on a Sunday afternoon by Japanese at Daijingu Temple, 61 Puiwa Road, Nuuanu Valley, Oahu.

Kanikapila: Hawaiian music festival staged for two nights at Andrews Outdoor Amphitheatre, University of Hawaii at Manoa campus.

Molokai-to-Oahu Canoe Race: International paddling competitors; race runs from Hale o Lono Harbor, Molokai, to Waikiki; greet the winner about noon at the Moana Hotel beachfront.

Honolulu Orchid Society Show: Grandest orchid show in the islands; at Blaisdell International Center; floral displays and sales, *lei* and corsage making, and oriental flower arrangement demonstrations.

Hawaii County Fair: Late October; commercial and agricultural exhibits, horse show and races, *lei* making contest, orchid and other floral displays, and Hawaiian arts and crafts.

Scottish-Hawaiian Traditional Games: At Waikoloa, Big Island.

Pro-Am Open Golf Tournament: At a designated course on the island of Maui.

November

Bull and Horse Show: Mid-November; Kamuela, Big Island. Announcements publicized in local newspaper.

Kona Coffee Festival: Four-day festivities in mid-November; Kailua, Big Island; includes judging of coffee recipes, Kona coffee farm tours, and local parade and pageantry. Check newspapers for announcements.

Mission Houses Museum Christmas Fair. — Late November. Handcraft fair featuring over 50 of Hawaii's finest craftspeople; a special display in the 1831 Chamberlain House, and free entertainment.

December

The Annual Honolulu Marathon: At the crack of dawn one morning every December, thousands of runners from all over the world set off from the Aloha Tower on a 26 mile, 385 yard AAU-certified marathon course along Oahu's south shore. The marathon ends at Kapiolani Park Bandstand. For more information, phone 531-2865.

7th: Pearl Harbor Day: In memory of those who were killed during the Japanese bombing of Oahu on December 7, 1941; memorial service is held at the USS *Arizona* Memorial.

Bodhi Day: Japanese day of Enlightenment on the first Sunday of the month; ceremonies at Buddhist temples.

Festival of Trees: Exhibit of decorated Christmas trees, including evergreens with handcrafted ornaments and island-style coconut palm branch "Christmas trees;" in early December at Blaisdell International Center.

Kamehameha Schools Christmas Song Festival: Sung in Hawaiian and English by this Hawaiian school's glee club accompanied by the school's orchestra; Blaisdell International Center; also televised.

Mission Houses Museum Candlelight Tour: A tour through the old-fashioned Christmas-decorated abodes of early Christian missionaries who brought Christ's teachings and Christmas to the islands; choral singing and hosts dressed in old-style missionary attire add to the holiday ambience.

24th: Kawaiahao Church Midnight Service: A memorable candlelit Christmas Eve service in this old coral church: choir sings in both Hawaiian and English.

Tours, Cruises, Places of Interest

Beyond peeking out at paradise from behind tinted tour bus windows, one can dip in and out of fantasy settings on scores of advertised glider, helicopter and small-prop plane tours, off-shore dinner and sunset-booze cruises, catamaran and glass-bottom boat rides, and even deep-sea fishing craft. All such commercial tours are advertised in the media. Provided below are some of the tours and instructions on how to get to major attractions by city bus from Waikiki. For more information about these tours and about other places of interest, consult the *Waikiki Beach Press, Island News, This Week on Oahu,* the daily newspapers' entertainment and community calendar sections, or call the Hawaii Visitors Bureau at 923-1811.

In Waikiki:

Rickshaws — three-wheeled pedicabs pedalled by bronze athletes — wait outside air-conditioned hotels to breeze you through another chapter of the Waikiki fantasy. Rickshaw rides begin at four dollars a person (price negotiable) for a 15 minute leisurely open-air cruise through Waikiki. The Tropical Trolley, meanwhile, runs a tour of Waikiki from King's Village to the Hilton Hawaiian Village Hotel between 9 a.m. to 3 p.m. Monday thru Saturday by reservation. Tickets, available at any hotel travel desk, are $5 for adults and $3 for youths under 12 and senior adults.

Kapiolani Park

At the foot of Diamond Head across Queen's Surf Beach. Features a special 1.8 mile jogging course, soccer field, driving range, archery cove, tennis courts, picnic tables, aquarium, amphitheatre, zoo, rose garden and bandstand.

Honolulu Zoo

Diamond Head end of Kalakaua Avenue in the Kapiolani Park complex. Open from 9 a.m. to 5 p.m. daily. Special shows during the summer at 6 p.m. on Wednesdays; admission free.

Kodak Hula Show

Off Monsarrat Avenue near the Waikiki Shell amphitheatre; showtimes 10 a.m. Tuesday, Wednesday, Thursday; and 10 a.m. Fridays during the summer; admission free.

Waikiki Aquarium

2777 Kalakaua Avenue, opposite Kapiolani Park; tel: 923-9741; 10 a.m. to 5 p.m. daily; admission: adults $1.00, youths under 16 free.

Elvis Presley Museum

2nd Floor, Mitsukoshi Building, 2155 Kalakaua Avenue; tel. 926-1147; 10 a.m. to 10 p.m.; admission: adults, $3.00; children 12 and under, $1.50.

U.S. Army Museum at Fort DeRussy

Ewa side of the Cinerama Reef Hotel inside Battery Randolph; tel: 543-2639; 10 a.m. to 4:30 p.m. Tuesday thru Sunday; admission free.

Downtown & Environs:

Iolani Place

The palace is located in downtown Honolulu with an entrance from King Street; tel: 536-6185. Tours are scheduled Wednesday through Saturday from 9 a.m. to 2:15 p.m. About 45 minutes. Admission: adults $4; youths 5-12, $1. No children under 5.

Chinatown Tour

Conducted by the Chinese Chamber of Commerce; tel: 533-3181; originates at 42 N. King Street, downtown; from 9:30 a.m. to noon Tuesday; $3 for persons over 13 years old, plus $4.00 for an optional six-course lunch at Wo Fat Restaurant; advance reservations suggested; take bus #2 or # 8 marked Airport or Airport/Hickam.

Mission Houses Museum

553 King St. Mission Houses Museum open daily, 9 a.m. to 4 p.m. Closed Thanksgiving, Christmas and New Year's Day. Adults, $3.50; children 6-15, $1.00; under 6 free. Admission to the Museum includes a guided tour of about 45 minutes through the historic houses.

Hawaiian Monarchy Promenade

Conducted by the Mission Houses Museum; tel: 531-0481; originates at 553 S. King Street, downtown; 9:30 a.m. to noon Monday thru Friday; admission: adults, $7; youths, 6-16, $2 (price includes Museum admission); advance reservations suggested; take bus #2 or #8 marked Airport or Airport/Hickam.

Passport to Polynesia

Excursion to the Bishop Museum and Planetarium (details below); offered by the Bishop Museum, 1355 Kalihi Street, Kalihi Valley: tel: 847-1443; 9 a.m. to 5 p.m. daily except Christmas: charge: adults, $10.00, youths 17 and under, $5.00, youths under 6, free (price entitles bus that shuttles between King's Village and the above attractions daily). For a "Diplomat's Passport to Polynesia" - the same tour escorted — the charge is $10 per adult, $5 per youth (17 and under), and free for youths under 6.

Bishop Museum & Planetarium

1355 Kalihi Street, Kalihi; tel: (Museum) 847-1443; 9 a.m. to 5 p.m. daily except Christmas: admission: adults 18 and older, $4.75, youths under 18 (museum only), $2.50; unescorted youths (museum only) 25 cents; Planetarium Show: at 11 a.m. and 3.15 p.m. Sunday and 8 p.m. Friday and Saturday; July and August only at 8 p.m. Wednesday and Sunday; admission: (to evening show) adults, $1.50; youths, 6–17, 75 cents. An entrance ticket entitles you to ride the red double-decker London Transport bus to and from the museum, or take bus #2 School Street and get off near Likelike Highway on School Street.

Falls of Clyde

A restored four-mast, fully rigged sailing ship museum; at Honolulu Harbor's Pier 7, tel: 536-6373; 9.30 a.m. to 4:30 p.m. daily; admission: adults, $3; youths 6-17, $2.50; under 6, free. Take bus #8 Airport/Hickam.

Aloha Tower

Pier 9 at Honolulu Harbor; 10th floor observation deck open from 8 a.m. to 9 p.m. daily; admission free; bus #8 Airport or Airport/Hickam.

Queen Emma Summer Palace

2913 Pali Highway, Nuuanu Valley; tel: 595-3167; 9 a.m. to 4 p.m. daily; admission $3 for adults; $1 for youths and 50 cents for children under 12. Bus #2 or #8 Airport or Airport/Hickam. Request a transfer. Transfer on Bethel Street downtown onto bus #4 Nuuanu/Dowsett.

Contemporary Arts Center of Hawaii

In the News Building, 605 Kapiolani Blvd; tel: 525-8000; 8 a.m. to 5 p.m. Monday thru Friday and 8 a.m. to noon Saturday; admission free; bus #8 Ala Moana Center. Request a transfer. Walk one block *mauka* to Kapiolani Blvd. Transfer onto bus #3 Navy Yard to end of Kapiolani Blvd.

Foster Botanic Garden

180 N. Vineyard Blvd. (entrance on Vineyard Blvd. at Nuuanu Stream); tel: 531-1939; 8:30 a.m. to 4 p.m. daily; admission free; bus 2 or 8 Airport or Airport Hickam. Request a transfer. Transfer on Bethel Street downtown onto bus 4 Nuuanu/Dowsett.

Honolulu Academy of Arts

900 S. Beretania Street, *mauka* of Thomas Square; tel: 538-3693; 10 a.m. to 4:30 p.m. Tuesday, Wednesday, Friday and Saturday and 2 p.m. to 5 p.m. Sunday; closed Monday; admission free; any bus #2.

Elsewhere on Oahu:

National Memorial Cemetery of the Pacific

In Punchbowl Crater, top of Puowaina Drive; September 30 thru March 1, 8 a.m. to 5:30 p.m. daily; March 2 thru September 29, 8 a.m. to 6:30 p.m. daily; Memorial Day, 7 a.m. to 7 p.m.; admission free; any bus #2. Request a transfer. Transfer on Alapai Street near downtown onto bus #15 Maikiki/Pacific Heights.

Dole Pineapple Cannery

650 Iwilei Road. Iwilei-Kalihi. between Nimitz Highway and Dillingham Boulevard; tel: 536-3411; open 8:30 a.m. to 8 p.m. weekdays; advance reservations advised; admission: adults, $2, youths 6-17, 50 cents. 5 and under, free; bus# 8 Airport or Airport/Hickam.

Royal Mausoleum

2261 Nuuanu Avenue, Nuuanu Valley; tel: 536-7602; 8 a.m. to 4:30 p.m. Monday thru Friday;

advance reservations requested; admission free; bus #2 or #8 Airport or Airport/Hickam. Request a transfer. Transfer on Bethel Street downtown onto bus #4 Nuuanu/Dowsett.

Tennent Art Foundation Gallery

203 Prospect Street, Makiki; tel: 531-1987; open 10 a.m. — noon Tuesday thru Saturday; 2 p.m. to 4 p.m. Sunday; admission free; bus #2 to corner of Beretania and Alapai Streets, transfer onto #15 Pacific Heights on Alapai Street.

U.S.S. Arizona Memorial Cruise

At Pearl Harbor, conducted by the State of Hawaii; tel: 471-3901; open 9 a.m.–3 p.m. Tuesday thru Sunday, except on rainy or windy days; admission free, but on a first come first-served basis; not admitted: children under 6 years old, barefooted and swimsuit-clad visitors; half hour shuttle ride and tour of the memorial conducted by a National Park Service guide; bus #5 Ala Moana/Manoa or #8 Ala Moana. Request a transfer. Transfer at Ala Moana Center onto bus #50 Ewa Beach, #51 Makaha, #52 Wahiawa Heights, or the Waipahu or Barbers Point buses. (Commercial Pearl Harbor boat tours which cruise by the USS *Arizona* Memorial leave from Kewalo Basin daily, but passengers on these tours are not permitted to board the Memorial. Advance reservations can be made at Waikiki hotel travel desks.)

U.S.S. Arizona Memorial Visitors Center

A new Arizona Memorial Visitor Center is located at Pearl Harbor, on Kam Highway, Route 90, about one-half mile east of Aloha Stadium. Limited parking for private vehicles. Tel: 471-3901 for recorded message. For further information call the Center at 422-2771. Open 8 a.m. to 3 p.m. except Monday. The National Park Service offers a continuous program which features a 20-minutes historical film and a Navy operated shuttle boat trip to the Arizona Memorial. Free tickets at Visitor Center lobby. No reservations.

University of Hawaii, East West Center, Center for Korean Studies

In Manoa Valley; tel: 948-7700; 8 a.m. to 4:30 p.m. Monday thru Friday; free hour-long student-guided tour; Monday thru Thursday; 1:30 p.m.; meet in front of Jefferson Hall (East–West Road); bus #4 Nuuanu/University/Waikiki or bus #6 Woodlawn/Ala Moana Center/Pauoa.

Paradise Park

3737 Manoa Road, Manoa Valley; tel: 988-2141; 9:30 a.m. to 5 p.m. daily; admission: adults, $6.95; youths 4-12, $3.50; bus #5 Manoa Ala Moana Center Waikiki.

Harold L. Lyon Arboretum

3860 Manoa Road, Manoa Valley; tel: 988-7378; open first Friday of every month 1 p.m. to 2:30 p.m. admission free; limited admission, so make advance reservations; bus #5 Manoa/Ala Moana Center/Waikiki.

Sea Life Park

At Makapuu Point; tel: 259-7933; 9:30 a.m. to 5 p.m. daily; admission: adults, $6.50, youths 7-12, $4.75; bus #57 Hawaii Kai Sea Life Park (bound *Diamond Head* on Kalakaua Avenue).

Koko Head Botanic Park

In Koko Head Crater; tel: 537-9373; 9 a.m. to 4 p.m., Monday thru Friday; (park is still under development but open); admission free; call for an escort; one hour hike or horse back ride into crater from Koko Crater Stables; 408 Kealahou; tel: 395-2628; 10:30 a.m. and 2 p.m. Tuesday thru Friday, 2 p.m. and 3 p.m. weekend; horseride to Koko Head Botanic Park, $10.00 an hour; make advance reservations; bus 57 Hawaii Kai/Sea Life Park (bound *Diamond Head* on Kalakaua Avenue).

Castle Park

Across from Aloha Stadium; tel: 488-6822; 9.30 a.m. to 10:30 p.m., Sun. — Thurs. Until 12:30 p.m. Fri. and Sat. Family fun and theme park. No general admission; each attraction has its own price.

Byodo-In Temple

47-200 Kahekili Highway on Windward Oahu; tel: 239-8811; 9 a.m. to 5 p.m. daily; admission: adults $1, youths 50 cents. Replica of a 900-year old Buddhist Temple at Kyoto, Japan.

Polynesian Cultural Center and Mormon Temple

At Laie on Oahu's North Shore; tel: 293-8561 or 923-1861; shows: 11:00 a.m., 3.00 p.m., 7 p.m. Monday thru Saturday; admission: adults, $14.00 (matinees), $15.00 (evening), dinner $13.00, youths 5–11, half price; bus 8 Ala Moana Center. Request a transfer. Transfer onto bus 52 Kaneohe/Wahiawa.

Waimea Falls Park

59-864 Kam Highway, at Waimea on Oahu's North Shore; arboretum, picnic sites, waterfall trail hike; tel: 638-8511; 10 a.m. to 5:30 p.m. daily; admission: adults $5.75; youths, 7-12, $3,75; 6 and under, free; bus #8 Ala Moana Center. Request a transfer. Transfer onto bus #52 Wahiawa/Kaneohe.

Suggested Readings:

Allen, Helena G., *The Betrayal of Liliuokalani*, Glendale, Clark, 1982. All important biography of Hawaii's last queen.

Armstrong, William Nevins, *Around the World With a King*, London, Heinemann, 1904. About King Kalakaua's 1881 circumnavigation of the globe.

Atlas of Hawaii, Department of Geography, University of Hawaii Press, University of Hawaii, Honolulu, Second Ed., 1983.

Baker, Ray Jerome. *Hawaiian Yesterdays*. Honolulu, Mutual Publishing, 1982. Edited by Robert E. Van Dyke with a text by Ronn Ronck. A wonderful collection of historic photographs by Hawaii's pioneer cameraman.

Barrow, T.: *Art and Life in Polynesia*, A.H. & A.W. Reed, Wellington, N.Z., 1972.

Beckwith, Martha Warren, *Hawaiian Mythology*, New Haven, Yale University Press, 1940, and University Press of Hawaii, 1970.

Bingham, Hiram, *A Residence of Twenty-one Years in the Sandwich Islands*, New York, Goodwin, 1855. Missionary memoirs.

Bishop, Isabella Lucy (Bird). *Six Months in the Sandwich Islands*, Tokyo, Tutffe, 1974. Comments by a traveling English lady who visited Hawaii in 1873.

Bone, Robert W., *The Maverick Guide to Hawaii*, New Orleans, Pelican. Revised annually. A consumer report-review of Hawaii.

Brown, De Soto, Ann Ellett and Gary Gienza. *Hawaii Recalls: Selling Romance to America*. Honolulu, Editions Limited, 1982. Nostalgic images of the Isles, 1910–1950.

Buck, Sir Peter, *Arts and Crafts of Hawaii*, Bishop Museum, 1957.

Buffet, Guy, *Guy Buffet's Hawaii*, San Francisco, Cameron and Co., 1980. A delightful book of Hawaii watercolor paintings reproduced with the artist's commentary.

Bushnell, Oswald, *Kaaawa*, University Press of Hawaii, 1972; *Molokai*, World Publishing Company, 1963; *The Return of Lono*, University Press of Hawaii, 1971; *A Walk Around old Honolulu*, Kapa, 1976; *The Stone of Kannon*, University Press of Hawaii, 1979; and *The Water of Kane*, University Press of Hawaii, 1980. Important works by a much-esteemed local man-of-letters.

Cameron, Robert, *Above Hawaii*, San Francisco, Cameron and Co., 1977. An aerial view of the Hawaiian Islands.

Charlot, Jean, *An Artist on Art*, The University Press of Hawaii, Honolulu, 1972.

Charlot, John, *Chanting the Universe*, Honolulu, Emphasis International, 1983. An examination of Hawaiian culture through its poetry and chants.

Chinen, Jon, *The Great Mahele*, University Press of Hawaii, 1958. About the great royal Hawaiian land divisions of 1848.

Chisholm, Craig, *Hawaiian Hiking Trails*, The Touchstone Press, 1977. A must for backpackers and nature-seekers.

Clark. John R.K., *The Beaches of Oahu*, 1977, and *The Beaches of Maui County*, 1980. University Press of Hawaii. Informative guides to Hawaii's shorelines.

Cook, Captain James, and King, James, *A Voyage to the Pacific Ocean, 1776–1780*, London, 1784, 3 vols. The first and still one of the best guidebooks about Hawaii and the Pacific. The official account of Cook's voyages, including the discovery of Hawaii.

Cox, J. Halley, with William H. Davenport, *Hawaiian Sculpture*, The University Press of Hawaii, Honolulu, 1974.

Cox, J. Halley, with Edward Stasack, *Hawaiian Petroglyphs*, Bishop Museum, 1970.

Daws, Gavan, *Shoal of Time*, New York, Macmillan, 1968. Hawaiian history from Cook's arrival to the 1960s; very enjoyable reading, true to scholarly sources.

Daws, Gavan, *Holy Man*, New York, Harper and Row. 1973. An entertaining and scholarly biography of Father Damien. Molokai's leper priest.

Day, A. Grove, *Books About Hawaii*, University Press of Hawaii, 1977. Reviews of the best books in Hawaii's literature.

Elbert, Samuel, and Keala, S.A., *Spoken Hawaiian*, University Press of Hawaii, 1970. Hawaiian language guide.

Elbert, Samuel, *Na Mele o Hawaii Nei*, University Press of Hawaii, 1970. A review of favorite Hawaiian folk songs.

Emerson, Nathaniel, *Unwritten Literature of Hawaii*, Tuttle, 1965. A scholarly look at the hula and ancient Hawaiian chants.

Feher, Joseph, *Hawaii: A Pictorial History*, Bishop Museum, 1969. A huge captioned collection of archival illustrations and photographs from the time of Cook and Kamehameha to the 1960's.

Finney, Ben R., *Surfing: The Sport of Hawaiian Kings*, Tuttle, 1965. A history of wave-riding.

Fornander, Abraham, *Fornander's Collection of Hawaiian Antiquities and Folklore; the Hawaiian Account of the Formation of Their Islands and Origin of Their Race with the Traditions of Their Migrations, etc., as Gathered from Original Sources;* Bernice Pauahi Bishop Museum, out of print; and *Selections from Fornander's Hawaiian Antiquities and Folk-lore.* University Press of Hawaii, 1959.

Fuchs, Lawrence H., *Hawaii Pono*, Harcourt, Brace, 1961. A social history of Hawaii.

Gosline, W.A. and Brock, Vernon, *Handbook of Hawaiian Fishes*, University Press of Hawaii. 1970. All you might want know about Hawaiian fish.

Handy, Edward Smith Craighill and Pukui, Mary Kawena (Wiggin), *The Polynesian Family System in Ka'u, Hawaii.* An important look by anthropologists at the belief systems and lifestyle of an old Hawaiian community on the Big Island of Hawaii.

Hawaii Audubon Society, *Hawaii's Birds*, Honolulu, 1981 A local birdwatcher's bible.

Holmes, Tommy, *The Hawaiian Canoe*, Kauai, Editions Limited, 1981. A definitive study.

Hopkins, Jerry, *The Hula*, Honolulu, Apa Productions, 1981. All you need to know about Hawaiian dance.

Joesting, Edward, *Hawaii: An Uncommon History*, New York, W.W. Norton, 1972. A behind-the-scenes look at Hawaii's history.

Jones, James, *From Here to Eternity*, Scribner, 1951. The famous novel (and subsequent movie) about Hawaii during World War II.

Judd, Gerrit Parmele, *Hawaii: An Informal History*; New York, Collier, 1961. A concise historical review by a *kamaaina* author.

Kamakau, Samuel Manaiakalani, *Ka Po'e Kahiko, the People of Old*, Bishop Museum, 1964; and *Ruling Chiefs of Hawaii*; Honolulu, Kamehameha Schools, 1961. Important memoirs by a 19th Century Hawaiian historian.

Kanahele, George S., *Hawaiian Music and Musicians*, University Press of Hawaii, 1979. An encyclopedia of Hawaii's musical heritage.

Korn, Alfons L., *The Victorian Visitors*, University Press of Hawaii, 1958. Fascinating look at the Hawaiian Kingdom during the reign of Kamehameha IV and his Queen Emma.

Kuck, Loraine E. and Tongg, Richard C., *A Guide to Tropical & Semitropical Floral*, Charles E. Tuttle, Japan, 1958. An easy to understand look at Hawaiian plants, illustrated.

Kumulipo, *The Kumulipo, a Hawaiian Creation Chant*, edited with commentary by Martha Warren Beckwith, Chicago, University of Chicago Press, 1951.

Kuykendall, Ralph Simpson, *The Hawaiian Kingdom*, University Press of Hawaii, 1938-1967, 3 v. The most important historical work about Hawaii during the 19th Century.

Kyselka, Will and Lanterman, Ray, *Maui: How it Came to Be*, University Press of Hawaii, 1980. A geologic history of the Valley Isle.

Lee, W. Storrs, *Hawaii: A Literary Chronicle*, Funk and Wagnalls, 1967. A collection of Hawaii impressions penned by prominent visiting authors of the late 18th and 19th centuries.

Liliuokalani, Queen of the Hawaiian Islands, *Hawaii's Story by Hawaii's Queen*, Boston, Lothrop, Lee & Shepard Co., 1898; and Rutland, Vermont & Tokyo, Charles E. Tuttle, 1964. Queen Liliuokalani's memoirs.

MacDonald. Gordon A., *Volcanoes in the Sea*, University of Hawaii Press, Second Ed., 1983. A historical and scientific look at Hawaii's spectacular volcanoes.

Malo, David, *Hawaiian Antiquities (Moolelo Hawaii)*, Bishop Museum Press, 1951.

Manhoff, Milton, and Uyehara, Mitsuo, *Rockhounding in Hawaii*, Hawaiiana Almanac Publishing Company, 1976.

McAllister, J. Gilbert, *Archaeology of Oahu*, Bishop Museum Press, 1933.

McGaw, Sister Mary Martha, *Stevenson in Hawaii*, University Press of Hawaii, 1950. A look at the Hawaiian wanderings and writings of the visiting storyteller Robert Louis Stevenson.

Merlin, Mark David, *Hawaiian Forest Plants*, Honolulu, Oriental Publishing Company, 1976. An editorial and photographic stroll past Hawaiian plants.

Michener, James, *Hawaii*, Random House, 1959.

Michener's epic novel about Hawaii from Genesis to the 1950s.

Mitchell, Donald D. Kilolani, *Hawaiian Treasures,* The Kamehameha Schools Press, Honolulu, 1978.

Morrison, Boone, and Chun, Malcolm, *Images of the Hula,* Volcano, Summit Press, 1983. Contemporary photographs of the *hula* with lively commentary.

Nordyke, Eleanor C., *The Peopling of Hawaii,* The University Press of Hawaii and The East-West Center, 1977. Who the people of Hawaii are, where they came from and how Hawaii's various ethnic groups are faring in the Hawaiian Islands.

Pierce, Richard A., *Russia's Hawaiian Adventure,* 1815–1817, Berkeley, California, University of California, 1965. The curious story about how a German physician working for the Russian-American Company tried to overthrow and claim Hawaii for Tzarist Russia.

Pukui, Mary Kawena (Wiggin), *Place Names of Hawaii,* University Press of Hawaii, 1966; *Nana I Ke Kumu (Look to the Source),* Hui Hanai, Honolulu, 1972; *The English-Hawaiian Dictionary,* University Press of Hawaii, 1964; and *The Hawaiian-English Dictionary,* University Press of Hawaii, 1965. Basic Hawaiian reference books by an esteemed Hawaiian scholar.

Rice, William Hyde, *Hawaiian Legends,* Bishop Museum Press, 1977. Attractive reprint of a 1923 classic, with new photographs by Boone Morrison.

Speakman, Cummins E., *Mowee,* Salem, Peabody Museum, 1978. A general history of Maui to the present day.

Stearns, Harold T., *Road Guide to Points of Geologic Interest in the Hawaiian Islands,* Palo Alto, Pacific Books, 1978.

Stephan, John J., *Hawaii Under the Rising Sun,* Honolulu, University of the Hawaii Press, 1983. Details Japan's plans to invade Hawaii after the attack on Pearl Harbor.

Stevenson, Robert Louis, *Travels in Hawaii,* University Press of Hawaii, 1973.

Sutherland, Audrey, *Paddling My Own Canoe,* University Press of Hawaii, 1978. A solitary pilgrimage exploring the wilderness beauty of Molokai's coastline.

Takaki, Ronald, *Pau Hana,* Honolulu, University of Hawaii Press, 1983. a history of plantation life and labor in Hawaii.

Twain, Mark (pseudonym for Samuel Langhorne Clemens), *Mark Twain's Letters from Hawaii,* New York, Appleton-Century, 1966. Master Twain's look at Hawaii in the 1860's, originally published as dispatches in the *Sacramento Union* newspaper.

Von Tempski, Armine, *Born in Paradise,* Duell, 1940. One of the best, if not the best, look at old Hawaii ranch life on the island of Maui.

Wenkam, Robert, *The Big Island Hawaii,* 1975, *Honolulu is an Island,* 1978, *Hawaii's Garden Isle: Kauai,* 1979, and *Maui No Ka Oi,* 1980, all Chicago, Rand McNally. Large-format photographic books with informative texts.

Hotels

The following list of hotels and facilities is reproduced by kind permission of the Hawaii Visitors Bureau.

OAHU

HOTEL	Facilities

ALA MOANA AMERICANA
Hotel (W)
410 Atkinson Drive
Honolulu, HI 96814
Phone 955-4811
Toll Free (800) 228-3278
   Total Units   1194
   Area A—Waikiki

Facilities:
100% Air Cond.
Parking
TV
Restaurants
Cocktail Lounges
Swimming Pool
Shops
Meeting Rooms

ALOHA PUNAWAI
Hotel Apts.
305 Saratoga Rd.
Honolulu, HI 96815
Phone 923-9222/923-5211
   Total Units   20
   Area A—Waikiki

ALOHA TOWERS
Condominium Apts. (W)
430 Lewers St.
Honolulu, HI 96815

   Hotel Units   8
   Area A—Waikiki

Facilities:
100% Air Cond.
Parking
Swimming Pools
Shop
Maid Service:
  On Request
Minimum Stay:
  5 Nights

APARTMENTS WAIKIKI
Condominium Apts. (W)
2233 Ala Wai, Apt. 2B
Honolulu, HI 96815
Phone (808) 923-4490
   Total Units   20
   Area A—Waikiki
   2 Blocks to Waikiki
   Beach

Facilities:
Air Cond.
Parking
TV
Swimming Pool
Tennis Court
Minimum Stay:
  3 Days

BAYVIEW APT. HOTEL
Apartment Hotel (W)
44-707 Puamohala St.
Kaneohe, HI 96744
Phone 247-3635
   Total Units   17
   Area E—Windward Oahu

Facilities:
Parking
TV
Swimming Pool
Minimum Stay:
  3 Days

BREAKERS HOTEL, THE
Hotel (W)
250 Beach Walk
Honolulu, HI 96815
Phone 923-3181
   Total Units   66
   Area A—Waikiki

Facilities:
100% Air Cond.
Parking
Swimming Pool
TV

COLONY SURF HOTEL
Condominium Apt. Hotel (W)
2895 Kalakaua Ave.
Honolulu, HI 96815
Phone 923-5751
Toll Free (800) 421-0530
          (800) 423-2922
          (800) 223-6625

Facilities:
Parking
TV
Restaurant
Cocktail Lounge
Children:
  12 or older

   Total Units   171
   Hotel Units   50
   Area A—Diamond Head
   On the Beach

COLONY SURF EAST HOTEL
Hotel (W)
2895 Kalakaua Ave.
Honolulu, HI 96815
Phone 923-5751
Toll Free (800) 421-0530
          (800) 423-2922
          (800) 223-6625
   Total Units   50
   Hotel Units   50
   Area A—Diamond Head

Facilities:
100% Air Cond.
Parking
TV
Restaurants
Cocktail Lounges
Children:
  12 or older

CONTINENTAL SURF
Apartment Hotel (W)
2426 Kuhio Ave.
Honolulu, HI 96815
Phone 922-2755
Toll Free (800) 227-4321
   Total Units   140
   Area A—Waikiki
   1 Block from
   Kuhio Beach

Facilities:
100% Air Cond.
Parking
TV

CORAL REEF HOTEL
Hotel (W)
2299 Kuhio Ave.
Honolulu, HI 96815
Phone 922-1262
Toll Free (800) 367-5124
   Total Units   247
   Hotel Units   209
   Area A—Waikiki

Facilities:
100% Air Cond.
Parking
TV
Restaurants
Cocktail Lounges
Swimming Pool
Shops

CORAL SEAS HOTEL
Hotel
250 Lewers St.
Honolulu, HI 96815
Phone 923-3881
Toll Free (800) 367-5170
   Total Units   110
   Area A—Waikiki

Facilities:
100% Air Cond.
Restaurants
Cocktail Lounge
Shops
TV
Parking
Swimming Pool

DIAMOND HEAD BEACH HOTEL
Hotel-Condominium Apts.
2947 Kalakaua Ave.
Honolulu, HI 96815
Phone 922-1928
Toll Free (800) 367-6046
   Total Units   61
   Hotel Units   61
   Area A—Waikiki
   Oceanfront

Facilities:
Parking
TV

DISCOVERY BAY
Condominium Apts. (W)
1778 Ala Moana
Honolulu, HI 96815
Phone 944-8555
   Total Units   665
   Hotel Units   70
   Area A—Waikiki
   One Block from
   Beach

Facilities:
100% Air Cond
Parking
TV
Restaurant
Cocktail Lounge
Swimming Pool
Shops
Maid Service:
  Every 3rd
  Day
Minimum Stay:
  5 Nights

DISCOVERY BAY RESORT
Hotel
1778 Ala Moana Blvd.
Honolulu, HI 96815
Phone 944-5588
   Total Units   665
   Hotel Units   150
   Area A—Waikiki
   1 Block from Beach
   and Lagoon

Facilities:
100% Air Cond.
Parking
Swimming Pool
Restaurant
Cocktail Lounge
Shop
Minimum Stay:
  2 Days

DISCOVERY BAY
Condominium Apts. (W)
1778 Ala Moana
Honolulu, HI 96815

   Total Units   665
   Hotel Units   25
   Area A—Waikiki

Facilities:
100% Air Cond.
Parking
TV
Restaurant
Cocktail Lounge
Swimming Pool
Shop
Maid Service:
  On Request
Minimum Stay
  5 Nights

EDGEWATER HOTEL
Hotel
2168 Kalia Rd.
Honolulu, HI 96815
Phone 922-6424
Toll Free (800) 367-5610
   Total Units   175
   Area A—Waikiki

Facilities:
95% Air Cond.
Parking
TV
Restaurants
Cocktail Lounges
Swimming Pool
Shops

EDMUNDS HOTEL APTS.
Apartment Hotel (W)
2411 Ala Wai Blvd.
Honolulu, HI 96815
Phone 923-8381
   Total Units   12
   Area A—Waikiki

Facilities:
TV

444 NAHUA
Condominium Apts. (W)
444 Nahua St.
Honolulu, HI 96815
Phone 923-9458
   Total Units
   Area A—Waikiki
   3 Blocks from
   Beach

Facilities:
100% Air Cond.
Parking
Swimming Pool

FOSTER TOWER
Condominium Apts. (W)
2500 Kalakaua Ave.
Honolulu, HI 96815

   Total Units   6
   Area A—Waikiki

Facilities:
Air Cond.
Parking
TV
Swimming Pool
Maid Service:
  On Request
Minimum Stay:
  5 Nights

FOUR STAR SERVICES OF HAWAII
Vacation Homes
3721 Kanaina St.
Suite 213
Honolulu, HI 96815
Phone 732-1121
   Total Units   12
   Area A—Kahala
   Oceanfront

GO NATIVE-HAWAII
Private Homes
130 Puhili St.
Hilo, HI 96720
Phone 961-2080
   Home Units   25
   Area F

HALE KOA HOTEL
Hotel—For Military Only (W)
2055 Kalia Rd.
Honolulu, HI 96815
Phone 955-0555
Toll Free (800) 367-6027
   Total Units   416
   Area A—Waikiki
   On the Beach

Facilities:
100% Air Cond.
Parking
TV
Restaurants
Cocktail Lounges
Swimming Pool
Tennis Courts
Shops
Meeting Rooms
Maximum Stay:
  30 Days

HALE PUA NUI HOTEL APT.
Apartment Hotel
228 Beach Walk
Honolulu, HI 96815
Phone 923-9693
   Total Units   22
   Area A—Waikiki

Facilities:
Parking
Minimum Stay:
  2 Days
Children:
  12 or older

HALE WAIKIKI APT. HOTEL
Apartment Hotel
2410 Koa Ave.
Honolulu, HI 96815
Phone 923-9012
   Total Units   15
   Area A—Waikiki

Facilities:
Maid Service:
  3 Times
  A Week

HALEKULANI HOTEL
Hotel (W)
2199 Kalia Rd.
Honolulu, HI 96815
Phone 923-2311
Toll Free (800) 545-4000
   Total Units   456
   Area A—Waikiki
   On a Sand Beach

Facilities:
100% Air Cond.
Parking
TV
Restaurants
Cocktail Lounges
Swimming Pool
Shops
Meeting Rooms

HAWAII DYNASTY HOTEL
Hotel (W)
1830 Ala Moana
Honolulu, HI 96815
Phone 955-1111
Toll Free (800) 421-6662
   Total Units   199
   Area A—Waikiki

100% Air Cond.
Parking
TV
Restaurant
Swimming Pool

HAWAIIAN KING
Apartment Hotel (W)
417 Nohonani St.
Honolulu, HI 96815
Phone 922-3894
Toll Free (800) 367-7042
   Total Units   65
   Hotel Units   65
   Area A—Waikiki
   1 Block to Beach

100% Air Cond.
TV
Restaurant
Cocktail Lounge
Swimming Pool
Shops

HAWAIIAN KING HOTEL
Apartment Hotel (W)
417 Nohonani St.
Honolulu, HI 96815
Phone 922-3894
Toll Free (800) 367-7042
   Total Units   67
   Hotel Units   64
   Area A—Waikiki

100% Air Cond.
Swimming Pool
Shop
TV
Cocktail Lounge

HAWAIIAN MONARCH HOTEL
Hotel
444 Niu St.
Honolulu, HI 96815
Phone 949-3911
Toll Free (800) 367-2351
RCA Telex 8367 HMH HR
   Total Units   278
   Hotel Units   278
   Area A—Waikiki

100% Air Cond.
Parking
TV
Restaurants
Cocktail Lounge
Swimming Pool
Shops
Meeting Rooms

HAWAIIAN MONARCH CONDOMINIUM
Condominium Apts. (W)
444 Niu St.
Honolulu, HI 96815
Phone 949-4089
Toll Free (800) 367-7042
   Total Units   424
   Hotel Units   120
   Area A—Waikiki
   2 Blocks to Beach

100% Air Cond.
Parking
TV
Restaurants
Cocktail Lounge
Swimming Pool
Shops
Meeting Room
Maid Service:
   On Request
Minimum Stay:
   3 Days

HAWAIIAN PRINCESS
Condominium Apts.
84-1021 Lahilahi St.
Makaha, HI 96792
Phone 696-6400
   Total Units   124
   Hotel Units   85
   Area D—Makaha
   On Beach

100% Air Cond.
Parking
TV
Swimming Pool
Tennis Court
Shop
Maid Service
   On Request

HAWAIIAN REGENT
Hotel (W)
2552 Kalakaua Ave.
Honolulu, HI 96815
Phone 922-6611
Toll Free (800) 367-5370
   Total Units   1,346
   Area A—Waikiki

100% Air Cond.
Parking
TV
Restaurants
Cocktail Lounges
Swimming Pools
Shops
Meeting Rooms
Tennis Court

HAWAIIANA HOTEL
Hotel (W)
260 Beach Walk
Honolulu, HI 96815
Phone 923-3811
Toll Free (800) 367-5122
   Total Units   95
   Area A—Waikiki

100% Air Cond.
Parking
Swimming Pools

HILTON HAWAIIAN VILLAGE
Hotel (W)
2005 Kalia Rd.
Honolulu, HI 96815
Phone 949-4321
   Total Units   2,612
   Area A—Waikiki
   On the Beach

100% Air Cond.
Parking
TV
Restaurants
Cocktail Lounges
Swimming Pools
Shops
Meeting Rooms

HOLIDAY INN-HONOLULU AIRPORT
Hotel (W)

100% Air Cond.
Parking
TV

3401 Nimitz Hwy.
Honolulu, HI 96819
Phone 836-0661
Toll Free (800) HOLIDAY
   Total Units   309
   Area C—Airport

HOLIDAY INN-WAIKIKI BEACH
Hotel
2570 Kalakaua Ave.
Honolulu, HI 96815
Phone 922-2511
   Total Units   636
   Area A—Waikiki

100% Air Cond.
Parking
TV
Restaurants
Cocktail Lounges
Swimming Pool
Shop
Meeting Rooms

HOLIDAY ISLE HOTEL
Hotel (W)
270 Lewers St.
Honolulu, HI 96815
Phone 923-0777
Toll Free (800) 367-5120
   Total Units   288
   Hotel Units   283
   Area A—Waikiki

100% Air Cond.
Parking
TV
Restaurant
Cocktail Lounge
Swimming Pool
Shops

HOTEL MIRAMAR HAWAII
Hotel (W)
2345 Kuhio Ave.
Honolulu, HI 96815
Phone 922-2077
Toll Free (800) 227-4320
Calif. (800) 622-0847
   Total Units   370
   Area A—Waikiki

100% Air Cond.
Parking
TV
Restaurants
Cocktail Lounges
Swimming Pool
Shops
Meeting Rooms

HYATT REGENCY WAIKIKI
Hotel (W)
2424 Kalakaua Ave.
Honolulu, HI 96815
Phone 922-9292
Toll Free (800) 228-9000
HI (800) 228-9005
   Total Units   1,234
   Area A—Waikiki
   Across Street from
   Beach

100% Air Cond.
Parking
TV
Restaurants
Cocktail Lounges
Swimming Pool
Shops
Meeting Rooms

ILIKAI
Condominium Apts (W)
1777 Ala Moana
Honolulu, HI 96815

   Hotel Units   4
   Area A—Waikiki

100% Air Cond.
Parking
TV
Restaurant
Cocktail Lounge
Swimming Pools
Tennis Courts
Shop
Meeting Room
Maid Service:
   On Request
Minumum Stay:
   5 Nights

IMPERIAL HAWAII RESORT
Condominium Hotel (W)
205 Lewers St.
P.O. Box 88235
Honolulu, HI 96815
Phone 923-2328
   Total Units   290
   Hotel Units   30
   Area A—Waikiki
   50 yds. to Beach

100% Air Cond.
Parking
TV
Restaurant
Cocktail Lounge
Swimming Pool
Shops
Maid Service:
   3 Times
   Per Week

IMPERIAL HAWAII RESORT
Condominium Hotel (W)
205 Lewers St.
P.O. Box B
Honolulu, HI 96815
Phone 926-2781
   Total Units   290
   Hotel Units   40
   Area A—Waikiki
   50 yds. to Beach

100% Air Cond.
Parking
TV
Cocktail Lounge
Cocktail Lounge
Swimming Pool
Shops
Maid Service:
   On Request

ISLAND COLONY HOTEL
Apt. Hotel (W)
445 Seaside Ave.
Honolulu, HI 96815
Phone 923-2345
Toll Free (800) 367-5124
   Total Units   740
   Hotel UNits   529

100% Air Cond.
Parking
TV
Restaurant
Cocktail Lounge
Swimming Pool
Meeting Rooms

   Area A—Waikiki
   2 Blocks from
   Beach

ISLAND COLONY HOTEL
Apt. Hotel (W)
445 Seaside Ave.
Honolulu, HI 96815
Phone 923-2345
   Total Units   740
   Area A—Waikiki
   2 Blocks from
   Beach

100% Air Cond.
Parking
TV
Restaurant
Cocktail Lounge
Swimming Pool
Meeting Rooms

KAHALA HILTON HOTEL
Hotel (W)
5000 Kahala Ave.
Honolulu, HI 96816
Phone 734-2211
Toll Free (800) 367-2525
   Total Units   347
   Area A—Kahala
   On the Beach

100% Air Cond.
Parking
TV
Restaurants
Cocktail Lounges
Swimming Pool
Shops
Meeting Rooms

KAILUANA: KAILUA BEACHFRONT VACATION HOMES
Cottages/3 BR Home
133 Kailuana Pl.
Kailua, HI 96734
Phone 261-3484
   Total Units   2
   Area E—Kailua
   On a Sand Beach

Parking
TV
Minimum Stay:
   5 Days
Maid Service:
   On Request

KUILIMA VACATION CONDOMINIUMS AT TURTLE BAY
Condominium Apts. (W)
Kahuku, HI 96731
Phone 293-2494
   Total Units   366
   Hotel Units   85
   Area E—Kahuku

Parking
TV
Swimming Pool
Golf Course
Tennis Courts
Maid Service:
   On Request
Minimum Stay:
   3 Days

LANILOA LODGE HOTEL
Hotel (W)
55-109 Laniloa St.
Laie, Oahu, HI 96862
Phone 293-9282
   Total Units   46
   Area E—Windward Oahu
   Across Road from Beach
   Next to Polynesian
   Cultural Center

100% Air Cond
Parking
Restaurant
Swimming Pool
Shops
TV

LEALEA HALE
Apartment Hotel
2423 Cleghorn St.
Honolulu, HI 96815
Phone 922-1726
   Total Units   26
   Area A—Waikiki

Partial Air Cond
Parking
Minimum Stay:
   2 Days
Maid Service:
   On Request
TV

LEISURE HERITAGE
Condominium Apts.
311 Ohua St.
Honolulu HI 96815
   Hotel Units   4
   Area A—Waikiki

Air Cond.
Parking
TV
Swimming Pool
Maid Service:
   On Request
Minimum Stay:
   5 Nights

MAILE COURT
Hotel-Condominium Apts. (W)
733 Bishop St., Suite 1600
Honolulu, HI 96813
Phone 523-0411
Toll Free (800) 367-6046
   Total Units   580
   Hotel Units   580
   Area A—Waikiki
   2 Blocks from Beach

Air Cond.
Parking
TV
Swimming Pool
Restaurant
Cocktail Lounge
Shop
Meeting Room

MAKAHA SHORES
Condominium Apts.
84-265 Farrington Hwy.
Makaha, HI 96792
Phone 696-7121
   Hotel Units   88
   Area D—Leeward Oahu
   Beachfront

Parking
TV
Swimming Pool
Minimum Stay:
   7 Days
Maid Service:
   Weekly

MAKAHA VALLEY TOWERS
Condominium Apts. (W)
84-1170 Farrington Hwy.
Makaha, HI 96792
Phone 695-9055
   Total Units   586
   Hotel Units   48
   Area D—Waianae/Makaha
   1 Mile to Beach
Air Cond.
Parking
Swimming Pool
Golf Courses
Maid Service:
  On Request
Minimum Stay:
  7 Days

MALIHINI HOTEL
Apartment Hotel (W)
217 Saratoga Rd.
Honolulu, HI 96815
Phone 923-9644
   Total Units   30
   Hotel Units   29
   Area A—Waikiki
Shop
Elec. Fans

MOANA HOTEL
Hotel (W)
2365 Kalakaua Ave.
Honolulu, HI 96815
Phone 922-3111
Toll Free (800) 325-3535
   Total Units   387
   Area A—Waikiki
   On the Beach
Partial Air Cond.
Parking (Nearby)
Restaurants
Cocktail Lounges
Shops
Meeting Rooms
TV

MOKULEIA BEACH COLONY
Cottages (W)
68-615 Farrington Hwy.
Waialua, HI 96791
Phone 637-9311
Toll Free (800) 367-7042
   Total Units   50
   Hotel Units   30
   Area E—North Shore
   On a Sand Beach
Parking
TV
Swimming Pool
Tennis Court
No Maid Service
Minimum Stay:
  7 Days

MONTE VISTA
Condominium Apts. (W)
320 Liliuokalani
Honolulu, HI 96815

   Hotel Units   4
   Area A—Waikiki
Air Cond
Parking
TV
Maid Service
  On Request
Minimum Stay:
  5 Nights

**NEW OTANI KAIMANA
BEACH HOTEL**
Hotel (W)
2863 Kalakaua Ave
Honolulu, HI 96815
Phone 923-1555
Toll Free (800) 421-8795
Calif. (800) 252-0197
Canada (800) 663-1118
   Total Units   156
   Area A—Waikiki
   On the Beach
100% Air Cond
Parking
TV
Restaurants
Cocktail Lounge
Shops
Meeting Rooms

OUTRIGGER EAST
Hotel
150 Kaiulani Ave.
Honolulu, HI 96815
Phone 922-5353
Toll Free (800) 367-5170
   Total Units   442
   Area A—Waikiki
100% Air Cond
Parking
TV
Restaurants
Cocktail Lounges
Swimming Pool
Shops
Meeting Room

THE OUTRIGGER PRINCE KUHIO
Hotel (W)
2500 Kuhio Ave.
Honolulu, HI 96815
Phone 922-0811
Toll Free (800) 367-5310 US
   Total Units   620
   Area A—Waikiki
   1 Block from Beach
100% Air Cond.
Parking
TV/Clock radios
Restaurants
Cocktail Lounges
Swimming Pool
Shops
Meeting Rooms

OUTRIGGER SURF
Hotel
2280 Kuhio Ave.
Honolulu, HI 96815
Phone 922-5777
Toll Free (800) 367-5170
   Total Units   251
   Area A—Waikiki
100% Air Cond.
Parking
TV
Restaurant
Cocktail Lounge
Swimming Pool

OUTRIGGER WAIKIKI HOTEL
Hotel
2335 Kalakaua Ave.
Honolulu, HI 96815
100% Air Cond.
Parking
TV
Restaurants

Phone 923-0711
Toll Free (800) 367-5170
   Total Units   530
   Area A—Waikiki
Cocktail Lounges
Swimming Pool
Shops
Meeting Room

OUTRIGGER WEST
Hotel
2330 Kuhio Ave.
Honolulu, HI 96815
Phone 922-5022
Toll Free (800) 367-5170
   Total Units   662
   Area A—Waikiki
100% Air Cond.
Parking
TV
Restaurants
Cocktail Lounges
Swimming Pool
Shops

PACIFIC BEACH HOTEL
Hotel (W)
2490 Kalakaua Ave.
Honolulu, HI 96815
Phone 922-1233
Toll Free (800) 367-6060
   Total Units   850
   Area A—Waikiki
100% Air Cond.
Parking
TV
Restaurants
Cocktail Lounges
Swimming Pool
Shops
Tennis Courts

PACIFIC GRAND
Condominium Apts. (W)
747 Amana St.
Honolulu, HI 96814
Phone 955-1531
   Total Units   360
   Hotel Units   75
   Area A—Waikiki
   Three Blocks from
   Ala Moana Beach Park
100% Air Cond.
Parking
TV
Restaurant
Cocktail Lounge
Swimming Pool
Maid Service:
  Every 3rd
  Day

**PACIFIC-HAWAII
BED & BREAKFAST
Private Homes**
19 Kai Nani Place
Kailua, HI 96734
Phone 262-6026
   Area E—Kailua

PACIFIC ISLAND ADVENTURES
Executive Home Rentals
150 Hakamua Ctr., Suite 323
Kailua, HI 96734
Phone 262-2210

PACIFIC MONARCH
Condominium Apts. (W)
142 Ulunui Ave.
Honolulu, HI 96815
Phone 923-9805
Toll Free (800) 367-6046
   Total Units   216
   Area A—Waikiki
   200 yds. to Beach
100% Air Cond.
Parking
TV
Swimming Pool
Cocktail Lounge

PAGODA HOTEL
Hotel (W)
1525 Rycroft St.
Honolulu, HI 96814
Phone 941-6611
Toll Free (800) 528-1234
   Total Units   340
   Area A—Ala Moana
   ½ Mile from Beach
100% Air Cond.
Parking
TV
Restaurants
Cocktail Lounge
Swimming Pools
Meeting Rooms

PARK SHORE HOTEL, THE
Hotel
2586 Kalakaua Ave.
Honolulu, HI 96815
Phone 923-0411
Toll Free (800) 367-2377
Canada (800) 663-1118
   Total Units   227
   Area A—Waikiki
100% Air Cond.
Parking
TV
Cocktail Lounge
Swimming Pool
Shopping Center

"PAT'S AT PUNALUU" CONDO
Condominium Apts. (W)
53-567 Kam Highway
Hauula, HI 96717
Phone 293-8111
   Total Units   136
   Hotel Units   30
   Area E—Windward Oahu
   On the Beach at Punaluu
Parking
TV
Restaurant
Cocktail Lounge
Swimming Pool
Maid Service:
  Twice Weekly
Minimum Stay:
  2 Days

**PLAZA HOTEL-HONOLULU
INTERNATIONAL AIRPORT**
Hotel (W)
3253 N. Nimitz Hwy.
Honolulu, HI 96819
Phone 836-3636
Toll Free (800) 367-2351
   Total Units   268
100% Air Cond.
Parking
TV
Restaurant
Cocktail Lounge
Swimming Pool
Shop
Meeting Rooms

Area C—Airport
8 Miles from
  Waikiki Beach

THE POLYNESIAN PLAZA
Apartments
2131 Kalakaua Ave.
Honolulu, HI 96815
Phone 923-4818
   Total Units   50
   Area A—Waikiki
   Near a Beach
100% Air Cond.
Cocktail Lounges
Swimming Pool
Minimum Stay:
  7 Days

PRINCESS KAIULANI HOTEL
Hotel (W)
120 Kaiulani Ave.
Honolulu, Hi 96815
Phone 922-5811
Toll Free (800) 325-3535
   Total Units   1,156
   Area A—Waikiki
100% Air Cond.
Parking
TV
Restaurants
Cocktail Lounges
Swimming Pool
Shops
Meeting Rooms

**QUALITY INN WAIKIKI-
DIAMOND HEAD**
Hotel
175 Paoakalani Ave.
Honolulu, HI 96815
Phone 922-4671; 922-3861
   Total Units   261
   Area A—Waikiki
   1 Block from Beach
100% Air Cond.
Parking
TV
Restaurant
Cocktail Lounge
Swimming Pools
Shops
Meeting Rooms

QUALITY INN WAIKIKI-PALI
Hotel
175 Paoakalani Ave.
Honolulu, HI 96815
Phone 922-4671; 922-3861
Toll Free (800) 228-5151
   Total Units   190
   Area A—Waikiki
   1 Block from Beach
100% Air Cond.
Parking
TV
Restaurant
Cocktail Lounge
Swimming Pools
Shops
Meeting Rooms

QUEEN KAPIOLANI HOTEL
Hotel (W)
150 Kapahulu Ave.
Honolulu, HI 96815
Phone 922-1941
Toll Free (800) 367-5004
   Total Units   315
   Area A—Waikiki
   ½ Block from Beach
100% Air Cond.
Parking
TV
Restaurant
Cocktail Lounge
Swimming Pool
Shops
Meeting Room

REEF HOTEL
Hotel (W)
2169 Kalia Rd.
Honolulu, HI 96815
Phone 923-3111
Toll Free (800) 367-5610
   Total Units   883
   Area A—Waikiki
   On the Beach
100% Air Cond.
Parking
TV
Restaurants
Cocktail Lounges
Swimming Pool
Shops
Meeting Rooms

REEF LANAIS
Hotel (W)
225 Saratoga Rd.
Honolulu, HI 96815
Phone 923-3881
Toll Free (800) 367-5170
   Total Units   109
   Area A—Waikiki
100% Air Cond.
Parking
Restaurant
Cocktail Lounge
TV

REEF TOWERS
Hotel
227 Lewers St.
Honolulu, HI 96815
Phone 923-3111
Toll Free (800) 367-5610
   Total Units   500
   Area A—Waikiki
95% Air Cond.
Parking
Restaurants
Cocktail Lounges
Swimming Pool
Shops

ROYAL GROVE HOTEL
Apartment Hotel (W)
151 Uluniu Ave.
Honolulu, HI 96815
Phone 923-7691
   Total Units   110
   Area A—Waikiki
Partial Air Cond.
Swimming Pool
TV

ROYAL HAWAIIAN HOTEL
Hotel (W)
2259 Kalakaua Ave.
Honolulu, HI 96815
Phone 923-7311
Toll Free (800) 325-3535
100% Air Cond.
TV
Restaurants
Parking
Cocktail Lounges
Swimming Pool

Total Units
Area A—Waikiki
On the Beach

Shops
Meeting Rooms

ROYAL KUHIO
Condominium Apts. (W)
2240 Kuhio Ave.
Honolulu, HI 96815
Phone 923-2502
Total Units 385
Hotel Units 49
Area A—Waikiki

100% Air Cond.
Parking
TV
Swimming Pool
Meeting Room
Maid Service:
Weekly

ROYAL KUHIO
Condominium Apts. (W)
2240 Kuhio Ave.
Honolulu, HI 96815
Total Units 385
Hotel Units 385
Area A—Waikiki

100% Air Cond.
Parking
Swimming Pool
Meeting Room

ROYAL KUHIO
Condominium Apts.
2240 Kuhio Ave.
Honolulu, HI 96815
Total Units 385
Hotel Units 5
Area A—Waikiki

100% Air Cond.
Parking
Swimming Pool
Maid Service:
On Request
Minimum Stay:
5 Nights

SHERATON MAKAHA RESORT AND COUNTRY CLUB
Hotel-Cottages Type (W)
P.O. Box 896
Waianae, Oahu, HI 96792
Phone 695-9511
Total Units 196
Area D—Leeward Oahu
Less than 1 mile from Beach at Makaha

100% Air Cond.
Parking
Restaurants
TV
Cocktail Lounge
Swimming Pool
Golf Course
Tennis Courts
Shops
Meeting Rooms

SHERATON-WAIKIKI
Hotel (W)
2255 Kalakaua Ave.
Honolulu, HI 96815
Phone 922-4422
Toll Free (800) 325-3535
Total Units 1,852
Area A—Waikiki
On the Beach

100% Air Cond.
Parking
TV
Restaurants
Cocktail Lounges
Swimming Pools
Shops
Meeting Rooms

SHERRY WAIKIKI
Condominium Apts.
334 Lewers St.
Honolulu, HI 96815
Phone 922-2771
Toll Free (800) 241-3848
Total Units 100
Hotel Units 100
Area A—Waikiki

100% Air Cond.
Parking
TV
Swimming Pool

SILVER'S PACIFIC MONARCH
Condominium Apts. (W)
142 Uluniu Ave.
Honolulu, HI 96815
Phone 922-4359
Toll Free (800) 367-2311
Total Units 216
Hotel Units 98
Area A—Waikiki
1 Block from Beach

100% Air Cond.
TV
Parking
Swimming Pool
Shop

SURFRIDER HOTEL
Hotel (W)
2353 Kalakaua Ave.
Honolulu, HI 96815
Phone 922-3111
Toll Free (800) 325-3535
Total Units 430
Area A—Waikiki
On the Beach

100% Air Cond.
Parking (Nearby)
TV
Restaurants
Cocktail Lounges
Shops
Meeting Rooms

TURTLE BAY HILTON AND COUNTRY CLUB
Hotel (W)
P.O. Box 187
Kahuku, HI 96731
Phone 293-8811
Total Units 487
Hotel Units 483
Area E—Windward Oahu
On the Beach at Kuilima Point

100% Air Cond.
Parking
TV
Restaurants
Cocktail Lounge
Swimming Pool
Golf Course
Tennis Courts
Shops
Meeting Rooms

2121 ALA WAI
Condominium Apts. (W)
2121 Ala Wai Blvd.
Honolulu, HI 96815
Hotel Units 3
Area A—Waikiki

VENTURE ISLE HOTEL APTS.
Apartment Hotel (W)
2467 Cleghorn St.
Honolulu, HI 96815
Phone 923-6363
Total Units 10
Area A—Waikiki

WAIKIKI BANYAN
Condominium Apts.
201 Ohua Ave.
Honolulu, HI 96815
Phone 922-0555
Total Units 660
Hotel Units 25
Area A—Waikiki
1 Block from Beach

100% Air Cond.
Parking
TV
Swimming Pool
Tennis Court

WAIKIKI BANYAN
Condominium Apts. (W)
250 Ohua Ave.
Honolulu, HI 96815
Phone 922-0555
Hotel Units 25
Area A—Waikiki

100% Air Cond.
Parking
TV
Swimming Pool
Maid Service:
On Request
Tennis Court
Minimum Stay:
5 Nights

WAIKIKI BEACHCOMBER
Hotel (W)
2300 Kalakaua Ave.
Honolulu, HI 96815
Phone 922-4646
Total Units 498
Area A—Waikiki

100% Air Cond.
Parking
TV
Restaurants
Cocktail Lounges
Swimming Pool
Shops

WAIKIKI CIRCLE HOTEL
Hotel (W)
2464 Kalakaua Ave.
Honolulu, HI 96815
Phone 923-1571
Total Units 100
Area A—Waikiki

100% Air Cond.
Parking
Restaurant
Cocktail Lounge

WAIKIKI GATEWAY HOTEL
Hotel (W)
2070 Kalakaua Ave.
Honolulu, HI 96815
Phone 955-3741
Toll Free (800) 367-5124
Total Units 200
Area A—Waikiki

100% Air Cond.
Parking
TV
Restaurant
Cocktail Lounge
Swimming Pool
Shops

WAIKIKI LANAIS
Condominium Apts.
2452 Tusitala St.
Honolulu, HI 96815
Phone 923-0994
Total Units 120
Area A—Waikiki
1 Block to Beach

100% Air Cond.
Parking
TV
Swimming Pool

WAIKIKI LANAIS
Condominium Apts.
2452 Tusitala St.
Honolulu, HI 96815
Phone 923-0994
Toll Free (800) 367-7042
Total Units 160
Hotel Units 65
Area A—Waikiki
1 Block to Beach

100% Air Cond.
Parking
TV
Swimming Pool
Maid Service:
On Request
Minimum Stay:
3 Days

WAIKIKI LEI APT. HOTEL
Apartment Hotel
241 Kaiulani Ave.
Honolulu, HI 96815
Phone 923-6656; 734-8588
Total Units 20
Hotel Units 10
Area A—Waikiki

100% Air Cond.
Parking
Minimum Stay:
6 Days
No Maid
Service
TV (Opt.)

WAIKIKI PACIFIC ISLE TRAVELODGE
Hotel (W)
1850 Ala Moana Blvd.
Honolulu, HI 96815
Phone 955-1567

100% Air Cond.
Parking
TV
Restaurant
Cocktail Lounges
Swimming Pool

Parking

Toll Free (800) 255-3050
Canada (800) 268-3330
Hawaii (800) 255-6411
Total Units 250
Area A—Waikiki
1 Block from
Hilton Beach

WAIKIKI PARK HEIGHTS
Condominium Apts. (W)
2440 Kuhio Ave.
Honolulu, HI 96815
Hotel Units 8

100% Air Cond.
Parking
TV
Restaurant
Cocktail Lounge
Swimming Pool
Maid Service:
5 Nights

WAIKIKI PLAZA HOTEL
Hotel (W)
2045 Kalakaua Ave.
Honolulu, HI 96815
Phone 955-6363
Toll Free (800) 367-2351
Total Units 247
Hotel Units 247
Area A—Waikiki

Air Cond.
Parking
Swimming Pool
Restaurant
Cocktail Lounge
Shops
Meeting Room

WAIKIKI PRINCE HOTEL
Hotel (W)
2431 Prince Edward St.
Honolulu, HI 96815
Phone 922-1544
Total Units 24
Area A—Waikiki
200 ft. from Beach

100% Air Cond.
Parking
No Maid
Service
TV

WAIKIKI RESORT HOTEL
Hotel (W)
2460 Koa Ave.
Honolulu, HI 96815
Phone 922-4911
Total Units 295
Area A—Waikiki
1 Block from Beach

100% Air Cond.
Parking
TV
Restaurants
Cocktail Lounge
Swimming Pool
Shops
Meeting Room

WAIKIKI SAND VILLA HOTEL
Hotel
2375 Ala Wai Blvd.
Honolulu, HI 96815
Phone 922-4744
Toll Free (800) 367-5072
Total Units 223
Area A—Waikiki
2 Blocks from Beach

100% Air Cond.
Parking
TV
Restaurant
Cocktail Lounge
Swimming Pool

WAIKIKI SHORES APARTMENTS
Apartment Hotel (W)
2161 Kalia Rd.
Honolulu, HI 96815
Phone 923-3283
Total Units 159
Hotel Units 100
Area A—Waikiki
On the Beach

Parking
Minimum Stay:
3 Nights
Maid Service:
Weekly
Children:
12 or older
TV

WAIKIKI SUNSET
Condominium Apts. (W)
229 Paoakalani Ave.
Honolulu, HI 96815
Phone 922-0511
Toll Free (800) 367-5124
Total Units 435
Hotel Units 375
Area A—Waikiki
1 Block to Beach

100% Air Cond.
Parking
TV
Swimming Pool
Snack Bar

WAIKIKI SUNSET
Condominium Apts.
229 Paoakalani Ave.
Honolulu, HI 96815
Total Units 435
Hotel Units 3
Area A—Waikiki
1 Block to Beach

100% Air Cond.
Parking
TV
Swimming Pool

WAIKIKI SUNSET
Condominium Apts. (W)
229 Paoakalani Ave.
Honolulu, HI 96815
Phone 922-0511
Total Units 435
Hotel Units 375
Area A—Waikiki
1 Block to Beach

100% Air Cond.
Parking
TV
Swimming Pool
Snack Bar

WAIKIKI SURF
Hotel
412 Lewers Ave.
Honolulu, HI 96815
Phone 923-7671
Toll Free (800) 367-5170
   Total Units   291
   Area A—Waikiki

100% Air Cond.
Parking
TV
Swimming Pool
Cocktail Lounge
Restaurant

WAIKIKI SURF EAST
Hotel
422 Royal Hawaiian Ave.
Honolulu, HI 96815
Phone 923-7671
Toll Free (800) 367-5170
   Total Units   103
   Area A—Waikiki

100% Air Cond.
Parking
TV
Swimming Pool

WAIKIKI SURF WEST
Hotel
412 Lewers St.
Honolulu, HI 96815
Phone 923-7671
Toll Free (800) 367-5170
   Total Units   110
   Area A—Waikiki

Air Cond.
Parking
TV
Swimming Pool

WAIKIKI SURFSIDE HOTEL
Hotel
2452 Kalakaua Ave.
Honolulu, HI 96815
Phone 923-0266
Toll Free (800) 367-5124
   Total Units   80
   Hotel Units   80
   Area A—Waikiki

100% Air Cond.
TV

WAIKIKI TERRACE APT. HOTEL
Apartment Hotel (W)
339 Royal Hawaiian Ave
Honolulu, HI 96815
Phone 923-3253
   Total Units   24
   Area A—Waikiki

Partial Air Cond.
Minimum Stay:
   2 Days
Parking
Maid Service:
   Weekly
TV Rental

WAIKIKI TOWER
(OF THE REEF HOTEL)
Hotel (W)
200 Lewers St.
Honolulu, HI 96815
Phone 922-6424
Toll Free (800) 367-5610
   Total Units   440
   Area A—Waikiki

100% Air Cond.
Parking
Restaurants
Cocktail Lounges
Swimming Pool
Shops
TV

WAIKIKI VILLAGE
Hotel
240 Lewers St.
Honolulu, HI 96815
Phone 923-3881
Toll Free (800) 367-5170
   Total Units   439
   Area A—Waikiki

100% Air Cond.
Parking
Restaurants
Cocktail Lounges
TV

WAIKIKIAN HOTEL
Hotel (W)
1811 Ala Moana Blvd.
Honolulu, HI 96815
Phone 949-5331
Toll Free (800) 367-5124
   Total Units   135
   Area A—Waikiki
   On the Beach

Partial Air Cond.
Parking
Restaurant
Cocktail Lounge
Swimming Pool
Shops
TV—Rentals

WAIPIOLANI HOTEL
Hotel Apt. (W)
95-023 Waihau St.
Wahiawa, HI 96786
Phone 625-1828
   Total Units   40
   Hotel Units   19
   Area D—Waipio Valley

Parking
TV
Restaurants
Shops

WESTIN ILIKAI, THE
Hotel (W)
1777 Ala Moana
Honolulu, HI 96815
Phone 949-3811
Toll Free (800) 228-3000
   Total Units   750
   Area A—Waikiki
   On the Beach

100% Air Cond.
Parking
TV
Restaurants
Cocktail Lounges
Swimming Pools
Tennis Courts
Shops
Meeting Rooms

WHITE SANDS WAIKIKI RESORT
Hotel (W)
431 Nohonani St.

100% Air Cond.
Parking
Swimming Pool

Honolulu, HI 96815
Phone 923-7336
   Total Units   78
   Area A—Waikiki

TV

HAWAII

ALII VILLAS
Condominium Apts.
75-6016 Alii Drive
Kailua-Kona, HI 96740
Phone 538-7145
Toll Free (800) 367-5205
   Total Units   125
   Hotel Units   6
   Area J—Kona
   Oceanfront

Parking
TV
Swimming Pool
Maid Service:
   Weekly
Minimum Stay:
   2 Days

COUNTRY CLUB VILLA
Condominium Apts.(W)
Kailua-Kona, HI 96740

   Hotel Units   3
   Area J
   On the Golf Course

Parking
TV
Swimming Pool
Tennis Court
Golf Course
Maid Service:
   On Request
Minimum Stay:
   5 Nights

DOLPHIN BAY HOTEL
Hotel (W)
333 Iliahi St.
Hilo, HI 96720
Phone 935-1466
   Total Units   18
   Area F
   Near Hilo Bay

Parking
TV (On Request)

GO NATIVE-HAWAII
Private Homes
130 Puhili St.
Hilo, HI 96720
Phone 961-2080
   Home Units   25
   Area F

HALE KAI O KONA
Condominium Apts. (W)
Alii Drive
Kailua-Kona, HI 96740
Phone
   Total Units   9
   Hotel Units   3
   Area J

Parking
TV
Minimum Stay:
   5 Nights

HALE KONA KAI
Condominium Apts. (W)
75-5870 Kahakai Rd.
Kailua-Kona, HI 96740
Phone 329-2155
   Total Units   39
   Hotel Units   24
   Area J—Kona
   Oceanfront

100% Air Cond.
Parking
TV
Swimming Pool
Maid Service:
   On Request
Minimum Stay:
   3 Days

HILO BAY HOTEL
Hotel (W)
87 Banyan Dr.
Hilo, HI 96720
Phone 935-0861
Toll Free

100% Air Cond.
Parking
TV
Restaurant
Cocktail Lounge
Swimming Pool

Hawaii (800) 442-5841
USA (800) 367-5102
   Total Units   150
   Area F
   On Hilo Bay

Shops

HILO HAWAIIAN HOTEL
Hotel (W)
71 Banyan Drive
Hilo, HI 96720
Phone 935-9361
Toll Free (800) 367-5004
   Total Units   290
   Area F
   On Hilo Bay

100% Air Cond.
Parking
TV
Restaurant
Cocktail Lounge
Swimming Pool
Shops
Meeting Room

HILO HUKILAU HOTEL
Hotel
126 Banyan Drive
Hilo, HI 96720
   Total Units   145
   Area F—Hilo
   Bayfront

Ceiling Fans
Parking
TV
Restaurant
Cocktail Lounge
Swimming Pool
Meeting Rooms

HILO LAGOON
Hotel
101 Aupuni St.
Hilo, HI 96720
Phone 536-4086
   (Direct from Oahu)
      935-9311 (Hilo)
   Total Units   120
   Hotel Units   115
   Area F

Partial Air Cond.
Parking
TV
Restaurant
Cocktail Lounge
Swimming Pool
Shops
Meeting Rooms

HOTEL KING KAMEHAMEHA
Hotel (W)
75-5660 Palani Rd.
Kailua-Kona, HI 96740
Phone 329-2911
   Total Units   460
   Area J
   On the Beach at
   Kailua

100% Air Cond.
Parking
TV
Restaurants
Cocktail Lounges
Swimming Pool
Tennis Courts
Shops
Meeting Rooms

KEAUHOU BEACH SUMMIT
HOTEL
Hotel (W)
78-6740 Alii Dr.
Kailua-Kona, HI 96740
Phone 322-3441
   Total Units   317
   Area J
   On Kahaluu Bay

100% Air Cond.
Parking
TV
Restaurants
Cocktail Lounges
Swimming Pool
Tennis Courts
Shops
Meeting Rooms

KEAUHOU RESORT
CONDOMINIUMS
Condominium Townhouses (W)
78-7039 Kamehameha III Rd.
Kailua-Kona, HI 96740
Phone 322-9122
Toll Free (800) 367-5286
         (800) 367-5287
   Total Units   47
   Hotel Units   39
   Area J—Kona Coast
   3 Minutes to Sandy Beach

Parking
TV
Swimming Pools
Maid Service:
   Weekly
Minimum Stay:
   5 Days
Golf Course

KONA BALI KAI
Condominium Apts. (W)
76-6246 Alii Dr.
Kailua-Kona, HI 96740
Phone 329-9381
Toll Free
   US (800) 243-2992
   Calif. (800) 272-3282
   Total Units   155
   Hotel Units   99
   Area J
   On Holualoa Bay

Partial Air Cond.
Parking
TV
Swimming Pool

KONA BAY HOTEL
Hotel (W)
75-5739 Alii Dr.
Kailua-Kona, HI 96740
Phone 329-1393
Toll Free
   Hawaii (800) 442-5841
   USA (800) 367-5102
   Total Units   125
   Area J
   Across from Kona Bay

100% Air Cond.
Parking
TV
Swimming Pool
Restaurant
Cocktail Lounge
Shops

KONA BY THE SEA
Condominium Apts.
75-6106 Alii Dr.
Phone 329-0200
   Total Units   30
   Area J
   Kailua Bay

100% Air Cond.
TV
Swimming Pools

KONA HILTON BEACH &
TENNIS RESORT
Hotel
Kailua-Kona, HI 96740
Phone 329-3111
Toll Free in Hawaii
  (800) 452-4411/12
   Total Units
   Area J
   On Kailua Bay

100% Air Cond.
Parking
TV
Restaurants
Cocktail Lounges
Swimming Pool
Tennis Courts
Shops
Meeting Rooms

KONA HUKILAU HOTEL
Hotel
75-5646 Palani Rd.
Kailua-Kona, HI 96740
Phone 367-7000
   Total Units   100
   Area J—Kona
   Bayfront

90% Air Cond.
Parking
TV
Swimming Pools
Shopping Plaza
Restaurant
Cocktail Lounge
Meeting Rooms

KONA ISLANDER INN
Condominium Apts. (W)
75-5776 Kuakini Hwy.
Kailua-Kona, HI 96740
Phone 329-3181
Toll Free (800) 367-5124
   Total Units   144
   Hotel Units   85
   Area J
   Kailua Bay

100% Air Cond.
Parking
TV
Swimming Pool

KONA ISLANDER INN
Condominium Apts. (W)
75-5776 Kuakini Hwy.
Kailua-Kona, HI 96740
Phone 329-3181
   Total Units   100
   Area J
   Kailua Bay

100% Air Cond.
Parking
TV

KONA LAGOON HOTEL
Hotel
78-6780 Alii Drive
Keauhou-Kona, HI 96740
Phone 322-2727
Toll Free (800) 367-5004
   Total Units   454
   Area J—Keauhou-Kona
   On the Beach

100% Air. Cond.
Parking
TV
Restaurant
Cocktail Lounge
Swimming Pool
Tennis Courts
Shops
Meeting Room

KONA MAGIC SANDS
Condominium Apts.
77-6452 Alii Dr.
Kailua-Kona, HI 96740
Phone 329-9177
   Total Units   37
   Hotel Units   26
   Area J
   On the Beach at
    Kailua-Kona

Parking
TV
Restaurants
Cocktail Lounge
Swimming Pool
Minimum Stay:
  4 Days
Maid Service:
  On Request

KONA MANSIONS
Condominium Apts. (W)
Alii Drive
Kailua-Kona, HI 96740

   Hotel Units   3
   Area J

Parking
TV
Swimming Pool
Maid Service:
  On Request
Minimum Stay:
  5 Nights

KONA SEASIDE HOTEL
75-5646 Palani Road
Kailua-Kona, HI 96740
Phone 329-1655
   Total Units   125
   Area J—Kona
   Bayfront

100% Air Cond.
Parking
TV
Restaurant
Cocktail Lounge
Swimming Pools
Shopping Plaza
Meeting Rooms

KONA SURF
Hotel (W)
Keauhou-Kona, HI 96740
Phone 322-3411
Toll Free (800) 367-5360

100% Air Cond.
Parking
TV
Restaurants
Cocktail Lounges

   Total Units   537
   Area J
   On Keauhou Bay

Swimming Pools
Golf Course
Tennis Courts
Shops
Meeting Rooms

KONA TIKI HOTEL
Hotel
P.O. Box 1567
Kailua-Kona, HI 96740
Phone 329-1425
   Total Units   17
   Hotel Units   15
   Area J
   On the Beach at Kailua Bay

Parking
Swimming Pool
100% Air Cooled
Minimum Stay:
  3 Days

KONA VILLAGE RESORT
Individual Cottages (W)
P.O. Box 1299
Kailua-Kona, HI 96740
Phone 325-5555
Toll Free (800) 367-5290
   Total Units   95
   Area J
   On the Beach at
    Kaupulehu

Parking
Restaurant
Cocktail Lounge
Swimming Pool
Tennis Courts
Shop
Meeting Room

KONA WHITE SANDS APT. HOTEL
Apts.-Hotel
P.O. Box 594
Kailua-Kona, HI 96745
Phone 329-3210
   Total Units   7
   Area J
   Across Street from Beach
    at White Sands

Parking
TV

MANAGO HOTEL
Hotel (W)
P.O. Box 145
Capt. Cook-Kona, HI 96704
Phone 323-2642
   Total Units   64
   Area J

Parking
Restaurant
Cocktail Lounge

MAUNA KEA BEACH HOTEL
Hotel (W)
P.O. Box 218
Kamuela, HI 96743
Phone 882-7222
Toll Free (800) 228-3000
   Total Units   310
   Area G
   On the Kohala Coast

100% Air Cond.
Parking
Restaurants
Cocktail Lounge
Swimming Pool
Golf Course
Tennis Courts
Shops
Meeting Rooms

MAUNA LANI BAY HOTEL
Hotel (W)
P.O. Box 4000
Kawaihae, HI 96743
Phone 885-6622
Toll Free (800) 367-2323
Hawaii (800) 992-7987
   Total Units   351
   Area G—S. Kohala Coast
   On a Sand Beach

100% Air Cond.
Parking
TV
Restaurants
Cocktail Lounges
Swimming Pool
Tennis Courts
Golf Course
Shops
Meeting Rooms

NANILOA SURF
Hotel (W)
93 Banyan Dr.
Hilo, HI 96720
Phone 935-0831
Toll Free (800) 367-5360
   Total Units   386
   Area F
   On Hilo Bay

100% Air Cond.
Parking
TV
Restaurants
Cocktail Lounges
Swimming Pool
Tennis Courts
Shops
Meeting Rooms

PARKER RANCH LODGE
Hotel (W)
P.O. Box 458
Kamuela, HI 96743
Phone 885-4100
   Total Units   10
   Area G—Kamuela
   Meadow and Mountain

Parking
Meeting Room

PUAKO BEACH APARTMENTS
Condominium Apts. (W)
3 Puako Beach Dr.
Kamuela, HI 96743
Phone 882-7711
   Total Units   38
   Hotel Units   19

Parking
TV
Swimming Pool
Maid Service:
  Twice a Week

Area G
Across Street from
  Beach at Puako

ROYAL SEA-CLIFF CLUB
Condominium Apts.
75-6040 Alii Drive
Kailua-Kona, HI 96740
Phone 329-8021
Toll Free (800) 331-8067
   Total Units   154
   Hotel Units   61
   Area J—Kona
   Oceanfront

100% Air Cond.
Parking
TV
Swimming Pools
Tennis Court
Maid Service:
  Every
  Other Day

SEAMOUNTAIN AT PUNALU'U
Condominium Cott. Apts. (W)
P.O. Box 70
Pahala, HI 96777
Phone 928-8301
   Total Units   76
   Hotel Units   33
   Area H—Punalu'u
   On Oceanfront Near
    Black Sand Beach
    at Punalu'u

Parking
TV
Restaurant
Cocktail Lounge
Swimming Pool
Tennis Courts
Golf Course
Meeting Rooms
Maid Service:
  Weekly
Minimum Stay:
  2 Days

SEA VILLAGE
Condominium Apts.
75-6002 Alii Dr.
Kailua-Kona, HI 96740
Phone 329-1000
Toll Free (800) 367-5205
   Total Units   131
   Hotel Units   72
   Area J—Kailua-Kona
   On Oceanfront

Parking
TV
Swimming Pool
Tennis Court
Maid Service:
  Weekly
Minimum Stay:
  3 Days

SHERATON ROYAL WAIKOLOA
Hotel
P.O. Box 5000
Waikoloa, HI 96743
Phone 885-6789
Toll Free US (800) 325-3535
Canada (800) 268-9330
   Total Units   543
   Area G
   On a Sand Beach

100% Air Cond.
Parking
TV
Restaurants
Cocktail Lounges
Swimming Pool
Tennis Courts
Golf Course
Shops
Meeting Room

SHIRAKAWA MOTEL
Motel (W)
P.O. Box 467
Naalehu, HI 96722
Phone 929-7462
   Total Units   13
   Area H

Parking

VOLCANO HOUSE
Hotel (W)
Hawaii Volcanoes Nat'l Park
  HI 96718
Phone 967-7321
Toll Free (800) 325-3535
  (HNL) (800)
   Total Units   37
   Area I

Parking
Restaurant
Cocktail Lounge
Gift Shop
Meeting Room

WAIKOLOA VILLAS
Condominium Apts.
P.O. Box 3066
Waikoloa Village Station
Kamuela, HI 96743
Phone 883-9588
Toll Free (800) 367-7042
   Total Units   104
   Hotel Units   40
   Area G—South Kohala

Parking
TV
Swimming Pools
Golf Course
Meeting Room
Maid Service:
  Every
  3rd Day
Minimum Stay:
  3 Days

WHITE SANDS VILLAGE
Condominium Apts. (W)
74-6469 Alii Drive
Kailua-Kona, HI 96740

   Hotel Units   6
   Area J
   Across Street
    from Beach

100% Air Cond.
Parking
TV
Swimming Pool
Tennis Courts
Maid Service:
  On Request
Minimum Stay:
  5 Nights

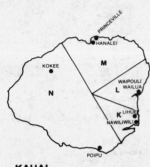

KAUAI

ALII KAI I
Condominium Apts.
P.O. Box 1109
Hanalei, Kauai, HI 96714
Phone 826-9833
  Total Units   59
  Hotel Units   5
  Area M—Princeville
  Oceanfront

Parking
TV
Swimming Pool
Golf Course
Tennis Courts
Maid Service:
  On Request
Minimum Stay:
  3 Days

ALII KAI II HANALEI
Condominium Apts. (W)
P.O. Box 3292
Lihue, Kauai, HI 96766
Phone 826-9988
  Total Units   56
  Hotel Units   56
  Area M
  On Hanalei Bluff

Parking
TV
Restaurant
Cocktail Lounge
Swimming Pool
Tennis Court
Golf Course
Shop
Maid Service:
  On Request
Minimum Stay:
  3 Days

AVERY HOME
Home
P.O. Box 1109
Hanalei, Kauai, HI 96714
Phone 826-9833
  Total Unit   1
  Hotel Unit   1
  Area M—Hanalei
  A Sand Beach
  Oceanfront
  Bay

Parking
Maid Service:
  On Request
Minimum Stay:
  3 Days

CLIFFS
Condominium Apts.
P.O. Box 1109
Hanalei, Kauai, HI 96714
Phone 826-9833
  Total Units   204
  Hotel Units   5
  Area M—Princeville
  Oceanfront

Parking
TV
Swimming Pool
Meeting Room
Golf Course
Tennis Courts
Maid Service:
  On Request
Minimum Stay:
  3 Days

CLIFFS AT PRINCEVILLE, THE
Apartment Hotel (W)
P.O. Box 1005
Hanalei, Kauai, HI 96714
Phone 826-6219
  Total Units   202
  Hotel Units   80
  Area M
  Oceanfront

Parking
TV
Restaurants
Cocktail Lounges
Swimming Pool
Tennis Court
Golf Course
Shop
Meeting Room

COCO PALMS RESORT HOTEL
Hotel (W)
P.O. Box 631
Lihue, Kauai, HI 96766
Phone 822-4921
  Total Units   416
  Area L
  Across Road from
    Wailua Beach

Partial Air Cond.
Parking
TV
Restaurants
Cocktail Lounge
Swimming Pools
Tennis Courts
Shops
Meeting Room

FAYE HOME
Home
P.O. Box 1109
Hanalei, Kauai, HI 96714
Phone 826-9833

Parking
Maid Service:
  On Request
Minimum Stay:
  3 Days

  Total Unit   1
  Hotel Units   2
  Area M—Hanalei
  A Sand Beach
  Oceanfront
  Bay

GARDEN ISLE BEACH COTTAGES
Apartment-Cottages
R.R. 1, Box 355
Koloa, Kauai, HI 96756
Phone 742-6717
  Total Units   9
  Area N
  On Lagoon

Parking
Minimum Stay:
  2 Days

GO NATIVE-HAWAII
Private Homes
130 Puhili St.
Hilo, HI 96720
Phone 961-2080
  Home Units   25
  Area F

HALE MOI
Condominium Apts.
P.O. Box 1109
Hanalei, Kauai, HI 96714
Phone 826-9833
  Total Units   40
  Hotel Units   1
  Area M—Princeville

Parking
Maid Service:
  On Request
Minimum Stay:
  3 Days

HALE PUMEHANA
Motel
P.O. Box 1828
Lihue, Kauai, HI 96766
Phone 245-2106; 245-6151
  Total Units   17
  Area K

Parking
Shop

HANALEI BAY RESORT
Hotel
P.O. Box 220
Hanalei, Kauai, HI 96714
Phone 826-6522
  Total Units   280
  Hotel Units   160
  Area M—Hanalei
  Bay

Parking
Swimming Pool
Restaurant
Cocktail Lounge
Shop
Meeting Room
Golf Course
Tennis Court
Minimum Stay:
  2 Days

HANALEI BAY RESORT
Hotel
P.O. Box 1109
Hanalei, Kauai, HI 96714
Phone 826-9833
  Total Units   124
  Hotel Units   5
  Area M—Princeville
  A Sand Beach
  Oceanfront

Parking
TV
Swimming Pools
Restaurant
Cocktail Lounge
Shop
Meeting Room
Golf Course
Tennis Courts
Maid Service:
  On Request
Minimum Stay:
  3 Days

HANALEI BAY RESORT
Condominium Apts. (W)
P.O. Box 220
Hanalei, Kauai, HI 96714
Phone 826-6522
  Total Units   200
  Hotel Units   4
  Area M
  Near Hanalei Bay

Parking
TV
Restaurant
Cocktail Lounge
Swimming Pool
Tennis Courts
Golf Course
Shops
Meeting Room
Maid Service:
  On Request
Minimum Stay:
  5 Nights

HANALEI COLONY RESORT
Condominium Apts. (W)
P.O. Box 206
Hanalei, Kauai, HI 96714
Phone 826-6235
Toll Free (800) 421-0767
  Total Units   49
  Area M
  On the Beach at Haena

Parking
Restaurant
Cocktail Lounge
Swimming Pool
Minimum Stay:
  3 Days
Maid Service:
  Every 3rd Day

ISLANDER ON THE BEACH
Hotel
484 Kuhio Hwy.
Kapaa, Kauai, HI 96746

100% Air Cond.
Parking
Swimming Pool

Phone 822-7417
  Total Units   151
  Area L
  On the Beach

KA' EO KAI
Condominium Apts.
P.O. Box 3099
Princeville Contract Station
Princeville, Kauai, HI 96722
  Total Units   64
  Hotel Units   44
  Area M—Princeville
  ¼ Mile from Anini
    Beach

Parking
TV
Swimming Pool
Golf Course
Maid Service:
  On Request
Minimum Stay:

KA' EO KAI
Condominium Apts.
P.O. Box 1109
Hanalei, Kauai, HI 96714
Phone 826-9833
  Total Units   64
  Hotel Units   3
  Area M—Princeville
  ¼ Mile from Anini
    Beach

Parking
TV
Swimming Pool
Golf Course
Maid Service:
  On Request
Minimum Stay:
  3 Days

KAHA LANI
Condominium Apts.
4460 Nehe Road
Wailua, Kauai, HI
Phone 822-9331
  Total Units   74
  Hotel Units   50
  Area L
  On the Beach

100% Air Cond.
Parking
TV
Swimming Pool
Tennis Court
Maid Service:
  Every 2nd Day

KAMAHANA
Condominium Apts.
P.O. Box 1109
Hanalei, Kauai, HI 96714
Phone 826-9833
  Total Units   30
  Hotel Units   4
  Area M—Princeville
  Oceanfront

Parking
TV
Swimming Pool
Golf Course
Maid Service:
  On Request
Minimum Stay:
  3 Days

KAPAA SANDS
Condominium Apts. (W)
P.O. Box 3292
Lihue, Kauai, HI 96766
Phone 822-4901
  Total Units   24
  Hotel Units   22
  Area L
  Oceanfront at Wailua

Parking
TV
Restaurant
Cocktail Lounge
Swimming Pool
Tennis Court
Golf Course
Shop
Maid Service:
  On Request
Minimum Stay:
  3 Days

KAPAA SHORE
Condominium Apts.
4-0900 Kuhio Hwy.
Kapaa, Kauai, HI 96746
Phone 822-3055
  Total Units   81
  Hotel Units   30
  Area L
  Oceanfront

Partial Air Cond.
Parking
TV
Swimming Pool
Tennis Court
Maid Service:
  Every 3rd Day

KAPAA SHORES
Condominium Apts. (W)
40-900 Kuhio Hwy.
Kapaa, Kauai, HI 96746
Phone 822-3055
  Total Units
  Hotel Units   3
  Area L
  On Beach

Parking
TV
Swimming Pool
Tennis Court
Maid Service:
  On Request
Minimum Stay:
  5 Nights

KAUAI BEACHBOY
Hotel (W)
Waipouli Beach
Kapaa, Kauai, HI 96746
Phone 822-3441
  Total Units   243
  Area L
  On the Beach at
    Waipouli

100% Air Cond.
Parking
TV
Restaurant
Cocktail Lounge
Swimming Pool
Tennis Court
Shops
Meeting Room

KAUAI BEACH VILLAS
Hotel-Condo. Apts. (W)
4330 Kauai Beach Rd.
Lihue, Kauai, HI 96766
Phone 245-7711

100% Air Cond.
Parking
TV
Swimming Pool
Restaurant

Toll Free (800) 367-5124
Total Units — 150
Hotel Units — 100
Area K—Lihue
A Sand Beach
Oceanfront
Shop / Tennis Courts

KAUAI RESORT HOTEL
Hotel (W)
3-5920 Kuhio Hwy.
Kapaa, Kauai, HI 96746
Phone 245-3931
Toll Free (800) 367-5004
Total Units — 242
Area L
200 yds from Beach at Wailua
100% Air Cond. / Parking / TV / Restaurant / Cocktail Lounge / Swimming Pool / Shops / Meeting Rooms

KAUAI SANDS HOTEL
Hotel
420 Papaloa Road
Coconut Plantation
Wailua, Kauai, HI 96746
Phone 822-4951
Total Units — 200
100% Air Cond. / Parking / TV / Restaurant / Cocktail Lounge / Swimming Pool / Shop / Meeting Rooms

KAUAI SURF
Hotel
P.O. Box 1729
Lihue, Kauai, HI 96766
Phone 245-3631
Toll Free (800) 367-5360
Total Units — 552
Area K
On the Beach at Kalapaki
100% Air Cond. / Parking / TV / Restaurants / Cocktail Lounge / Swimming Pool / Golf Course / Tennis Courts / Shops / Meeting Rooms

KIAHUNA BEACHSIDE
Condominium Apts. (W)
P.O. Box 368
Koloa, Kauai, HI 96756
Phone 742-7262
Total Units — 333
Hotel Units — 50
Area N
On the Beach
Parking / Restaurant / Cocktail Lounge / Swimming Pool / Tennis Court / Golf Course / Shop / Maid Service: Every 2nd Day / Minimum Stay: 3 Nights

KIAHUNA PLANTATION
Hotel
R.R. 1 73
Koloa, Kauai, HI 96756
Phone 748-6411
Total Units — 333
Hotel Units — 230
Area N—Koloa
A Sand Beach
Parking / Swimming Pool / Cocktail Lounge / Cocktail Lounge / Meeting Room / Golf Course / Tennis Court

KIAHUNA PLANTATION
Condominium Apts. (W)
R.R. 1 Box 73
Koloa, Kauai, HI 96756
Phone 742-6411
Total Units — 333
Hotel Units — 25
Area N
On Poipu Beach
Parking / Restaurant / Cocktail Lounge / Swimming Pool / Tennis Court / Golf Course / Shop / Meeting Room / Maid Service: 3 Times Weekly / Minimum Stay: 5 Nights

KOKEE LODGE
Cabins
P.O. Box 819
Waimea, Kauai, HI 96796
Phone 335-6061
Total Units — 12
Area N
Parking Cabin / Restaurant / Cocktail Lounge / Shop / No Maid Service

LAE NANI
Condominium Apts. (W)
410 Papaloa Rd.
Kapaa, Kauai, HI 96746
Phone 822-4938
Toll Free (800) 367-6046
Total Units — 84
Area L
On the Beach at Wailua
Parking / TV / Swimming Pool / Tennis Court

LAE NANI
410 Papaloa Road
Kapaa, Kauai, HI 96746
Parking / TV / Swimming Pool

Total Units — 87
Hotel Units — 6
Area L
On the Beach

MAKAI CLUB COTTAGES & CONDOMINIUMS at Princeville
Condominiums & Cott.
P.O. Box 121
Hanalei, Kauai, HI 96714
Phone 826-6561
Toll Free (800) 367-7090
Total Units — 57
Hotel Units — 40
Area M—Princeville
Above the Valley
Partial Air Cond. / Parking / TV / Restaurants / Cocktail Lounges / Swimming Pool / Tennis Courts / Golf Course / Shops / Meeting Rooms

MAUNA KAI
Condominium Apts.
P.O. Box 1109
Hanalei, Kauai, HI 96714
Phone 826-9833
Total Units — 26
Hotel Units — 2
Area M—Princeville
¼ Mile from Anini Beach
Parking / TV / Swimming Pool / Golf Course / Maid Service: On Request / Minimum Stay: 3 Days

NIHI KAI VILLAS
Condominium Apts.
1870 Hoone Road, RRI
Koloa, Kauai, HI 96756
Phone 742-6458
Toll Free (800) 367-5314
Total Units — 70
Hotel Units — 35
Area N—Poipu
200 yds. to Beach
Parking / TV / Swimming Pool / Tennis Court / Maid Service: Every Other Day

OCEAN VIEW MOTEL
Motel
3445 Wilcox Rd.
Lihue, Kauai, HI 96766
Phone 245-6345
Total Units — 21
Area K 2 Blocks from Kalapaki Beach
Parking / Refrigerators

PALI KE KUA at Princeville
Condominium Apts. (W)
P.O. Box 899
Hanalei, Kauai, HI 96714
Phone 826-9066
Toll Free (800) 367-7042
Total Units — 99
Hotel Units — 60
Area M—Princeville
Oceanfront
Parking / TV / Restaurant / Swimming Pool / Golf Course

PALI KE KUA
P.O. Box 1109
Hanalei, Kauai, HI 96714
Honolulu, HI 96714
Phone 826-9833
Total Units — 98
Hotel Units — 7
Area M—Princeville
A Sand Beach
Oceanfront
Parking / TV / Swimming Pool / Restaurant / Cocktail Lounge / Golf Course / Maid Service: On Request / Minimum Stay: 3 Days

PALIULI COTTAGES
Cottages
P.O. Box 351
Hanalei, Kauai, HI 96714
Phone 826-6264
Total Units — 8
Area M—Princeville
Near Hanalei Beach
Parking / Restaurants / Cocktail Lounge / Swimming Pools / Tennis Court / Golf Course / Shop / TV / Minimum Stay: 3 Days

PANIOLO
Condominium Apts.
P.O. Box 1109
Hanalei, Kauai, HI 96714
Phone 826-9833
Total Units — 26
Hotel Units — 3
Area M—Princeville
¼ Mile from Anini Beach
Parking / Swimming Pool / Golf Course / Maid Service: On Request / Minimum Stay: 3 Days

---

PLANTATION HALE
Condominium Apts. (W)
484 Kuhio Hwy.
Kapaa, Kauai, HI 96746
Phone 822-4941
Toll Free (800) 367-6046
Total Units — 160
Hotel Units — 155
Area K—Kapaa
In Coconut Plantation
100% Air Cond. / Parking / TV / Restaurants / Cocktail Lounges / Swimming Pool / Shops

POIPU BEACH HOTEL
Hotel (W)
Koloa, Kauai, HI 96756
Phone 742-1681
Toll Free US (800) 227-4700
CA (800) 622-0838
Total Units — 138
Area N
On the Beach at Poipu
100% Air Cond. / Parking / TV / Restaurants / Cocktail Lounges / Swimming Pool / Tennis Courts / Shops

POIPU EXECUTIVE BEACH RENTALS
Condo. Apts.-Cott.
P.O. Box 996
Koloa, Kauai, HI 96756
Phone 742-1243
Total Units — 12
Hotel Units — 12
Area N—Poipu
TV / Swimming Pools / Tennis Court / Maid Service: On Request

POIPU KAI
Condominium Apts. (W)
R.R. 1. Box 173
Koloa, Kauai, HI 96756
Phone 742-6464
Toll Free (800) 367-6046
(800) 423-2922
Calif. (800) 272-3282
Total Units — 240
Hotel Units — 100
Area N—Poipu
On a Sand Beach
Parking / TV / Restaurant / Cocktail Lounge / Swimming Pools / Tennis Courts / Meeting Room

POIPU KAPILI
Condominium Apts
R.R. 1. Box 272
Koloa, Kauai, HI 96756
Phone 742-6449
Total Units — 60
Hotel Units — 25
Area N—Poipu
Oceanfront
Parking / Swimming Pool / Tennis Court / Minimum Stay: 2 Days

POIPU SHORES RESORT
Condominium Apts (W)
RRI Box 95
Koloa, Kauai, HI 96756
Phone 742-6522
Toll Free (800) 367-5686 87
Total Units — 38
Area N—Poipu
Parking / TV / Cocktail Lounge / Swimming Pool / Maid Service: Once Weekly / Minimum Stay: 3 Days

PONO KAI
Condominium Apts.
1250 Kuhio Hwy.
Kapaa, Kauai, HI 96746
Phone 822-9831
Toll Free (800) 367-5124
Total Units — 217
Hotel Units — 74
Area L—Kapaa
On the Beach
Parking / TV / Swimming Pool / Tennis Courts

PONO KAI
Condominium Apts.
P.O. Box 310
1250 Kuhio Hwy.
Kapaa, Kauai, HI 96746
Phone 822-9831
Total Units — 217
Hotel Units — 74
Area L—Kapaa
On the Beach
Parking / TV / Swimming Pool / Tennis Courts

PRINCEVILLE MAUNA KAI
P.O. Box 3292
Lihue, Kauai, HI 96766
Phone 826-6855
Total Units — 46
Hotel Units — 46
Parking / TV / Restaurant / Swimming Pool / Tennis Court / Golf Course

Area M
On Hanalei Bluff

PUAMANA
Condominium Apts.
P.O. Box 1109
Hanalei, Kauai, HI 96714
Phone 826-9833
Total Units 98
Hotel Units 22
Area M—Princeville
¼ Mile from Anini
Beach

Parking
TV
Swimming Pool
Meeting Room
Golf Course
Maid Service:
On Request
Minimum Stay:
3 Days

PU'U PO'A
at Princeville
Condominium Apts.
P.O. Box 1185
Hanalei, Kauai, HI 96714
Phone 826-9602
Toll Free (800) 367-7042
Total Units 56
Hotel Units 15
Area M—Hanalei
Oceanfront

Parking
TV
Swimming Pool
Tennis Court
Golf Course
Maid Service:
On Request
Minimum Stay:
3 Days

PU'U PO'A
Condominium Apts.
P.O. Box 1109
Hanalei, Kauai, HI 96714
Phone 826-9833
Total Units 56
Hotel Units 5
Area M—Princeville

Parking
TV
Swimming Pool
Tennis Courts
Maid Service:
On Request
Minimum Stay:
3 Days

SANBORN HOME
Home
P.O. Box 1109
Hanalei, Kauai, HI 96714
Phone 826-9833
Total Unit 1
Area M—Princeville
A Sand Beach
Oceanfront
Bay

Parking
TV
Maid Service:
On Request
Minimum Stay:
3 Days

SANDPIPER VILLAGE
Condominium Apts.
P.O. Box 460
Princeville, Kauai, Hi 96714
Phone 826-9613
Toll Free (800) 367-5314
Total Units 74
Hotel Units 18
Area M
2 Blocks from Beach

Parking
Swimming Pool
Maid Service:
Every
Three Days

SEA LODGE
Condominium Apts.
P.O. Box 1109
Hanalei, Kauai, HI 96714
Phone 826-9833
Total Units 86
Hotel Units 3
Area M—Princeville
Oceanfront

Parking
TV
Swimming Pool
Golf Course
Maid Service:
On Request
Minimum Stay:
3 Days

SEA LODGE AT PRINCEVILLE
Condominium Apts. (W)
Hanalei, Kauai, HI 96714

Hotel Units 12
Area M
Near Hanalei Pay

Parking
Swimming Pool
Golf Course
Maid Service:
On Request
Minimum Stay:
5 Nights

SHERATON COCONUT BEACH HOTEL
Hotel (W)
Coconut Plantation
Kapaa, Kauai, HI 96746
Phone 822-3455
Toll Free US (800) 334-8484
Canada (800) 268-9330
(800) 325-3535
Total Units 311
Area L—Waipouli
On a Sand Beach

100% Air Cond.
Parking
TV
Restaurant
Cocktail Lounge
Swimming Pool
Tennis Courts
Shops
Meeting Room

SHERATON KAUAI HOTEL
Hotel (W)
Rt. 1, Box 303

100% Air Cond.
Parking
TV

Koloa, Kauai, HI 96756
Phone 742-1661
Toll Free (800) 325-3535
Total Units 344
Area N
On the Beach at Poipu

SUNSET KAHILI CONDO APT.
Condominium Apts. (W)
R.R. 1, Box 96
Koloa, Kauai, HI 96756
Phone 742-1691
Total Units 36
Hotel Units 28
Area N
On the Ocean at Poipu

Parking
TV
Swimming Pool
Minimum Stay:
3 Days
Maid Service:
Weekly
Meeting Room

TIP TOP MOTEL
Motel
3173 Aikahi St.
Lihue, Kauai, HI 96766
Phone 245-2333; 245-2761
Total Units 34
Hotel Units 31
Area K—Lihue

100% Air Cond.
Parking
Restaurant
Cocktail Lounge

WAILUA BAYVIEW
Condominium Apts. (W)
P.O. Box 3292
Lihue, Kauai, HI 96766
Phone 822-3651
Total Units 45
Hotel Units 44
Area L
Oceanfront

Parking
TV
Restaurant
Cocktail Lounge
Swimming Pool
Maid Service:
On Request
Minimum Stay:
3 Days

WAILUA BAY VIEW
Condominium Apts. (W)
320 Papaloa Road
Kapaa, Kauai, HI 96746
Phone 822-3651

Parking
Restaurant
Swimming Pool
Maid Service:
On Request
Minimum Stay:
5 Nights

WAIOHAI RESORT, THE
Hotel
RR1, Box 174
Koloa, Kauai, HI 96756
Phone 742-9511
Toll Free USA (800) 227-4700
Canada (800) 622-0838
Total Units 434
Area N—Poipu
On the Beach at Poipu

100% Air Cond.
Hotel
Parking
TV
Restaurants
Swimming Pools
Tennis Courts
Shops
Meeting Room

MAUI

FOUR STAR SERVICES OF HAWAII
Vacation Homes (W)
3721 Kanaina St.
Suite 213
Honolulu, HI 96815
Phone 732-1121
Total Units 12
Area R, Q & T
Lahaina, Hana & Wailea
Oceanfront

GO NATIVE-HAWAII
Private Homes
130 Puhili St.
Hilo, HI 96720
Phone 961-2080
Home Units 25
Area F

Restaurants
Cocktail Lounges
Swimming Pools
Shops
Meeting Rooms

HALEAKALA SHORES RESORT
Condominium Apts. (W)
2619 S. Kihei Rd.
Kihei, Maui, HI 96753
Phone 879-1218
Toll Free (800) 367-5224
Total Units 76
Hotel Units 50
Area T
Across Street from
Beach at Kihei

Partial Air Cond.
Parking
TV
Swimming Pool
Minimum Stay:
3 Days
"On Season"
7 Days
Maid Service:
On Request

HALE KAI O KIHEI
Condominium Apts.
1310 Uluniu Rd.
Kihei, Maui, HI 96753
Phone 879-2757
Total Units 59
Hotel Units 35
Area T
On the Beach on Kihei

Parking
TV
Swimming Pool
Minimum Stay:
7 Days
Maid Service:
On Request
Children:
6 or older

HALE MAUI APT. HOTEL
Apartment Hotel (W)
P.O. Box 516
Lahaina, Maui, HI 96761
Phone 669-6312
Total Units 13
Area R
On the Beach at
Honokowai

Parking
TV (rental)
Minimum Stay:
3 Nights
Maid Service:
Weekly

HALE NAPILI
Condominium Apts.
65 Hui Road H
Lahaina, Maui, HI 96761
Phone 669-6184
Total Units 18
Area R
Oceanfront —
Napili Bay

Parking
TV
Minimum Stay:
3 Days

HALE ONO LOA
Condominium Apts. (W)
3823 L. Honoapiilani Rd.
Lahaina, Maui, HI 96761
Phone 669-6362
Toll Free (800) 367-2927
Total Units 67
Hotel Units 40
Area R
Oceanfront at
Honokowai

Parking
TV
Swimming Pool
Minimum Stay:
3 Days
Maid Service:
Weekly

HANA KAI RESORT APTS.
Condominium Apts.
P.O. Box 38
Hana, Maui, HI 96713
Phone 248-8435
Total Units 19
Area Q
On the Ocean at
Hana Bay

Parking
Swimming Pool

HOLOLANI CONDO RESORT
Condominium Apts. (W)
4401 Honoapiilani Rd.
Lahaina, Maui, HI 96761
Phone 669-8021
Toll Free (800) 367-5032
Total Units 63
Hotel Units 22
Area R—Lahaina
On a Sand Beach

Parking
TV
Swimming Pool
Maid Service:
On Request
Minimum Stay:
3 Days
Shop

HONOKEANA COVE
Condominium Apts.
5255 L. Honoapiilani Rd.
Lahaina, Maui, HI 96761
Phone 669-6441
Total Units 38
Hotel Units 36
Area R
On the Ocean at
Honokeana

Parking
TV
Swimming Pool
Minimum Stay:
3 Days
Maid Service:
Weekly

HONO KAI RESORT
Condominium Apts.
RR1 Box 389
Wailuku, Maui, HI 96793
Phone 244-7012
Toll Free (800) 367-6084
Total Units 46
Hotel Units 36

100% Air Cond.
Parking
TV
Swimming Pool
Maid Service:
On Request
Minimum Stay:
5 Days

Area T—Maalaea Bay
On a Sand Beach

HOTEL HANA-MAUI
Hotel (W) — Parking
P. O. Box 8 — Restaurant
Hana, Maui, HI 96713 — Cocktail Lounge
Phone 248-8211 — Swimming Pool
  536-7522 — Golf Course
(Honolulu Direct Line) — Tennis Courts
Total Units 71 — Shop
Area Q — Meeting Room
¼ Mile from Hana Bay — TV (in lobby)

HOTEL INTER-CONTINENTAL MAUI-WAILEA
Hotel (W) — 100% Air Cond.
P.O. Box 779 — Parking
Kihei, Maui, HI 96753 — TV
Phone 879-1922 — Restaurants
Toll Free (Hawaii) — Cocktail Lounges
(800) 537-5589 — Swimming Pool
USA (800) 367-2960 — Golf Course
Total Units 600 — Tennis Courts
Hotel Units 540 — Shops
Area T — Meeting Rooms
On the Beach at Wailea

HOYOCHI NIKKO
Condominium Apts. (W) — Partial Air Cond.
3901 Lower Honoapiilani Rd. — Parking
Lahaina, Maui, HI 96761 — TV
Phone 669-8343 — Swimming Pool
In Canada (604) 922-9740 — Minimum Stay:
Total Units 18 — 3 Days
Area R — Maid Service:
On Oceanfront Garden — On Request

HYATT REGENCY MAUI
Hotel (W) — 100% Air Cond.
Kaanapali Beach Resort — Parking
Kaanapali, Maui, HI 96761 — TV
Phone 667-7474 — Restaurants
Toll Free (800) 228-9000 — Cocktail Lounges
Total Units 815 — Swimming Pool
Area R — Tennis Courts
Oceanfront & — Golf Course
Sand Beach — Shops
— Meeting Rooms

ISLAND SURF
Condominium Apts. (W) — Parking
1993 S. Kihei Road
Kihei, Maui, HI 96753 — Restaurant
Phone 879-1683 — Cocktail Lounge
Toll Free (800) 367-5232 — Swimming Pool
Total Units 82 — Minimum Stay:
Hotel Units 64 — 5 Days
Area T — Maid Service:
Across Street from Beach — On Request

KAANAPALI ALII
Condominium Apts. — 100% Air Cond.
50 Nohea Kai Dr. — Parking
Kaanapali, Maui, HI 96761 — TV
Phone 667-1400 — Swimming Pools
Toll Free US (800) 367-6090 — Tennis Courts
Total Units 264 — Golf Course
Hotel Units 250
Area R

KAANAPALI BEACH HOTEL
Hotel (W) — 100% Air Cond.
2525 Kaanapali Parkway — Parking
Lahaina, Maui, HI 96761 — TV
Phone 661-0011 — Restaurants
Total Units 430 — Cocktail Lounges
Area R — Swimming Pool
On the Beach — Golf Courses
— Shops
— Tennis Court

KAANAPALI PLANTATION
Condominium Apts. (W) — Parking
150 Puukolii Road — TV
Lahaina, Maui, HI 96761 — Swimming Pool
Phone 661-4446 — Tennis Court
Total Units 62 — Minimum Stay:
Condo Units 20 — 3 Days
Area R
¼ Mile from Beach

KAANAPALI ROYAL
Condominium Apts. — 100% Air Cond.
2560 Kekaa Drive — Parking
Lahaina, Maui, HI 96761 — TV
— Swimming Pool

Phone 667-7200
Total Units 105
Hotel Units 27
Area R—Kaanapali

KAANAPALI ROYAL
2560 Kekaa Dr. — 100% Air Cond
Kaanapali, Maui, HI 96761 — Parking
Phone 667-7200 — TV
Toll Free (800) 367-2922 — Swimming Pool
Total Units 105 — Tennis Courts
Hotel Units 40
Area R
On the Golf Course

KAANAPALI SHORES RESORT
Apartment Hotel (W) — 100% Air Cond.
100 Kaanapali Shores Place — Parking
Lahaina, Maui, HI 96761 — TV
Phone 667-2211 — Restaurant
Toll Free (800) 367-5124 — Cocktail Lounge
Total Units 463 — Swimming Pool
Hotel Units 415 — Tennis Courts
Area R — Shop
On the Beach

KAANAPALI SHORES RESORT
Apartment Hotel (W) — 100% Air Cond.
100 Kaanapali Shores Place — Parking
Lahaina, Maui, HI 96761 — TV
Phone 667-2211 — Restaurant
Toll Free (800) 367-5124 — Cocktail Lounge
Total Units 463 — Swimming Pool
Area R — Tennis Courts
On the Beach — Shop

KAANAPALI SHORES RESORT
Condominium Apts. — 100% Air Cond.
100 Kaanapali Shores Place — TV
Lahaina, Maui, HI 96761 — Parking
— Restaurant
— Swimming Pool
Total Units 463 — Tennis Courts
Hotel Units 8 — Shop
Area R — Maid Service:
— On Request
On Beach — Minimum Stay:
— 5 Nights

KAHALELANI APTS.
at Sugar Beach Resort — 100% Air Cond.
Condominium Apts. — Parking
145 N. Kihei Rd. — TV
Kihei, Maui, HI 96753 — Swimming Pool
Total Units 218 — Shops
Hotel Units 6 — Maid Service:
Area T—Kihei — On Request
On a Sand Beach — Minimum Stay:
— 4 Days

KAHANA VILLA
Condominium Apts. (W) — Ceiling Fans
4242 Lower Honoapiilani Rd. — Parking
Lahaina, Maui, HI 96761 — TV
Phone 669-5613 — Restaurant
Toll Free (800) 367-2974 — Cocktail Lounge
Total Units 100 — Swimming Pool
Hotel Units 80 — Tennis Court
Area RT — Shop
50 Feet to Beach

KAMAOLE SANDS
Condominium Apts. — Parking
2695 S. Kihei Rd. — TV
Kihei, Maui, HI 96753 — Swimming Pool
Phone 879-0666 — Tennis Courts
Toll Free (800) 367-6046 — Maid Service:
Total Units 440 — Daily
Hotel Units 440
Area T—Kihei
Across from Beach

KANA'I A NALU CONDO.
Condominium Apts. (W) — Parking
% Oihana Prop. Mgt. — TV
2145 Wells St., Suite 205 — Swimming Pool
Wailuku, Maui, HI 96793 — No Maid
Phone 242-4466 — Service
Toll Free (800) 367-5234 — Minimum Stay:
Total Units 80 — 5 Days
Hotel Units 7
Area T—Maalaea
On a Bay

KAPALUA BAY HOTEL & VILLAS
Hotel (W) — 100% Air Cond.
One Bay Drive — Parking
Kapalua, Maui, HI 96761 — TV
Phone 669-5656 — Restaurants
Toll Free (800) 367-8000 — Cocktail Lounge
Total Units 327 — Swimming Pool
Area R — Tennis Courts
— Golf Course
— Shops

KAPALUA VILLAS
Condominium Apts. (W) — Parking
500 Bay Drive — TV
Lahaina, Maui, HI 96761 — Restaurants
— Cocktail Lounge
— Swimming Pool
— Golf Course
Hotel Units 8 — Shop
Area R — Maid Service:
On the Beach — On Request
— Minimum Stay:
— 5 Nights

KAUHALE MAKAI
Condominium Apts. (W) — 100% Air Cond.
% 2145 Wells St. — Parking
Suite #205 — TV
Wailuku, Maui, HI 96793 — Swimming Pools
Phone 242-4476 — Minimum Stay:
Total Units 168 — 5 Days
Hotel Units 12 — Winter
Area T — 4 Days
Oceanview at Kihei — Summer

KEALIA CONDOMINIUM
Condominium Apts. (W) — 100% Air Cond.
191 N. Kihei Rd. — Parking
Kihei, Maui, HI 96753 — TV
Phone 879-9159 — Swimming Pool
Toll Free (800) 367-5222 3 — Maid Service:
Total Units 36 — On Request
Area T — Minimum Stay:
Beachfront — 4 Days

KIHEI BEACH RESORT
Condominium Apts. — Partial Air Cond
36 S. Kihei Rd. — Parking
Kihei, Maui, HI 96753 — TV
Phone 879-2744 — Swimming Pool
Toll Free: — Minimum Stay:
USA (800) 367-6034 — 3 Days
Calif. (800) 252-0078
Canada (800) 663-3602
Total Units 54
Hotel Units 25
Area T
Near the Beach

KIHEI KAI
Condominium Apts. — 100% Air Cond.
61 N. Kihei Rd. — Parking
Kihei, Maui, HI 96753 — TV
Phone 879-2357 — Minimum Stay:
Total Units 24 — 4 Days
Hotel Units 20 — Swimming Pool
Area T
On the Beach at Kihei

KIHEI RESORT
Condominium Apts. — Parking
777 S. Kihei Rd. — TV
Kihei, Maui, HI 96753 — Swimming Pool
Phone 879-7441 — Maid Service:
Toll Free US (800) 367-6006 — On Request
Canada (800) 663-1118
Total Units 64
Hotel Units 60
Area T—Kihei
Across Street from Beach

KIHEI SANDS
Condominium Apts. (W) — 100% Air Cond.
115 N. Kihei Rd. — Parking
Kihei, Maui, HI 96753 — TV
Phone 879-2624 — Swimming Pool
Total Units 30 — Minimum Stay:
Hotel Units 22 — 3 Days
Area T — No Maid
On the Beach at — Service
Maalaea Bay

KIHEI SURFSIDE RESORT
Condominium Apts. (W) — Parking
2936 S. Kihei Rd. — TV
Kihei, Maui, HI 96753 — Swimming Pool
— Maid Service:

355

Phone 879-1488
Toll Free (800) 367-5240
  Total Units 83
  Hotel Units 43
  Area T—Kihei
  Oceanfront

KOA RESORT
Condominium Apt. (W)
811 S. Kihei Rd.
Kihei, Maui, HI 96753
Phone 879-7879
Toll Free (800) 367-5224
  Total Units 54
  Hotel Units 34
  Area T—Kihei
  Across Street from Beach

Parking
TV
Swimming Pool
Tennis Court
Maid Service:
  On Request

KULAKANE
Condominium Apts.
3741 Lower Honoapiilani Rd.
Lahaina, Maui, HI 96761
Phone 669-6119
Toll Free (800) 367-6088
  Total Units 42
  Area R
  Oceanfront at Honokowai

Parking
TV
Swimming Pool
Minimum Stay:
  3 Days
Maid Service:
  On Request

LAHAINA SHORES HOTEL
Condominium Apts. (W)
475 Front Street
Lahaina, Maui, HI 96761
Phone 661-4835
Toll Free (800) 367-2973
  Total Units 199
  Hotel Units 150
  Area R
  On a Sand Beach

100% Air Cond.
Parking
TV
Swimming Pool
Tennis Court

LEINA'ALA CONDO.
Condominium Apts.
998 S. Kihei Rd.
Kihei, Maui, HI 96753
Phone 879-2235
Toll Free (800) 367-5234
  Total Units 24
  Hotel Units 12
  Area T—Kihei
  Oceanfront

Partial Air Cond.
Parking
TV
Swimming Pool
Tennis Court
No Maid
  Service
Minimum Stay:
  5 Days

LEINA'ALA CONDO.
Condominium Apts. (W)
% Oihana Prop. Mgmt.
2145 Wells St., Suite 205
Wailuku, Maui, HI 96793
Phone 242-4466
Toll Free (800) 367-5234
  Total Units 20
  Hotel Units 7
  Area T—Kihei
  Oceanview

Partial Air Cond.
Parking
TV
Swimming Pool
Tennis Court
No Maid
  Service
Minimum Stay:
  5 Days

LIHI KAI COTTAGES
Cottages-Apt. Hotel
2121 Iliili Road
Kihei, Maui, HI 96753
Phone 879-2335
  Total Units 25
  Area T
  Across Street from Beach

Parking
TV
Minimum Stay:
  3 Days

LUANA KAI
Condominium Apts. (W)
940 S. Kihei Rd.
Kihei, Maui, HI 96753
Phone 879-1268
Toll Free (800) 367-7042
  Total Units 110
  Hotel Units 65
  Area T
  On a Sand Beach

Parking
TV
Swimming Pool
Tennis Court
Maid Service:
  Every 3rd Day
Minimum Stay:
  3 Days

LUANA KAI
Condominium Apts. (W)
940 S. Kihei Rd.
Kihei, Maui, HI 96753
Phone 879-1268
  Total Units 110
  Hotel Units 3
  Area T
  On a Sand Beach

Parking
TV
Swimming Pool
Tennis Court

MAALAEA BANYANS CONDO.
Condominium Apts. (W)
% Oihana Prop. Mgt.

Parking
TV
Swimming Pool

2145 Wells St., Suite 205
Wailuku, Maui, HI 96793
Phone 242-5668
Toll Free (800) 367-5234
  Total Units 76
  Hotel Units 30
  Area T—Maalaea
  Bayfront

No Maid
  Service
Minimum Stay:
  5 Days

MAHANA
Condominium Apts. (W)
110 Kaanapali Shores Place
Lahaina, Maui, HI 96761
Phone 661-8751
Toll Free USA (800) 367-5124
  Total Units 216
  Hotel Units 100
  Area R
  On the Beach at
  Kaanapali

100% Air Cond.
Parking
TV
Swimming Pool
Tennis Courts
Shop
Minimum Stay:
  3 Days

MAHANA
Condominium Apts.
110 Kaanapali Shore Pl.
Lahaina, Maui, HI 96761

  Hotel Units 7
  Area R
  On the Beach

100% Air Cond.
Parking
TV
Swimming Pool
Tennis Courts
Shop
Maid Service:
  On Request
Minimum Stay:
  5 Nights

MAKANI A KAI CONDOMINIUM
Condominium Apts. (W)
R.R. 1, Box 400
Maalaea Village
Maui, HI 96793
Phone 244-5627
Toll Free (800) 367-6084
  Total Units 24
  Hotel Units 17
  Area T
  On the Beach at Maalaea

Air Cond.
Parking
TV
Swimming Pools
Minimum Stay:
  Days
Maid Service:
  On Request

MAKANI SANDS
Condominium Apts. (W)
3765 Honoapiilani Rd.
Lahaina, Maui, HI 96761
Phone 669-8223; 669-8268
  Total Units 30
  Hotel Units 23
  Area R
  On the Beach at
  Honokowai

Parking
TV
Swimming Pool
Minimum Stay:
  3 Days
Maid Service:
  Every 4th Day

MANA KAI-MAUI
Condominium Apt. Hotel (W)
2960 S. Kihei Rd.
Kihei, Maui, HI 96753
Phone 879-1561
Toll Free (800) 525-2025
  Total Units
  Area T
  On the Beach at Kihei

Parking
TV
Restaurant
Cocktail Lounge
Swimming Pool
Shops
Meeting Room

MAUI BEACH HOTEL
Hotel (W)
Kahului, Maui, HI 96732
Phone 877-0051
Toll Free (800) 367-5004
  Total Units 154
  Area U
  On Kahului Bay

100% Air Cond.
Parking
Restaurants
Cocktail Lounge
Swimming Pool
Shop
Meeting Room
TV

MAUI ELDORADO RESORT
Condominium Apts.
Kaanapali Beach
Lahaina, Maui, HI 96761
Phone 661-0021
  Total Units 204
  Hotel Units 120
  Area R

100% Air Cond.
Parking
TV
Swimming Pool
Golf Course
Shop

MAUI ELDORADO RESORT
Condominium Apts. (W)
Kaanapali Beach
Lahaina, Maui, HI 96761

  Total Units 204
  Hotel Units 4
  Area R
  On the Beach

100% Air Cond.
Parking
TV
Swimming Pool
Golf Course
Maid Service:
  On Request
Minimum Stay:
  5 Nights

MAUI HILL
Condominium Apts.
2881 S. Kihei Rd.
Kihei, Maui, HI 96753
Phone 879-6321
Toll Free (800) 367-5314
  Total Units 140
  Hotel Units 85
  Area T

100% Air Cond.
Parking
TV
Swimming Pool
Tennis Court
Maid Service:
  Every
  Other Day

MAUI HUKILAU HOTEL
Kahului, Maui, HI 96732
Phone 877-3311
  Total Units 79
  Area U
  White Sand Beach

Ceiling Fans
Parking
TV
Restaurant
Cocktail Lounge
Swimming Pool
Shopping Plaza

MAUI ISLANDER
Apartment Hotel
660 Wainee
Lahaina, Maui, HI 96761
Phone 667-9766
Toll Free (800) 367-5226
  Total Units 324
  Hotel Units 324
  Area R—Lahaina
  2 Blocks to Waterfront

100% Air Cond.
Parking
TV
Swimming Pool
Tennis Court

MAUI KAI CONDOMINIUM
Condominium Apts. (W)
106 Kaanapali Shores
Lahaina, Maui, HI 96761
Phone 661-0002
Toll Free (800) 367-5635
  Total Units 79
  Hotel Units 38
  Area R
  On the Beach at
  Kaanapali

100% Air Cond.
Parking
TV
Swimming Pool
Minimum Stay:
  2 Nights
Maid Service:
  Twice Weekly

MAUI LU RESORT
Hotel
575 S. Kihei Rd.
Kihei, Maui, HI 96753
Phone 879-5881
Toll Free (800) 367-5244
Toll Free (800) 592-3351
  Total Units 150
  Area T
  On the Beach

100% Air Cond.
Parking
TV
Restaurant
Cocktail Lounge
Swimming Pool
Tennis Courts
Shops

MAUI MARRIOT RESORT
Hotel (W)
100 Nohea Kai Drive
Lahaina, Maui, HI 96761
Phone 667-1200
Toll Free (800) 542-6821
      (800) 228-9290
  Total Units 720
  Area R
  On the Beach

100% Air Cond.
Parking
TV
Restaurants
Cocktail Lounges
Swimming Pool
Tennis Courts
Shops
Meeting Rooms

MAUI PALMS
Hotel
170 Kaahumanu Ave.
Kahului, Maui, HI 96732
Phone 538-6817
  Total Units 103
  Area U
  Near Kahului Bay

Partial Air Cond.
Parking
TV
Swimming Pool
Restaurant
Cocktail Lounge
Shop
Meeting Room

MAUI SANDS
Condominium Apts. (W)
3559 Lower Honoapiilani Rd.
Lahaina, Maui, HI 96761
Phone 669-4811
Toll Free (800) 367-5037
  Total Units 76
  Hotel Units 56
  Area R
  On the Beach at
  Honokowai

Partial Air Cond.
Parking
TV
Swimming Pool
Minimum Stay:
  4 Nights
  Off Season
  7 Nights
Maid Service:
  Every
  Other Day

MAUI SEASIDE HOTEL
Kahului, Maui, HI 96732
Phone 877-3311
  Total Units 108
  Area U

100% Air Cond.
Parking
TV
Restaurant
Cocktail Lounge
Swimming Pool
Shopping Plaza

MAUI VISTA CONDO.
Condominium Apts. (W)
% Oihana Prop. Mgt.
2145 Wells St., Suite 205
Wailuku, Maui, HI 96793
Phone 242-4466
Toll Free (800) 367-5234
Total Units 280
Hotel Units 10
Area T—Kihei
100 yds. to Beach

Parking
TV
Swimming Pools
Tennis Courts
No Maid
Service
Minimum Stay:
5 Days

MAUI SURF
Hotel (W)
2365 Kaanapali Parkway
Lahaina, Maui, HI 96761
Phone 661-4411
Toll Free (800) 367-5360
Total Units 556
Area R

100% Air Cond.
Parking
TV
Restaurants
Cocktail Lounge
Swimming Pool
Golf Courses
Tennis Courts
Shops
Meeting Rooms

MAUIAN HOTEL, THE
Apartment Hotel
P.O. Box 1684
Lahaina, Maui, HI 96761
Phone 669-6205
Toll Free (800) 367-5034
Total Units 44
Hotel Units 44
Area R—Napili
Oceanfront

Parking
Swimming Pool
Maid Service:
On Request
Minimum Stay:
3 Days

NANI KAI HALE
Condominium Apts. (W)
73 N. Kihei Rd.
Kihei, Maui, HI 96753
Phone 879-9120
Toll Free (800) 367-6032
Total Units 46
Hotel Units 30
Area T
On a Sand Beach

Parking
TV
Swimming Pool
No Maid
Service
Minimum Stay:
3 Days:
Low Sn.
7 Days:
High Sn.

NAPILI KAI BEACH CLUB
Hotel (W)
5900 Honoapiilani Rd.
Lahaina, Maui, HI 96761
Phone 669-6271
Toll Free (800) 367-5030
Total Units 136
Area R
On Napili Bay

Partial Air Cond.
Parking
TV
Restaurant
Cocktail Lounge
Swimming Pools
Tennis Courts
Shops
Meeting Rooms

NAPILI POINT
Condominium Apts. (W)
5295 Honoapiilani Hwy.
Napili, Maui, HI 96761
Phone 669-9222
Toll Free (800) 367-5124
Total Units 115
Hotel Units 72
Area R—Napili
On Oceanfront

Parking
TV
Swimming Pools

NAPILI POINT
Condominium Apts. (W)
5295 Honoapiilani
Lahaina, Maui, HI 96761

Total Units 115
Hotel Units 4
Area R
Oceanfront

Parking
TV
Swimming Pool
Maid Service:
On Request
Minimum Stay:
5 Nights

NAPILI PUAMALA
Apartment Hotel (W)
% Napili Surf Beach Resort
50 Napili Pl.
Napili Bay, Maui, HI 96761
Phone 669-8002
Total Units 18
Area R
200 ft. from Beach

Parking
TV
Swimming Pool
Minimum Stay:
3 Days

NAPILI SHORES RESORT
5315 Honoapiilani Hwy.
Lahaina, Maui, HI 96761
Phone 669-8061
Toll Free (800) 367-6046
Total Units 152
Area R

Parking
TV
Restaurant
Cocktail Lounge
Swimming Pools
Shop

NAPILI SHORES
Condominium Apts. (W)
5315 Honoapiilani
Lahaina, Maui, HI 96761
Total Units 152
Hotel Units 25
Area R
On the Beach

Air Cond.
Parking
TV
Restaurants
Cocktail Lounge
Swimming Pools
Shop
Maid Service:
On Request
Minimum Stay:
5 Nights

NAPILI SUNSET
Condominium Apts. (W)
46 Hui Dr.
Lahaina, Maui, HI 96761
Phone 669-8083
Toll Free (800) 421-0680
Total Units 41
Area R
On the Beach at
Napili Bay

Parking
TV
Swimming Pool
Minimum Stay:
3 Days

NAPILI SURF BEACH RESORT
Condominium Apts. (W)
50 Napili Pl.
Napili Bay, Maui, HI 96761
Phone 669-8002
Total Units 36
Area R
On the Beach at
Napili Bay

Parking
TV
Swimming Pool
Minimum Stay:
3 Days

NOELANI
Condominium Apts. (W)
4095 Honoapiilani Rd.
Lahaina, Maui, HI 96761
Phone 669-8374
Toll Free (800) 367-6030
Total Units 50
Hotel Units 41
Area R
Oceanfront at
Mahinahina

Parking
TV
Swimming Pools
Minimum Stay:
3 Days
Maid Service:
Weekly

NOHONANI RESORT
Condominium Apts. (W)
RR 1
Lahaina, Maui, HI 96761
Phone 669-8208
Total Units 28
Hotel Units 24
Area R   On the Beach at
Honokowai

Parking
TV
Swimming Pool
Minimum Stay:
3 Days
Maid Service:
On Request

PAKI MAUI VACATION CONDOMINIUMS
Condominium Apts.
3615 L. Honoapiilani Hwy.
Lahaina, Maui, HI 96761
Phone 669-8235
Total Units 108
Hotel Units 65
Area R
On a Sand Beach

Parking
TV
Swimming Pool
Meeting Room
Maid Service:
Every 4th Day
Minimum Stay:
3 Days

PAPAKEA BEACH RESORT
Condominium Apts. (W)
Kaanapali, Maui, HI 96761
Phone 669-4848
Toll Free (800) 367-5637
Total Units 364
Hotel Units 190
Area R
On the Beach at
Kaanapali

Parking
TV
Swimming Pools
Tennis Courts
Maid Service:
Every
Other Day
Minimum Stay:
5 Days

PAPAKEA BEACH RESORT
Condominium Apts. (W)
3543 Honoapiilani
Lahaina, Maui, HI 96761
Total Units 364
Hotel Units 33
Area R
On the Beach

Parking
TV
Swimming Pool
Tennis Courts
Maid Service:
On Request
Minimum Stay:
5 Nights

PIONEER INN
Hotel
658 Wharf St.
Lahaina, Maui, HI 96761
Phone 661-3636
Total Units 48
Area R
On Lahaina Harbor

Partial Air Cond.
Restaurants
Cocktail Lounge
Swimming Pool
Shops

POHAILANI MAUI RESORT (W)
4435 Honoapiilani Rd.
Kahana, Maui, HI 96761
Phone 669-6125
Toll Free (800) 367-6038
Total Units 114
Hotel Units 30
Area R
Oceanfront

Parking
TV
Swimming Pools
Tennis Courts
Minimum Stay:
3 Days
Off Season
5 Days
Winter

POLYNESIAN SHORES
Condominium Apts. (W)
3975 Honoapiilani Way
Lahaina, Maui, HI 96761
Phone 669-6065 (Collect)
Total Units 52
Rental Units 33
Area R
On the Beach at
Mahinahina

Parking
TV
Swimming Pool
Minimum Stay:
3 Days
No Maid
Service

PUAMANA
Condominium Apts. (W)
P.O. Box 515
Lahaina, Maui, HI 96761
Phone 667-2551
Total Units 228
Hotel Units 64
Area
On south edge of
Lahaina

Partial Air Cond.
Parking
TV
Swimming Pool
Tennis Court
Maid Service:
Limited

ROYAL LAHAINA HOTEL
Resort (W)
2780 Kekaa Dr.
Lahaina, Maui, HI 96761
Phone 661-3611
Total Units 514
Area R
On the Beach at
Kaanapali

100% Air Cond.
Parking
TV
Restaurants
Cocktail Lounges
Swimming Pools
Golf Courses
Tennis Courts
Shops
Meeting Rooms

SHERATON MAUI HOTEL
Hotel (W)
Kaanapali Beach
Lahaina, Maui, HI 96761
Phone 661-0031
Toll Free (800) 325-3535
Total Units 522
Hotel Units 503
Area R
On the Beach at
Kaanapali

100% Air Cond.
Parking
TV
Restaurants
Cocktail Lounges
Swimming Pools
Golf Course
Tennis Courts
Shops
Meeting Rooms

SHORES OF MAUI
Condominium Apts. (W)
2075 S. Kihei Rd.
Kihei, Maui, HI 96753
Phone 879-9140
Total Units 50
Hotel Units 33
Area T—Kihei
Ocean Across Street

Partial Air Cond.
Parking
TV
Swimming Pool
Tennis Court
Minimum Stay:
3 Days
Maid Service:
On Request

STOUFFER'S WAILEA BEACH, THE
Hotel (W)
Wailea, Maui, HI 96753
Phone 879-4900
Toll Free (800) 228-3000
Total Units 350
Area T
On the Beach at
Wailea

100% Air Cond.
Parking
TV
Restaurants
Cocktail Lounge
Swimming Pool
Tennis Courts
Golf Course
Shops

SUGAR BEACH RESORT
Condominium Apts. (W)
145 N. Kihei Rd.
Kihei, Maui, HI 96753
Phone 879-4421
Total Units 260
Hotel Units 50
Area T
On Sandy Beach

100% Air Cond
Parking
TV
Cocktail Lounge
Swimming Pool
Tennis Court
Shops
Maid Service:
Every 3rd Day
Minimum Stay:
5 Nights —
Winter Season
12 15 - 4 3

SUGAR BEACH RESORT
Condominium Apts.
145 N. Kihei Rd.
Kihei, Maui, HI 96753

100% Air Cond.
Parking
TV
Swimming Pool
Tennis Courts

Hotel Units 20
Area T
On the Beach

Shops
Maid Service:
  On Request

SUNSEEKER RESORT
Apartment Hotel
551 S. Kihei Rd.
Kihei, Maui, HI 96753
Phone 879-1261
  Total Units 6
  Hotel Units 6
  Area T
  On a Sand Beach

Parking
TV
Maid Service:
  On Request
Minimum Stay:
  3 Days

VALLEY ISLE RESORT
Condominium Apts.
4327 Honoapiilani Rd.
Lahaina, Maui, HI 96761
Phone 669-5511
  Hotel Units 20
  Area R
  On Oceanfront Sandy
    Beach

Partial Air Cond.
Parking
TV
Restaurant
Cocktail Lounge
Swimming Pool
Maid Service:
  Every 3rd Day

VALLEY ISLE
Condominium Apts. (W)
4327 Honoapiilani
Lahaina, Maui, HI 96761

  Hotel Units 2
  Area R
  On the Beach

100% Air Cond.
Parking
TV
Restaurant
Cocktail Lounge
Swimming Pool
Shop
Maid Service:
  On Request
Minimum Stay:
  5 Nights

WAILANA SANDS
Apartment Hotel (W)
25 Wailana Pl.
Kihei, Maui, HI 96753
Phone 879-2026
  Total Units 10
  Area T
  ¼ Block from Beach

Parking
TV
Swimming Pool
Minimum Stay:
  3 Days
No Maid
  Service

WAILEA CONDOMINIUMS
Condominium Apts.
Kihei, Maui, HI 96753

  Hotel Units 10
  Area T
  On the Beach or
    Golf Course

Parking
TV
Restaurant
Cocktail Lounge
Swimming Pool
Tennis Court
Golf Course
Maid Service:
  On Request
Minimum Stay:
  5 Nights

**THE WHALER ON
KAANAPALI BEACH**
Condominium Apts. (W)
2481 Kaanapali Parkway
Lahaina, Maui, HI 96761
Phone 661-4861
Toll Free (800) 367-2963
  Total Units 360
  Hotel Units 203
  Area R
  On a Sand Beach

100% Air Cond.
Parking
TV
Swimming Pool
Tennis Courts
Golf Course
Shop
Meeting Room
Minimum Stay:
  3 Days

WHALER AT KAANAPALI BEACH
Condominium Apts. (W)
2481 Kaanapali Parkway
Lahaina, Maui, HI 96761
  Total Units 360
  Hotel Units 24
  Area R
  On the Beach

100% Air Cond.
Parking
TV
Swimming Pool
Tennis Court
Shop
Maid Service:
  On Request
Minimum Stay:
  5 Nights

ISLAND OF MOLOKAI

HOTEL MOLOKAI
Cottage
P.O. Box 546
Kaunakakai, Molokai, HI 96748
Phone 553-5347
Phone HNL 531-4004
  Total Units 55
  Area W
  Oceanfront

Parking
Restaurant
Cocktail Lounge
Swimming Pool
Shop

MOLOKAI SHORES
Condominium Apts. (W)
Star Route
Kaunakakai, Molokai, HI 96748
Phone 553-5954
Toll Free (800) 367-7042
  Total Units 102
  Hotel Units 81
  Area W
  On the Beach

Parking
TV
Swimming Pool
Shop
Minimum Stay:
  2 Days

PANIOLO HALE
Condominium Apts. (W)
P.O. Box 146
Maunaloa, Molokai, HI 96770
Phone 552-2731

Parking
TV
Swimming Pool
Golf Course
Maid Service:

Toll Free (800) 367-2984
  Total Units 76
  Hotel Units 40
  Area W
  On Kepuhi Beach

Weekly
Minimum Stay:
  3 Days

PAU HANA INN
Cottage Type Inn
P.O. Box 860
Kaunakakai, Molokai, HI 96748
Phone 553-5342
    536-7545
  (Honolulu Direct Line)
Toll Free (800) 367-5072
  Total Units 39
  Area W
  On the Ocean at
    Kaunakakai

Parking
Restaurant
Cocktail Lounge
Swimming Pool

SHERATON MOLOKAI HOTEL
Hotel
P.O. Box 1977
Maunaloa, Molokai, HI 96770
Phone 552-2555
Toll Free (800) 325-3535
  Total Units 292
  Area W
  On Kepuhi Beach

Parking
TV
Restaurants
Cocktail Lounge
Swimming Pool
Golf Course
Tennis Courts
Shops
Meeting Rooms

WAVECREST RESORT
Condominium Apts. (W)
Star Route
Molokai, HI 96748
Phone 558-8238
Toll Free (800) 367-2980
  Total Units 126
  Hotel Units 45
  Area W—Molokai
  Oceanfront

Parking
TV
Swimming Pool
Tennis Courts
Shop
Meeting Room
Maid Service:
  Every 3rd Day
Minimum Stay:
  2 Days
Age Restriction:
  12 years

ISLAND OF LANAI

HOTEL LANAI (W)
P.O. Box A-119
Lanai, HI 96763
Phone 565-6605
  Total Units 10
  Area Y—Lanai

Parking
Restaurant
Cocktail Lounge

ART/PHOTO CREDITS

Cover   Hans Hoefer; *wili lei* (made of *likolehua, pua lehua, uluhe, pukiawe, maile, pala palai, a'alii, hau,* and *ti*) by Treva Spencer; model, Leialoha Ma'a.

End paper front   "Hula Girl" by Ray Jerome Baker, from the Bernice Pauahi Bishop Museum.

1   Frank Salmoiraghi.
2-3   Ken Sakamoto.
6-7   Steve Wilkings.
10-11   Ray Jerome Baker lantern slide, from the Robert Van Dyke Collection.
12   Jacques Arago, from the Don Severson Collection.
14   John Webber, 1779, from the Don Severson Collection.
16   Andrew Pellion, from the Don Severson Collection.
17   John Webber, from the Don Severson Collection.
18   John Webber, from the Don Severson Collection.
19   Jacques Arago, from the Don Severson Collection.
20-21   The first Western map of Hawaii, from Cook, Captain James, and King James, *A Voyage to the Pacific Ocean, 1776-1780*, London, 1784, V. 3; from the Peter Hutton Collection.
22-23   John Webber, from the Don Severson Collection.
24   Lantern slide, from the Robert Van Dyke Collection.
25·   State of Hawaii Archives.
26   John Webber, from the Don Severson Collection.
27   John Webber, from the Don Severson Collection.
28   Sarah Stone, from the Don Severson Collection.
29   Map from a *Voyage Round in the Years MD CC XL, I, II, III, IV by George Anson, Esq*—from one of 42 copper plates by John and Paul Knapton, Ludgate St. London, 1784; the Robert Van Dyke Collection.
30-31   Lithograph by Lauvergne, *Scene De Danse Auy Iles Sandwich*, 1836; the Don Severson Collection.
32   Louis Choris, from the Don Severson Collection.
33   Louis Choris, from the Don Severson Collection.
35   Louis Choris, *Port d' Honarourou*, from the Don Severson Collection.
36   John Hayter lithograph, from the Robert Van Dyke Collection.
37   Jacques Arago, from the Don Severson Collection.

38   From *Corvetten Galathea's Jordomseiling — Reise Amkring Jorden 1845, 46, og 47;* from the Robert Van Dyke Collection
39   Louis Choris, from the Don Severson Collection.
40   From the Robert Van Dyke Collection.
41   Engraving by W. J. Linton, from the Robert Van Dyke Collection.
42-43   From *Fregatten Eugenies, Resa Omkring, Jorden, Aren 1851—1853;* the Robert Van Dyke Collection.
44   The Robert Van Dyke Collection.
45–L   State of Hawaii Archives.
45–R   The Robert Van Dyke Collection.
46   The Robert Van Dyke Collection.
47   The Robert Van Dyke Collection.
48   J. J. William, from the Robert Van Dyke Collection.
49   Lantern slide, from the Robert Van Dyke Collection.
50   Lantern slide, from the Robert Van Dyke Collection.
50-51   The Bernice Pauahi Bishop Museum.
52   State of Hawaii Archives
53   State of Hawaii Archives
54   The Robert Van Dyke Collection.
55   The Don Severson Collection.
56-57   U. S. Navy, *Honolulu Star Bulletin,* from the Robert Van Dyke Collection.
58   Lantern slide, from the Robert Van Dyke Collection.
59   The Kimo Wilder McVay Collection.
60   The Robert Van Dyke Collection.
61   U.S. Navy
62   *The Honolulu Star Bulletin,* from the Robert Van Dyke Collection.
63   *The Honolulu Advertiser,* from the Robert Van Dyke Collection.
64   *The Honolulu Advertiser.*
65   ıState of Hawaii, Dennis Fuji.
66-67   *see* cover page credit.
69   Lantern slide by Ray Jerome Baker, from the Robert Van Dyke Collection.
70   Jim Haas.
71   Leonard Lueras.
72   ·Frank Salmoiraghi.
73   Leonard Lueras.
74   Frank Salmoiraghi.

75   Leonard Lueras.
76   Hans Hoefer.
77   Ray Jerome Baker lantern slide, from the Robert Van Dyke Collection.
78   Ray Jerome Baker, from the Robert Van Dyke Collection.
79   Jim Haas.
80   Hans Hoefer.
81   Ray Jerome Baker lantern slide, from the Robert Van Dyke Collection.
82   Leonard Lueras.
83   Yukie Yoshinaga.
84-5   The Robert Van Dyke Collection.
86   Hans Hoefer.
87   Hans Hoefer.
88   Leonard Lueras.
89   Nedra Chung Collection.
90   Government of South Korea
91   Leonard Lueras.
92   Corky Trinidad.
93   Ray Jerome Baker Lantern slide, from the Robert Van Dyke Collection.
94   Ronni Pinsler.
95   Corky Trinidad.
96   Leonard Lueras.
97   Jim Haas.
98   Jim Haas.
104-5   Hans Hoefer
106-7   Jerry Chong
110   Leonard Lueras.
111   Jim Haas.
112   Ken Sakamoto.
113   Ken Sakamoto.
116   Ray Jerome Baker lantern slide, from the Robert Van Dyke Collection.
117   Peter Simon.
118   Hans Hoefer.
119   Hans Hoefer.
120   Hans Hoefer.
121   Jim Haas.
122   The Robert Van Dyke Collection.
123   Edgeworth Photo, from the Robert Van Dyke Collection.
124   Jim Haas.
125   Steve Wilkings.
126   Eric Yanagi.
127   Hans Hoefer.
128   The Don Ho Collection.
129   Marcus Lee
132   Jerry Chong.
133   The Robert Van Dyke Collection.
134   Jim Haas.
135   Jim Haas.
136   Jim Haas.
137   Eric Yanagi.
138–L   Leonard Lueras.
138–R   State of Hawaii Archives.
139   Eric Yanagi.
140   Jim Haas.
141–L   State of Hawaii Archives.
141–R   Jim Haas.
142–L   Leonard Lueras.
142–R   Hans Hoefer.

143 The Thurston Twigg-Smith Collection.
144 Hans Hoefer.
145 Eric Yanagi.
146 Jim Haas.
147 Jim Haas.
148-9 Hans Hoefer.
150 Jim Haas.
151 Eric Yanagi.
152 Hans Hoefer.
153 Ray Jerome Baker, from the Robert Van Dyke Collection.
154 The Kimo Wilder McVay Collection.
155 Leonard Lueras.
156 The Jerry Hopkins Collection.
157 The Robert Van Dyke Collection.
158 Ray Jerome Baker lantern slide, from the Robert Van Dyke Collection.
159 Jim Haas.
160 Leonard Lueras.
161 Jim Haas.
162 Leonard Lueras.
163 Affandi.
164 Jerry Chong.
165 Hans Hoefer.
166 Ken Sakamoto.
167 Steve Wilkings.
168 Steve Wilkings.
169 Steve Wilkings.
170 Mike and Bettan Dorn.
170–L Ray Jerome Baker lantern slide, from the Robert Van Dyke Collection.
171–R Leonard Lueras.
172 Leonard Lueras.
173 Jim Haas.
174 Jerry Chong.
175 Hans Hoefer.
176-7 Steve Wilkings.
177–R Steve Wilkings.
178-9 Hans Hoefer.
180 Ray Jerome Baker lantern slide, from the Robert Van Dyke Collection.
181 Jim Haas.
182 Warren Roll.
183 Hans Hoefer.
184 The Robert Van Dyke Collection.
185 Craig Kojima.
186 Eric Yanagi.
187 Steve Wilkings.
188 Steve Wilkings.
189 Hans Hoefer.
190 Hans Hoefer.
191 Warren Roll.
192-3 Hans Hoefer.
196 Leonard Lueras.
197 Hans Hoefer.
198-9 Eric Yanagi.
200 J. Moynet, 1873, from the Robert Van Dyke Collection.
201 Hans Hoefer
202 Chris Newbert
203 "Pulling Teeth" —ca. late 1830s, sketch by Francis

Allyn Olmsted, from the Robert Van Dyke Collection.
204 Hans Hoefer.
205 Hans Hoefer.
206 Hans Hoefer.
207 Frank F. Fasi
208 Eric Yanagi.
209–L Hans Hoefer.
209–R Eric Yanagi.
210 U.S. Navy.
211 Frank Salmoiraghi.
212-3 Hans Hoefer.
214 Hans Hoefer.
215 Frank Salmoiraghi.
216-7 Hans Hoefer.
218-9 Hans Hoefer.
222–L Frank Salmoiraghi.
222–R Frank Salmoiraghi.
223 Frank Salmoiraghi.
224 Frank Salmoiraghi.
225 Frank Salmoiraghi.
226 Frank Salmoiraghi.
227 Frank Salmoiraghi.
228 Frank Salmoiraghi.
229 Frank Salmoiraghi.
230 Frank Salmoiraghi.
231 Frank Salmoiraghi.
232 Frank Salmoiraghi.
233 Frank Salmoiraghi.
234 Frank Salmoiraghi.
235 Frank Salmoiraghi.
236-7 Hans Hoefer.
237-8 Hans Hoefer.
239-40 Hans Hoefer.
244 Leonard Lueras.
245 Frank Salmoiraghi.
246 Ray Jerome Baker lantern slide, from the Robert Van Dyke Collection.
247 Hans Hoefer.
248 Frank Salmoiraghi.
249 Frank Salmoiraghi.
250 Walter Andreae.
251 Hans Hoefer.
252 Hans Hoefer.
253 Frank Salmoiraghi.
254 State of Hawaii Archives.
256 James Sloan.
257–L Hans Hoefer.
257–R Chris Neubert.
258 Boone Morrison.
259 Frank Salmoiraghi.
260–L Hans Hoefer.
260–R Martin Charlot.
261 Boone Morrison.
262 Hans Hoefer.
264–L Leonard Lueras.
264-R Hans Hoefer.
265 Hans Hoefer.
266-7 Hans Hoefer.
270 Boone Morrison.
271 Rothschild study, from the Don Severson Collection.
272-3 Hans Hoefer.
274 J. Moynet, about 1873, from Robert Van Dyke Collection.
275 Walter Andreae.
276–L Hans Hoefer.
276–R Hans Hoefer.
277 Hans Hoefer.

278 Hans Hoefer.
279 Hans Hoefer.
280 Hans Hoefer.
281 Hans Hoefer.
283 Hans Hoefer.
284-5 Boone Morrison
287 The Don Severson Collection.
288–L The Bernice Pauahi Bishop Museum.
288–R The Bernice Pauahi Bishop Museum.
290 The Robert Van Dyke Collection.
291 Paul Emmert, ca. 1852, from the Don Severson Collection.
292 The Robert Van Dyke Collection.
293 Theodore Kelsey, from the Don Severson Collection
294 The Robert Van Dyke Collection.
295 Keystone View Co., from the Don Severson Collection.
296 The Panini Productions Collection.
297 Hans Hoefer.
298 Ray Jerome Baker, from the Robert Van Dyke Collection.
299 Ray Jerome Baker lantern slide, from the Robert Van Dyke Collection.
300 Leonard Lueras.
301 The Robert Van Dyke Collection.
302 Ray Jerome Baker lantern slide, from the Robert Van Dyke Collection.
303 Boone Morrison.
304 Radio control and "camera board" photo by Steve Wilkings.
306 State of Hawaii Archives.
307 E. Riou, from the Robert Van Dyke Collection.
308 Steve Wilkings.
309 Steve Wilkings.
310-1 Steve Wilkings, motor-drive sequence.
312 From the Swedish *Corvetten Galathea's* voyage, ca. 1847: from the Robert Van Dyke Collection.
313 The Robert Van Dyke Collection.
314 The Robert Van Dyke Collection.
315 Ronni Pinsler.
316 *Kumu Hawaii*, from the Don Severson Collection.
319 *Ke Au Hou*, from the Don Severson Collection.
321 Jerry Chong.
322-3 Chris Newbert underwater studies.

End paper "Hula Girl" by Hans Hoefer.
Back

All art reproductions by Hans Hoefer.

On Speaking Hawaiian

In its development the Hawaiian language has acquired several interesting grammatical complications and a sound system known for its complex vowel combinations and small number of consonants. Hawaiian, as afore-mentioned, has eight consonants, each roughly equivalent in pronunciation to their equivalent letter symbols in English, with the exception of w and '.

h	hula	(Hawaiian dance)
k	kai	(sea)
l	lani	(heaven)
m	manu	(bird)
n	niho	(tooth)
p	pua	(flower)
w	wa'a	(canoe)
'	'ala	(fragrance)

The symbol w varies in pronunciation among Hawaiians between a w and v sound. To English speakers this w symbol often sounds more like an English v after a stressed vowel as in the place names Hale'iwa and Hawi. At the beginning of a word or after an unstressed vowel the w symbol sounds more like an English w as in the place names Waikiki and Wahiawa.

Meanwhile, the consonant symbolized ' and called the 'okina in Hawaiian represents a glottal stop. The glottal stop indicates a stop-start-again type of pronunciation. It is common to Hawaiian, but is also found in several dialects of English such as in the Cockney pronunciation of a little bottle of beer (which comes out a li'l bo'l a beer) and the American English pronunciation of button (bu'n) and cotton (co'n).

The five Hawaiian vowels come in both short and long duration forms. Long duration vowels are marked by a bar termed the kahako in Hawaiian (and macron in English) and sometimes differ from short vowels in quality as well as duration.

	Short Form
a as in cut	mana (power)
e as in bet	hele (go)
i as in beet	pili (a grass)
o as in boat	holo (run)
u as in boot	hulu (feather)
	Long Form
ā as in father	nānā (look)
ē as in hay	nēnē (native bird)
ī as in beet	wīwī (skinny)
ō as in boat	lōlō (paralyzed)
ū as in boot	pūpū (hors d'oeuvre)

If you would like more kokua (help) with the rudimentary Hawaiian language you'll be learning, refer to three key books on the subject: Spoken Hawaiian, by Samuel Elbert; Let's Speak Hawaiian, by Dorothy Kahananui and A. Anthony; and The Hawaiian Dictionary, by Samuel Elbert and Mary Kawena Pukui. These should be available at any good island bookstore.

Also, refer to the following Index-Glossary, which includes the phonetic pronunciation and definition of Hawaiian words used in this book.

HONOLULU MARATHON

The Honolulu Marathon Association and the City and County of Honolulu invite you to participate in the world-famous Honolulu Marathon held annually each December. The race has grown from 162 starters in 1973 to now over 7,500.

The official course, shown below, begins adjacent to Aloha Tower, goes through Waikiki to Kapiolani Park, around Diamond Head and down Kahala Avenue, along Kalanianaole Highway, acdrcles Hawaii Kai and then reverses the route again to Kapiolani Park for the finish. Fifteen aid stations are placed at two-mile intervals to help runners. The entry fee is $10.

FURTHER INFORMATION: Write or telephone the Honolulu Marathon Association, P.O. Box 27244, Chinatown Station, Honolulu, HI 96827, Telephone (808) 734-7200 between 9:00 a.m. and 12:00 noon, Hawaiian Standard Time, Monday, Wednesday, and Friday, when volunteers are available. Other calls will be recorded and returned as soon as possible. We are all volunteers. Please be patient if we are delayed in responding.

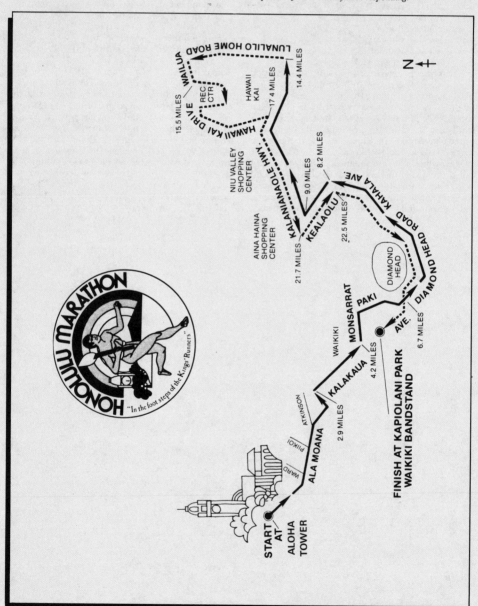

INDEX-GLOSSARY

367